To Brendan,

Many Blessings,

Roberta King

Jan 6, 2017

art for faith's sake series

SERIES EDITORS:

Clayton J. Schmit
J. Frederick Davison

This series of publications is designed to promote the creation of resources for the church at worship. It promotes the creation of two types of material, what we are calling primary and secondary liturgical art.

Like primary liturgical theology, classically understood as the actual prayer and practice of people at worship, primary liturgical art is that which is produced to give voice to God's people in public prayer or private devotion and art that is created as the expression of prayerful people. Secondary art, like secondary theology, is written reflection on material that is created for the sake of the prayer, praise, and meditation of God's people.

The series presents both worship art and theological and pedagogical reflection on the arts of worship. The series title, *Art for Faith's Sake,** indicates that, while some art may be created for its own sake, a higher purpose exists for arts that are created for use in prayer and praise.

OTHER VOLUMES IN THIS SERIES:

Senses of the Soul by William A. Dyrness
Dust and Prayers by Charles L. Bartow
Dust and Ashes by James L. Crenshaw
Preaching Master Class by William H. Willimon
Praying the Hours in Ordinary Life by Clayton J. Schmit and Lauralee Farrer
Mending a Tattered Faith: Devotions with Dickinson by Susan VanZanten
Blessed: Monologues for Mary by Jerusha Matsen Neal
Senses of Devotion: Interfaith Aesthetics in Buddhist and Muslim Communities by William A. Dyrness
Sanctifying Art: Inviting Conversations between Artists, Theologians, and the Church by Deborah Sokolove
Dance in Scripture: How Biblical Dancers Can Revolutionize Worship Today by Angela Yarber.
ReVisioning: Critical Methods of Seeing Christianity in the History of Art edited by James Romaine and Linda Stratford

**Art for Faith's Sake* is a phrase coined by art collector and church musician, Jerry Evenrud, to whom we are indebted.

(un)Common Sounds

(un)Common Sounds

*Songs of Peace and Reconciliation
among Muslims and Christians*

EDITED BY
Roberta R. King
and Sooi Ling Tan

CASCADE *Books* · Eugene, Oregon

(UN)COMMON SOUNDS
Songs of Peace and Reconciliation among Muslims and Christians

Art for Faith's Sake

Cascade Books
An Imprint of Wipf and Stock Publishers
199 W. 8th Ave., Suite 3
Eugene, OR 97401
www.wipfandstock.com

ISBN 13: 978-1-62564-488-6

Cataloging-in-Publication data:

(un)Common sounds : songs of peace and reconciliation among Muslims and Christians / edited by Roberta R. King and Sooi Ling Tan.

xviii + 330 p. ; 23 cm. —Includes bibliographical references and index(es).

Art for Faith's Sake

ISBN 13: 978-1-62564-488-6

1. Ethnomusicology. 2. Religions—Relations. 3. Peace—Songs and Music. I. Title. II. Series.

ML3798 U66 2014

Manufactured in the U.S.A.

Contents

Resource Links and Accompanying Multimedia

Resource Links:

A companion website based on the materials captured at and during the two research consultations in Beirut, Lebanon, and Yogyakarta, Indonesia by a professional film crew can be found at www.songsforpeaceproject.org. The website provides materials to enhance classroom teaching, seminar, and personal use. It includes interviews with contributing authors, participating musicians, excerpts from concerts performed in Lebanon and Indonesia, and information on various peace projects that also look at music and the arts. Audio clips on the website also include musical examples referenced in book chapters: for example, cantillation and *tawshīḥ* as well as photographs of consultations, concerts, and cultural art. In addition, abstracts of each chapter are available on the website in the following languages: English, Arabic, French, and Indonesian.

Accompanying Multimedia:

A professionally made documentary film of the "story behind the story," with on-location footage from all three concerts, consultation interactions, relevant contexts, interviews with priests and sheiks, and unique locations, such as Muslim boarding schools in Indonesia, complements the material in this volume. Miroslav Volf, esteemed professor on conflict resolution, peacemaking, and Muslim-Christian relations at Yale University, provides an external voice and commentary. Trailer for the documentary can be found on the website at www.songsforpeaceproject.org. Information for purchasing *(un)Common Sounds*, the fifty-eight-minute DVD as shown on national US television (ABC), is also available on the www.songsforpeaceproject.org website.

List of Illustrations

Chapter 11

Chapter 12

Chapter 13

Chapter 14

Notes on Transliteration and Translation

This text makes frequent reference to terms in Arabic, Bahasa Indonesian, and French. Unless otherwise indicated, all translations are those of the contributor within each chapter. The *ALA-LC Romanization Tables: Transliteration Schemes for Non-Roman Scripts* approved by the Library of Congress and the American Library Association was used for transliteration from the Arabic into English. See http://www.loc.gov/catdir/cpso/roman.html.

No adjustment in the transliteration was made in the following cases:

1. common enough English words, sometimes even bearing English suffix (as in Qur'anic, Sunnis, Sufism): Islam, Qur'an, Sunni, Shi'i, Hadith, Sufi, imam, ulama;

2. less common but also treated as English words: Ibadi, Isma'ili, Khariji;

3. English words whose form differs significantly from the Arabic equivalent: Umayyad, Abassid, Fatimid, caliph, Druze;

4. words in quoted passages or cited titles;

5. place names that have familiar English spellings; local spellings of place names;

6. proper names of people, assuming the form given is the individual's preferred spelling;

7. Indonesian words derived from Arabic, such as "Syari'ah" instead of "Sharī'ah."

Additional exceptions include where a singular Arabic word made plural by adding "s" takes "-s" (unitalicized), as in "*ūd*-s" in order to avoid confusion. Both Muḥammad or Muhammad were used interchangeably although Muḥammad is the correct transliteration.

Notes on Contributors

Nidaa Abou Mrad, PhD, is professor of musicology and director of the Higher Institute of Music and of the Centre of Languages, Université Antonine, Baabda, Lebanon, and Chief Editor of the *Revue des Traditions Musicales des Mondes Arabe et Méditerranéen* (RTMMAM).

Bernard Adeney-Risakotta, PhD, is professor of religion and social science, international representative, Indonesian Consortium for Religious Studies (ICRS), at Gadjah Mada University, Yogyakarta, Indonesia. His publications include *Dealing with Diversity: Religion, Globalization, Violence, Gender and Disaster in Indonesia* and *Strange Virtues: Ethics in a Multicultural World.*

Rev. Marcel Akiki, PhD, is Assistant Professor, Faculty of Pedagogy, Lebanese University, Lebanon.

Irwansyah Harahap is a faculty member, Ethnomusicology Department, University of North Sumatra. His publications include *Hata ni Debata: Etnografi Spiritual-Musikal Parmalim Batak Toba* and *Fajar Di Atas Awan* (music album).

Jared Holton is assistant lecturer, Music Department, University of Tripoli, Libya.

Mustafa Said is Director of the Arab Music Archive and Research Foundation, Lebanon, and Instructor, Higher Institute of Music, Université Antonine (UA), Baabda, Lebanon. His music albums include *Rubaiyat El Khayyam* and *Asil.*

Jon Hoover, PhD, is associate professor of Islamic studies, The University of Nottingham, England. His publications include *Ibn Taymiyya's Theodicy of Perpetual Optimism* and several articles on Christian-Muslim relations and medieval Islamic theology.

Rithaony Hutajulu is a faculty member, Ethnomusicology Department, University of North Sumatra. Her publications include "Gondang Batak Toba and Tourism's Impact on Toba Batak Ceremony."

Roberta R. King, PhD, is associate professor of communication and ethnomusicology, Fuller Theological Seminary, School of Intercultural Studies, California, USA. Her publications include *Pathways in Christian Music Communication: the Case of the Senufo of Côte d'Ivoire* and *Music in the Life of the African Church*.

James R. Krabill, PhD, is adjunct professor of missions, Anabaptist Mennonite Biblical Seminary, Indiana, USA. His publications include *Anabaptists Meeting Muslims: A Calling for Presence in the Way of Christ* and *Mission and Worship for the Global Church: An Ethnodoxology Handbook*.

Sahiron Syamsuddin, PhD, is professor in Islamic studies, UIN (State Islamic University), Yogyakarta, Indonesia. His publications include *Die Koranhermeneutik Muhammad Šahrūrs und ihre Beurteilung aus der Sicht muslimischer Autoren,* and "Muhkam and Mutashābih: an Analytical Study of al-Tabarī's and al-Zamakhsharī's Interpretation of Q. 3:7."

Sooi Ling Tan, PhD, is an adjunct assistant professor, Fuller Theological Seminary, and adjunct lecturer, Malaysia Baptist Theological Seminary, Malaysia. Her publications include *Transformative Worship among the Salako, Sarawak, Malaysia* and "Transformative Worship In the Malaysian Context."

Foreword

This splendid collection of studies reflects on a series of encounters between members of different religious traditions in which music played a key role. Music, of course, has played a central role in all religious traditions, from Buddhist chants, to Muslim calls to prayer, to Evangelical praise choruses. The music of the great faiths has the rare ability to capture the heart of these faiths and give believers, as Rumi the Sufi poet says, the taste of being at home: "The value of a human being can be measured by what he or she most deeply wants. Be free of possessing things. Sit at an empty table. Be pleased with water, the taste of being at home."[1]

Rumi's enormous influence on people of many faiths illustrates the potential role of aesthetics and art for interreligious encounter. But it is safe to say that these encounters have not taken sufficient advantage of this potential. In the midst of the stereotypes that today threaten our polarized world, it is especially important to attend not only to the beliefs of each other, but more often and more centrally, to the music of our neighbor's faith, along with other aesthetic practices. Of course art can induce conflict, as in the Danish cartoon episodes, and it can incite divisions, as Islamist art has done in Iran. But historically the encounter with the imagery of other religious traditions has often been positive and mutually enriching, and this is especially true of the music produced by these traditions.

We have now in this volume a wonderful example of how such mutual listening can contribute to understanding and reconciliation. What I found especially moving in these studies was the ability of music to open up participants to each other, and encourage a mutual hospitality, one that is willing to receive the gifts of another. Surely, after we have sat together in the presence of a haunting melody or a sonorous call to prayer, it will be more difficult for us to look on our neighbor with suspicion and distrust. Cynical observers of the violence in our world might wonder if such a meeting could really happen, or, if it did, if it would make any difference. The studies in this

---

1. Jalal al-Din Rumi, *The Glance: Songs of Soul Meetings*, trans. Coleman Banks (New York: Penguin, 2001) 85.

book, by world-class musicians and leaders of their traditions, are evidence not only that this can happen but that it *is* happening. And the authors have offered this gift to us in the hopes that this mutual gift-giving will continue to flourish.

William Dyrness
Professor of Theology and Culture
Fuller Theological Seminary

Foreword

I am honored and humbled to be writing a foreword for this new volume, *(un)Common Sounds: Songs of Peace and Reconciliation among Muslims and Christians*. This project is noteworthy in its contribution to interreligious education and peacebuilding on four different levels:

1. The research recognizes the importance of lived religion, and that the texts of human consumption include the holy Scriptures that are then rendered into being by engagement with the spiritual dimensions of imaginative thought and action. Too many books on religious peacebuilding stay bounded to the confines of a text and ignore the rich emanations of that text in the lives of humans. This book contributes greatly to a methodology for producing descriptive forms of literature that show the practice of peace and religion in their full glory and form.

2. As a scholar who teaches Muslim and Christian peacemaking both in their independent and conjoined interfaith iterations, this book is exciting because it explores theological, liturgical, and spiritual dimensions that are authentic to each tradition. One may use this book to demonstrate case studies in which music, peace, and culture are shown in their authentic realms of specific and interfaith ecosystems. This attention to richness of context provides the reader with an exciting window into worlds that may be deeply embedded in religious spaces not often open to the inquiry of a student.

3. The articles in the book span Arab and Southeast Asian communities. It cannot be overstated how often the Christian-Muslim framing is limited to a few sections of the Middle East. As a book of comparative ethnomusicology, this book functions also as a comparative theological text. Very often, if one is teaching in a seminary setting, a professor looks for examples of spiritual formation that are legitimate within a tradition and allow for a student to envision interreligious cooperation as a possibility. This text does this beautifully by speaking within and

across traditions, assuming each has the resources for building peace inherent in its texts and cultural production.

4. As a reader, one is drawn into the community and author's recognition that there is no universal, monolithic interpretation of an Islamic or Christian way of being. One of the most damaging aspects of Islamophobia has been the perception of Islam as a religion incapable of adjusting to social and dynamic forces of specific contemporary needs. The impact of these collective essays will assist students with the development of a conflict-assessment lens that includes culture, religion, geography, popular discourse, and historical analysis all as tools for developing a critical eye.

It is not often that one waits for a book so eagerly to join the canon of literature that contributes to interfaith and intercultural understanding. I am delighted to join you on your journey as you read this text!

Najeeba Syeed-Miller
Assistant Professor of Interreligious Education
Claremont School of Theology

Acknowledgments

It is nearly impossible to adequately acknowledge and recognize the multiple people who have so generously contributed to this project exploring "Songs of Peace and Reconciliation among Muslims and Christians" in countless ways. We want to thank the following people and institutions.

- Henry B. Luce Foundation for their generous research grant that made this project possible. We are also grateful to Lynn Szwaja who guided us so wisely through the proposal process.

- The Brehm Center for Worship, Theology, and the Arts, Fuller Theological Seminary, and in particular Kathleen Tiemubol for her invaluable administrative support.

- Fred Davison, Director of the Brehm Center, Fuller Theological Seminary and co-editor of the Art for Faith's Sake series with Cascade.

- Douglas C. McConnell, Provost, Fuller Theological Seminary, who helped to envision the project.

- Bill and Dee Brehm, who sponsored a three-year post-doctoral fellowship for Dr. Sooi Ling Tan

- School of Intercultural Studies, Fuller Theological Seminary for providing research travel funds to Morocco.

- Clayton J. Schmit, Provost, School of Theology, Lenoir-Rhyne University and Lutheran Theological Southern Seminary, and co-editor of the Art for Faith's Sake series with Cascade.

- Martin Accad, Director of The Institute of Middle East Studies (IMES) and the staff of the Arab Baptist Theological Seminary (ABTS), Beirut, Lebanon, who hosted us and showed legendary Lebanese hospitality. We thank Dany Chaloub for his excellent photography.

- Bernie and Farsijana Adeney-Risakota who hosted and introduced us to the ICRS (International Consortium for Religious Studies) and their warmly welcoming staff, in particular Elis Zuliati Anis and Maria Ingrid.

- Irfan Amalee, Eric Lincoln and Peace Generation, Bandung, Indonesia, for allowing us to share in their peacebuilding ventures.

- Kirk-Evan Billet, for his excellent and tireless help in Arabic translation and transliteration.

- Numerous consultation participants, colleagues, and friends who contributed in countless ways: W. Robert Hodges, Nizar Fares, Jean Ngoya Kidula, Katherine Holton, Marsius Tinambunan, Sue Whittaker, and Habib Chirzin.

- Craig Detweiler of Pepperdine University and his film crew, James O' Keefe and Donald Hale, who not only made a wonderful documentary, but also was an encouraging presence and conversation partner.

- Eric Bigoness and Oliver Lo for their creative *(un)Common Sounds* website design.

- As lead investigator and scholar of this challenging, rewarding, and long project, Roberta wants to especially thank Sooi Ling for her excellent administrative gifting, leadership in organizing the consultations, editorial contributions, and patient perseverance in helping to bring this project that has lasted well beyond her three-year post-doctoral fellowship to completion.

- To our creator God who profoundly longs for peace and reconciliation among all peoples.

Prologue

. . . from Beirut to Yogyakarta

by Roberta R. King and Sooi Ling Tan

In every heart there is a hunger for words of peace.[1]

In an era when violence and war is overwhelming, something new and unusual is taking place. From Beirut to Yogyakarta a reshaping of the imagination and possibilities for coming together through diverse musical performances in new configurations is emerging. Musicians and scholars at two academic consultations in Lebanon and Indonesia collaborated and revealed how Muslims and Christians are creating musical spaces for coming together, for relating with one another, and for building sustainable peace. What took place?

Beirut, Lebanon: "Songs of Divine Love: an Islamic/Christian Spiritual Concert."[2]

The Sunni *shaykh*[3] raises his lone voice in a clarion call, offering a cantillation of a verse from the Holy Ḥadīth, a part of the Islamic divine tradition. In highly ornamented Arabic recitation, he declares the sacred text:

1. Participant, Songs of Peace and Reconciliation Colloquium, Beirut, Lebanon, April 4, 2009.

2. The "Songs of Divine Love: An Islamic/Christian Spiritual Concert" took place on April 3, 2009.

3. Shaykh Salah Yammut, a Qur'anic reciter, is an authorized official cantor of the Sunni inshād.

1

I was a hidden treasure. I wanted to be known, so I created men and through Me they knew Me.

Toward the end of his extended, *a cappella* melisma, the ensemble surrounding him offers its appreciation of the *shaykh*'s exceptional recitation. They softly and appreciatively exclaim, "Allah,"[4] and in so doing acknowledge God as the source of profound interiority.[5] Now the leader and founder of the Classical Arabic Music Ensemble, Nidaa Abou Mrad, takes up his violin. Mustafa Said from Egypt joins him on the *'ūd* (the short-necked lute) as does Ghassan Sahhab on the *qānūn* (the plucked zither). They respond with *"Bashraf Murabbaʿ Bayyātī nawā,"* an instrumental composition from the Arabic renaissance based on the *Bayyātī maqām*.[6] Improvisations (*taqāsīm*) extend the instrumental development with the musicians playing deeper into the theme of the evening as they offer an instrumental improvisation that serves as a cantillation of Hymn 16 from *Hymns of Divine Love by St. Symeon the New Theologian* (Constantinople, 949–1024). The text, although not vocalized, lays out their prayer:

> I frequently cast glances all around to see my Beloved
>
> And He, the invisible One, never shows Himself to me.
>
> But when I begin to weep, as desperate, then
>
> He shows Himself and He looks at me, He who contemplates all creatures.

So began the evening's concert, "Songs of Divine Love: An Islamic/Christian Spiritual Concert." The performance of common and related sacred texts through cantillation and instrumental interludes takes the audience into profound arenas of Arabic musical traditions that speak into their contemporary setting. A renewal process and reconfiguration is occurring wherein long, historical, and common roots, both musical and liturgical, are engendering a revival of heritage that addresses contemporary realities among highly religious peoples. Where barriers between people have come to exist, they are being torn asunder through musical performance of common musical traditions. The audience and performers find themselves in musical spaces that allow them to come together in new ways.

---

4. Although often associated with Islam, the term "Allah" is the Arabic word for "God."

5. Nidaa Abou Mrad discussing the concept of ṭarab (ecstasy) as "immobility, silence, and interiority" at the Songs of Peace and Reconciliation Colloquium, Beirut, Lebanon, April 4, 2009.

6. Arabic modal scale centered on D.

The concert setting itself is strikingly sparse, even ascetic. Yet, it is also rife with profound metaphorical significance. From the back of the stage in the Ahajar Auditorium, hang three banners, each proclaiming Christian symbolism of the institution: a flame on one banner is representative of the Holy Spirit, an abstract cross quilted on the second banner, plus the insignia of the Near East School of Theology[7] is embroidered on the middle banner. The grand piano, closed and protected with a black cover, looms in the background pushed toward the rear of the stage. However, front and center on stage is the performing group, or *takht*, constituted in this case of violin, *qānūn*, and *'ūd*, of the Classical Arabic Music Ensemble. The ensemble, founded in 1998 by Nidaa Abou Mrad and since 2002 based at the Higher Institute of Music at the Antonine University in Lebanon, also includes two vocal performers. While it is already somewhat unusual to listen to a traditional Arabic music ensemble in a protestant setting, what is even more striking is the composition of the two cantillator-singers: Shaykh Salah Yammut is a Qur'anic reciter and Mikael Hourani, an Orthodox singer. Indeed, the whole ensemble is a surprisingly mixed group composed of Muslims and Christians of various traditions who perform and record together on a regular basis. The mixed blend on the stage increases even further when Shaykh Shafik Jaradeh, representing the local Shia community, arrives later and joins the ensemble, taking a chair next to the grand piano and becoming totally involved in deep listening to the performance. It is indeed an unusual setting. Many people in the audience, composed of visiting scholars from across the Middle East and the United States plus local residents, have not previously imagined how Muslim and Christian performers could come together on the same stage in Beirut. Beirut, Lebanon, is a city that has known religious conflict, such as its long civil war (1975–1990) and is currently laced with further tensions and sporadic eruptions into the twenty-first century (Gavlak 2006, 130–32; Haddad 2001, 131–42; Peleikis 2001, 400–429; Joseph 1978). For many, Lebanon serves as a symbol of Muslim-Christian encounters.

7. Located on Sourati St., Hamra district of Beirut.

**Figure 1: Beirut: Songs of Divine Love Concert with the
Classical Arabic Music Ensemble**

As the concert notes explain, the performance is based on a "musical tradition heavily influenced by spiritual hermeneutics: the Arab-Oriental art music tradition in its encounter with ecclesiastical Antioch Orthodox tradition." Seeking to find common focus drawn from their religious heritages this encounter takes place through shared spiritual desires where "Christian and Muslim mystical paths have as their goal the sanctifying union of humans with the divine light. These paths serve a quest of human love for God, which responds to the infinite and inconceivable love which God bears for humankind."[8] In total, the evening is organized around the cantillation of biblical and Qur'anic verses plus excerpts from the Hadith. Mystical texts from recognized poets and theologians from both Christianity (Syméon the New Theologian) and Islam (al-Husayn ibn Mansur al-Hallaj, Muhyi d-Din ibn 'Arabi, and 'Umar ibn al-Farid) are also drawn upon.

Mutuality and recognition of each tradition during the concert proceeds with the alternation of cantillation and singing between the two religious liturgical specialists, along with instrumental statements that function in some ways as interludes for further reflection. As an outside observer of the performance I am drawn to a striking similarity of the performance alternation of sacred texts typical of that found in the structure of many of the

8. From the program notes for the Concert: "Songs of Divine Love: An Islamic/ Christian Spiritual Concert."

Psalms, sacred texts common to all three Abrahamic faiths. In essence, the performance of common musical traditions encompasses content conveyed across generations through intersecting vectors of transmission pregnant with a renewal of heritage in current lived settings. Such authenticity and renewal through spiritual, hermeneutical practice that impacts current realities lies at the foundation of the ensemble's performative purpose.[9]

As the evening continues, Shaykh Shafik Jaradeh, representing the local Muslim Shia community, offers a religious reflection on the significance of the arts. He begins by confessing that he is passionate about the arts, especially since he has learned through Professor Abou Mrad that "art is part of the deeper knowledge of life, . . . spiritual knowledge." He speaks of how the spirit of God was placed in Mary, and the spirit became word, "*logos*," with the existence of Christ. He continues by making critical links between melody and art as means for reaching God. He comments further, "And if the melody is the word of silent presence, then the melody and art is the means of those who are in love with God as well." Finally, he reveals his main purpose for attending the event:

> So when I heard that as part of your conference you had a dialogue of silence, which is the dialogue of art and melody, knowing that such a dialogue can only be about peace and reconciliation, and reconciliation with God, my passion and my desire was to share with you in this dialogue so that perhaps my heart would be united with yours as we come together as people seeking the melody of the heart. And may this diagnosis of the heart and this dialogue of the spirit be among the people of religion and the lovers of peace.[10]

The *shaykh's* reflection is then immediately followed by a cantillation of the well-known Light Verse from the Qur'an (24:35):

> Allah is the Light of the heavens and the earth. The similitude of His light is as a niche wherein a lamp is. The lamp is in a glass. The glass is as it were a shining star. (This lamp is) kindled from a blessed tree, an olive neither of the East nor of the West, whose oil would almost glow forth though no fire touched it. Light upon light, Allah guideth unto His light whom He will. And

9. "Musical Traditions from the Arab World," CD-Sampler, Notes, p. 11, the Taqālīd Collection, Nidaa Abou Mrad, Artistic Director, Beirut, Lebanon. The Taqālīd Collection constitutes seven albums produced in Lebanon in 2009.

10. Translation of reflection from the concert, "Songs of Divine Love," by Dr. Martin Accad.

Allah speaketh to mankind in allegories, for Allah is knower of all things.[11]

The famous Qur'anic passage is immediately followed by the *Doxastikon* (Glory . . . both now . . .) of the Aposticha from the Antiochene ecclesiastical tradition.[12] Within the *takht* ensemble, Professor Abou Mrad participates by crossing himself and folding his hands in prayer as the recitation from his own religious tradition fills the musical space. The alternation of mystical poems and sacred texts moves the concert forward and includes a cantillation of Saint Paul's "Hymn to Love" (1 Cor 13):[13]

> If I speak in the tongues of men and of angels, but have not love, I am only a resounding gong or a clanging cymbal. If I have the gift of prophecy and can fathom all mysteries and all knowledge, and if I have a faith that can move mountains, but have not love, I am nothing. If I give all I possess to the poor and surrender my body to the flames, but have not love, I gain nothing. Love is patient, love is kind. It does not envy, it does not boast, it is not proud. It is not rude, it is not self-seeking, it is not easily angered, it keeps no record of wrongs. Love does not delight in evil but rejoices with the truth. It always protects, always trusts, always hopes, always perseveres.[14]

The evening concludes with concert attendees who have not previously experienced the performance of their common musical religious traditions asking where they can purchase recordings of the Classical Arabic Music Ensemble. Having been profoundly impacted, they are longing once again to listen deeply to the musical interfaith dialogues: from cantillation to instrumental "dialogues of silence." Significant paradigm shifts and the breaking of stereotypes have occurred through performance in musical spaces, resulting in the expansion of limited knowledge of each other's religious tradition.

While the "Songs of Divine Love: An Islamic/Christian Spiritual Concert" took place in Lebanon, the musical traditions performed are characteristic of Christian, Muslim, and Jewish musical traditions of the Mediterranean basin from the first millennium. Broadly situated beyond

11. From the program notes for the Concert: "Songs of Divine Love: An Islamic/ Christian Spiritual Concert."

12. Doxastikon (Glory . . . Both now . . .) of the Aposticha (By the Nun Kassiani)— Great Wednesday Matins, in Tone 8 (Arabic adaptation: Dimitry Murr).

13. Performed as a cantillation of an Arabic version of verses from 1 Cor 13 in the eighth ecclesiastical mode (Nisabur) of the Orthodox music tradition.

14. Text from concert program notes, 3.

Lebanon, they are also considered "equally relevant to the great art-music traditions of Eastern Arab, Persian, and Ottoman cities and also to the folk music traditions from the East and South of the Mediterranean basin and beyond."[15] Indeed, with the expansion of Arab traders and Islam into the South Asia regions, many similar musical characteristics have taken root in places such as Indonesia. As in Beirut, a concert in Yogyakarta revealed emerging new configurations among musicians in musical performance that were expressive of their unique, local contexts and religious-historical heritage.

Yogyakarta, Indonesia: A Concert on "Common Sounds: Songs of Peace and Reconciliation"[16]

As the drone sound from the *sruti* box pulsated during the closing bars of the final song of the concert, *Kita Berbagi* (We Share), the guitar and *djembe* wove in their own musical patterns providing a steady rhythm and chordal structure. Mustafa Said began to improvise lightly on the *'ūd*. And over this, individual voices rose up melodically. Dr. William Hodges and Jared Holton sang, "O Sacred Head Now Wounded" and "O Lord You are my God" together with vocal improvisations from other members of Suarasama. It was a mesmerizing moment of harmony of sound as musicians from different nations and different faith traditions set aside their religious and ethnic differences, yet remained true to their religious and musical beliefs, and locked their hearts together to sing for peace.

Figure 2: Yogyakarta Concert: Singing *Kita Berbagi* Together

15. See concert program notes and/or CD notes.

16. The "Common Sounds: Songs of Peace and Reconciliation" concert took place on April 1, 2010.

This powerful moment concluded "Common Sounds: Songs of Peace and Reconciliation", a concert fully sponsored by the Henry Luce Foundation grant. It featured Muslim and Christian artists, ensembles and choirs, with participants coming from Egypt, North Africa, Sumatra, Yogyakarta, and the United States. Held at *Lembaga Indonesia-Perancis* or the Indonesian-French Cultural Center, Jogjakarta, on April 1, 2010, the vision for the concert was to find a common sound (of peace) through music and performing arts.

Sitting there as an organizer and observer, I noticed the breadth of diversity present. The performers and audiences came from different walks of life: Muslims, Christians and other religious faiths, young children to mature adults, world-renowned musicians, university professors and students, and local women and children from the outskirts of Yogyakarta. Musically, the styles drew from various music genres: Indonesian folk and cultural music, popular music, classical Arabic music, *shallawat*, and a hybridity of world music. Instruments featured included the *'ūd, gambus, khendang, sruti* box, electronic keyboard, *djembe*, and *bonang*. What did these diverse performers, instruments, and musical styles from various parts of the world have in common? Interestingly what emerged with each successive performance was the common sound of instruments, movement and voices in dialogue and expressing their hopes and reasons for peace. This common sound became a shared hope and a uniting factor.

Figure 3: Yogyakarta Concert: Children Contribute.

The concert also provided a platform to communicate the vision and hope of peace. This message was conveyed most overtly by the children's performance. As the children from *Gabungan Komunitas Pondok Tali Rasa*, *Pondok Anak Sewon*, and *Pondok anak-anak Taman Terban*[17] took to the stage in their brightly multicolored costumes in traditional design, they engaged the audience in a sincere, simple and yet touching rendition of dance and mime. On stage, they initially danced and played local Indonesian games in harmony. However, this harmony is disrupted as, in due course, quarrels break out and conflict escalates. The conflict is, however, resolved and the children re-gather to dance and finally fly balloons as an affirmation of their desire to seek to live peaceably and for life.

The concert had opened with a set of four songs by Suarasama, a music ensemble based in Sumatra and founded by Irwansyah Harahap and his wife, Rithaony Hutajulu, the principal vocalist. With the delicate plucking of the guitar by Irwansyah, accompanied by soft percussion of the ensemble and the silky voice of Rithaony, the audience quieted down and was absorbed in the harmony of voices and instruments in their songs, *Bahtera* (Sails), *Lebah* (Bee), and *Fajar di Atas Awan* (Dawn Above the Clouds).

An arresting piece was their third song, "Untuk Mu Yang Berperang" (For Those who go to war), a strong piece sardonically dedicated to those who go to war. Inspired by an African tradition, *Chedo*, it draws its inspiration from an African saying, "If you are angry, you are not thinking. If you are making music, you are thinking." The song text poetically describes the negative consequences of war with the use of strong imagery such as "black iron spreads all over, the smell of the blood of death." The author's voice is heard as the lament is sung and hopes ascribed:

> "For you it is power, for us it is suffering.
> For you it is pride, for us, it is stupidity.
> Your legacy is only hateful vengeance."
> What we desire is to sit and to walk together,
> Saying to everyone, never to war again."[18]

The songs and cultural performances also provided moments of transcendence, inclusion, and camaraderie. Mustafa Said, a prolific 'ud player from Egypt, sang and played a *waslah* (sequence of pieces) based on five of El Khayyam's quatrains. Impacted by the intellect, asceticism, profound

17. The children are from three communities: Pondok Tali Rasa, Pondok Anak Sewon, Pondok anak Taman Terban.

18. *Untuk Mu yang Berperang*" (For Those Who Go to War). Lyrics and music by Harahap.

vision, and philosophy of El Khayyam (1048–1131), a renowned Persian scientist, traveler, and poet, Mustafa drew us into the world of the poet's wisdom. Drawing excerpts from his album "Roubaiyat El Khayyam," in a *waṣlah* played in *ramal* rhythm, Mustafa expresses the poet's reminder that love is central to a person's existence. In another *waṣlah,* he reminded us of the wisdom that knowledge is limited for the human person, or, "he only knows one thing, that he does not know anything." What is striking about the performance is the creativity of the *taqāsīm* and Mustafa's mastery of the *'ūd,* as he moves seamlessly between different rhythms and the *maqāmāt.* His versatility and impeccable musical technique combined with El Khayyam's deep and profound philosophical poetry fostered moments of transcendence among many of his listeners.

Duta Voice, a thirty-member choir from Duta Wacana Christian University under the direction of Mr. Marsius Tinambunan, the choir director, gave a stirring performance of three Indonesian folk songs that drew the audience into the diverse cultural worlds of Indonesia. Dressed in traditional clothing representing the various ethnic groups in Indonesia, they performed in perfect harmony and synchronized dance movements. The first song, *Sayang Kene,* was feisty and strongly upbeat with beautiful alliteration of poetic language from the island of Maluku.

Figure 4: Yogyakarta Concert: Dutawacana Christian University.

Accompanied only by an electronic keyboard, the choir soared with their voices in unison and harmony, accompanied by occasional ululations and small but strong dance moves. The *bonang* and *khendang* accompanied the next song performance of "Soyang," a song from Central Java.

Clearly, there was a natural and close cooperation among Muslim and Christian performers that night. This was demonstrated when twenty-nine ladies from the Indonesian Women's Coalition, who came from the villages in the outskirts of Yogyakarta, performed two songs. Farsijana Adeney-Risakotta, the spokesperson, explains that the purpose of this organization is to help people understand how women can be a part of decision-making in Indonesian society. These ladies, from different economic and religious backgrounds, singing together in one common voice, gave a memorable performance. Farsijana describes how practicing for this performance allowed Muslim ladies to connect with Christians. In fact the leader of the group, who also leads the reading of the Qur'an in their local mosque, played an instrumental role in convincing the Muslim women of the need to sing together with Christians. In particular, this group's heart-filled rendition of *Tanah Air Ku* (My Homeland), a patriotic song written by Ibu Soed, evoked a common longing, love, and appreciation for their homeland. Farsijana aptly summarizes, "We live together in this green and beautiful land. We need to share what we have together. Indonesia is a precious resource and there is a need to maintain peace in Indonesia so that we can all share in this resource."

Another example of cooperation was the next performance when Dr. William (Rob) Hodges took to the stage to sing *L'Agli-nNabi* (For the Sake of the Prophet), accompanied by Mustafa Said. A poignant moment of musical interconnectedness was demonstrated as a Muslim (Mustafa Said) and a Christian (William Hodges) made music together. There were instances when Mustafa sang together with Rob at the chorus. At other times, the vocal and the *'ud* would weave in and out, each listening to the other, and each giving space for the other to either take the lead in improvisation or to fall back in a supporting role.

Suarasama masterfully capped the evening with a final set of four songs. What was striking was the identification of the commonality of Abraham as the forefather between Islam and Christianity. The first three songs were thus a trilogy dedicated to the three icons of the Islamic tradition: Prophet Muhammad (*Habibullah, Muhammad Ya Rasullullah* [Beloved of God, Muhammad Apostle of God]); Abraham (*Ibrahim Alaihissalam* [Abraham, Upon Him be Peace]); and Jesus (*Isa Alaihissalam* [Jesus, Upon Him be Peace]), two of whom intersect with those of the Christian faith and both based on the Abrahamic tradition. Significantly, all three religious leaders included in this musical trilogy came to bring peace on earth.

Perhaps the final song for the concert, *"Kita Berbagi,"* written by Irwansyah Harahap, specially commissioned for the consultation and concert most reflected the possibilities and aspirations of the project in bringing together people from diverse musical cultures, ethnicities, and religions to sing and perform together in and for peace. The lyrics share this hope:

> We should be as one, sharing this life
>
> We should be without suffering, without anger
>
> We should be of one voice, no longer quarrelling
>
> Sending forth to all, love for one another.

The longing and hope expressed in the song, *"Kita Berbagi,"* is found in varying local contexts around the world and most often expressed in differing local ways. While interreligious encounters in Indonesia have a broader religious diversity than the Middle East, both arenas find themselves confronted in the twenty-first century by conflict among adherents of Abrahamic religions. In the Middle East, the birthplace of all three Abrahamic faith traditions, historical roots point to hotly contested arenas of interreligious encounters and conflicts. Indonesia, as the most populous Muslim nation in the world, and Lebanon with its history of interreligious-political conflict, know the injustice, heartbreak, and suffering of clashes, especially between Muslims and Christians. Not only did the "(un)Common Sounds Concert" in Yogyakarta reveal longings and initiatives in pursuing peace via cultural musics and the arts, but the concert the year before in Beirut, Lebanon, courageously engaged overcoming religious barriers and divides by seeking common sounds and liturgical practices. Indeed, from Beirut to Yogyakarta, new configurations of peoples are coming together with a desire for peacemaking through music and the arts.

How This Book Came About

This work emerged out of a desire to begin to understand the global-local dialectic of the twenty-first century. World religions are no longer limited to certain regions of the world, but are increasingly interacting with and confronting one another on the global stage. Based at a theological seminary where interfaith dialogue is valued and practiced between various religions, we began to consider how music and the arts could contribute to such critical dialogues. We knew that intimate, expressive links between music, art, and world religions provide rich resources for understanding the belief systems of peoples and their influence on society and daily living. We therefore began asking if and how they function in bringing about peace and reconciliation. Out of these initial considerations emerged what has become a challengingly rich journey of musical and scholarly encounters that form the core of this book. Sponsored by a generous three-year grant from the Henry B. Luce Foundation, an international collaboration of twenty-one scholars and numerous musicians from the Middle East, North Africa, Indonesia, and the United States gathered together to discuss the role of music and related arts in building sustainable peace.

Two consultations took place in areas of the world where Muslims and Christians have lived together peacefully for centuries, yet have also known extreme violence. Beirut, Lebanon, based in the Middle East, began our journey where we held our first consultation (April 2009) followed by further dialogues on our topic in Yogyakarta, Java, located in Arab-influenced Indonesia (Southeast Asia), the highest populated Muslim nation in the world (March 2010). We felt each site offered unique contributions to make to the global community through academic research and musical exchange. Although they are not the only places where interreligious conflicts have taken place, both countries offer contexts where the dynamics of interreligious living among and between Christians and Muslims provide fertile soil for learning the lessons of sustainable peacebuilding. In addition, there is an interconnectedness that exists between these regions of the world that provide common and comparative elements, such as religion (Islam and Christianity in the midst of multiple religions), Arabic heritage, and political influence. Finally, both countries possess richly prolific music and artistic traditions critical for researching our topic.

The overall goal of each consultation was to listen and to learn about music and song as social activism within local contexts. Our desire is to give voice to scholars in these regions of the world who are making their contribution to society through music-making in their local contexts. In particular, we sought to research, think, and reflect together about the roles music and the arts can and do play in forging sustainable peace. Second, we sought to engage with each local scene about the ways music and the arts foster peace. Thus, we sponsored music concerts that demonstrated and revealed peacebuilding processes that are quietly taking place. Our ultimate desire was to discover, research, experience, and then offer global and local audiences opportunities to learn about one another and to demonstrate ways to build interconnectedness that foster mutual understanding and growing, dynamic relationships that are critical to sustaining peace.

Regarding the selection of scholars, the criteria were Christian and Muslim scholars who are experts in the fields of religion and ethnomusicology, and/or are active participants in peace work through the arts. We agreed on diversity, in terms of religious streams, ethnicity, gender, age, and social standing, as a guideline. We believed that by affirming similarities and by embracing differences that result in creative tension, the project would be enriched.

As such, this book features Dr. James Krabill, a Mennonite theologian involved in peace studies from the United States in dialogue with his counterpart Dr. Sahiron Syamsuddin, an Islamic Qur'anic Scholar from the State Islamic University, Yogyakarta. It involves conversations between senior scholar and peace practitioner such as Dr. Bernard T. Adeney Risakotta (Director of the Indonesian Consortium for Religious Studies, Yogyakarta) and Dr. Habib Chirzin (President, Islamic Forum on Peace, Human Security and Development, Indonesia) with two younger authors, Mr. Mustafa Said, a young, widely respected 'ūd player and instructor from Egypt, and Mr. Jared Holton, a scholar and accomplished pianist and musician who was teaching at that time in Libya.

Since we (Dr. Roberta King and Dr. Sooi Ling Tan) also wanted to highlight local voices with musicologists writing about their own musical traditions, we set out on our own individual journeys to visit Lebanon and Indonesia respectively, to scour for potential, local scholar-musicians. With the help of Dr. Martin Accad, Roberta came into contact with several musicologists from Lebanon, Dr. Marcel Akiki, Dr. Nidaa Abou Mrad, and Mr. Nizar Fares. In Indonesia, Irwansyah Harahap and Rithaohny Hutajulu, ethnomusicologists and widely acclaimed musicians from Sumatra agreed to join the project. In Bandung, Indonesia, through Dr. Jon and Judi Culver, Sooi Ling connected with Eric Lincoln and Peace Generation.

Subsequently, Dr. Farsijana Adeney-Risakkota's participation as an anthropologist involved in peace work through music in Maluku, Indonesia, and Dr. Jon Hoover's experiences as a scholar of Islam based in Beirut and now teaching Islamic Studies at the University in Nottingham, England, added more facets to the already present disciplines of ethnomusicology, history, peace studies, theology, and communication.

What This Book Is Not About

Recognizing the immensely sophisticated musical traditions along with the historical and political complexities of each region where we have held consultations, we do not endeavor to be comprehensive. Rather, we have sought to identify selective topics via the intersection of ethnomusicology and music cultures, theology and religious studies, and peacebuilding that contribute to living together with our neighbors.

Our main goals are to listen to and learn from two contrasting contexts of interreligious dimensions, where we find diverse expressions of two world religions. We recognize that each setting is much more complex than the simple monolithic representations presented on popular levels. Although each faith tradition claims to be universal, the variety of expression, musical *praxis*, and theological positions is staggering. We do not attempt to cover the full range of variability, but have chosen instead to focus on local contexts found in three major regions of the world: the Middle East, North Africa, and Southeast Asia, in order to begin to understand the dynamics of "musicking" (Small 1998, 9) in ways that impact societies toward peace.

Why Read This Book?

In these current times when sensationalism and conflicts are highlighted in the news, a book on peacebuilding can seem somewhat futile. Yet, growth in world population figures among Muslims and Christians provides compelling and challenging statistics, where, "in 1800, Christians and Muslims together accounted for just under 33 percent of the world's population. By 1900 this figure had increased to 47 percent, and by 2000 it was 53 percent" (Barrett 2001). Further projections point to 58 percent by 2025, rising up to as much as 66 percent by 2100—two-thirds of the world's population (ibid.). How, then, can we come together through music and the arts?

There are unheard voices that value, speak of, sing, and advocate for peace in the world today. These voices are playing significant roles in their local contexts and need to be heard. This book provides that venue. In a passionate statement at the Beirut consultation, Rev. Dr. Marcel Akiki said, "Us being here is a sign that a culture of peace is present and can be stronger than a culture of death and destruction"; while one of the observers at the Beirut consultation remarked, "The subject is what matters; if we put this as the first step, then we're going to the right place. Lebanese people have been looking for peace since we were born."

Thus, this book seeks to present the first steps toward interfaith dialogue and peace. Our ultimate goal is to initiate conversations that will encourage and promote sustainable peacebuilding through music and the performing arts. It is our desire that, as Dr. William Hodges aptly put it, "voices presenting a paper, or praising God in song [as in this project] is a source of strength" for those of us seeking peace. We offer this work as a seed of hope for today's world and for future generations. Not only is there a hunger for words of peace,[19] but what we discovered is that:

In every heart there is a hunger for songs of peace.

FOR DISCUSSION

1. How can music overcome real or perceived barriers, both interpersonal and intrapersonal, which lead to conflicts? Skim through the table of contents, read several chapter précis, and predict the different ways this book might explore how ethnomusicology relates to peacebuilding within Muslim-Christian contexts.

References Cited

Barrett, David B., et al. 2001. *World Christian Encyclopedia*. New York: Oxford University Press.

Gavlak, Dale. 2006. "They Know We are Christians: Lebanese Christian Compassion Impresses Muslims During Bloody Conflict." *Christianity Today* 50, no. 10: 130–32.

Haddad, Simon. 2001. "Christian-Muslim Relations and Attitudes towards the Lebanese State." *Journal of Muslim Minority Affairs* 21, no. 1: 131–48.

Joseph, Suad, and Barbara L. K. Pillsbury. 1978. *Muslim-Christian Conflicts: Economic, Political, and Social Origins*. Boulder, CO: Westview.

Peleikis, Anja. 2001. "Shifting Identities, Reconstructing Boundaries: The Case of a Multi-Confessional Locality in Post-War Lebanon." *Die Welt des Islams* 41, no. 3: 400–429.

Small, Christopher. 1998. *Musicking: The Meanings of Performing and Listening (Music Culture)*. Middletown, CT: Wesleyan University Press.

19. Participant, Songs of Peace and Reconciliation Colloquium, Beirut, Lebanon, April 4, 2009.

Introduction

Pursuing Songs of Peace and Reconciliation

By Roberta R. King

"We do not grow by knowing all of the answers,
but rather by living with the questions."

—MAX DePREE (DE PREE 1990, 58)

Setting the Stage

In an era of heightened globalization, extremist acts of violence appear to be on the rise linking global and local contexts in new ways. Indeed, the uncommon, explosive sounds of international terrorist attacks on September 11, 2001 in New York City coupled with an ever-growing litany of bombings from Bali (2002), to Madrid (2004), London (2005), and Mumbai (2006) demonstrate the conditions of a globalized world with its "expansion and intensification of social relations and consciousness across world-time and world-space" (Steger 2009, 15). Thus, global and local conflicts are no longer separated from one another. Rather, they are often interlinked in ways that influence and exacerbate arenas of tension. At the same time, world religions and their heightened encounters in the western hemisphere, often deemed as playing major roles in conflict, are generating an increased urgency to learn how to engage with followers of various religious traditions in ways that nurture peaceful coexistence.

While interreligious differences are not the source of all conflicts, certainly in the first decades of the twenty-first century they are perceived by

numerous peoples in the public domain as lying at the center of many conflicts. What can help to change this rising tide? Questions about the role of
music in conflict, conflict transformation, and peacemaking are taking on
magnified significance. In *(un)Common Sounds* we ask, what contributions
do music and the arts make toward understanding such emerging interactions in all their complexity? How does one go beyond religious differences
to engage with neighbors previously unknown or unrecognized? As globalization continues unabated, peoples of all faiths are moving onto the global
stage in new configurations, crisscrossing around the world, and living next
door to one another. Local contexts where peoples of differing faiths have
peacefully lived together for long periods of time are also experiencing dissonance within their own communities, including Egypt in the Arab Spring
era (Nelson February 25, 2012), Lebanon (MacKey 2006), and Indonesia.[1]
We ask, what roles do music and the performing arts bring to creating understanding and engaging one another in musical spaces that impact societies in positive ways? More specifically, focusing on music's transformative
role in conflict and post-conflict settings, we examine a single but endlessly
complex question: How is music and song used in our faiths and daily lives
to foster peace and reconciliation? Such questions lie at the heart of our
study.

   (un)Common Sounds is an investigation lying in the realm of applied
ethnomusicology. It is a collaborative work based on mutually reflective
academic dialogue between scholars and music practitioners as they seek
to identify and generate new approaches to pursuing peacemaking through
music and the arts. As Araujo (2006, 291) points out, the strength of collaborative research is "the opening of a possibility of a new kind of knowledge about social forms such as music and music-making—one that may
even subvert academic knowledge as it has been traditionally legitimated."
Indeed, such approaches afford local scholars occasions and opportunities
to reflect on academic levels previously unattainable within global arenas.
For us, as outside researchers who were coming into new contexts, our main
goal was to learn from and listen to those who have experienced war and
protracted conflict as well as those who are currently living and co-existing
with their neighbors in the midst of flaring tensions and threats.

   To be more precise, *(un)Common Sounds* is based on scholarly consultations, writings, and concerts that took place in parts of the world where

---

1. See for example, http://www.yale.edu/gsp/index.html; http://www.
voanews.com/content/rising-religious-violence-threatens-democracy-in-indone-
sia-116221519/167054.html; http://www.trust.org/alertnet/news/violence-against-
indonesias-religious-minorities-surges-hrw/. Based on a google search on 'violence in
Indonesia': August 8, 2012, 12:35 pm.

Muslims and Christians interact with one another on a daily basis. Beirut, Lebanon, was the sight of our first consultation in 2009. It is a city located in a country that experienced a horrific fifteen-year civil war (1975–1990) and continues to know political tensions and sporadic outbursts. Yogyakarta, Indonesia, on the other hand, was the location for the second consultation in 2010. It served as a base in a land of contested areas such as Aceh, Bandung, and the Moluccas (Spice Islands). With the immense religious diversity distributed throughout the Middle East and across Southeast Asia, these sites did not in any way represent the full spectrum of local contexts or variables when it comes to music-making, peacebuilding, and Muslim-Christian relations. Rather, they offered accessible venues to initiate much needed conversations with local, regional, and global implications.

This chapter addresses music and interreligious studies with a view toward sustainable peacebuilding. Three main arenas of academic discourse are required to critically consider the multivalent issues that arise when pursuing songs of peace and reconciliation. These streams are 1) the music-in-war-and-peacemaking continuum; 2) peacebuilding; and 3) interreligious studies and interfaith dialogue. Following the discussion of these streams, we provide a framework and overview of each scholar's contribution to the academic discourses contained in this volume and their implications for the development of an initial model for employing music in peacebuilding and interfaith dialogue.

Music, Peacebuilding, and Interreligious Studies

Exploring Muslim-Christian relations in light of contemporary contexts and conflicts, the intersection with music and peacebuilding requires negotiating multiple streams of academic inquiry within larger disciplinary arenas. Inherent in music studies is the coalescence of multiple tributaries that are gathered together in the dialectic between sound and society, imposing a dauntingly, mammoth task. Our original intent was to study song texts in light of religious *praxis*. Both Muslim and Christian traditions put great significance on sanctioned sacred texts, including the Bible, the Qur'an, and the Hadith as well as poetry, sacred texts embedded in hymns, and the performative practice of cantillation. Yet, dealing only with texts, in a manner similar to orientalism's literary approach is highly problematic. Although an important place to begin for peoples of religious conviction, we soon realized that our approach required taking broader roads. Our goal was to attain deeper understandings of how and in what ways music and the arts nurture relational spaces for sustainable peacebuilding. As van

Zanten argues about Islamic musics in Indonesia, one needs to go beyond the contents of a holy book and sacred written traditions by also looking at "the actual practices of the people involved" (2011, 260). Both the study of context plus text are required in order to access critical concerns intermingled in the complex task of music-making as peacebuilding. In other words, song texts divorced from their local context and religious ideologies are severely limited in revealing the complexity of religious *praxis,* no less interreligious encounters.

Thus, we were drawn into studying music events and music performance as a means to understanding broader social interactions of societies, with the hope of offering "perspectives on the relationship between sound and society" (Castelo-Branco 2010, 252). Christopher Small's concept of *musicking* took on significant implications for our studies as we opened up the range of topics normative of traditional ethnomusicological studies (2011, vii–xviii). Small maintains that "the meaning of a song, or indeed of any piece of music, is not just that of the text on the page." He argues, "Only when a song is performed will its multiple layers of meaning reveal themselves" (ix). Conceived as an action, not an object, "musicking" serves as an action verb where "to music is to take part, in any capacity, in a musical performance" (x).[2] Small emphasizes further that music is not only a mere activity but is also "a form of human encounter in which everyone who is present is taking part, and for whose success or failure as an event everybody who is present has some responsibility" (x). Thus, the ramifications of "musicking" offer essential links to human encounters, ones potentially lying at the heart of effective peacebuilding. Taking "musicking" in combination with the exigencies of studying local contexts, then, three major streams of academic discourse, music in war and peacemaking, peacebuilding, and interreligious studies (in particular Muslim-Christian relations), became critical issues that inform this study.

Music in War and in Peacemaking

Music in war and peacemaking is for the most part an unexplored arena of investigation. John O'Connell, noted investigator in the field, argues, "The study of music in war and music for peace has received surprisingly little attention in ethnomusicology" (O'Connell 2011, 112). This situation stands in stark contrast to the fields of anthropology and folklore, cognate

---

2. "To music is to take part, in any capacity, in a musical performance, whether by performing, by listening, by rehearsing or practicing, by providing material for performance (what is called composing), or by dancing" (Small 2011, 9).

disciplines to ethnomusicology, where applied studies have been firmly established (see Goldschmidt 1986; Nordstrom 1992; Mach 1993; Spradley 2000). Similarly, it follows that theoretical studies of conflict and music are also largely neglected (Araujo 2006, 289).[3] Yet, in the current post-9/11 era, an emergent literature among ethnomusicologists is emerging with a call for fuller development of applied ethnomusicology and musical advocacy within the discipline (See McDonald 2009, 58–85; Mendonca 2010, 369–94; Kartomi 2010, 452–83; and Van Buren 2010, 202–23). Scholars are seeking to identify means for investigating music and the performing arts in broad ways that ultimately contribute to resolving war and pursuing peacemaking.

The study of music in conflict, its resolution, and music for peace presents a knotty dilemma. The roles and functions of music are infinitely multitudinous in ways that elicit and yield ambivalence to its pursuit. The researcher must repeatedly consider multiple factors as to how to conduct investigations and to identify the point of departure in beginning one's investigation. As O'Connell (2011, 117) reveals, music poses as

> a double-edged sword used both as a point to excite hostility
> and as a potion to foster friendship. In the continuum that exists
> between war and peace, music occupied an ambiguous position,
> at once providing a contested space for conveying dissent while
> at the same time providing a common space for promoting as-
> sent. (117)

Thus, investigations must be tempered with the realization of a range of interpretations of music performed and heard. O'Connell further argues, "a peaceful song for one person could be a warlike song for another" (117). Known investigations into music in war, beginning with Arnold's 1993 classic study of art and military music in the West, through to more recent publications such as *Music and Conflict* (O'Connell 2010), focus on exploring "the significance of music for understanding conflict" (O'Connell and Castelo-Branco 2010, vii). Notably, major studies addressing music in war and for peace were just beginning to emerge as our research project, "Songs of Peace and Reconciliation among Muslims and Christians" began in 2008 (see O'Connell 2011). Although we encountered multiple layers of ambiguity and ambivalence, the significance of the project acquired further import. With ever-increasing conflicts, it became even more pressing to seek to make a contribution to peacebuilding via studies in the interplay between sound and society.

---

3. At the time of initiating our investigation (2008), the literature on music and peacemaking and also music and world religions was very sparse, almost non-existent.

What then is the intersection of music in war and peacemaking studies? Where does *(un)Common Sounds* situate itself in the music in war and peace continuum? We turn first to two streams of academic discourse: music and conflict, and music in conflict transformation and peacemaking.

Music and Conflict

Musical responses to violence and terror offer opportunities to observe and reflect on the multiple ways in which peoples in various contexts employ music in the midst of conflict and process traumatic events. The September 11, 2001 terrorist attack in New York City, for example, served as an arena of investigating music in response to terror. Based on a range of musical reactions to the attacks and eventual involvement in Afghanistan and Iraq, a set of densely layered cultural studies of music-in-performance create a "provisional map of music in the post-9/11 world" (Ritter 2007, xxi).[4] Originally intended as a purely ethnomusicological investigation, and similar to the evolution of *(un)Common Sounds*, the work morphed into a broader interdisciplinary study, expanding the spectrum of studies to include musicology, music theory, folklore, popular music and communication, American studies, and music journalism. Indeed, the parameters and intersection of music-in-performance touch on multiple aspects of society, addressing studies in critical societal components. The range of investigation resulted in the defying of compartmentalized restrictions within established disciplinary boundaries. While the first half of Ritter's work investigates music in the United States, most particularly popular music and the role of the media after 9/11, the second half turns to international studies and the impact of 9/11 on the global stage. Of particular note is Grippo's exposition of the music videos and songs by Sha'ban 'Abd al-Rahim, a popular Egyptian *sha'bī* singer. In "I'll tell you why we hate you!" Grippo provides an analysis of popular songs that unearth stereotypes and attitudes commonly found in popular Arab media. His findings reveal a sharp critique of American policies in the Middle East (Grippo 2007, 255–76). Additionally, of particular note is Blumenfeld's chapter about Sufis making music after 9/11 in "Exploding Myths in Morocco and Senegal" (Blumenfeld 2007, 209–24). Although the intersection of music and religion is not fully developed, the recognition of Muslim musicians within the Sufi tradition seeking interfaith dialogue and their critique on Muslim extremism provides a "myth-exploding" corrective to the demonization of Islam as singularly terrorist.

---

4. See also Ritter and Daughtry's edited volume (2007).

This exemplifies how the intimate links between sound, society, and religion are beginning to position themselves within academic discourse.

In a more wide-ranging series of studies, *Music and Conflict* seeks to "explore the significance of music for understanding conflict" (O'Connell 2010, vii). Engaging diverse geographical locations, topics, and theories, ethnomusicologists from around the world develop and critically address conflict arenas through ethnographical studies. From Kosovo to Northern Ireland, Brazil, Iran, Indonesia, Germany, and the United States, they investigate the ways in which music can be used to identify and resolve conflict. In these more fully developed ethnographic case studies, the ultimate goal was to contribute to an ethnomusicology of conflict and violence in order to offer "a framework for the public engagement of ethnomusicologists in conflict resolution as mediators and advocates" (Castelo-Branco 2010, 252). Similar to the "Songs of Peace and Reconciliation" project, the studies highlight how music can serve as a catalyst for imagining conflict resolution and the role of performance as a platform for dialogue among otherwise contentious groups. The emergence of religious studies and music in conflict situations in relation to world religions is beginning to appear on a more regular basis. Cooper, for example, in "Fife and Fiddle: Protestants and Traditional Music in Northern Ireland" addresses issues of religious allegiance and cultural identity in Northern Ireland in relation to music serving as a point of contention. Beeman (2010) and Rasmussen (2010), on the other hand, address issues of music and ideology in relation to Islam, a contentious issue often surrounding Islamic musical discourses. They reveal a continuum of Muslim musical practices that range from musical censorship to prolific musical performances representative of the plurality of local Islamic contexts worldwide. Although beyond the geographical arena for our studies, Seeger presents a particularly striking and cogent concept in musical diplomacy from Brazil where the Suyá people in their unique way "sing their enemies' songs and make them their own" (Seeger, 109). Seeger argues that such reciprocity through performing and paying attention to one another's performance plays a significant role in peaceful encounters with outsiders.

Music in Conflict Transformation and Peacemaking

While O'Connell and Castelo-Branco's work focuses on music and conflict, some issues related to solving conflict are also addressed. In *Music and Conflict Transformation: Harmonies and Dissonances in Geopolitics* (Urbain 2008), on the other hand, conflict resolution becomes the main topic. In an attempt to address the expansive, multivalent influences of music in society, a range of topics and case studies explore the significance of music for promoting peace. Of particular note is the identification of two theoretical concepts critical to peacemaking: empathy (Laurence 2008) and societal values. Each of these concepts is intrinsically and extrinsically embedded within musical experience in cross-cultural contexts as Boyce-Tillman argues (2008, 42–43). Not only is music in conflict transformation investigated but music healing and education serve as major foci for restoration processes. While a number of excellent concepts are offered, such as "collective vulnerability" for healing cultural violence (see Jordanger 2008, 128–46), there is a lack of in-depth analysis of the unique ways in which music directly contributes to resolving conflict. This is perhaps a reflection of the fact that, other than one musicologist, the majority of the scholars are specialists in peace studies. While music and religion is not directly addressed, two chapters address music and peacemaking in the Middle East (Abi-Ezzi in Urbain, 2008), a context that inherently implicates interreligious dynamics. It is commendable that peace specialists are recognizing music as a medium for facilitating conflict transformation. New patterns of coalescing disciplines are beginning to emerge.

More recently, Laurence and Urbain[5] address topics of peace and the policies required in employing music in conflict transformation in *Music and Solidarity* (2011). Published as an issue of *Peace and Policy (Volume 15)*, concepts and theories are aggregated with a focus on solidarity, universality, consciousness, and connection. Intermusicality, diversity, dialogue, and identity contribute to the conceptual base that address the paucity of serious theoretical engagement. Seeking to find ways to pursue peacemaking, the authors also speak into the void of applied studies in effectively employing music in peacemaking. Significantly, the place of "musicking" becomes much more developed with Small's substantial prologue to the work. Key issues toward an initial framework for exploring the intersection of music and peacemaking are identified (Lawrence 2011, vii–xviii). In spite of this, O'Connell laments that studies on "relevant themes that include . . . critical examination(s) of music and violence, music and dispossession, and music and ideology, an in-depth evaluation of music in peace negotiations is not extant" (2011, 117). Yet, scholars continue to note that, "The war-peace continuum is a particularly suitable ground for rethinking the "barriers between academic and applied work" and are greatly needed (2010, 189). Thus, in *(un)Common Sounds,* we seek to bridge the academic and applied

---

5. Laurence and Urbain were main contributors to the first volume, *Music and Conflict Transformation*, discussed above.

arenas through scholarly investigations related to peacemaking. More precisely, we began to address music and peacebuilding as our investigations continued over a period of time. Thus, our ultimate goal became to suggest an initial framework (model) for implementing sustainable peacebuilding through music and the performing arts. Like researchers before us, we discovered our studies extending beyond sound and text, moving into the societal dynamics surrounding music-making and musical performance. The significant role of music as and for peacebuilding emerged, to which we now turn.

Music and Peacebuilding

At the juncture of music and peacebuilding lies the core value of fostering human relationships as they promote sustainable peace and is practiced at differing stages of conflict, most notably in post-conflict settings. Peacebuilding in *praxis* reframes "the context of violence by viewing conflict as an opportunity to improve upon broken relationships and accentuate(s) areas of commonalities and mutual interests" (Huda 2007, 169). It works toward transforming human lives and healing broken relationships and communities, especially through strategic dialogue. As Huda notes further, peacebuilding "is a relational approach to increase dialogue, (and) facilitates interaction toward further mutual understanding and trust between conflicting groups" (2007, 169). Conflict resolution, on the other hand, works at changing the paradigm of conflict via behavioral change to one of mutual existence and tolerance (see Huda 2007, 169). Conflict transformation, like peacebuilding, is a process-structure set in place to develop quality relationships of mutual understanding and respect in face-to-face interactions and in the structuring of society. John Paul Lederach, leading scholar in the field of peacebuilding, astutely argues that "conflict transformation views peace as a continuously evolving and developing quality of relationships. Peace work, therefore, is characterized by intentional efforts to address the natural ebb and flow of human conflict through nonviolent approaches" (2003, 20–21). Recognizing the dynamic nature of human interaction, Lederach thus opens possibilities for a natural intersection with music.

Music-making, music performance, and *musicking,* offer critical spaces of human interaction as nonviolent means to pursue peace in profound ways. It is only recently that the field of peacebuilding has begun to recognize the oft-neglected arts-based processes that can serve as vehicles for improving relations between conflicting parties. Lederach (2005), after long years of study (see Lederach 1997) and in seeking to articulate an effective means to peacebuilding, introduces the concept of the "moral imagination." With this concept he addresses a tension he has found in his discipline and work ethos over the years. His continuing concern is the question of how to move from destructive violence to constructive social engagement. Behind the theory and *praxis* of peace work, he has found himself returning to a "wellspring" of his long-term experience, that of the "moral imagination." For him, the moral imagination is the "*capacity to imagine something rooted in the challenges of the real world yet capable of giving birth to that which does not yet exist*" (2005, ix*)*. It is at this juncture that music and the arts make a substantial contribution to the peacebuilding process, for as ethnomusicologists are quick to point out music occurs within space and time in real world contexts. Music and related arts provide social spaces, for imagining the possibilities of change within arenas of tension and conflict.[6]

Significantly, the realm of the imagination becomes Lederach's driving focal point. For him the moral imagination is an essential key to the envisioning of positive relationships that foster peace. He argues that without a "capacity to imagine the canvas of mutual relationships and situate oneself as part of that historic and ever-evolving web (of interconnected relationships), peacebuilding collapses" (35). He then identifies essential roles of music and the arts. He notes:

> The artistic five minutes, I have found rather consistently, when it is given space and acknowledged as something far beyond entertainment, accomplishes what most of politics has been unable to attain: It helps us return to our humanity, a transcendent journey that, like the moral imagination, can build a sense that we are, after all, a human community. (153)

Here we note that music and the performing arts inherently get to the root of sociological concerns and foster diverse peoples recognizing and respecting each other as human beings. Although not directly aimed at politics, Lederach implies that political realms are engaged and addressed. Further, his intuition serves him well on two levels. He acknowledges music's incredible power to bring us into transcendent journeys that remind us of our coexisting as a human community. Indeed, as we will learn throughout this study, music and the arts help us to locate our identities and to provide spaces for profound social engagement with peoples coming from different communities. Second, Lederach recognizes that the arts function beyond mere entertainment and points to their power to communicate and reconcile people in the inner recesses of their very beings. Ethnomusicologist Thomas Turino, for example, observes that "musical participation and

6. See King, "Musical Gateways to Peace and Reconciliation," below.

experience are valuable for the processes of personal and social integration that make us whole" (2008, 1). In a manner reminiscent of Lederach, Turino further contends that music and the arts distinguish themselves with their "propensity to fire the imagination and create sensory, emotional, and physical effects" (13). In a holistic way that engages the whole person set in community, the "firing of the imagination" engenders a reintegration of both self and social groups to envision the possibilities of something new taking place within existing realities. Herein lies the hope of moving from destructive violence to constructive social engagement in nonviolent ways. Taking the concept of imagination further, Lederach maintains that "the moral imagination requires the capacity to imagine ourselves in a web of relationships that includes our enemies; the ability to sustain a paradoxical curiosity that embraces complexity without reliance on dualistic polarity; the fundamental belief in and pursuit of the creative act; and the acceptance of the inherent risk of stepping into the mystery of the unknown that lies beyond the far too familiar landscape of violence" (2005, 5). Significantly, music has an important role to play at this point. It is our contention in *(un) Common Sounds,* that music provides spaces for nurturing webs of relationships along a full spectrum of social interactions, among friends, neighbors, and enemies in bold and courageous ways with opportunities for shifting paradigms from negative attitudes of exclusivity to positive inclusive ones.[7]

Interethnic interaction via music is among the most obvious arenas where significant positive steps in the peacebuilding process have been documented. For example, Brinner's insightful and profound work, *Playing Across a Divide,* focuses on Israelis and Palestinians playing across their ethnic divides through musical encounters and thus underscores the importance of music-making within such encounters (2009, 305). Brinner furthers the inter-ethnic and music argument by persuasively asserting that two seemingly distinct components—sociopolitical and musical—are, in fact, intertwined. As he notes, musicians in the ethnic music scene in Israel are thus participating in Erlmann's (1996, 467–87) "reconfiguration of space and cultural identity" (Brinner 2009, 305). Recognizing the limited powers of musicians and the destruction that new outbreaks of violence impose on the public's already fragile possibilities of peacefully living together, he contends that the need for coexistence through music is even more evident. He further asserts that, "at some level, people who see and hear these musicians become aware of possibilities for other ways of being within the Israeli/ Palestinian sociocultural sphere" (ibid.). Here Brinner inadvertently evokes

---

7. See Lederach and Lederach 2010 for further development of musical application to peacebuilding.

Lederach's concept of the moral imagination in tandem with the musical imagination in fostering changes of perception across ethnic boundaries.

Imagining that peoples can live together or coexist through music and the performing arts offers critical steps toward peacebuilding. Indeed, some scholars recognize that the arts in post-conflict societies can be useful tools of transition in moving the process forward (Huda 2007, 691). In our own work, the two consultations for the "Songs of Peace and Reconciliation Project" took place in post-conflict locations, Lebanon and Indonesia. In addition to studies from these contexts, our scholars from further afield also address local, specific sites of previous conflict and, in some cases, where tensions are still palpable and recovery from conflict is continuing. Huda, however, questions beyond post-conflict arenas as to how the arts can also contribute toward peacebuilding in times of inactive or nascent conflict (ibid.). He then adds an oft ignored dimension to the mix when he questions, "More importantly, can the arts contribute to the inner peace and spiritual formation of members of society to prevent and mediate potential conflicts?" (ibid.). With this, the specter of interreligious tensions and issues arise. Similarly, in this investigation we acknowledge a dominant presence of an additional seemingly distinct arena of investigation—that of interreligious, interfaith dynamics. Not only sociopolitical and musical elements are intertwined, but underneath and often running alongside lies an underground tributary—that of interreligious dynamics.

Through an Interreligious Lens

Most certainly, in light of the nature of global and local conflicts in the early twenty-first century, a heightened urgency for interreligious studies has arisen in tandem with the entrance of religion into the global public discourse. With the resurgence of what have been designated as "world religions," such as Islam, Hinduism, Buddhism, and Christianity, migrating peoples are reconfiguring nation states and societies into increasingly pluralistic contexts. In reality, around the world and including the United States, "religious belief is often central to people's lives—a direct contradiction of expectations created by the Enlightenment three centuries ago. Despite the complaints of its most ardent despisers, religion is not going away" (Niebuhr 2008, xx). For many peoples worldwide, religion plays a major factor in their identities on both personal and collective levels.[8] In response, national leaders, government institutions, and religious training institu-

---

8. See Hoover, "Muslim-Christian Relations and Peacemaking in the Arab World," below.

tions[9] are coming to the realization that "ignorance of religious differences can be perilous, for the obvious reason that what one does not know about other people can provide a blank slate on which demagogues can write with great, destructive effect" (ibid.). Although not the main reason for conflict, religion remains a contributing factor in a wide array of countries: from Northern Ireland to the Balkans, the Middle East, Nigeria, Sudan, Indonesia, and Kashmir. Religion is one factor among "several interrelated causal factors such as ethnicity, economic disparities, regional differences" (Smock 2002, 127), as well as injustice.

Scholars are recognizing, however, that, while religion is most often noted for inflaming conflict, "religion also has the power to transform."[10] Indeed, reconfigurations of institutions and academic programs are taking place. For example, a major participant in this study was the Indonesian Consortium of Religious Studies, an Indonesian higher academic institution that graciously served as the host of our second consultation in Yogyakarta (April 2010). Their curriculum is centered around "a Religious Studies Ph.D. Program that is co-sponsored by Muslim, Christian, and national universities."[11] Thus, with a similar focus on Muslim-Christian relations set within contemporary contexts and global conflicts taking place in the twenty-first century, we have chosen to explore interfaith relations. We are investigating local contexts where violence has been done in the name of religion and has had tragic polarizing effects. It is such arenas that we are seeking to understand. Our original intention was to investigate music and peacebuilding among all three Abrahamic faiths. We soon realized, however, that the scope of such a study was too large for the parameters of our project. We thus limited our investigations to Muslim-Christian encounters, a mammoth topic and daunting task in and of itself. We recognize that in a pluralistically diverse religious world, there are more religious encounters that also merit such investigations. If you see Hinduism or Buddhism in relation to Indonesia mentioned in these chapters, we have chosen to nar-

9. "Organizations such as the United States Institute of Peace, the World Conference on Religion and Peace, and the Community of sant'Egidio have identified an urgent need to convene Christians, Muslims, and Jews internationally to help defuse tension and forestall wider religious conflict" (Smock 2002, 4).

10. Najeeba Syeed-Miller, "Religious Education for the 21st Century," Lecture notes, May 16, 2012. For further information, see http://blog.pe.com/multicultural-beat/2012/05/16/muslim-professor-to-speak-on-religious-education-dialogue/.

11. http://icrs.ugm.ac.id/who-we-are, accessed July 2, 2012. "The Indonesian Consortium for Religious Studies (ICRS-Yogya) is a consortium of three universities: Gadjah Mada University (UGM), State Islamic University Sunan Kalijaga (UIN), and Duta Wacana Christian University (UKDW). Together they offer an integrative, international PhD program in interreligious studies.

row our focus on two religions where violence is and has been done in the name of religion. We see this study, then, as an initial first step to begin the conversations and lay out a framework for initiating further investigations.

Geographically and in light of our focus on Muslim-Christian relations, *(un)Common Sounds* turned first to the Arab world in the Middle East and North Africa, in particular Lebanon, Libya, Morocco, and Egypt, all countries where Arab music draws from a vast music tradition shared by Christians, Muslims, and Jews.[12] We then extended our investigations into the wider Muslim world as seen in the contrasting nation of Indonesia. Recognized to have the largest Muslim population in the world, we focused on Java (Yogyakarta and Bandung) and Sumatra (Aceh). Rich with undeniable diversity, some anthropologists argue that both regions in many ways and at certain points represent a single, cohesive sociocultural arena with the presence of shared key cultural symbols, their variants, and historical circumstances (Eickelman 1989, 9). This can notably be observed in Rasmussen's, *Women, the Recited Qur'an, and Islamic Music in Indonesia* (2010b) and Harnish and Rasmussen's, *Divine Inspirations: Music & Islam in Indonesia* (2011). Both works demonstrate music-making and experiencing of music through intersecting music culture components between the two regions. Each of these regions have had significant cultural interaction that has resulted in the integrating of theoretical components of music—such as scales, rhythms, and forms—material culture with families of related instruments, and shared aesthetic ideologies, most often in religious domains (Rasmussen 2010a). These two contrasting regions, the Arab world and Southeast Asia, provided our study a first-hand glimpse of Muslim-Christian relations in the richness of common expressions, music, and the performing arts, laced with the nuanced particularities of vast diversity.

Music and Interreligious Studies: Critical Issues

Numerous critical issues surrounding Muslim Christian interfaith dynamics are at play when moving throughout the Arab world, Southeast Asia, and extended arenas of interreligious encounter. Prominent among them are postcolonial discourses as generated by Said's incisive critique surrounding *orientalism* (1978). The orientalist critique addresses the problems of pejorative, prejudicial attitudes toward the "other" and issues of power. Additionally, anthropological studies of religions argue for acknowledging a diversity of religious discursive traditions shaped by local *praxis* to such an extent that scholars contend, for example, that there is not one, monolithic Islam, but many Islams (Asad 1986).

12. See Abou Mrad, "Cantillation as a Convergence Point," below.

Postcolonial Considerations

Arising out of colonial discourse, Edward Said launched raging debates and critiques in his landmark volume, *Orientalism* (1978), a seminal work that continues to significantly influence contemporary postcolonial studies (Kennedy 2000, 162–73). In it, Said exposed Western manipulation of knowledge of and power over the Orient, specifically "as a Western style for dominating, restructuring, and having authority over the Orient" (2006a, 25). He argued that Orientalism has "constructed" a false, demeaning, and self-serving representation of the Orient. His thoughts revolved around a dualistic distinction between "Us" and "Them" (Swanson 2004, 107) that pitted Orientals through imaginative portrayals in negative, sub-standard ways over against ascribed, self-gratulatory superiority on the part of Occidentals. In his castigation of ethnocentrism, he contended, "It is more rewarding—and more difficult—to think concretely and sympathetically, contrapuntally, about others than only about 'us'" (Said 2006b, 98). His observation contains significant implications for contemporary Muslim-Christian relations and dialoguing with the "Other."[13]

The growth of postcolonial studies continues unabated, with classical themes such as migration, slavery, suppression, resistance, representation, and difference drawing from the theory of Said and his contemporaries and include Spivak and Bhabha whose works remain prominent in contemporary postcolonial studies (Ashcroft 2006, 5). Acknowledging forms of colonial and neocolonial power operating in contemporary settings, "postcolonial" as a concept has been adopted in a variety of fields of study and disciplines, among them politics, sociology, anthropology, religious studies, and ethnomusicology. Of particular relevance for this study are the discussions of the music cultures of the Middle East and Arab-influenced music. Shannon, in his discussion of music and modernity in contemporary Syria (2006), addresses the critique of "how Orientalist thought participated in colonial regimes of knowledge and power." He moves beyond it and argues that "[t]he 'Orient' and the 'Oriental' served as a mirror in which Europeans created their own self images to the extent that what we label 'modern European culture' was a product of the interaction ... of Europe with its colonies" (62). While in Indonesia and her discussion of women and the recitation of the Qur'an, Rasmussen maintains that "the recognition, imagination, appropriation, adaptation, and modification of Arab art forms

13. It is noteworthy that Said also wrote extensively about music, including *Musical Elaborations* (1991); *Parallels and Paradoxes: Explorations in Music and Society* (2004) (with the Argentine-Israeli conductor Daniel Barenboim); and his last book, *On Late Style: Music and Literature against the Grain* (2006).

are accomplished through a process resembling the framework of orientalism, the paradigm originally identified by Edward Said" (2010b, 62). At the same time, debates surrounding traditional and sacred belief of colonized, indigenous, and marginalized peoples were emerging in significance (Donaldson 2002; King 1999; Sugirtharajah 2001; Treat 1996; Van der Veer 2004; Viswanathan 1998). Previously ignored and left unanalyzed, debates about the sacred have become even more urgent in the twenty-first century. Scholars currently recognize that "[a]nalyses of the sacred have been one of the most neglected, and may be one of the most rapidly expanding areas of post-colonial study" (Ashcroft 2006, 8).

Islam and Christianity as Discursive Traditions

Nestled within postcolonial discourses is the critical concept of essentialism, where some investigators claim to have discovered the "essence" of their object of study. Richard King, in his discussion of orientalism in relation to religion argues that "works that purport to explain the 'Oriental mind-set' . . . presuppose that there is a homogeneous, and almost Platonic 'essence' or 'nature' that can be directly intuited by the . . . expert" (1999, 531). He reasons that not only does such essentialism misrepresent the heterogeneity of the subject matter but that it also leads to "the construction of a cultural stereotype that may then be used to subordinate, classify and dominate the non-Western world" (ibid.). This indeed can be the case when presenting or representing a religion and its devotees. It is a danger when investigating interrelations between Muslims and Christians, one that we are seeking to avoid in this study. Talal Asad's position is helpful to combatting such dangers. His critique is that anthropologists often fall prey to essentialism when addressing the notion of an anthropology of Islam; he argues that their scope is too wide and all encompassing. This is the case of orientalists, the conventional authorities on Islam, who are accused of insensitivity to "change, negotiation, development, and diversity that characterizes lived Islam" (Anjum 2007, 656).[14] Thus, Asad argues for beginning from the concept of a *discursive tradition* that investigates lived practices while at the same time includes and relates itself to the founding sacred texts, such as the Qur'an and Hadith. He contends, "Islam is neither a distinctive social structure nor a heterogeneous collection of belief, artefacts, customs, and morals. It is a tradition" (Asad 1986, 14). Drawing from MacIntyre, he builds on the concept of a lived tradition as "an historically extended, socially embodied argument, an argument precisely in part about the goods which constitute

---

14. Geertz's work, *Islam Observed* (1968), has been accused of essentialism.

that tradition" (MacIntyre 1984, 222). An Islamic discursive tradition for Asad "is simply a tradition of Muslim discourse that addresses itself to conceptions of the Islamic past and future, with reference to a particular Islamic practice in the present" (1986, 14).

Thus, a lived Islamic tradition, is set within local contexts, investigates practitioners' traditions of "apt performance" in light of the past and the future in current lived situations. Asad cautions that, although Muslim practices are not homogenous, their heterogeneity does not indicate a lack of certain commonality among them. Rather they aspire to achieve coherence. He further argues, "An anthropology of Islam will therefore seek to understand the historical conditions that enable the production and maintenance of specific discursive traditions, or their transformation—and the efforts of practitioners to achieve coherence" (17). This can be observed, for example, in the Islamic musical arts[15] of Indonesia, where a plurality of religious expression flourishes through the generation of diverse streams of lived musical religious experience. Rasmussen, for example, identifies two of these streams. The first is what she references as "traditional, Javanese Islam" where the performers and their audience[16] derive power from and simultaneously empower the so-called grassroots" (2010a, 155). Drawing from Arabic-language poetry and song combined with liturgical, paraliturgical elements, traditional and popular Javanese gamelan-based music, and world pop, the various strands of their unique history weave together a unique lived tradition as they seek to achieve coherence within their local religious context and the broader Muslim world.[17] A strikingly distinct second stream locates itself in the *nasyid* tradition, a much more western *a cappella* sound comprised of small, all-male unaccompanied vocal ensembles, and "allies itself with the upper-middle class, urban, university campus-based pious" (Rasmussen 2010a, 156).[18] The *nasyid* genre also reveals great diversity, yet is balanced with a coherence based on historical traditions as it engages with the present twenty-first-century context.

Notably, heterogeneity located within local lived religious expression is not limited to Islamic traditions. Asad does not limit his attack on essentialism to "Islam as a discursive Tradition." On the contrary, he also turns

15. "Seni Musik Islam" is the local Bahasa Indonesia term for Islamic musical arts as used by Rasmussen 2010, 156.

16. This is based on Rasmussen's analysis and interpretation of Emha Ainun Nadjib and his ensemble, Kiai Kanjeng (2010a, 155–74).

17. See Rithaony, "Voices of Peace and Reconciliation in Contemporary Islamic Music," below.

18. For further ethnomusicological studies related to the intersection of music and Islam in Indonesia, see also Rasmussen 2010b, and Harnish 2011.

to Christianity in *Genealogies of Religion: Discipline and Reasons of Power in Christianity and Islam* (1993) underlining that discursive traditions are also found among a plurality of Christians. It is a topic that is more recently being addressed in the newly emerging field of the anthropology of Christianity (Robbins 2003).[19] Of particular note is Hann's study of *Eastern Christians in Anthropological Perspective* (Hann 2010), wherein scholars focus on select Eastern Orthodox groups who celebrate their rituals in regions that occupy the borderlands between Western Christendom, the Orthodox world, and Islam. Hann investigates the influences and impacts of living in borderlands among peoples of various faiths. As with Asad and his interlocutors, the emphases is on the study of "the living experience" of religious people, but applied in this case to Orthodoxy. One also observes a drive toward coherence among Orthodox believers through their retaining of traditional patterns of worship and customs practiced historically, yet appropriated in expressions that are unique and relevant to their local contemporary contexts.

With this in mind, then, *(un)Common Sounds* provides studies of Muslims and Christians in the plurality of their musical religious experience as lived traditions and practiced in the twenty-first century. We have sought to move beyond the essentialism and resultant cultural, religious, and musical stereotypes that so gravely depersonalize peoples, the practices of their faiths, and daily lives. A major way to pursue this is through interfaith dialogue as peacebuilding intersecting with music-making and "musicking," yet another critical arena of interreligious engagement.

Interfaith Dialogue as Peacebuilding

Interfaith dialogue serves as one of the principle practices in facilitating harmonious interreligious relationships and peacebuilding. The 1990s and into the twenty-first century has experienced a sharp rise in the practice and numbers of investigations in peacemaking within interreligious contexts (Smock 2002; Little 2007; Abu-Nimer 1996; Assefa 1993; Gopin 2000). Increasingly and similar to postcolonial studies, scholars and practitioners in peacebuilding are exploring the potential impact of religion as a source of peacemaking rather than studying it only as a source of violence and war (Abu-Nimer 2002, 16). Abu-Nimer, noted scholar in interfaith dialogue and peacebuilding, notes how nongovernmental organizations in conflict arenas are shifting from peacebuilding through the typical focus on interethnic

19. Robbins is currently co-editor of the journal *Anthropological Theory* and editor of the University of California Press book series "The Anthropology of Christianity," http://anthro.ucsd.edu/Faculty_Profiles/robbins.html, accessed July 20, 2012.

relations "to initiating interfaith training and dialogue workshops to promote peacebuilding from a religious perspective" (16). Rather than looking
only at the ways religion may promote violence, scholars and practitioners
have turned to studying ways in which religion can be a positive influence.
Scholars in the United States Institute for Peace,[20] a nonpartisan institute
with an initiative in Religion and Peacemaking, maintain that interfaith dialogue provides avenues for increasing mutual understanding and reducing
the likelihood of widespread interfaith animosity and conflict (Smock 2002,
4). They contend that, "when two or more faiths come together to explore
or promote the possibility of peace, the effects can be especially potent"
(Smock 2002, viii).

> Not only are postcolonial studies and peacebuilding engaging
> the sacred, there is rapid growth of scholarly studies and ap-
> plied dimensions of interfaith dialogue and peacebuilding
> (Abu-Nimer 2009; Esposito 2010; Volf 2010). Recognizing the
> "intensity and urgency of the interfaith challenge today is un-
> precedented" (Kärkkäinen 2010, 3), scholars and theologians
> alike are addressing a multitude of questions that emerge in
> religiously pluralistic societies, both in the midst of conflict and
> violence and also in learning to live together in ways that foster
> sustainable peace. Thus, interfaith dialogue, peacebuilding, and
> interreligious studies are growing arenas of prominence in the
> academy, including religious seminaries.[21]

In particular, three distinctive features of interfaith dialogue, lie in the
realms of spirituality, rituals, and Scripture and sacred texts (Abu-Nimer
2002, 16–19). Abu-Nimer (16) argues that spirituality located at the center
of interfaith encounters can prompt changes in attitude toward the "other."
Furthermore, he notes that participants draw from their spiritual identities
(beliefs and values) in their pursuit of transformation or perceptual changes
in regards to conflict. This significantly points to deeper human connections via spiritual encounters that impact change. He argues:

> When this "deeper spiritual connection" is made in the inter-
> faith dialogue, it becomes the main source for the individual's

20. The United States Institute of Peace USIP is the independent, nonpartisan
conflict management center created by Congress to prevent and mitigate international
conflict without resorting to violence. USIP works to save lives, increase the government's ability to deal with conflicts before they escalate, reduce government costs, and
enhance our national security. http://www.usip.org/about-us#manage, accessed August
12, 2012; 1:52 pm.

21. See the *Evangelical Interfaith Dialogue* journal initiated and published by students at Fuller Theological Seminary, www.evangelicalinterfaith.com.

commitment to social change, peace work, and taking the risks
to confront one's own evil. (17)

Thus, spiritual connections distinguish interfaith dialogue from secular or interethnic dialogue. Additionally, learning another religion's rituals and symbols provide windows into the meaning system of the "other," while Scripture and sacred texts not only enrich interfaith dialogue, but also provide a level of "certainty" and "truth" that grounds people in their own faith. If practiced as they are in the midst of interreligious encounter, the process of such demythologization is often disorienting (18). Throughout *(un)Common Sounds,* our investigations interact with the force of and implications of these three aspects of interfaith dialogue through music and the performing arts and thus underscore the profound dynamics of interreligious engagement.

Some of the first questions that arise among Christian theologians are, for example: Who is the "other"? How do we relate to each "other"? Miroslav Volf, employing the term "other" differently from Said, identifies the "other" as constituted most often of "people of different races, religions, and cultures, who live in proximity and with whom we are often in tension and sometimes in deadly conflict" (2005, 9). He further shows how these "neighborly" others, often living at the edges of our communities and within our nations, are redefining our common social spaces as increasingly pluralistic, both culturally and religiously (3). It is a social reality with which we must contend. Volf ascribes not just to interfaith dialogue but also to an interpersonal approach for relating to the "other." He boldly argues that

> living with the other in peace is an expression of our God-given humanity. We are created not to isolate ourselves from others but to engage them, indeed, to contribute to their flourishing, as we nurture our own identity and attend to our own well-being. (12–13)

Human relations, conceived as relating with one another in healthy and nourishing ways as noted above, are central to pursuing peace and constitute one of the most fundamental and imperative aspects of peacebuilding. Kärkkäinen has recently taken up a clarion call that pushes the concept of "other" beyond objectification of individuals to mutual involvement with each other.[22] He calls for interreligious encounters that challenge people to

22. Here Kärkkäinen calls for turning the noun "other" into a verb, "othering" meant to be a positive term. This could, however, be misleading for some. Both Volf and Kärkkäinen are speaking into long scholarly debates surrounding the concepts of "other" and the "Other," in the discipline of philosophy, and more recently in gender and post-colonial studies. Notably, Edward Said, in his work on *Orientalism* (1979),

recognize "the importance of seeing the religious Other not as a counter-object," and extends the challenge to actively engage in the demanding and risky dynamic process of relating to people outside of one's own group (2010, 6). Such involvement demands "the capacity to listen to the distinctive testimony of the Other, to patiently wait upon the Other, and make for him or her a safe space" (ibid.). This is critical because patient involvement in safe spaces produces multiple benefits, among them helping each group to overcome fears of the "Other" and to deflate the demonization of others based on their religious beliefs. A key finding of *(un)Common Sounds* is that the spaces of music-making and performance generate safe spaces for interacting with one another, a finding that we will discuss later.

Common elements between Kärkkäinen and Volf are their mutual concern for interfaith dialogue as it facilitates mutual understanding, reconciliation, and the importance of developing harmonious relationships. In no way are they suggesting that either party give up their identity; it is important rather that people remain committed to their beliefs and also maintain a sincere openness to listen carefully to the "Other," a position maintained by all scholars in the field (Smock 2002). Vital to one's self-identity, it is critical for us to recognize both "what distinguishes us from others" (Volf 2005, 9) as well as finding what we have in common. Both Volf and Smock are, in essence, pointing to interfaith relations that elicit broader approaches to interfaith dialogue, dialogues that do not ignore sacred spaces but that also move beyond into holistic approaches to societal living. Revealing a close affinity to the goals of peacebuilding, one expanded arena for interfaith engagement lies in the *dialogue of life*, where there is an *intentional* commitment "to get to know one another as human beings, as neighbors and as fellow citizens" (Zago 2000, 10). Such "dialogues of life" open up space for engagement between religious "others" beyond doctrinal exchange, as important as that is, and foster building peace among divergent peoples. Paralleling much of what Abu-Nimer posits in interfaith dialogue and peacebuilding, Bevans and Schroeder have identified a typology of dialogues for interreligious interaction that align well with the processes inherent in music-making and "musicking". These include 1) dialogues of spiritual experience; 2) dialogues of theological exchange; 3) dialogues of action (social); and 4) dialogues of life (Bevans 2004, 383–84). Taken together they suggest an initial framework for identifying music as a dialogical partner in peacebuilding. We will later

---

used it in a distancing negative way that has become common rhetoric among scholars of multiple disciplines. In post-colonial studies, for example, use of the term "othering" often includes a demonization and dehumanization of groups (see Ashcroft, Griffiths, and Tiffin 1998, 167–173). In deference to such sensibilities, I have chosen to avoid use of Kärkkäinen's positive use of the term, "othering," in order to avoid confusion.

return to and develop this framework as a fundamental component in our suggested model of musical pathways contributing toward peacebuilding.[23]

While there is a plethora of scholars, clerics, and practitioners pursuing interfaith dialogue as peacebuilding as a viable means for improving relationships, there is at the same time a negative dimension. Many readily admit that interfaith dialogue has its challenges. There are, for example, calls to set aside platitudes and superficial politeness that overlook and ignore religious differences and knowing one another on the basis of a people's identity within a tradition along with what one truly believes (Yoffie 2011). If such concerns are not addressed, interfaith sessions can degenerate into extreme arguments (Smock 2002, 8–9) and become a dangerous business (Abu-Nimer 2002, 15). At the heart of this problem lies the flaw of relying solely on the use of the spoken word as a principle means of peacemaking (Gopin 2002). Gopin, for example, asserts, "Neither in practice nor in principle do words open us up to the vast range of possibilities in terms of how human beings change internally or how they transform their relationships externally with adversaries" (33). He highlights the tendency of Abrahamic religions in the West to overemphasize the power of the word over the power of deed in spite of the deeply embedded nature of deed and ritual within each of these faiths. He notes that interfaith dialogue is only good to the degree that it generates good relations that also lead to good deeds and thus impacts peace and justice. Significantly, Gopin contends that dialogue, as reconciliation, must be pursued through a wide range of means, especially in terms of deed, symbol, and emotional communication (45). In this he implies and recognizes another dimension for pursuing peacebuilding as also acknowledged above in Lederach's concept of the "moral imagination" (Lederach 2005). Here the parallels with music and the arts, rich in symbol, emotional communication, and the generation of good deeds evoke significant implications for the dynamic intersection of music-making and "musicking" in interfaith dialogue and the peacebuilding process. Thus, throughout *(un)Common Sounds* our major goal is to study how and in what ways music and the arts foster positive and nurturing interfaith relationships of trust, respect, and dignity that significantly contribute to sustainable peacebuilding in ways that incorporate but also move beyond words alone.

In summary, in all three areas of study, music, peacebuilding, and interreligious studies, there is a growing consensus of the need to address the contribution of music and the performing arts in fostering sustainable peacebuilding through an interreligious lens. This is the focus of our work.

23. See King and Tan, "Musical Pathways toward Peace and Reconciliation," below.

Organization of This Volume

In addressing the multiple issues and dimensions latent within "musicking" and music-making in interreligious contexts, we invited a cohort of
international scholars and practitioners to participate. Each scholar identifies religiously with or is involved in a local faith community. Since our
religions are taunted for bringing violence while claiming to bear peace, we
have sought to understand and unveil dynamics that are not otherwise considered. We have assumed religious identities as a playing card in conflict.
As Muslims and Christians collaborating together, we are not analyzing the
effect of religion on conflict; rather, we have assumed interaction among
Muslims and Christians and together are seeking to learn and understand
how to move beyond prejudices and stereotypes that impede living together
as neighbors. Thus, this is a phenomenological study that explores what is
happening in current lived contexts across the Muslim world, in particular
the Middle East and Southeast Asia, where Christians are also present. We
are investigating how music is moving and working in diverse, often dispa-
rate, environments. As such this book gives voice to different local contexts
with their unique aspects. Voices from local communities are given space
to reflect on the depth of their experience and expertise on the global academic stage. The advantage is that scholars living on location and highly
recognized and esteemed within their academic institutions and local communities have a lifetime of experiences that bring a depth to the topics we
are addressing that might not have been attained otherwise. On the other
hand, there is a range of approaches to the topic, including divergent writing styles, all issues inherent when working on a transnational basis and in
multiple languages (French, Arabic, Bahasa Indonesia, and English). More
significantly, however, is that when we as nonwestern and western scholars
joined together, we found ourselves practicing interfaith dialogue, both aca-
demically and in music performance, employing a dialogic research mode
that impacted each of us (Gourlay 1978; Rice 1997). As we listened to and
learned from one another, we found ourselves living out and demonstrating
collaboration across religious faiths and three regions of the world that was
mutually enriching and, for some, life transforming. We found ourselves
putting into practice and operating in three areas of interreligious dialogue
as suggested by Swidler: "the practical, where we collaborate to help humanity; the depth or 'spiritual' dimensions, where we attempt to experience the
partner's religion or ideology 'from within'; the cognitive, where we seek
understanding [of] the truth" (Smock 2002, 6). It was an incredible, mutually enriching experience.

This volume is organized into four distinct yet fluid and interconnecting sections: 1) Historical Contexts, 2) Theological Considerations, 3)
Multi-Disciplinary Explorations, and 4) Pathways Toward Peace.

Part One: Historical Contexts explores the multiple intertwined factors critical to investigating the significance of music and the arts in peacebuilding in two major regions of the world. Jon Hoover's opening chapter,
"Muslim-Christian Relations and Peacemaking in the Arab World," traces
the history of Christian-Muslim relations in the Arab world from the beginnings of Islam to the present. Set within a complex demographic and
political reality where "religion constitutes a legal and political identity into
which one is born," Hoover explains how Christians and Muslims have
lived together. He lays out a framework for peacemaking efforts desiring to
overcome injustice, insecurity, and sectarianism that continue to afflict local
interrelational dynamics in the region.

In contrast to the Arab world, Berney Adeney-Risakotta's chapter,
"Peacemaking in the Indonesian Context," lays out the unique historical and
religious underpinnings that have influenced Muslim-Christian relations in
Southeast Asia's 17,000-island multireligious nation of Indonesia, a country
that has enjoyed thousands of years of relatively peaceful relations between
religious communities. Recognized as the most populous Muslim nation
in the world, he cites three paradigmatic events of violence—two of local
magnitude, and one on a global scale that, when combined, cast doubt on
Indonesia's religious tolerance: 1) the mass killings of suspected communists
in 1965–1966; 2) the violent conflict between religious and ethnic groups
after the fall of Soeharto (1997–2004); and 3) the "War on Terrorism" that
constructed a bipolar view of the world as a conflict between Islam and
the West. In his analysis of these events, Adeney-Risakotta offers insights
and understanding of the complex national and global context of religions,
violence, and diversity in Indonesia through which he sets an agenda for
peacemaking via the musical arts found in Indonesia.

Part Two: Theological Considerations speaks directly to the concepts
and notions of peace as articulated in the sacred texts of Muslims and
Christians. How do Muslims and Christians perceive peace within their respective traditions and what are their implications as they interact with one
another? What do the sacred texts of each tradition teach? James Krabill, in
"Biblical Approaches to Peace," examines God's vision for "reconciling all
things" and "setting things right with the world." He does so by studying in
detail the rich Hebrew term *shalom* and its interrelated meanings for peace,
justice, and wholeness. He then points to implications for the church in
pursuing peacemaking through music. In counterpoint to *shalom*, a striking Muslim perspective that argues for peace over and above war or *jihād*

is offered next. Sahiron Syamsuddin, in "A Peaceful Message beyond the Permission of Warfare (*jihād*): An Interpretation of Qur'an 22:39–40," takes on the concepts of peace, reconciliation, and *jihād* as taught in the Qur'an. Arguing for exegetical rigor, Syamsuddin offers an analysis of two key verses from the Qur'an that provide a nuanced articulation of the concepts revealing a message that upholds strong moral and ethical values. He shows how the Qur'an prioritizes peace and reconciliation over war, and if war then only as "justified" war (*jihād*) for overcoming oppression.

Nidaa Abou Mrad's chapter brilliantly demonstrates the inextricable link between liturgical music and theology. In "Cantillation as a Convergence Point of the Musical Traditions of the Abrahamic Religions," Abou Mrad offers deep insights into the shared musical tradition of cantillation (sung Scripture recitation) as practiced among all three Abrahamic faiths. He contends that cantillation constitutes an important intersection of traditional, cultural, and musical practices in the Mediterranean. Integrating musicological, liturgical, theological, and philosophical considerations, Abou Mrad underscores the ways music functions as a catalyst for fruitful interreligious encounters. He also provides commentary on how he has effectively brought together Muslims and Christians in performance in the *Classical Arab Music Ensemble* that he founded and currently directs in Beirut.

Part Three: Multi-Disciplinary Explorations provides a range of regional case studies that address specific cultural and musical issues critical in peacebuilding and interfaith dialogue within two major world regions addressed in this work, the Middle East and North Africa, and Indonesia.

The Middle East and North Africa: Roberta King's chapter, "Musical Gateways to Peace and Reconciliation: The Dynamics of *Imagined Worlds of Spirituality* at the Fes Festival of World Sacred Music," investigates the role transnational music festivals play in bringing about understanding of the "other" in world religions and discusses the communication dynamics inherent in such events that often elicit transformed attitudes and behavior toward people of differing faiths. Based on ethnographic research at Morocco's Fes festival, King focuses on the social spaces of the festival venues and the interrelational dynamics generated between and among performers and their audiences. She argues and shows how safe social spaces engendered by music performance can serve as entryways into peaceful relations among religious peoples on the global stage.

Jared Holton, in "Performing towards Peace: Investigations into the Process of Peacebuilding through Shared Music in Libya," moves us from the transnational to a local setting. Living and working as an American music teacher in Libya, he provides an examination of his own evolving relationship with Libyan musicians with whom he interacted on a one-to-one sharing of music and musical performance. After giving an account of various conflicts of historical opposition and contemporary misperception between two nations, he identifies a five-level schematic for moving toward mutual understanding. Starting with "mutuality" (Clark 2005) in listening and moving toward public performance between engaged musicians, Holton demonstrates the extended possibilities for doing ethnomusicological work and further investigations in peacebuilding.

Mustafa Said, on the other hand, provides a musical analysis of *tawshīḥ*, a vocal form deriving from the *inshād* religious and Sufi parareligious tradition of the Arab-oriental area. In his study of intra-cultural music communication, Said contends that the responsorial form reveals and influences cooperation among performers wherein the acceptance of ideas and thoughts other than one's own collaborate and merge together in producing music.

Then, dealing with lived experiences, Father Doctor Marcel Akiki, in his chapter, "Music for Peace and Reconciliation from Lebanon," highlights the multiple approaches that he has witnessed and experienced in his work in Lebanon during and after the Lebanese fifteen-year civil war, 1975–1990. Based on historical practices, Akiki argues the importance of musicians and educators taking on intermediate roles in peacebuilding via music; in essence they function as music peace catalysts. Drawing from his lifetime of musicological research in the collection and analysis of traditional, neo-traditional, and popular genres of Lebanese song, Akiki delineates two major approaches to implementing songs for peace and reconciliation: a spiritual-musicological approach and an anthropological-musicological approach that ultimately function to bring about mutual understanding and to foster coexistence.

Indonesia: In the first of three case studies, "Voices of Peace and Reconciliation in Contemporary Islamic Music: the Kyai Kanjeng and Suarasama Music Ensembles," Rithaony Hutajulu explores the spirit of peace and reconciliation expressed by each of these two music ensembles. Through her analysis of song lyrics, musical sounds, processes of music making, and philosophical ideas behind the two bands, she shows how music expresses and transfers the energy of peace and feelings of reconciliation among performers and their listeners. Further, Hutajulu addresses how peacebuilding is attempted and realized through the processes of musical interaction and music-making based on the perspectives of two Indonesian Muslim musician-composers in relating to other non-Islamic religions, especially Christianity. She argues for the power of music as a vehicle of mutual understanding and interfaith dialogue between Muslims and Christians. In the second case study, "A Samanic Messenger: Interfaith Dialogue through Art Performance," Irwansya Harahap addresses interfaith dialogue through analysis of the *saman*, a traditional Muslim dance genre and its innovative adaptation by Marzuki Hasan for new uses and functions related to peacebuilding in the volatile region of Aceh. He points to the significance of learning from the artist's experiences as a means of gaining a depth of understanding of how the *saman,* as an art expression and a way of communication, contributes to a mutuality of understanding among diverse peoples.

Finally, countering a climate of violence in Indonesia's recent history, Sooi Ling Tan examines a peace education program in "Peacesongs: Forging Musical Peace *Communitas* among the Youth of Indonesia." Peace Generation, a program set in the context of Bandung, Indonesia, seeks to inculcate peace values within a new younger generation through multiple media formats that appeal to youth, among them comic books and music. In particular, Tan examines how music impacts the personal and collective affect, evokes sympathy and understanding that brings about a collective vulnerability, trust, and unity, and subsequently facilitates peacebuilding. She argues that the relational dimensions of collaborative music-making lead to the emergence of a musical peace *communitas.*

Part Four: Pathways Toward Peace brings together the multiple strands and themes derived from the findings of the study. Seeking to make sense of the multivalent ways in which music and the arts contribute to interfaith dialogue as peacemaking, King and Tan in "Musical Pathways Toward Peace and Reconciliation" analyze the aggregate of studies in *(un)Common Sounds;* they develop an initial model for living together as neighbors through music and the performing arts. Based on a convergence of empirical evidence from the investigations and analyzing them through the theoretical lenses of "musicking" (Small 1998) and communication theory, they identify and discuss the interactive dynamics of five key musical pathways that combine together in moving toward sustainable peacebuilding: 1) music events that foster relationships; 2) music-making that lays a sonic foundation for processing life; 3) music convergences that heighten and intensify musical experiences; 4) the spiraling circle of ongoing musical dialogues, creating a taxonomy of musical dialogues that include musical collaboration, spiritual experiences, theological exchange, social action, and everyday life; and, finally, 5) the significant leadership roles of music peace catalysts, that is, musicians and composers who compose, create, and live their expressive art for peaceful purposes. Within each of these pathways critical functions of music that move forward relational, transformative dynamics between people are highlighted. While maintaining that each musical pathway is dynamically interlinked, King and Tan argue that musical pathways comprise a broad totality of music components and dynamic processes that enhance and strengthen transformational impact in peacebuilding. In the final chapter, "Employing Musical Pathways for Peace and Reconciliation," King and Tan further conclude the study with approaches to doing applied ethnomusicology and employing music in fostering sustainable peace. They delineate artistic practices for bridging differences and building community, for moving from perspectives of enmity toward the "other" to seeing one another as neighbors, and for building webs of relationship through music and the arts in ways that foster sustainable peacebuilding with the hopeful intention of activating paradigm shifts that transform the (un)Common sounds of "others' into common sounds of neighbors.

FOR DISCUSSION

1. "The future of the world depends on peace between Muslims and Christians." Analyze Volf's statement in light of current events and geopolitical discussions. Do you agree or disagree? Give support for your reasoning.

2. What is the difference between peacemaking and peacebuilding? Relate your thinking to the process of conflict transformation, as described in this chapter. Also, how does Lederach's "moral imagination" affect these processes?

3. Helpful dialogue between individuals or communities will always involve discussion of both commonalities and differences. Why is this important to the process of creating and sustaining harmony and mutual understanding in conflicted areas of the world? Why is this important for interfaith dialogue?

4. PROJECT: Muslims and Christians are interacting within local contexts worldwide. Research Muslims living in the USA, the Middle East, and Southeast Asia. Collect as much demographic information as possible. Create a map of where groupings of Muslims are living, include their place of origin, i.e., Indonesia, Lebanon, etc., and, if possible, the type of Islam that they follow (Shia, Sunni, or Sufi). What are the implications for your own involvement in local peacebuilding?

References Cited

Abi-Ezzi, Karen. 2008. "Music as a Discourse of Resistance: The Case of Gilad Atzmon." In *Music and Conflict Transformation: Harmonies and Dissonances in Geopolitics,* edited by Olivier Urbain, 93–103. Toda Institute Book Series on Global Peace and Policy. London: Tauris.

Abu-Nimer, Mohammed. 1996. "Conflict Resolution and Islam: Some Conceptual Questions." *Peace and Change* 21: 22–40.

———. 2002. "The Miracles of Transformation through Interfaith Dialogue: Are You a Believer?" In *Interfaith Dialogue and Peacebuilding,* edited by David R. Smock, 15–32. Washington, DC: United States Institute of Peace.

Anjum, Ovamir. 2007. "Islam as a Discursive Tradition: Talal Asad and His Interlocutors." *Comparative Studies of South Asia, Africa and the Middle East* 3: 656–72.

Araujo, Samuel, and Members of the Grupo Musicultura. 2006. "Conflict and Violence as Theoretical Tools in Present-Day Ethnomusicology: Notes on a Dialogic Ethnography of Sound Practices in Rio de Janeiro." *Ethnomusicology* 50: 287–313.

Asad, Talal. 1986. "The Idea of an Anthropology of Islam." *Center for Contemporary Arab Studies,* Occasional Papers Series. http://ccas.georgetown.edu/87058.html. Accessed on January 16, 2012.

Ashcroft, Bill, Gareth Giffiths, and Helen Tiffin. 2006. *The Post-Colonial Studies Reader.* 2nd ed. New York: Routledge.

Ashcroft, Bill, Gareth Giffiths, and Helen Tiffin. 1998. *Key Concepts in Post-colonial Studies.* London: Routledge.

Assefa, Hizkias. 1993. *Peace and Reconciliation as a Paradigm.* Nairobi: Nairobi Peace Initiative.

Beeman, William O. 2010. "Music at the Margins: Performance and Ideology in the Persian World." In *Music and Conflict,* edited by John M. O'Connell and Salwa El-Shawan Castelo-Branco, 141–54. Urbana: University of Illinois Press.

Bevans, Stephen B., and Roger P. Schroeder. 2004. *Constants in Context: A Theology of Mission for Today.* Maryknoll, NY: Orbis.

Blumenfeld, Larry. 2007. "Exploding Myths in Morocco and Senegal: Sufis Making Music after 9/11." In *Music in the Post-9/11 World,* edited by Jonathan and J. Martin Daughtry Ritter, 209–24. New York: Routledge.

Boyce-Tillman, June. 2008. "Music and Value in Cross-Cultural Work." In *Music and Conflict Transformation: Harmonies and Dissonances in Geopolitics,* edited by Olivier Urbain, 40–52. Toda Institute Book Series on Global Peace and Policy. London: Tauris.

Brinner, Benjamin. *Playing Across a Divide: Israeli-Palestinian Musical Encounters.* New York: Oxford University Press, 2009.

Castelo-Blanco, Salwa El-Shawan. 2010. Epilogue. In *Music and Conflict,* edited by John Morgan and Salwa El-Shawan Castelo-Branco O'Connell. Urbana: University of Illinois Press,

Clark, Eric F. 2005. *Ways of Listening: An Ecological Approach to the Perception of Musical Meaning.* Oxford: Oxford University Press.

Donaldson, Laura E., and Kwok Pui-Lan. 2002. *Postcolonialism, Feminism and Religious Discourse.* London: Routledge.

Erlmann, Veit. 1996. "The Aesthetics of the Global Imagination: Reflections on World Music in the 1990s." *Public Culture* 8: 467–87.

Esposito, John L., and Ihsan Yilmaz. 2010. *Islam and Peacebuilding: Gülen Movement Initiatives*. New York: Blue Dome.

Geertz, Clifford. 1968. *Islam Observed: Religious Development in Morocco and Indonesia*. Chicago: University of Chicago Press, 1968.

Gopin, Marc. 2000. *Between Eden and Armageddon: The Future of World Religions, Violence, and Peacemaking*. New York: Oxford University Press.

Grippo, James R. 2007. "'I'll Tell You Why We Hate You!' Sha'ban 'Abd Al-Rahim and Middle Eastern Reactions to 9/11." In *Music in the Post-9/11 World*, edited by Jonathan Ritter and J. Martin Daughtry, 255–76. New York: Routledge.

Hann, Chris, and Hermann Goltz. 2010. *Eastern Christians in Anthropological Perspective*. Berkeley: University of California Press.

Huda, Qamar-ul. 2007. "Memory, Performance, and Poetic Peacemaking in Qawwali." *Muslim World* 97 no. 4: 678–700.

Jordanger, Vegar. 2008. "Healing Cultural Violence: 'Collective Vulnerability' through Guided Imagery with Music." In *Music and Conflict Transformation: Harmonies and Dissonances in Geopolitics*, edited by Olivier Urbain, 128–46. Toda Institute Book Series on Global Peace and Policy. London: Tauris.

Kartomi, Margaret. 2010. "Towards a Methodology of War and Peace Studies in Ethnomusicology: The Case of Aceh, 1976–2009." *Ethnomusicology* 54 no. 3: 452–83.

Kärkkäinen, Veli-Matti. 2010. "Theologies of Religions: A Position Paper for Edinburgh 2010." *Evangelical Interfaith Dialogue* 1, no. 2: 3–7.

King, Richard. 1999. *Orientalism and Religion: Postcolonial Theory, India and the "Mystic East."* London: Routledge.

Laurence, Felicity. 2008. "Music and Empathy." In *Music and Conflict Transformation: Harmonies and Dissonances in Geopolitics*, edited by Olivier Urbain, 13–25. Toda Institute Book Series on Global Peace and Policy. London: Tauris.

Lawrence, Felicity, and Olivier Urbain, ed. 2011. "Music and Solidarity: Questions of Universality, Consciousness, and Connection." Special issue, *Peace & Policy* 15.

Lederach, John Paul. 1997. *Building Peace: Sustainable Reconciliation in Divided Societies*. Washington, DC: United States Institute of Peace Press.

———. 2003. *The Little Book of Conflict Transformation*. Good Books: Intercourse, PA.

———. 2005. *The Moral Imagination: the Art and Soul of Building Peace*. Oxford: Oxford University Press.

Lederach, John Paul, and Angela Jill Lederach. 2010. *When Blood and Bones Cry Out: Journeys through the Soundscape of Healing and Reconciliation*. Oxford: Oxford University Press.

Little, David. 2007. *Peacemakers in Action: Profiles of Religion in Conflict Resolution*. Cambridge: Cambridge University Press.

MacIntyre, Alisdair. 1984. *After Virtue*. 2nd ed. Notre Dame: University of Notre Dame Press.

Mach, Zdzislaw. 1993. *Symbols, Conflict, and Identity: Essays in Political Anthropology*. Albany: State University of New York Press.

MacKey, Sandra. 2006. *Lebanon: A House Divided*. New York: Norton.

McDonald, David. 2009. "Poetics and the Performance of Violence in Israel/Palestine." *Ethnomusicology* 53, no. 1: 58–85.

Mendonca, Maria. 2010. "Gamelan in Prisons and Scotland: Narratives of Transformation and the 'Good Vibrations' of Educational Rhetoric." *Ethnomusicology* 54, no. 2: 369–94.

Nelson, Soraya Sarhaddi. February 25, 2012. "In Egypt, Christian-Muslim Tension Is On the Rise." http://www.npr.org/2012/02/25/147370689/in-egypt-christian-muslim-tension-is-on-the-rise. Accessed August 6, 2012.

Nordstrom, Carolyn, and JoAnn Martin. 1992. *The Paths to Domination, Resistance, and Terror.* Berkeley: University of California Press.

O'Connell, John Morgan. 2011. "Music in War, Music for Peace: A Review Article." *Ethnomusicology* 55, no. 1: 112–27.

O'Connell, John Morgan, and Salwa El-Shawan Castelo-Branco, eds. 2010. *Music and Conflict.* Urbana: University of Illinois Press.

Pettan, Svanibor. 2010. "Music in War, Music for Peace: Experiences in Applied Ethnomusicology." In *Music and Conflict,* edited by John Morgan and Salwa El-Shawan Castelo-Branco O'Connell, 177–92. Urbana: University of Illinois Press.

Rasmussen, Anne K. 2010. "Performing Religious Politics: Islamic Musical Arts in Indonesia." In *Music and Conflict,* edited by John Morgan and Salwa El-Shawan Castelo-Branco O'Connell, 155–76. Urbana: University of Illinois Press.

Ritter, Jonathan, and J. Martin Daughtry, eds. 2007. *Music in the Post-9/11 World.* New York: Routledge.

Robbins, Joel, ed. 2003. "The Anthropology of Christianity." Special issue, *Religion* NS 33, no. 3.

Seeger, Anthony. 2010. "The Suyá and the White Man: Forty-five Years of Musical Diplomacy in Brazil." In *Music and Conflict,* edited by John Morgan and Salwa El-Shawan Castelo-Branco O'Connell, 109–125. Urbana: University of Illinois Press.

Shannon, Jonathan Holt. 2006. *Among the Jasmine Trees: Music and Modernity in Contemporary Syria.* Middletown, CT: Wesleyan University Press.

Small, Christopher. 1998. *Musicking: The Meanings of Performing and Listening.* Music Culture. Middletown, CT: Wesleyan University Press.

———. 2011. "Prologue: Misunderstand and Reunderstanding." In "Music and Solidarity: Questions of Universality, Consciousness, and Connection," edited by Felicity and Olivier Urbain Laurence. *Peace & Policy* 15.

Smock, David R., ed. 2002. *Interfaith Dialogue and Peacebuilding.* Washington, DC: United States Institute of Peace.

Spivak, Gayatri Chakravorty. 1996. *The Spivak Reader: Selected Works of Gayatri Chakravorty Spivak.* Edited by Donna Landry and Gerald MacLean. New York: Routledge.

Spradley, James, and David W. McCurdy. 2000. *Conformity and Conflict: Readings in Cultural Anthropology.* Boston: Allyn and Bacon.

Steger, Manfred B. 2009. *Globalization: A Very Short Introduction.* Oxford: Oxford University Press.

Sugirtharajah, R. S. 2001. *The Bible in the Third World: Precolonial, Colonial, Postcolonial Encounters.* Cambridge: Cambridge University Press.

Syeed-Miller, Najeeba. 2012. "Religious Education for the 21st Century." Lecture notes, May 16.

Treat, James. 1996. *Native and Christian: Indigenous Voices on Religious Identity in the United States and Canada.* New York: Routledge.

Turino, Thomas. 2008. *Music as Social Life: The Politics of Participation*. Chicago: University of Chicago Press.

Urbain, Olivier, ed. 2008. *Music and Conflict Transformation: Harmonies and Dissonances in Geopolitics*. Toda Institute Book Series on Global Peace and Policy. London: Tauris.

Van Buren, Kathleen J. 2010. "Applied Ethnomusicology and HIV and AIDS: Responsibility, Ability and Action." *Ethnomusicology* 54, no. 2: 202–23.

Van der Veer, Peter. 2004. *Global Conversions*. Edited by Gareth and Jamie S. Scott Griffiths. Mixed Messages: Materiality, Textuality, Missions. New York: Palgrave Macmillan.

Viswanathan, Gauri. 1998. *Outside the Fold: Conversion, Modernity and Belief*. Princeton: Princeton University Press.

Volf, Miroslav. 2005. "Living with the 'Other.'" In *Muslim and Christian Reflections on Peace: Divine and Human Dimensions*, edited by J. Dudley Woodberry, Osman Zümrüt, and Mustafa Köylö, 3–22. Lanham, MD: University Press of America.

Volf, Miroslav, Ghazi bin Muhammad, and Melissa Yarrington. 2010. *A Common Word: Muslims and Christians on Loving God and Neighbour*. Grand Rapids: Eerdmans.

Yoffie, Eric H. 2011. "Why Interfaith Dialogue Doesn't Work--and What We Can do About It." *Huffington Post*, http://www.huffingtonpost.com/rabbi-eric-h-yoffie/why-interfaith-dialogue-d_b_867221.html (accessed July 11, 2012).

Zago, Marcellos. 2000. "The New Millennium and the Emerging Religious Encounters." *Missiology: An International Review* 28, no. 1: 10.

PART ONE

Historical Contexts

CHAPTER 1

Muslim-Christian Relations and Peacemaking in the Arab World[1]

by Jon Hoover

Muslims and Christians in the Contemporary Arab World

The Arab world extends from Mauritania in the west to Iraq and Oman in the east and is home to some 300 million people. Most of these are Sunni Muslims, but there are Shiʻi majorities in Iraq and Bahrain and sizable Shiʻi minorities in Lebanon, Yemen, and Saudi Arabia. Most Muslims in Oman belong to a third group called the Ibadis. Whether Sunni, Shiʻi or Ibadi, the Muslims of the region vary widely in spirituality, culture and political persuasion, and some have secularized. The Christians of the Arab World are found mainly in Egypt and the Levant. Egypt's Christians, known as Copts, are the largest in number, comprising 6–10 percent of the country's 80 million people. The vast majority is Coptic Orthodox, although there are important Coptic Catholic and Coptic Evangelical (Protestant) communities as well. Lebanon has the highest ratio of Christians to Muslims, with 30–35 percent of the 4 million population adhering to an array of Christian confessions, the largest being the Maronite (Catholic aligned with Rome) and then the Greek Orthodox. Christians make up about 10 percent of the population in Syria, and there are significant minorities of Christians in Jordan, Iraq, and Palestine/Israel and much smaller groups in North Africa. Also, good numbers of both Arab and non-Arab Christians

---

1. I would like to thank Jacqueline Hoover for reviewing an earlier draft and drawing my attention to sources on Egypt.

are found among the millions of migrant workers in the Gulf countries.[2] The Christians of the Arab world vary widely in their religiosity and political commitments just as Muslims do. What is consistent across the board however is that religion constitutes a legal and political identity into which one is born. Religion is not simply a matter of faith commitment as it is for many in other parts of the world.

The Egyptian revolution of January 25, 2011 helpfully motivates the dynamics of Christian-Muslim relations within this complex demographic and political reality. Egyptian Christians and Muslims joined together in peaceful demonstrations against the regime of President Hosni Mubarak. Moreover, the security vacuum precipitated by the besieged government's withdrawal of police from their posts and release of criminals from prisons drew ordinary people out into the streets of Cairo to protect their neighborhoods from harm. Suspicion between Christian and Muslim neighbors dissipated as they met—some for the first time—and worked together to give order to their local affairs. It was a proud moment for Muslim-Christian unity in Egypt.

Yet, with the resignation of President Mubarak more than two weeks later on February 11, Egyptians found themselves facing a profoundly difficult question: What kind of nation did they want to become? It was clear to everyone that an amended constitution must limit the number of presidential terms. No president could serve thirty years again. But what about the constitution's second article, which specified that Islam was the religion of the state and the principles of *Sharī'ah* the chief source of law?[3] Some secular intellectuals and a few Christian leaders called for removal of this article and establishment of a secular state that made no distinction on the basis of religion. Not only would this abolish the preferential place given to Islam in

2. For detail on religious demographics, see the Pew Forum on Religion and Public Life report, "Mapping the Global Muslim Population: A Report on the Size and Distribution of the World's Muslim Population" (2009), http://pewforum.org/Muslim/Mapping-the-Global-Muslim-Population.aspx; and the religion entries under national population in the CIA World Fact Book, https://www.cia.gov/library/publications/the-world-factbook/index.html. For introductions to the major Christian groups in the region, see O'Mahony and Loosley 2010. For a survey of research on Christianity in the region, see Robson 2011.

3. Article 2 of the constitution reads in full, "Islam is the religion of the state. Arabic is the official language. The principles of the Islamic Sharī'ah are the chief source of legislation." This is my translation of the Arabic text from the Egyptian government website: www.egypt.gov.eg/arabic/laws/constitution/chp_one/part_one.aspx. The government translation is at: www.egypt.gov.eg/english/laws/constitution/chp_one/part_one.aspx. The new Egyptian constitution of 1971 was the first to indicate that the *Sharī'ah* was a chief source of legislation. This was amended in 1980 to say that the *Sharī'ah* was the chief source.

Egypt; it would also grant legal status to adherents of all religions or none, not just Muslims, Christians, and Jews. Muslim voices ranging from the Muslim Brotherhood and Salafi groups to leading officials of the renowned al-Azhar University quickly drowned out this call for a secular state, and Christian leaders cautioned their followers not to expect too much from the revolutionary moment. By the end of February 2011, the Islamic identity of Egypt as a legal fact was no longer in serious question.[4]

These events reveal two competing accounts of Christian-Muslim relations in Egypt: one of national unity and the other of Islamic precedence. The Egyptian national unity narrative asserts that Christians and Muslims live and work harmoniously side by side as equal citizens in society. This discourse has a venerable tradition in Egypt going back at least to the secular nationalist ideology of the Wafd party and its drive for Egyptian independence from the British in the late 1910s and early 1920s. In more recent decades, the former Egyptian government and numerous Muslim and Christian intellectuals frequently underlined national unity to alleviate pressure from assertive Islamism (Hasan 2003; Makari 2007; Scott 2010). That so much was made of Christian-Muslim unity in the 2011 Egyptian revolution speaks in fact of a crisis in Egypt's national unity narrative at the hands of an alternative vision of society giving precedence to Islam.

The Islamic precedence narrative insists that Islam be the defining constituent of the Egyptian state. As we will see below, Muslims enjoyed political control over the Arab world and beyond from very early in their history, and this heritage inspires Islamists of various kinds in contemporary Egypt to advance the cause of Muslim priority. The flip side of Muslim assertions of precedence is a Coptic story of victimization in the face of discriminatory laws and social practices. Yet, Muslims also complain of victimization at the hands of the more powerful West, especially the United States, which is seen to undermine Muslim interests and give unstinting support to the state of Israel.

Similar tensions around Christian-Muslim coexistence, Muslim precedence and external interference appear elsewhere in the Arab World today, and I will return later in this chapter to touch on the case of modern Lebanon. The intervening discussion traces the history of Christian-Muslim relations in the Arab world from the beginnings of Islam to the present. My purpose overall is to explain how Christians and Muslims have lived together and to set the stage for peacemaking efforts that might ameliorate

---

4. The archives of the Arab West Report, 2011, Weeks 5–9 (http://www.arabwestreport.info/), provide thorough documentation of these events.

some of the injustice, insecurity, and sectarianism that plague their ongoing interaction.

Muslims and Christians in the Early Islamic Era

The strong religious identities characteristic of Muslims and Christians in the Arab world have their roots in late antiquity and the emergence of religions making universal claims and maintaining clear communal boundaries through religious ritual, moral comportment, polemics, and occasionally violence. The main religions of late antiquity were Zoroastrianism, Manichaeism, Judaism, Christianity, and paganism. Paganism and Manichaeism both lasted several centuries into the Muslim era before dying out. Zoroastrianism was the dualistic national religion of Persia and the religion of the Sasanian Empire, which stretched from southern Iraq eastward beyond Persia. Zoroastrianism declined rapidly under Islam, but a small community of Zoroastrians remains.

Judaism in the ancient world was missionary through the late 300s, and Jews spread throughout the Mediterranean basin and into Egypt, Iraq, and Arabia. With the rise of the rabbis in Babylonia/Iraq, Judaism gave increasing attention to polemic against Christianity and clarifying the boundaries of its community. This coincided with polemic from the Christian side and the increasing size and power of the Christian community, especially following the conversion of the Roman Emperor Constantine in 312. Egypt was 80 percent Christian by the early 400s, and Christians probably constituted the largest religious community in Iraq by the late 500s. Christianity expanded eastward even after the seventh-century Arab conquests with Nestorian missions through the 1200s. There were also communities of Jews through the 300s who worshiped Jesus yet rejected the label "Christian." However, the ever-sharpening boundary between Jew and Christian eventually deprived these communities of their viability (Berkey 2003, 10–38).

The work of Thomas Sizgorich provides insight into how Christians of late antiquity buttressed their identities. He observes that Christian clergy preached against Judaism to curb Christian fascination with Jewish synagogues as repositories of sacred power, and he focuses especially on the role of militant monks in preserving the gains of earlier Christian martyrs for the faith. From the fourth century onward, the monks in their extreme piety and asceticism became the new martyrs, and some took to violent intervention to reestablish blurring borders either between Jews and Christians or between orthodox Christians and heretics. Sizgorich sees in these warrior monks a precedent for the ascetic *jihādī*-s of early Islam, a matter to which I will return below (Sizgorich 2009, 21–143).

Islam emerged into this world of well-bounded religious communities in the early 600s. In the traditional Muslim account, the Prophet Muhammad received the first revelation of the Qur'an in 610 and formed a group of followers in the west Arabian city of Mecca adhering to the monotheistic religion of Islam. The young Muslim community eventually suffered persecution at the hands of the Meccan polytheistic elite and thus emigrated from Mecca to Medina in 622. In Medina the Muslim community matured into a viable political entity, removed the Jews from their midst on charges of treachery, and eventually conquered Mecca in 629. Following Muhammad's death in 632, Arab armies advanced rapidly throughout the Near East—under God's blessing according to early Muslim sources—to open up new lands for Islam. The Sasanian Empire of Iraq and Persia fell rapidly. The Byzantine Empire, the bastion of what is now Greek Orthodox Christianity, quickly lost Syria, Palestine, and Egypt, but remained strong in Anatolia and southeastern Europe for centuries to come. The center of Muslim power shifted firmly from Arabia to Damascus with the Umayyad caliphate (661–750), and then to Baghdad in 750 with the Abbasid caliphate.

In the traditional account of Islamic origins, Islam and the Muslim community appear clearly delineated from rival religious traditions from the outset. Historians are not agreed that this is exactly what happened, and alternative proposals have been set forth. For example Fred Donner has suggested that the Prophet Muhammad (d. 632) led not only Arab pagans but also Jews and Christians in an ecumenical revival movement of "Believers" that called for rigorous monotheism and then rapidly conquered the ancient Near East. In Donner's account the "Believers" movement only became a clearly separate community of Muslims under the reign of Caliph 'Abd al-Malik (d. 705) who built the Dome of the Rock in 691–692 on the Temple Mount in Jerusalem to claim space sacred to Judaism and overshadow the Church of the Holy Sepulcher sacred to Christians. It is at this point, not before, that Islam was clearly distinguished from Christianity and Judaism (Donner 2010).[5] Whether Islam emerged in accord with the traditional Muslim narrative or developed along lines closer to a theory like Donner's, Muslims eventually did come to resemble their religious counterparts in late antiquity. They had their own distinctive beliefs, rites of worship, patterns of life, and polemics against other religions to demarcate their community from the others. One could not be a Jewish or Christian follower of Muhammad; there were only Muslim adherents of Islam.

---

5. For a critique of Donner, see Crone, August 10, 2010.

The work of Sizgorich mentioned above highlights two different Muslim strategies for fortifying this identity, both with precedents in the Christianity of late antiquity. Sizgorich argues that Muslims found in the trope of the Christian monk-warrior a model for the ascetic piety of their *jihād* fighters who spread Islamic rule from Spain to central Asia in the first Islamic century and thereafter vigilantly guarded the frontier with the Byzantine Empire. It was the piety of the *jihādī* that brought God's blessing in war against the unbeliever. In words attributed to the Prophet Muhammad, "Every community has its monasticism, and the monasticism of my community is *jihād* for the sake of God" (Sizgorich 2009, 144–95).[6] Sizgorich observes that the asceticism of the *jihādī*-s also rendered them exemplars of piety for city-dwellers just as much as for those living at the frontiers. However, turning *jihādī* violence inward against wayward Muslims or even against the non-Muslim majority living under Muslim rule could well have destroyed the Muslim community (196–230).[7] Another way of marking religious boundaries within Muslim domains had to be found, and here Sizgorich turns to the example of the Baghdadi religious scholar Ahmad ibn Hanbal.

Ibn Hanbal (d. 855) was a stern ascetic famous for his steadfast resistance to the Inquisition (*miḥnah*) of the Abbasid caliph al-Ma'mun. The Umayyad and Abbasid caliphs claimed the right to speak for Islam, but scholars of prophetic traditions and law (functionally equivalent to Jewish rabbis) slowly gained strength and challenged caliphal religious authority. Al-Ma'mun imposed his Inquisition in 833 to silence these scholars. Most acquiesced, but Ibn Hanbal held out despite imprisonment and torture. The Inquisition came to naught in the late 840s, and the caliphal prerogative to define Islam was broken for good. Religious authority now resided firmly with the scholars; the job of the caliph or Muslim ruler was reduced to protecting the teaching and practice of Islam, defending his borders, and administrating the political affairs of his domain. With this it may be said that the Islamic community achieved the separation of religion from the state.[8]

Ibn Hanbal's vision of Islamic faith and identity was challenged not only by caliphal power but also by the daily interchange between religious communities. The early Muslim conquerors did not require their new subjects to convert to Islam, and Muslims were not yet a majority in Iraq in Ibn

6. The tradition is quoted in Sizgorich 2009, 161 and 180, from a collection of 'Abd Allah b. al-Mubarak (d. 797).

7. Sizgorich explains that this was the threat posed by the Kharijis. The Kharijis emerged in the first Muslim civil war of 656–661 and violently attacked Muslims who deviated from the rigorous standards of their own belief and practice.

8. On the Inquisition, see further Nawas 1994; Nawas, 1996; and Lapidus 1975.

Hanbal's day. Thus, interaction with non-Muslims was an inevitable part of Ibn Hanbal's world. Sizgorich vividly portrays the "cultural clutter" that Ibn Hanbal faced:

> [Muslims of Ibn Hanbal's time] had Christian mothers, Jewish fathers, Magian neighbors, non-Muslim comrades on raiding expeditions against the enemies of Islam, non-Muslim partners in business, Christian slaves, Christian lovers, Jewish clients, and Magian students . . . The intimacy of Muslim and non-Muslim ran from the battlefields of the Syrian frontier to the *sūq-s* [markets], bedrooms, and birthing places of the Muslim world. (259)

In the midst of this plurality, Sizgorich explains, Ibn Hanbal permitted interacting with non-Muslims for humanitarian purposes but yet prescribed practices aimed at protecting the boundaries of Muslim identity. A Muslim could greet a Christian or Jew, but not with the Muslim greeting of "peace." Muslims could visit with Christians and Jews, but only with the intention to invite them to Islam. A Muslim could bury a non-Muslim, but not perform a funeral prayer for him. Ibn Hanbal also enjoined Muslims to upbraid each other in the event that one of their number transgressed these bounds. This served as well to tighten the bonds of communal solidarity but without resort to violence against outsiders. Sizgorich observes that Ahmad ibn Hanbal's approach is much in the spirit of good fences making good neighbors, with Muslim-affirming practices providing the fences from behind which Muslims could interact closely with non-Muslims without jeopardizing their distinctive identity (254–71).

Ibn Hanbal's nonviolent approach to boundary maintenance through distinctive practice has resonated with numerous Muslims down through history, and it opens the door to conceiving Muslim identity as primarily communal rather than territorial. However, Ibn Hanbal himself was embedded in a wider story of Muslim territorial conquest, political dominance, and religious superiority that classified non-Muslims as protected peoples (*ahl al-dhimmah* / *dhimmī-s*) and subjected them to various encumbrances. The *dhimmī* was distinguished primarily by payment of an annual poll tax (*jizyah*) to the Muslim ruler, which was interpreted both as remuneration for protection services—*dhimmī-s* were exempt from military duties—and as punishment for not converting to Islam. Christians and Jews were also subject to Islamic blasphemy laws and regulations preventing their men from marrying Muslim women.

A document called the Pact of 'Umar outlined further obligations and restrictions on Christians. This pact presents itself as a Christian surrender agreement before the second Sunni caliph 'Umar ibn al-Khattab (d. 644), but it probably dates later to the eighth or ninth century. The Pact of 'Umar stipulates that Christians should treat Muslims with deference, limit the public display of Christian worship, distinguish themselves from Muslims in clothing, not proselytize, not prevent conversion to Islam, and not build new churches (Levy-Rubin 2009; Freidenreich 2009; Friedmann 2003). While application of the Pact of 'Umar through the Islamic middle periods was often lax, it proved especially useful for reigning in Christians during periods of sectarian tension, and its conditions became standard features in manuals of medieval Islamic law.

Although Christians in the Arab Middle East were disadvantaged politically in the early Islamic centuries, many continued to flourish culturally and religiously. Moreover, Muslims needed the skills of the non-Muslims in their midst as scribes, doctors, and scholars. Most famously, the Christian doctor and philosopher Hunayn ibn Ishaq (d. 873) led the Abbasid-financed movement to translate Greek medical and philosophical texts into Arabic. This gave rise to both Christian and Muslim philosophical discourse in Arabic and prepared the way for the transmission of the Greek philosophical tradition from Arabic to Latin in twelfth- and thirteenth-century Europe. Christians also developed their own liturgies and theologies in Arabic, and they exchanged apologetic and polemic with Muslims over matters of prophecy and the nature of God. Christian apologists addressed especially the Muslim rejection of the core Christian doctrines of the Trinity and incarnation and neutralized Muslim claims for Muhammad's definitive prophethood. Muslims for their part found Muhammad prophesied in the Bible and appropriated much Jewish and Christian biblical lore into an Islamic framework. Each community developed ways to retain its own theological integrity and blunt the truth claims of the other (Griffith 2008; Bertaina 2011).

While the churches of the Arab Middle East survive to the present day, Christianity eventually disappeared from North Africa west of Egypt. The Islamic advance across North Africa in the late 600s and early 700s encountered opposition from Berber tribes, some of whom were Christians. Substantial Christian communities remained for several centuries after the coming of Islam, but over the course of time some Christians converted to Islam while many others immigrated to Europe. The last trace of indigenous Christian presence comes from Tunisia and dates to the early 1400s (Talbi 1990; Courbage and Fargues 1997, 29–43; Speight 1995). Christianity returned to North Africa in the 1800s following French colonization.

Muslims and Christians from the
Islamic Middle Periods to Modernity

Returning to the Arab Middle East, Abbasid power declined from Ibn Hanbal's day onward, and the Buyids, supporters of Twelver Shi'ism, took control of Iraq in 945. The Fatimids, who were Isma'ili Shi'is, conquered Egypt in 969 from their base in Tunisia. The Byzantine Empire revived and reconquered parts of Syria in the late 900s. For the most part the Buyids and Fatimids allowed Christians and Jews to thrive and Sunni Muslims to continue in their confession. In Egypt Christians still constituted nearly half of the population, and they exercised considerable power over the administration of the country. However, the Fatimid ruler Al-Hakim Bi-Amr Allah (d. 1021) was exceedingly harsh with both Muslim and non-Muslim subjects, and he gained notoriety even in Europe for his persecution of Christians and his destruction of the Church of the Holy Sepulcher in Jerusalem in 1009. He nonetheless employed Christian scribes, a practice that rulers in Egypt continued into the 1300s (Samir 1996; Thomas 2010).[9] In 1055 the Turkish Seljuqs displaced the Buyids in Baghdad and threw their weight behind Sunni Islam to counter the Fatimids. The Seljuqs also defeated the Byzantines decisively at Manzikert in eastern Anatolia in 1071.

Al-Hakim's destruction of the Holy Sepulcher and the Byzantine loss to the Seljuqs set the stage for the Crusades from the west. The Byzantine emperor called on Rome for help, and Pope Urban II responded by preaching the First Crusade in 1095 with the express purpose of liberating Christian pilgrimage destinations from the Muslims.[10] The Seljuqs had weakened by this time, and the First Crusade captured Jerusalem in 1099. The crusaders set up a series of states along the Levantine coast, but further crusades in the following two centuries achieved little. There was much cultural and economic exchange between the crusaders and the Muslims, and open conflict was the exception rather than the rule (Dajani-Shakeel 1990; Dajani-Shakeel 1995). Nonetheless, the crusading movement hardened Latin Christian hostility toward Muslims, poisoned relations between Muslims and eastern Christians, and eventually evoked a Muslim revival of

9. For an account of Al-Hakim's reign by the medieval historian al-Maqrizi, see Lewis 1974, 46–59.

10. The readiness of Western Christians to undertake such a massive enterprise requires explanation beyond that of Muslim control of Christian holy places and a Byzantine cry for help. Mastnak 2002, 1–54, 96–117, plausibly argues that the Crusades emerged from the western church's efforts to limit violence among Christians and channel it toward pious ends externally. Out of this crystallized the notion of western Christendom set against Islam as the normative adversary. Other explanations are surveyed in Housley 2006, 24–47.

jihād among the Ayyubid dynasty in Syria. The renowned Ayyubid Salah al-Din (Saladin) supplanted the Fatimids in 1171 and captured Jerusalem from the crusaders in 1187. The Mamluks then came to power in Egypt and Syria in 1260 and drove out the last crusaders from the Levant in 1302 (Riley-Smith 1991; Hillenbrand 1999).

While the Crusades were a tragic moment in medieval Christian-Muslim relations, much more momentous were the Mongol invasions from the east. The Mongols emerged as a world power in the early 1200s under Ghenghis Khan (d. 1227), and they swept westward across the Asian steppes into Eastern Europe and south into Persia, eventually conquering Baghdad in 1258. The conquest was welcomed by Christians who saw the Mongols as liberators from Islam. The Mongols, with Christians among their ranks, moved on to capture Damascus in 1260, and local Christians again welcomed this as a victory over Islam. Christian jubilation was short-lived, however, as later in 1260 Mamluk armies defeated the Mongols at 'Ain Jalut in Palestine. Mongol armies invaded Syria several more times into the early 1300s but were repelled by the Mamluks. Mongol efforts to form an alliance with the Christian west against the Mamluk state also failed. The Mongols eventually converted to Islam, but this did nothing to endear them to the Mamluk regime (Morgan 1986; Baum and Winkler 2003; Bundy 1996).

The Copts in Egypt fared reasonably well under the Ayyubids and Mamluks through the Crusades and the Mongol invasions. However, the fourteenth century saw a sharp reversal of their fortunes as the Mamluks turned inward to sure up their Islamic credentials. Elite Copts played a prominent role in the running of the Mamluk bureaucracy, and their ostentatious displays of wealth provoked protests among the Muslim masses in the early 1300s and then riots in 1321. The 1321 riots involved the burning of sixty churches and monasteries and a counter-wave of mosque burnings. The Mamluk Sultan typically sought to appease the Muslim masses by imposing the Pact of 'Umar. Christians for example had to wear blue turbans and Jews yellow turbans, and non-Muslims in the administration had to convert to Islam or lose their posts. Enforcement of these measures was short-lived, and Copts returned to their positions with the passing of hostilities, paving the way for another round of Muslim protests. This cycle came to an end when Coptic ostentation again triggered riots in 1354 leading to Christian deaths and church burnings. The Mamluks responded much more harshly this time, confiscating Christian pious endowments and breaking the back of Coptic power in the bureaucracy. Conversion reduced the Christian proportion of the population to the roughly 6–10 percent that is found in Egypt today (Little 1976).[11] The Ottoman conquest of Egypt in 1517 did little to improve the situation of the Copts, but over time they developed contacts with the west through Catholic and, later on, Protestant missionaries, and some leading Copts attained positions of influence with the ruling authorities and were able to intervene on behalf of their poorer coreligionists as needed (Armanios 2011).[12]

In Syria Christians bore Mamluk repercussions for supporting the invading Mongols, and the Christian communities of both Syria and Iraq suffered much loss at the hands of Tamerlane's devastating invasions in the late 1300s. By the time of the Ottoman invasion of Syria in 1516, Muslims and non-Muslims had little in common apart from daily commerce. Ottoman policy solidified this by encouraging clear separation of religious communities: Muslims were superior, and for most Muslims Christians lay outside the bounds of their social and political concern. However, Christians in Aleppo gradually caught Muslim attention by working with emerging European trading missions in the seventeenth and eighteenth centuries, and affiliating with the Catholic Church in Rome. The Ottoman rulers then favored the Greek Orthodox Church in the 1700s and gave them political privileges to counter the rising Catholic influence. Most Syrian Christians remained poor, but the increasing power of the Syrian Christian merchant elite disturbed Muslims' sense of their superior place in society and contributed to spasms of violence in Syria and Lebanon in the mid-1800s (Masters 2001, 16–168).

The 1800s also saw the Ottoman government press forward with modernization in order to keep up with increasing European power to the west. Moreover, the Ottomans issued the Hatt-i Humayun under European pressure in 1856 abolishing the *dhimmī* status of their non-Muslim minorities and regulations going back to the Pact of 'Umar. Islam remained the state religion of the Ottoman Empire, but Muslims and non-Muslims were now granted equal status as citizens. Muslims generally did not welcome this reform as they saw local Christian ascendency coming at their expense (137–40, 161–63).[13] Power continued to slip from Muslim hands as the

11. Little suggests that the Muslim masses targeted Copts in the Mamluk administration as scapegoats for oppressive Mamluk policies, but he says that demonstrating this would require a more extensive study. While much has been made of the Copts' demographic decline under the Mamluks, Swanson 2010, 129–32, highlights the resilience of the Coptic Orthodox Church in enabling the Copts to survive.

12. Hamilton 2006, examines the role of Catholic missionaries in Egypt and seeks to neutralize earlier historiography presenting Copts as little more than an isolated and persecuted minority. Sharkey 2008 examines Protestant mission in Egypt.

13. The proportion of Christians in the Fertile Crescent (but not Egypt) also tripled from the late 1500s to the early 1900s, only to decline again to earlier levels through the

British eventually took control of Egypt, Iraq, and Palestine and the French took Syria, Lebanon, and North Africa. What was left of the Ottoman Empire became the modern secular state of Turkey in 1923. Syrian Christians led the way in promoting Arab nationalism to replace Ottoman and European colonial rule. Arab nationalism as a movement of secular Muslim and Christian elites was largely successful, leading to the eventual independence of modern Arab states in the mid-twentieth century. Almost all of these states had clear Muslim majorities, and Islam was seen as integral to what it meant to be Arab on at least the cultural level. That aside, Arab nationalism provided more room for Christians in the public sphere than they had enjoyed for centuries.

The 1917 British Balfour Declaration promising Palestine to the Jews as a homeland and the establishment of the Jewish state of Israel in Palestine in 1948 constituted the height of imperial imposition in the eyes of both Christian and Muslim Arabs. Arab opposition to Israel was unsuccessful, and Israel's defeat of Arab armies in the 1967 Six-Day War dealt Arab nationalism a major setback. Muslims turned increasingly to Islam as the way forward in subsequent decades. The Islamic revival of the 1970s onward has created an increasingly uncertain environment for Christians as they wonder whether they can find a *modus vivendi* with an assertive Islamist agenda. This is especially so when Islamic extremism rears its head. The 2003 American military intervention in Iraq may have successfully removed Saddam Hussein from power. However, it also opened a Pandora's box of sectarian strife and had the unintended effect of decimating Iraq's Christians as al-Qaʿida in Mesopotamia forced them to pay the *jizyah* tax, drove them out of the their homes, or killed them (Amos 2010, 24–29). Christians in other parts of the Arab world rarely face this level of immediate threat. Nonetheless, they cannot evade the question of how to position themselves in their Muslim contexts. Do they trust Muslims to give them the legal and political provisions that they need to live well? Or do they resist Muslim assertiveness in the name of a distinctly Christian political identity? (Sabra 2006)

The formation of modern Lebanon casts these questions into sharp relief as the Maronites opted for the second approach. Like the Catholic merchants of Syria, the Maronite Christians of Mount Lebanon prospered in the 1800s politically, economically, and culturally. In 1920 the French— apparently under Maronite pressure—created a much larger Lebanon than had ever been conceived before. To Mount Lebanon was annexed the traditionally Sunni coastal cities of Tripoli, Sidon, and Beirut, as well as the

---

course of the 20th century. On this, see Fargues 1998, 48–66.

heavily Shi'i regions of the Biqa' Valley to the east and Jabal 'Amil to south. The result was the borders of present-day Lebanon. The new entity provided a far more robust economic base than Mount Lebanon alone, but with a population that was barely majority Christian.

Muslims were not pleased to be absorbed into a majority Christian state, but moderating leadership on both the Christian and Sunni sides paved the way to the Lebanese National Pact and full Lebanese independence from France in 1943. Although the Pact affirmed Christian dominance in politics with the president a Maronite, it defined Lebanon as Arab and gave Muslims partnership with Christians in the running of the country. However, later presidents asserted the Christian character of the country more strongly, abused their powers to amass wealth and influence, and marginalized Muslim participation in government. This, along with the arrival of the Palestinian Liberation Organization following its expulsion from Jordan in 1971, led to the Lebanese civil war of 1975–1990 (Zamir 1985; Trablousi 2003).

The Ta'if Accord that ended the civil war sharply curtailed the authority of the Maronite president, shifted more power to the Sunni prime minister, and scaled back the ratio of Christian/Muslim representation in Parliament from 6/5 to 5/5. The back of Christian power was broken even if Christian precedence remained in name. However these adjustments failed to consider the rise of the Lebanese Shi'is from the dregs of society—in the eyes of the Christians and the Sunnis—to a powerful demographic, political, and military force from the 1970s to the present. In 2008 the Shi'i Hizbullah established itself decisively as the primary military and political power in Lebanon. Neither Sunnis nor Christians are inclined to grant Shi'is larger representation in Lebanon's parliament as long as Shi'i political leadership is primarily clerical rather than secular. Yet, this blockage in the Lebanese political structure only serves to stoke further frustration in the Shi'i community.

Peacemaking among Muslims and Christians in the Arab World Today

This historical survey of Christian-Muslim relations in the Arab world has focused on the military, the political, and the social. That is of course not the whole story. Next to nothing has been said about the rich spirituality and strong morality found among both Muslims and Christians in the region, and little has been noted of the largely peaceful day-to-day sharing of life between the two communities. Yet, apart from the Jewish dominated state of Israel and Lebanon, which is politically half-Christian/half-Muslim, that daily interaction takes place within a context of Muslim demographic and political dominance gained through a long history of competition with external and internal rivals and persistent belief in God's sanction. Moreover, following the decline of Arab nationalism as an ideological force, Islam has become the primary civil religion both *de jure* and *de facto*. No other more inclusive civil religion is on offer, and secular visions of political life have insufficient traction to achieve precedence.

So, the question at this moment in history is not whether Christians and Muslims in the Arab world will live together within Islamic polities. Rather, it is a matter of what kind of Islamic polities these will be. This is a crucial question facing those aspiring to peacemaking among Christians and Muslims in the region. Given the history of Christian *dhimmī* status to the mid-1800s, Christians are understandably apprehensive with increasing Islamization. However, the Islam of the past need not be the Islam of the future. Muslims could leave aside belief that peace comes through coercion and the narrative of Islamic precedence that supports it in favor of more life-affirming peacemaking paradigms that stress equity, conciliation, and nonviolence (Funk and Said 2009). Additionally, *dhimmī* regulations, the *jizyah* tax, and the Pact of 'Umar could be shelved permanently as historical artifacts unessential to Islamic politics in favor of egalitarian notions of citizenship and human rights. Finally, Islam could be conceived as most fundamentally communal rather than territorial, freeing Muslims from the need to tie Islam to the fates of particular states and nations. Some Muslims readily embrace and advocate these proposals while others vehemently reject them. Yet others try to find some kind of middle way. As for Christians in the region, some are skeptical that such proposals could ever prevail in the long run, while others are more sanguine. Peacemaking among Christians and Muslims in the Arab world must be alert to the debate over these issues and open to the ongoing process of negotiating what Islam means in contemporary society, not just what it has meant to past generations. The Christian communities as well face the task of discerning their contributions to peacemaking in society and envisioning new ways of interacting with Muslims that rise above destructive patterns of the past.

Many Muslims and Christians in the Arab world are actively involved in peacemaking to reconcile enemies and overcome barriers to more just and equitable societies, and it is worth mentioning a few of these efforts. A wide array of non-governmental organizations (NGOs), some secular and some religious, seek to build bridges between religious communities and offer essential services to those in need. Prominent in this regard is the Coptic Evangelical Organization for Social Services (CEOSS) in Egypt

(Makari 2007). Pre-civil war Lebanon provided the incubator for interreligious dialogue efforts spearheaded by the Catholic Church and the World Council of Churches, and post-civil war Lebanon hosts perhaps the richest dialogue culture in the region with nearly all major confessions initiating discussions. The Muslim initiated *A Common Word* coming out of Jordan in 2007 evoked much fruitful dialogue with English-speaking Christians in the West, although it had regrettably little impact within the Arab world (Hoover 2009). Given the integral role that religion plays in Arab political identity, it is perhaps inevitable that politicians also initiate interreligious dialogue. In 2008, for example, King Abdullah of Saudi Arabia launched a dialogue effort to bring religions together around universal values essential to them all (Royal Embassy of Saudi Arabia 2008).

Interreligious dialogue in the Arab world often suffers from miscommunication as Muslims and Christians bring different agendas to the table. Research on Syria before the 2011 uprising observes that Muslim religious leaders typically enter dialogue seeking to improve the image of Islam and decry fanaticism and immorality, while Christians more often hope to identify common theological ground and nurture neighborly love (Szanto 2008; Scheffler 2007). Despite such difficulties, it is essential that Christians and Muslims meet to talk and share life. This provides opportunity to bear witness to the truth as each understands it, negotiate difference peaceably and equitably, and develop solidarity across communal lines.

Music, the focus of the present volume, is one of many realms of life around which Christians and Muslims in the Arab world can and do gather for conversation. Music of many different kinds permeates Arab society, from heavy metal rock to the powerful love songs of the Lebanese diva Fairuz (Levine 2008; Stone 2008), but it is perhaps fitting to close this chapter by describing an event In Lebanon sponsored by the (un)Common Sounds project that brought together Christians and Muslims to share in specifically religious music. Gathering Muslims and Christians around religious music is not a straightforward undertaking. While music and musical instruments are integral to worship for most Christians, they are not part of the central Muslim rituals of five daily prayers and Friday mosque attendance, and some Muslims associate music and its emotive power with folly and vice. Nonetheless, Sufi and Shi'i Muslims have developed music for devotional purposes to varying degrees. The repertoire of Shi'i music is especially rich in commemorating the tragic martyrdom of Husayn at Karbala' in Iraq in 680, and many Sufis have long used music as an aid to heighten religious feeling in their recollection of God (*dhikr*).

The Songs of Divine Love concert held in Beirut on April 3, 2009 as part of the (un)Common Sounds Songs of Peace and Reconciliation

Colloquium featured similar Sufi and eastern Christian traditions of cantillation and mystical spirituality. The audience was treated to powerful
renditions of several Sufi favorites: the well-known hadith, "I was a Hidden
Treasure, and I longed to be known. So, I created the creatures that I might
be known"; the famous Qur'anic Light Verse, "God is the light of the heavens and the earth . . ." (Qur'an 24:34); and verses from great Sufi poets such
as Ibn al-Farid (d. 1235) and Ibn al-'Arabi (d. 1240). On the Christian side
were moving performances of poems and hymns from church fathers such
as St. Roman the Melodist (d. 551) and St. Symeon the New Theologian (d.
1024) and an entrancing cantillation of St. Paul's love hymn, "If I speak in
the tongues of men and of angels, but have not love . . ." (1 Cor 13). At an
interlude in the musical program, the prominent Lebanese Shi'i religious
scholar Shaykh Shafiq Jaradeh spoke on the elevated communion with God
that both Christians and Muslims seek.

This concert cut across many of the usual religious boundaries in
Lebanon. The concert was hosted by the Near East School of Theology, a
Lebanese Protestant seminary, and it brought together Lebanese Christians,
Sunnis, and Shi'is of different persuasions, as well as several foreign visitors
participating in the Songs of Peace and Reconciliation Colloquium. While
everyone present at the Songs of Divine Love concert could surely appreciate the quality of the music, differences were apparent. The restraint and refinement of the Christian hymns contrasted with the emotive and exuberant
improvisation in the cantillation of the Sufi poetry, and the music evoked
far deeper resonances for those rooted in Arab culture than those of western
culture. It also could not be taken for granted that everyone welcomed the
mystical love spirituality that was celebrated. For some, the theology articulated may have bordered on the heretical. Nonetheless, even for skeptics
the event provided opportunity to learn of the riches in the Christian and
Islamic mystical and musical traditions and to meet, greet and nurture relationships that engender forbearance and amicable negotiation of religious
and political difference.

FOR DISCUSSION

1. Identify historical episodes of violence and nonviolence within this chapter's broad overview of Christian-Muslim interaction in the Arab world. How has history repeated itself within a contemporary perspective? Which historical patterns, do you believe, could assist in fostering peace in today's contexts?

2. Compare and contrast the social, political, and religious climates of Egypt and Lebanon as described in this chapter. What were the most important historical events or leaders that have influenced these countries today? Use current news to give support to your argument.

3. "The Islam of the past need not be the Islam of the future." Discuss this perspective from the chapter's conclusions by reflecting on how various Christian and Muslim sects living both inside and outside the Middle East and North Africa might respond.

4. PROJECT: Interview several Christians and/or Muslims living in your area, asking them to identify any historical events they know about that have significantly influenced contemporary Christian-Muslim relations. Are these the same events as those in this chapter? If not, why are these events remembered in your area more than others? Analyze these reasons and share your conclusions with your class or study group.

References Cited

Amos, David. 2010. *Eclipse of the Sunnis: Power, Exile, and Upheaval in the Middle East.* New York: Public Affairs.

Armanios, Febe. 2011. *Coptic Christianity in Ottoman Egypt.* Oxford: Oxford University Press.

Bertaina, David. 2011. *Christian and Muslim Dialogues: The Religious Uses of a Literary Form in the Early Islamic Middle East.* Piscataway, NJ: Gorgias.

Baum, Wilhelm, and Dietmar W. Winkler. 2003.*The Church of the East: A Concise History.* London: RoutledgeCurzon.

Bundy, David.1996. "The Syriac and Armenian Christian Responses to the Islamification of the Mongols." In *Medieval Christian Perceptions of Islam*, edited by John Victor Tolan, 33–54. New York: Routledge.

Berkey Jonathan P. 2003. *The Formation of Islam: Religion and Society in the Near East, 600–1800.* Cambridge: Cambridge University Press.

CIA *World Fact Book*. https://www.cia.gov/library/publications/the-world-factbook/index.html.

Courbage, Youssef, and Philipe Fargues. 2012. *Christians and Jews under Islam*. Translated by Judy Mabro. London: Tauris.

Crone, Patricia. August 10, 2010. "Among the Believers: A new look at the origins of Islam describes a tolerant world that may not have existed." *Tablet*. http://www.tabletmag.com/news-and-politics/42023/among-the-believers/. Accessed July 14, 2014.

Dajani-Shakeel, Hadia. 1995. "Some Aspects of Muslim-Frankish Christian Relations in the Sham Region in the Twelfth Century." In *Christian-Muslim Encounters*, edited by Yvonne Yazbeck Haddad and Wadi Z. Haddad, 193–209. Gainesville: University of Florida Press.

———. 1990. "Natives and Franks in Palestine: Perceptions and Interaction." In *Conversion and Continuity: Indigenous Christian Communities in Islamic Lands Eighth to Eighteenth Centuries*, edited by Michael Gervers and Ramzi Jibran Bikhazi, 161–84. Toronto: Pontifical Institute of Mediaeval Studies.

Donner, Fred M. 2010. *Muhammad and the Believers: At the Origins of Islam*. Cambridge, MA: Belknap.

Egyptian government website: www.egypt.gov.eg/arabic/laws/constitution/chp_one/part_one.aspx. The government translation is at: www.egypt.gov.eg/english/laws/constitution/chp_one/part_one.aspx.

Fargues, Philippe. 1998. "The Arab Christians of the Middle East: A Demographic Perspective." In *Christian Communities in the Arab Middle East: The Challenge of the Future*, edited by Andrea Pacini, 48–66. Oxford: Clarendon.

Freidenreich, David M. 2009. "Christians in early and classical Sunnī law," Vol. 1 (600–900), edited by David Thomas and Barbara Roggema. Leiden: Brill.

Friedmann, Yohanan. 2007. *Tolerance and Coercion in Islam: Interfaith Relations in the Muslim Tradition*. Cambridge: Cambridge University Press.

Funk Nathan C., and Abdul Aziz Said. 2009. *Islam and Peacemaking in the Middle East*. Boulder, CO: Rienner.

Griffith, Sidney H. 2008. *The Church in the Shadow of the Mosque: Christians and Muslims in the World of Islam*. Princeton: Princeton University Press.

Hamilton, Alastair. 2006. *The Copts and the West 1439–1822: The European Discovery of the Egyptian Church*. Oxford: Oxford University Press.

Hasan, S. S. 2003. *Christians versus Muslims in Modern Egypt: The Century-Long Struggle for Coptic Equality*. Oxford: Oxford University Press.

Hillenbrand, Carol. 1999. *The Crusades: Islamic Perspectives*. Edinburgh: Edinburgh University Press.

Hoover, Hoover. 2009. "*A Common Word*: 'More Positive and Open, Yet Mainstream and Orthodox.'" *Theological Review of the Near East School of Theology* 30, no. 1: 50–77.

Housley, Norman. 2006. *Contesting the Crusades*. Oxford: Blackwell.

Lapidus, Ira M. 1975. "The Separation of State and Religion in the Development of Early Islamic Society." *International Journal of Middle East Studies* 6, no. 4: 363–85.

Levine, Mark. 2008. *Heavy Metal Islam: Rock, Resistance, and the Struggle for the Soul of Islam*. New York: Three Rivers.

Levy-Rubin, Milka. 2009. "The Pact of 'Umar." In *Christian-Muslim Relations: A Bibliographical History*, edited by David Thomas and Barbara Roggema, 1: 360–64. Leiden: Brill.

Lewis. Bernard. 1974. *Islam from the Prophet Muhammad to the Capture of Constantinople*. Vol. 1, *Politics and War*. New York: Harper & Row.

Little, Donald P. 1976. "Coptic Conversion to Islam under the Bahri Mamluks, 692–755/1293–1354." *Bulletin of the School of Oriental and African Studies*, 39: 552–69.

O'Mahony, Anthony, and Emma Loosley. 2010. *Eastern Christianity in the Modern Middle East*. New York: Routledge.

Makari, Peter E. 2007. *Conflict & Cooperation: Christian-Muslim Relations in Contemporary Egypt*. Syracuse, NY: Syracuse University Press.

Masters, Bruce. 2001. *Christians and Jews in the Ottoman Arab World: The Roots of Sectarianim*. Cambridge: Cambridge University Press.

Mastnak, Thomaz. 2002. *Crusading Peace: Christendom, the Muslim World, and Western Political Order*. Berkeley: University of California Press.

Morgan, David. 1986. *The Mongols*. Oxford: Blackwell.

Nawas, John A. 1994. "A Reexamination of Three Current Explanations for al-Ma'mun's Introduction of the *Mihna*." *International Journal of Middle East Studies* 26, no. 4: 615–29.

———. 1996. "The Mihna of 218 A.H./833 A.D. Revisited: An Empirical Study." *Journal of the American Oriental Society* 116, no. 4, 698–708.

Riley-Smith, Jonathan. 1991. *The Atlas of the Crusades*. London: Times.

Robson, Laura. 2011. "Recent Perspectives on Christianity in the Modern Arab World." *History Compass* 9, no. 4: 312–25.

Royal Embassy of Saudi Arabia in Washington, D.C. 2008. "Saudi King Abdullah Commences Interfaith Dialogue Conference in Madrid, Spain." July 17, 2008: www.saudiembassy.net/press-releases/press07170801.aspx. Accessed April 28, 2011.

Sabra, George. 2006. "Two Ways of Being a Christian in the Muslim Context of the Middle East." *Islam and Christian-Muslim Relations* 17, no. 1: 43–53.

Samir Khalil Samir. 1996. "The Role of Christians in the Fatimid Government Services of Egypt to the Reign of al-Hafiz." *Medieval Encounters* 2, no. 3: 177–92.

Scheffler, Thomas. 2007. "Interreligious Dialogue and the Ambivalence of Peace Building in the Middle East." In *From Baghdad to Beirut . . . Arab and Islamic Studies in Honor of John J. Donohue S.J.*, edited by Leslie Tramontini and Chibli Mallat, 407–25. Beirut: Orient-Institut.

Scott, Rachel M. 2010. *The Challenge of Political Islam: Non-Muslims and the Egyptian State*. Stanford, CA: Stanford University Press.

Sharkey, Heather J. 2008. *American Evangelicals in Egypt: Missionary Encounters in an Age of Empire*. Princeton: Princeton University Press.

Sizgorich, Thomas. 2009. *Violence and Belief in Late Antiquity: Militant Devotion in Christianity and Islam*. Philadelphia: University of Pennsylvania Press.

Speight, R. Marston. 1995. "Muslim Attitudes toward Christians in the Maghrib during the Fatimid Period, 297/909–358/969." In *Christian-Muslim Encounters*, edited by Yvonne Yazbeck Haddad and Wadi Z. Haddad, 180–92. Gainesville: University of Florida Press.

Stone, Christopher. 2008. *Popular Culture and Nationalism in Lebanon: The Fairouz and Rahbani Nation*. London: Routledge.

Swanson, Mark. 2010. *The Coptic Papacy in Islamic Egypt (641-1517)*. Cairo: American University in Cairo Press.

Szanto Ali-Dib, Edith. 2008. "Inter-religious Dialogue in Syria: Politics, Ethics and Miscommunication." *Political Theology* 9, no. 1: 93–113.

Talbi, Mohamed. 1990. "Le Christianisme maghrébin de la conquête musulmane à sa disparition une tentative d'explication." In *Conversion and Continuity: Indigenous Christian Communities in Islamic Lands Eighth to Eighteenth Centuries*, edited by Michael Gervers and Ramzi Jibran Bikhazi, 313–51. Toronto: Pontifical Institute of Mediaeval Studies.

Thomas, David. 2010. "Muslim Regard for Christians and Christianity, 900–1200." In *Christian-Muslim Relations. A Bibliographical History*, edited by David Thomas and Alex Mallett, 2:15–27. Leiden: Brill..

Trabloulsi, Fawwaz. 2003. *A History of Modern Lebanon*. London: Pluto.

Zamir, Meir. 1985. *The Formation of Modern Lebanon*. Ithaca, NY: Cornell University Press.

CHAPTER 2

Peacemaking in the Indonesian Context

by Bernard Adeney-Risakotta

Introduction: The History of Religions in Indonesia

In recent years, Indonesia has been known as a place of conflict and violence, including deadly violence between religious and ethnic groups (Colombijn and Lindblad 2002). In contrast, for thousands of years, this Southeast Asian archipelago of 17,000 islands has been proud of its long history of religious tolerance and peace. There is not space to explore this contradiction in detail. If we take a long view, Indonesia has enjoyed much more peaceful relations between religious groups than has Europe. For hundreds of years, Europeans unleashed terrible wars and persecutions on the basis of religion. The major religions of Europe tried, unsuccessfully, to annihilate each other in the name of Truth.[1]

In contrast, hundreds of local religions and six or seven world religions have co-existed in Indonesia for centuries. During the first millennium, Hinduism and Buddhism made their way across the Bay of Bengal and established major empires based in Java and Sumatra, which once ruled most of southeast Asia (Coedes 1968). In the fourteenth century Islam rapidly spread, largely through peaceful means, while Buddhism faded and Hindu kingdoms retreated to remoter areas of Java and Bali (Ricklefs 1993). In the sixteenth century, Catholic Christianity came with the Portuguese

---

1. The Europe Religious Wars were a series of wars in Europe from ca. 1524–1648, started by German's Peasant war in 1524 and ended by Peace of Westphalia in 1648. See Henkel and Knippenberg, *The Changing Religious Landscape of Europe*. See also: http://en.wikipedia.org/wiki/European_wars_of_religion (accessed on 9 May 2012)

and Spanish who sought fabulously valuable spices that only grew in the Moluccan islands (Aritonang and Steenbrink 2008). Prominent missionaries included Francis Xavier. They were soon followed by the Dutch and English bringing versions of Protestant Christianity. Eventually the Dutch established domination throughout most of Indonesia and drove out their competitors. The first Protestant church was established in Ambon in 1605.[2]

In 1942 the Dutch were driven out by the Japanese. In 1945, the Japanese surrendered and Indonesian nationalists issued a Declaration of Independence. The Dutch tried to force their way back into power between 1945 and 1949, but the Indonesians remained firm and gained their freedom.

Currently, Indonesia defines six religions as officially recognized and supported by the state. They are Islam, Protestantism, Catholicism, Hinduism, Buddhism, and Confucianism. Indonesia includes the largest Muslim community in the world with over 200 million Muslims, which is more than all the Middle Eastern countries put together. There are approximately 25 million Christians in Indonesia, equal to the entire population of Malaysia. Hindus include over 7 million people and Buddhists and Confucianists have 1–2 million followers each.[3] For most of Indonesian history and in most places, these communities have lived side by side in peace. Many families include members of different religions. Most Indonesians perceive themselves as tolerant and open to people of other faiths. This is valuable "social capital" that sets a backdrop for peace and reconciliation between religious communities in Indonesia.

Peacemaking and Music in Indonesia

Music is a vital part of the process of building and maintaining peace in Indonesia. Traditions of music are as diverse as the many different cultural, religious, and ethnic groups in this vast archipelago. There is no one musical tradition associated with each major religion but rather dozens. Musical traditions interpenetrate and influence each other. Javanese Muslims play gamelans to tell stories of war and reconciliation that are drawn from

2. There is strong evidence that Nestorian Christians resided in Sumatra in the seventh century, but did not establish a lasting presence. See Aritonang and Steenbrink 2008.

3. These statistics are my estimates based on the assumption that government (BPS) statistics slightly over-report the Muslim population. See Adeney-Risakotta, forthcoming. According to 2010 BPS Census: Muslims: 207.176.162, Christians: 16.528.513, Catholics: 6.907.873, Hindus: 4.012.116, Buddhists: 1.703.254, Confucianists: 117.091, and others: 299.617. See http://sp2010.bps.go.id/index.php/site/tabel?search-tabel=Pe nduduk+Menurut+Wilayah+dan+Agama+yang+ Dianut&tid=321&search-wilayah=I ndonesia&wid=0000000000&lang=id (accessed on 6 May 2012).

ancient Hindu epics (Spiller 2008). Balinese Hindus have a very different style of gamelan music, but tell stories of tragedy, violence, and peace that were composed by Muslim mystics. Other Muslims draw more on Middle Eastern styles of music, but often with local flavor. Santri (religious students) from Islamic boarding schools sway back and forth as they chant the Qur'an to the beat of drums. Qur'anic recitation contests take on the characteristics of high art as the Arabic is chanted with great emotional depth and subtlety. Sometimes erotic songs that date back to local fertility rituals are performed by beautiful women wearing Islamic head coverings. Meanwhile the influence of Western music slips in everywhere, with drums and guitars replacing or supplementing gamelan. *Campur Sari* (mixed music) combines Portuguese guitars, ukuleles, and violins with drums and electric keyboards. Religious themes mix in with stories of love and betrayal.

Meanwhile Javanese Christians play eighteenth-century Dutch Reformed music in their churches, but sing it with the slow pace and cadence of traditional Javanese music. Bataks forget their conflicts when they open their mouths to sing wonderful German Lutheran hymns, translated into Batak, in perfect harmony. Papuans know how to dance, as African rhythms mix with tribal songs to either heighten or resolve conflict. I once observed the most remarkable synthesis of musical styles when I was met, in a remote village in Ambon, Moluccas, by an entire orchestra of Western style instruments, including a pipe organ, which were all constructed from bamboo. Needless to say, the haunting melodies sounded nothing like Western music.

Sometimes Muslims and Christians influence each other's styles. On television there are now Muslim singing groups and choirs that look and sound like Western church music. Meanwhile our Javanese church uses a gamelan in the Javanese worship service. In our neighborhood, every Sunday afternoon a loudspeaker blares out children's songs that sound just like Sunday school choruses, except that they have Muslim lyrics. In Yogyakarta a Christian music director recently formed a gospel-type choir made up of Muslim women singing Islamic songs. In some cases, Muslims and Christians sing together, locking their voices into melodies to bridge their conflicts and create peace. We had a wonderful experience of seeing Muslims and Christians from the Moluccas come together in our home even as civil war still smoldered in their homeland. They started with stories, moved on to prayers, and ended with songs. Most impressive were traditional Moluccan ballads, in which everyone took turns making up verses to express their solidarity.

Pancasila as the Legal Context
for Peace and Reconciliation since 1945

Indonesia is not a secular state that attempts to exclude religion from public life. Nor is it a monoreligious state that affirms one religion as the official religion. In 1945, Indonesia proclaimed the five basic principles of *Pancasila* as the foundation of the new Republic. These five principles are: 1. The Great Unity of Deity; 2. Universal Humanitarianism; 3. National Unity and Solidarity; 4. Sovereignty of the People (democracy); and 5. Social Justice for All (Dharmaputera 1987). These admirable principles are capable of being interpreted in ways that preserve religious diversity or suppress it. The first principle, the great unity of deity, established Indonesia as an essentially monotheistic state. Religious freedom of conscience is guaranteed in the constitution. But in practice everyone is pressured to adopt one of the six recognized religions and interpret it in a monotheistic way.

After the fall of Soeharto in 1998, democratization and new freedoms of expression and association opened the door for hitherto banned organizations to express their own religious identity and demand recognition (Taylor 1993). In light of a bipolar world view linked to postcolonialism, the "war on terror," and perceptions of a clash of civilizations, some groups demanded that Indonesia redefine its normative religious identity as predominantly Muslim. Minimum demands included revision of Pancasila to restore the seven words deleted from the original draft of the Jakarta Charter, i.e., "the obligation for Muslims to obey Syari'ah." Maximum demands called for the implementation of Syari'ah (Islamic Law) as the national law of Indonesia. Neither of these demands has gained support from the majority of Indonesian Muslims (Hefner 2000). While particular versions of Syari'ah are being implemented in the Province of Aceh and in certain local districts elsewhere, most Indonesians are not keen on a religiously narrow state, even if it is their own religion. In the last election (2009) over 80 percent of voters chose non-Islamic parties.

Three Paradigmatic Events that Influence Peacemaking
in Indonesian History

The Attempted Coup of 1965 and its Aftermath

Prior to his effective downfall at the end of 1965, President Sukarno attempted to unify the thousands of incredibly diverse islands and communities of the Indonesian archipelago in three different ways. The first was through uniting against a common enemy: Western imperialism and in particular Dutch colonialism. The second was through a common and uniquely Indonesian ideology of Pancasila. The third was through the concept of *NASAKOM*, an acronym for Nationalism, Religion, and Communism (*Nasionalisme, Agama, & Komunisme* [Effendy 1998]).

Nationalism united all groups in opposition to colonialism. A unified concept of "Religion" was based on an Islamic doctrine that God revealed the truth to humankind throughout history. Therefore all "universal" religions are considered fundamentally monotheistic and good. All Indonesians, regardless of their particular religion, were construed as monotheists and were to be respected in spite of their differences. Communism, according to Sukarno, was not dogmatic Marxism, but rather an expression of the hunger for social equality and justice, especially for the poor (See Paget 1975). In Sukarno's synthetic mind, the three elements of nationalism, religion and communism were not really separate or distinct but rather three aspects of the same thing. All true religions united the people as a nation in opposition to colonialism, capitalism, and social injustice.

Nevertheless, *NASAKOM* also expressed the reality of profound divisions within Indonesian society. Groups whose main focus was secular nationalism did not get along well with those whose main concern was religion (Islam). Even more critical were the cracks in society between Islamic groups and the Communists (PKI). Indonesia had the largest Communist party in the world, outside of China. In 1965 PKI claimed 27 million members in its related mass organizations (Ricklefs 1993, 279). The whole world was gripped in the bipolar fears of the Cold War, which was constructed as a fight to the death between the Communist block and the West. In Indonesia, the fight to the death was more likely to be construed as between Islam and Communism. Sukarno rejected this bipolar world. Internationally he championed the Non-Aligned Movement for countries who refused domination by either the West (former colonialist capitalists) or the totalitarian Communists. Locally, Sukarno himself was a nationalist who tried to unify the country in his own person by affirming the value of both Islam and Communism.

During the early 60s the world came to the brink of a nuclear war with the Cuban missile crisis and America became embroiled in the Vietnam War to prevent the spread of Communism in Asia. In Indonesia, severe economic hardship and unilateral implementation of radical land-reform policies threatened to overturn traditional structures of economic, social, and religious power. Bitter memories of the 1948 "Madiun Affair," in which thousands of pious Muslims (*santri*) were killed by peasant (*abangan*) communists in a failed coup attempt against the nationalist government, lent credence to widespread fears that the new coup attempt of 1965 might lead to another bloodbath against those who opposed Communism (See Ricklefs 1993). On September 30, 1965, leftist army officers captured and killed 6 out of 7 of Indonesia's top generals. The brutal, failed coup attempt, referred to as G30S PKI (an acronym for *Gerakan 30 September Partai Komunis Indonesia*), led to one of the most massive slaughters of the twentieth century. Estimates of the death toll range from 200,000 to over 2 million suspected communists killed in just a few months (Crib 1990, 12). Most scholars believe at least 500,000 people were killed. Communism and atheism were banned and millions of people were imprisoned or lost their political and civil rights (Roosa 2006). This article makes no attempt to analyse these complex and controversial events. Nor do I suggest that the current situation in Indonesia is analogous to the events of 1965–66. We live in a different world.

However the events of 1965–66 are an eradicable element in the collective memory of Indonesia. No matter how one evaluates this tragedy—*Time* magazine once referred to it as, "The West's best news in Asia for years" (Crib 1990, 5)—it forms an inevitable backdrop to the question of how Indonesia should deal with diversity. Sukarno's attempt at *NASAKOM* failed. Diversity was eliminated by the physical slaughter, imprisonment, and repression of a sizable portion of the Indonesian population. Even today, tolerance for diversity does not extend to communists or atheists. Religious freedom only applies to those who hold a recognized, "universal" religion, not to those who do not.

The Fall of Soeharto, Decentralization and Communal Violence in 1998–2004

A second grand event that influences how Indonesians think about diversity is the birth of the "Reformation" period. Fortunately there is currently very little threat of Indonesia further reducing diversity by means of genocide or religio-ethnic cleansing.[4] Following the fall of Soeharto in 1998, the power vacuum at the center combined with severe economic conditions and a climate of fear to produce mass violence in many parts of Indonesia (Colombijn and Lindblad 2002). Some groups attempted to reduce diversity by

---

4. Some persecuted followers of minority Islamic sects, such as Aḥmadīyah, might not agree with this interpretation, since they have experienced mass violence against them recently. Fortunately there has not been mass killing and it is hard to imagine the Indonesian government or the wider society allowing mass killing. Unfortunately the government seems to tolerate oppression and discrimination against groups seen as threatening to Islamic orthodoxy as defined by MUI (Majelis Ulama Indonesia).

killing their ethnic or religious rivals.[5] However the scale of mass violence in 1998–2003 was much smaller than in 1965–66 and remained relatively localized. In the past twelve years Indonesia has slowly come through a long transition period and developed social, economic, and political structures that can maintain stability while permitting much wider latitude for diversity. Nevertheless, opponents of diversity are still ready to use violence to suppress those they perceive of as threatening their conception of a moral community. The attacks and threats against Irshad Manji, a Canadian, liberal, lesbian Muslim are a recent example.[6]

Mass violence as an instrument of religious and social purification feeds off of apocalyptic fears and utopian hopes. Elimination of a perceived enemy relieves fear of a terrible threat and offers hope for a new world of prosperity and justice. However, economic, political, and social conditions within Indonesia have improved to the point where neither apocalyptic fears nor utopian hopes appeal to the vast majority of Indonesians. Unfortunately Indonesia is part of a global context in which transcendent fears and absolutist hopes flow like a virus on the information highway around the world. The challenge of religious diversity and freedom in Indonesia is intimately related to its position within a global context. To understand that context, the problem of religion, violence and diversity in Indonesia must also be located in relation to the paradigmatic events of September 11, 2001.

September 11, 2001 as a Paradigmatic Event that Shapes the World Context of Religious Diversity in Indonesia

There are some remarkable parallels between the events of September 30, 1965, May 22, 1998, and September 11, 2001. All three were national events that were influenced by international actors. All three identified a transcendent threat from a powerful, mysterious enemy (Communists, Soeharto, and Muslim Terrorists). All three signalled the bloody end to tolerance toward cosmic enemies. All three were preceded by attempts to construct a unified world in which there is no enemy and all members of the society are seen as valuable. Prior to 1965, the new nation experienced exhilarating triumph in

5. This is an oversimplification. The killings were often part of a power struggle and/or influenced by fears of being killed, losing land or loss of identity.

6. See *The Jakarta Post*, May 10, 2012. Another example is the banning of the fourth Asian Regional Conference of ILGA (International Lesbian, Gay, Bisexual, Trans and Intersex Association) in Surabaya on March 25, 2010, which was cancelled because of pressure from Islamic organizations. See http://www.thejakartaglobe.com/home/indonesian-islamists-vow-that-gay-conference-will-not-proceed/365899 (accessed 9 May 2012).

freeing itself from 350 years of Dutch colonialism and dreamed of a unified nation of peace, justice, and prosperity, as movingly expressed by Sukarno's impassioned rhetoric. Prior to 1998 the New Order state postulated a nation without opposition to a unified vision of *Pancasila*, Progress, and Development. Prior to 2001 the West experienced an exhilarating triumph in freeing itself from the cosmic threat of "totalitarian communism." The iron curtain was ripped away and Western democratic capitalism proclaimed its ability to unify the world in peace and prosperity. In Fukuyama's infamous phrase, it was the "end of history." There need not be any more serious conflicts because Western liberalism had won (Fukuyama 1992).

Of course many scholars did not believe this optimistic picture prior to 2001 any more than most observers believed that NASAKOM could resolve the incredible diversity of Indonesia in 1965 or that *reformasi total* could resolve all religio-ethnic conflicts that broke out following the monetary crisis. In all three cases, cataclysmic, violent events brought an end to the dream of diversity without conflict. G30S 1965 PKI led to the mass slaughter of hundreds of thousands of "Communists," formerly Indonesian brothers and sisters; the forced "retirement" of Soeharto led to communal violence in many parts of Indonesia; September 11, 2001 led to the attacks on Afghanistan, Iraq, and the "War on Terror." G30S PKI identified a cosmic enemy who must be totally eliminated, namely, the Communists. But in 1998 and 2001 there was less agreement on who is the real enemy. President Bush in the United States identified the new global enemy as Islamic radicalism. However, many in Indonesia are more likely to fear globalization, Western neo-colonialism, and capitalism (Adeney-Risakotta 2004).

Unlike the unadulterated horror experienced in the West, the destruction of the World Trade Center and attacks on the Pentagon on September 11, 2001 provoked an ambivalent response in Indonesia. Almost all Muslim groups condemned the attacks and disassociated Islam from terrorism. However the American response in attacking Afghanistan and Iraq, and proclaiming a worldwide "War on Terrorism," also provoked condemnations by almost all religious groups. Even though the attacks on September 11, 2001 were acknowledged as brutal and in violation of "religion," they also evoked a fearful admiration at such an audacious attack on the symbols of global capitalism and American military dominance (Adeney-Risakotta 2004, 331). Western economic and military hegemony are widely regarded as unjust and oppressive, especially to the poor. Even if the means of September 11, 2001 were unjustifiable, the targets were symbolic representations of a dominating and unjust world system.

Furthermore, the attacks on Afghanistan and Iraq and the War on Terror were widely perceived as attacks on Islam. Even though almost all

Indonesians repudiated terrorism, they also recognized the radical Muslims targeted by the West as part of their own community. September 11, 2001 is a paradigmatic event, in part because it created a new way of seeing the world. Substantial numbers of Indonesian Muslims were drawn to the infamous Huntington thesis that the world is locked in a perennial and (almost) eternal "clash of civilizations" (Huntington 1997). Instead of perceiving the West as the defenders of democracy, freedom, human rights, and justice, defending itself against the irrational, brutal totalitarianism of Islam, many Muslims see those in the West as greedy imperialists, defending a decadent and unjust, capitalist world system against the oppressed inheritors of a high and moral Islamic civilization. Prior to September 11, 2001, America enjoyed an astounding 75 percent approval rating among Indonesians. After the attack on Iraq, the approval rating plummeted to 15 percent (Pew Research 2010). A discourse about peacemaking and reconciliation in Indonesia must take into consideration how September 11 and the subsequent War on Terror changed how many Indonesian Muslims view the world. The aftermath of September 11, combined with natural disasters and severe economic difficulties, continued to strengthen the position of groups who thrive on apocalyptic fears and utopian hopes. The fears relate to perceptions that the immoral and decadent West is intent on crushing Islam. The attack on Islam is not only through military power and economic injustice, but also through domination of information through the mass media and the rapid spread of a Western "immoral" way of life. Utopian hopes relate to the conviction that if humankind will only return to the way of life delineated by God's revelation through the final prophet, then all of the complex problems of the modern world will be solved.[7]

Most Indonesian Muslims do not subscribe to such an over-simplified worldview. However increasing numbers do feel that it is at least partially true. While militant groups agitate for the imposition of Syari'ah and declaration of Indonesia as an Islamic state, more tolerant Muslims emphasize the need to build a substantial Islamic civilization in Indonesia that will answer human needs far more adequately than Western capitalism (e.g., Nurcholis Madjid). A minority of Muslims want to impose Islamic values on Indonesian society by force, using state power if possible, and other kinds of coercion and violence if necessary. However the great majority of Muslim groups emphasize education and tolerance as the primary means for building Islamic civilization. There are significant differences in how the content of an Islamic civilization is defined. Some Muslims emphasize using law (coercion) to impose Islamic symbols, morality, and practices. Others

---

7. For Islamic utopian hope, see Nielsen and Christoffersen 2010; Demant 2006.

stress that the substance of Islam is what matters and it can be established by public discourse that includes non-Muslims in the conversation (Madjid 1988).

In summary, I have argued in this section that three major paradigmatic events are relevant for understanding the national and global context of religion, violence, and diversity in Indonesia. The first is the trauma or tragedy of 1965–66. In 1965–66, Indonesians dealt with increasing conflict and irreconcilable diversity by physically and politically eliminating a major portion of Indonesian society. In a sense, this strategy was successful. Indonesians, who were construed as atheist-communists, were annihilated as a recognizable group in Indonesia. Citizenship in the Republic was redefined to exclude them from public life. Political, economic, social, educational, religious, and cultural institutions all banned them (and their offspring) from participation. In the collective memory of Indonesians they were redefined through thirty-two years of public discourse as a dangerous threat to the meaning and identity of Indonesian society.

In the repertoire of Indonesian social responses to apocalyptic fear of the other, the strategy of annihilating the enemy is still a live option. The dramatic end to the New Order Regime of Soeharto was followed by the extreme brutality of the ethno-religious mass violence that broke out in Kalimantan, Java, Ambon, North Moluccas, and Poso. The violent aftermath of *Reformasi* witnesses to the fact that this strategy is still a possibility in Indonesia. The unsuccessful attempts to militarily annihilate separatists in East Timor, West Papua, and Aceh provide further examples. Even the brutal killing of petty thieves by villagers provides evidence that physical annihilation of the common social enemy is part of Indonesian consciousness (Colombijn and Lindblad 2002). It is part of the repertoire of social responses to painful diversity or threat. In my opinion, the inability of most Indonesians to face and condemn the massive killings of 1965–66, keeps these events alive as a dangerous memory and contributes to the willingness of some groups to use violence to oppose their perceived enemies.

On the other hand, unlike the massacres of 1965–66, none of the outbreaks of mass ethno-religious violence in recent years succeeded in eliminating the other. In every case, the mass violence yielded no clear winner and both sides sustained agonizing losses. To a greater or lesser extent, substantial progress has been made in achieving reconciliation through negotiation and compromise. After a cataclysmic earthquake and tsunami, even Aceh ended the violent conflict and began the difficult process of peacefully negotiating power sharing between formerly irreconcilable groups. The fact that ethno-religious conflicts remained relatively localized (in time and place), and Indonesia succeeded in forming a stable, democratically elected government that includes almost all sectors of Indonesian society, provides strong grounds for optimism that mass violence to eliminate diversity is less and less likely. Radical groups still use or threaten violence to attack groups that infringe on their conception of an ideal community. But so far their activities are severely constrained by lack of public support or governmental toleration. Most Indonesian communities recognize that the attempt to eliminate another substantial group by violence is just not worth the cost.

The third paradigmatic event was September 11, 2001 and the War on Terror. The War on Terror helped revive a bipolar worldview in which Islam is construed as under violent attack from the West (apocalyptic fear). This view is supplemented by conviction that only in Islam is there hope of building a just and moral society (utopian hope). The hopes and fears of this worldview are sustained by a particular reading of the global situation. In other words, Muslims who partially or wholly subscribe to this reading, do not justify it only on the basis of the concrete situation of the *reformasi* era of Indonesia, but rather with reference to Palestine, Iraq, Afghanistan, and Iran (Adeney-Risakotta 2004). A post-9/11 reading of the global situation informs Indonesians where they fit within a newly conceived, bipolar world. As the largest Muslim population in the world, Indonesia has experienced a remarkable renaissance of Islamic inspired civilization. Many Muslims believe (or hope), that Indonesia is (or may become) a new center of Islamic civilization and the key to its worldwide revival.

A post-9/11 bipolar worldview presents a new challenge to the discourse about reconciliation and peace building in Indonesia. On the one hand, fears of globalization, Western cultural hegemony, American militarism, capitalist neo-imperialism, and Christian proselytism can lead to violent attempts to protect the Muslim community against an outside enemy. Hopes for the rise of Islamic civilization can lead to vigorous efforts to purge the society of non-Islamic, polluting influences, such as churches, bars, and heretical sects.

On the other hand, the majority of Muslims in Indonesia, even if they accept some elements of a post-9/11 bipolar worldview, do not believe that true Islamic civilization can or should be imposed by violence. In fact many believe that Indonesia's greatest contribution to global Islamic discourse and practice is of a unique Islamic civilization that demonstrates substantive Islamic values of peace, tolerance, human rights (and responsibilities), justice, and respect for diversity. On this reading, Western civilizations have failed to live up to their own ideals, many of which are compatible with Islamic ideals. They believe it is time for an Islamic majority country like Indonesia to demonstrate a different way of life that succeeds where the West has failed.

FOR DISCUSSION

1. Pancasila is a particular political milieu in Indonesia. In your opinion, how might this affect peacebuilding efforts, on various societal levels, between Muslims and Christians?

2. Has Indonesia been successful in creating an environment where there is tolerance for diversity? Why or why not? If yes, argue in support of certain practices or political dicta that would work in Western countries.

3. Contrast the Arab world of the Middle East and North Africa with the most populous Muslim nation of Indonesia. What have been the external influences that have created today's contexts for Muslim-Christian interaction?

4. PROJECT: Create a concise chart that explores the similarities between the three paradigmatic events in modern Indonesian history described by Adeney-Risakotta. After analyzing your results, choose one of the three events you believe to be most effective in forming present-day Indonesian opinions regarding the role of peacemaking among religions. (You may need to talk with several Indonesians online or in your area, as well as read op-ed pieces in newspapers, to research political opinions.)

References Cited

Adeney, Bernard. 1994. "Liberalism Protects Dignity of Indonesians." *Jakarta Post.* March 1.

Adeney-Risakotta, Bernard. 1998. "Reformasi Gereja dan HAM." *Orientasi Baru: Jurnal Filsafat dan Teologi* 11: 60–75.

———. 2004. "The Impact of September 11 on Islam in Southeast Asia." In *Islam in Southeast Asia: Political, Social, and Strategic Challenges for the 21st Century,* edited by K. S. Nathan and Mohammad Hashim Kamali, 325–45. Singapore: Institute of Southeast Asian Studies.

———. 2005. "Power from Below: Deconstructing the Dominant Paradigm." *Asian Journal of Social Science* 33, no. 1: 23–45.

———. 2012. "Christians and Politics in 21st Century Indonesia." Unpublished manuscript.

Adeney-Risakotta, Farsijana R. 2005. "Politics, Ritual and Identity in Indonesia: A Moluccan History of Religion and Social Conflict." PhD diss., Radmoud University Nijmegen.

Anderson, Benedict R. O'G. 1990. *Language and Power: Exploring Political Cultures in Indonesia*. Ithaca, NY: Cornell University Press.

An-Na'im, Abdullahi Ahmed. 1990. *Toward an Islamic Reformation: Civil Liberties, Human Rights and International Law*. Syracuse, NY: Syracuse University Press.

Aritonang, Jan Sihar, and Karel Steenbrink. 2008. *A History of Christianity in Indonesia*. Leiden: Brill.

Badan Pusat Statistik. 2010. "Population by Region and Religion, Indonesia." http://sp2010.bps.go.id/index.php/site/tabel?search-tabel=Penduduk+ Menurut+Wilayah+dan+Agama+yang+%20Dianut&tid=321&search- wilayah=Indonesia&wid=0000000000&lang=id. Accessed May 6, 2012.

Bourchier, David, and John Legge. 1994. *Democracy in Indonesia: 1950s and 1990s*. Clayton, Australia: Monash University.

Bourdieu, Pierre. 2001. *Masculine Domination*. Translated by Richard Nice. Stanford, CA: Stanford University Press.

Coedès, George. 1968. *The Indianized States of Southeast Asia*. Honolulu: University of Hawaii Press.

Colombijn, Freek, and J. Thomas Lindblad. 2002. *Roots of Violence in Indonesia*. Leiden: KITLV.

Cribb, Robert. 1990. *The Indonesian Killings of 1965–1966: Studies from Java and Bali*. Monash Papers on Southeast Asia 21. Clayton, Australia: Monash University.

Demant, Peter. 2006. *Islam vs. Islamism: The Dilemma of Muslim World*. Westport, CT: Praeger.

Dharmaputera, Eka. 1987. *Pancasila: Identitas dan Modernitas*. Jakarta: BPK Gunung Mulia.

Effendi, Bachtiar. 1998. Islam dan Negara: Transformasi Pemikiran dan Praktik Politik Islam di Indonesia. Jakarta: Penerbit Paramadina.

Foucault, Michel. 1980. *Power/Knowledge*. New York: Pantheon.

Fukuyama, Francis. 1992. *The End of History and the Last Man*. New York: Free.

Hefner, Robert. 2000. *Civil Islam*. Princeton: Princeton University Press.

Henkel, Reinhard and Hans Knippenberg. 2005. "Secularisation and the Rise of Religious Pluralism: Main Features of the Changing Religious Landscape of Europe." In *The Changing Religious Landscape of Europe*, edited by Hans Knippenberg, 1–13. Amsterdam: Spinhuis.

Huntington, Samuel P. 1997. *The Clash of Civilisation and the Remaking of World Order*. New York: Touchstone.

Lubis, Todung Mulya. 1993. *In Search of Human Rights*. Jakarta: Gramedia Pustaka Utama.

Madjid, Nurcholis. 1998. "The Necessity of Renewing Islamic Thought and Reinvigorating Religious Understanding." In *Liberal Islam: A Sourcebook*, edited by Charles Kurzman, 284–94. New York: Oxford University Press.

Niebuhr, Reinhold. 1932. *Moral Man and Immoral Society*. New York: Scribner's Sons.

Nielsen, Jorgen S., and Lisbeth Christoffersen. 2010. *Shari'a As Discourse: Legal Traditions and the Encounter with Europe*. Farnham, UK: Ashgate.

Paget, Roger K. 1975. *Indonesia Accuses! Soekarno's Defense Oration in the Political Trial of 1930*. Oxford: Oxford University Press.

Pew Research. June 17, 2010. http://www.pewglobal.org/2010/06/17/obama-more- popular-abroad-than-at-home/.

Rawls, John. 1971. *A Theory of Justice*. Cambridge MA: Harvard University Press.

Ricklefs, M. C. 1993. *A History of Modern Indonesia since c. 1300*. 2nd ed. Stanford, CA: Stanford University Press.

———. 2007. *Polarizing Javanese Society: Islamic and Other Visions (c: 1830-1930)*. Singapore: NUS.

Roosa, John. 2006. *Pretext for Mass Murder: The September 30th Movement and Suharto's Coup d'Etat in Indonesia*. Madison: University of Wisconsin Press.

Runzo, Joseph, and Nancy Martin. 2003. *Human Rights and Responsibilities: The Contribution of the World Religions*. Oxford: Oneworld.

Spiller, Henry. 2008. *Focus: Gamelan Music of Indonesia*. 2nd ed. New York: Routledge.

Stackhouse, Max. 1984. *Creeds, Society and Human Rights: A Study in Three Cultures*. Grand Rapids: Eerdmans.

Taylor, Charles. 2004. *Modern Social Imaginaries*. Durham, NC: Duke University Press.

Taylor, Charles, et al. 1992. *Multiculturalism and "The Politics of Recognition."* Edited by Amy Gutmann. Princeton: Princeton University Press.

Walzer, Michael. 1983. *Spheres of Justice: A Defense of Pluralism and Equality*. New York: Basic.

———. 1994. *Thick and Thin: Moral Arguments at Home and Abroad*. Notre Dame: University of Notre Dame.

Wikipedia. April 19, 2014. http://en.wikipedia.org/wiki/European_wars_of_religion. Accessed May 9, 2012.

Zurbuchen, Mary S. 2005. *Beginning to Remember: The Past in the Indonesian Present* Singapore: Singapore University Press.

PART TWO

Theological Considerations

CHAPTER 3

Biblical Approaches to Peace

by James R. Krabill

In the last days,
the mountain of the Lord's temple will be established
>   *as chief among the mountains;*
>   *it will be raised above the hills,*
>   *and all nations will stream to it.*
Many peoples will come and say,
>   *"Come, let us go up to the mountain of the LORD,*
>   *to the house of the God of Jacob.*
>   *He will teach us his ways,*
>   *so that we may walk in his paths."*
>   *The law will go out from Zion,*
>   *the word of the LORD from Jerusalem.*
He will judge between the nations
>   *and will settle disputes for many peoples.*
>   *They will beat their swords into plowshares*
>   *and their spears into pruning hooks.*
>   *Nation will not take up sword against nation,*
>   *nor will they train for war anymore. (Isa 2:2–4)*[1]

---

1. All biblical passages quoted in this chapter will be from the New International Version of the Bible, published by Zondervan Bible Publishers, Grand Rapids, Mich., 1973 unless otherwise indicated.

The Bible is a book of both history and theology. Within its pages, writes Howard H. Charles, "we find a record of what *has happened* and a vision of what *ought to be*" (Charles 2005, 56; emphasis added). In the poetic picture painted above by the Old Testament prophet Isaiah, we clearly have a vision of what ought to be, though it is not presented as an unrealistic passing whim of wishful thinking, but as a description of where the God of history is taking the nations.

In this chapter we will examine in more detail this vision God has for "reconciling all things" and "setting things right with the world." We will do so by looking first at the narrative nature of the Scriptures and the relationship of the written Word as recorded in the Bible to the Living Word as known to us in Jesus, the Messiah. We will further examine in some detail the rich meaning of the Hebrew word *shalom* in order to grasp the full scope of God's reconciling initiative and then conclude with some reflections on what this means for those who wish to take seriously the Messiah—the One who "came and preached peace" (Eph 2:17).

The Bible—the Holy Scriptures for the Christian Church

People today are so accustomed to seeing the Bible as a book bound in one single volume that they sometimes forget about the many smaller books that make up its content. These shorter books were written by many different authors who were inspired by the Holy Spirit of God and lived in diverse cultural and sociopolitical contexts throughout various periods of ancient history. At least a thousand or more years, in fact, separated the earliest writers from the later ones.

Many of the books of the Bible took shape and circulated independently before being gathered together into groups of compiled writings. Eventually a collection of collections was brought together. The first such grouping is referred to by Christians as the Old Testament and is comprised of books of the law and history and of poetic and prophetic writings. The second collection, called the New Testament, came into being following the earthly life and ministry of Jesus and the birth of the church. There are twenty-seven books in this collection, comprised of four Gospels, the Acts of the Apostles, twenty-one letters, and the Revelation to John.

The Bible—this book of *many* books—contains a vast variety of literary types and styles: historical narratives, short stories, parables, liturgies, gospels, laws, sermons, poetic materials, letters, prayers, prophetic utterances, genealogies, wise sayings, apocalyptic visions, and, of course, songs, found in their greatest numbers in the Old Testament Psalter. Furthermore, there is a wide spectrum of pictorial images and descriptions in the Bible, something in fact for every mood and aspect of the human experience. As Edward P. Blair puts it:

> One can skip through lush meadows to music of the birds, drink from sparkling fountains, and loll under the cedars of Lebanon (Psalm 104). One can ride the waves in a ship of Solomon's fleet in search of the gold of Ophir (1 Kings 9). One can dawdle in the pleasure gardens of kings, sipping wine from golden goblets and watching maidens from the royal harem entertain the banqueters (Esther 1–2). One can enter into the awful silence of the temple, cry out for mercy before a majestic and holy God, and depart with sins forgiven and a mission to perform (Isaiah 6). One can vent his anger over the rank injustices in life, lament the day of his birth, and perhaps battle his way to faith (Job and Jeremiah) or turn to bitter pessimism (Ecclesiastes). One can spend his life in unselfish service and know the agony of vicarious suffering and death (Isaiah 53 and the Gospels). One can peer into the future with prophets and seers, tremble before the great white throne, and shout "hallelujah" with the redeemed or wail with the damned (Daniel and Revelation). (Blair 1975, 25–26)

Yet while the Bible is diverse by its many books, in its many parts, and through its many images, moods and styles, it is also fundamentally and rather amazingly *one* book with *one* primary and pervading theme: God's purposes and activity in redeeming the world through a chosen people, called out to be a blessing to all peoples of the world as a model and messenger of God's will and ways.

This explains why the Bible is first and foremost, and from beginning to end, a *story*—a narrative account of God's people, promised to Abraham, delivered from slavery, confirmed at Mount Sinai, blessed when obedient, disciplined when rebellious, and expanded in the New Testament beyond its biological boundaries to include people of all tribes and nations who embrace God's peacemaking work in Jesus.

For this reason, Christians do not view the Bible as a "flat" book, a non-historical or a-historical collection of divine laws and wise sayings, but rather as a narrative progressing through various stages of God's encounter with his people. The storyline of this people begins in the very first book of the Scriptures with God's call to Abraham (Gen 12) and culminates with the birth and growth of a "new" people grafted into Abraham's descendants and comprised of all those from all nations who gather around Jesus as Messiah.[2]

This progression moves from the Old Testament to the New, from the "promise" of a Messiah to the "fulfillment" of that hope in Jesus. It is one story, but a story in two parts. The life, teachings, and ministry of Jesus do not downplay, denigrate, or destroy the first part of the story; rather, they show us its deeper meaning, its true and original intentions. As Jesus himself taught:

> "Do not think that I have come to abolish the Law or the Proph-
> ets; I have not come to abolish them but to fulfill them. I tell
> you the truth, until heaven and earth disappear, not the smallest
> letter, not the least stroke of a pen, will by any means disappear
> from the Law until everything is accomplished." (Matt 5:17–18)

Written Word, Living Word: The Relation of Jesus to the Scriptures

The Christian faith has always been the faith of a book. Cradled in Judaism, the worship practice and experience of early Christianity was centered in the synagogue. And the center of the synagogue service was, as William Barclay reminds us, the reading of the Scripture:

> That is what the service existed for. It began with a recital of the
> creed of Judaism and with the offering of a series of prayers. It
> ended with an address by a Rabbi or a distinguished stranger.
> But right in the middle there came the reading of Scripture, and
> it was for this that the people had assembled. (See Rogerson
> 1972, 47)

The gospel narratives of the New Testament clearly indicate that Jesus fully accepted the authority of the Old Testament—the only Scripture he knew! —as the Word of God. In many cases, he openly quoted it and appealed to its authority in his teaching.[3] At the same time, notes David Schroeder, "Jesus sees himself as the one who fulfills the law and as having authority in regard to the Old Testament" (1966, 49). Thus, where the Law of Moses had permitted divorce, Jesus did not hesitate to proclaim this as nothing other than second best, as a concession to the hardness of human hearts. "But it was *not* this way from the beginning," Jesus reminds his listeners. "I tell you that anyone who divorces his wife, except for marital un-

2. This theme is developed in numerous passages of the New Testament; see e.g., Rom 3:21–31; 1 Pet 2: 9–10; and Rev 5.

3. For two examples, see Mark 10:17–19; and Luke 24:44–49.

faithfulness, and marries another woman commits adultery" (Matt 19:8–9; italics mine).

Jesus, however, takes us still deeper in defining his relation to the written Word of the Old Testament. In a remarkable story at the very end of his time on earth, Jesus encounters two disciples walking along the road, perplexed by what they had thought were hopeful messianic promises of the Old Testament Scriptures and the contradictory, confusing, and disheartening events transpiring around them. Jesus listens to the disciples, and then joins the conversation as teacher of the Scriptures, making this astonishing claim:

> "How foolish you are, and how slow of heart to believe all that the prophets have spoken! Did not the Messiah have to suffer these things and then enter his glory?" And beginning with Moses and all the Prophets, he explained to them what was said in *all* the Scriptures *concerning himself.* (Luke 24:25b–27; italics mine)

Shortly thereafter, Jesus appeared to a larger group of disciples and reminded them in similar terms:

> "Everything must be fulfilled that is written *about me* in the Law of Moses, the Prophets and the Psalms." Then he opened their minds so they could understand the Scriptures. (Luke 24:44b–45; italics mine)

As the disciples reflected on these remarkable claims in the days and months and years to follow, they came to understand that the promises made to their forebears had been fulfilled in Jesus, the Messiah. They came to see the "old" as best understood in light of the "new," the written Word as setting the stage for the Living Word in the person of Jesus. One of the gospel writers described it this way: "The Word became flesh and lived for a while among us" (John 1:14).

The ultimate significance of this remarkable insight for Jesus' followers was the gradual shift to understanding all things—including the Word of God they had received in the "Old" Testament—through the lens of the Living Word of God they had experienced in Jesus, the Messiah. Jesus thus became the barometer, the standard, the point of reference by which all that had gone before must be interpreted and understood (for more see Yoder Neufield 2009, 49–61). This firm belief, central to Christian thought and practice, will help us to approach the theme of "peace" as it is presented to us throughout the Scriptures, both Old and New.

Peace—God's Answer to a Broken World

Several years ago an informal survey was conducted among graduating students in a number of North American high schools, asking them to identify what they believed would be their greatest challenges as they faced the twenty-first century. Not surprisingly, the challenges highlighted were almost as numerous and varied as the students themselves. They ranged from world poverty, societal trends (divorce, suicide), and distressing diseases (e.g., AIDS), to growing materialism, family crises, and the quest for personal happiness and fulfillment.

These students had judged things correctly. The issues they were to face would be both global and local, societal as well as personal. In the view of the biblical writers, there is in fact *no part* of the human condition that remains untouched by the profound sense of brokenness permeating our world at every level. "Brokenness," from a biblical perspective, must be understood in at least three ways: it is, first of all, a *universal* phenomenon; secondly, it is *comprehensive* in nature and scope; and, thirdly, it *runs deep*—far, far back and beyond our current reality into the near-mythical past of the human experience. We will say a word about each of these to broaden our understanding.

Brokenness runs deep

Many cultures of the world have within their collective memory stories of a *Paradise Lost*—an original state of harmony and bliss disturbed and destroyed when something went drastically wrong. These stories take us back in time, back beyond the actual memory of clan historians, back to the earliest days of human origins when, out of deceit, arrogance, jealousy, or some other kind of disruptive, disobedient, or ignorant behavior, brokenness entered the world and changed the human story forever. Though these ancient accounts vary greatly in detail, they share this message in common: the world has been living in brokenness for a very long time—so long, in fact, that humans cannot even imagine what their existence would be like without it. Brokenness runs deep. It is a fact of life. It is "the way things are." And, for all practical purposes, it is the way they have always been.[4]

Brokenness is universal

The specific shape of brokenness is determined in part by the culture or society in which it finds expression. In some cultural contexts, this translates into alienation or loss of meaning in life. In other settings, it takes the

---

4. The biblical version of this is found in Gen 1:1—4:16. For a West African version, see "The Day God Got a Black Eye," in Krabill 2005, 90–93.

form of materialistic obsession, political oppression, or evil spirit possession. Whatever the particulars of brokenness in any given place and among
any people, it is clear that no culture or society can claim immunity to the
problem. For in every human setting, there are those who lie and deceive,
those who take things belonging to someone else, those who cheat on their
spouses, unmercifully beat their children, and treat others in ways that defy
all sense of human dignity.

Brokenness is comprehensive
The problem, seen from the biblical perspective, is not only deep within
the human past; it is deep within every human being. And no part of that
being—body, soul, or mind—has emerged unscathed from the effects of this
devastating blow. Healing is needed all around—a comprehensive healing
that alone can bring peace of mind, soundness of body, and joy to the heart.
For such a colossal problem, a solution of equal size and proportion is required. The Bible makes it abundantly clear in numerous passages that God
has an accurate and intimate awareness of the world he has created, as well
as of the mess that has been made of it. And it is for this precise reason that
God has put in place a plan to heal the world's brokenness, to bring peace
out of conflict, and to make things right, once and for all, with his creation.

References to God's peace initiative are scattered all throughout the
biblical text:

- **The Old Testament prophesied it:** A successor to King David would
  be born and he would rule as the Prince of *Peace*.[5]

- **An angel choir at Jesus' birth proclaimed it:** *Peace* on earth! A Savior
  is born![6]

- **Jesus himself pronounced it:** The blessed ones are those working for
  peace.[7]

- **The first Christians preached it:** In Christ (the Messiah), we have
  peace with God and with each other.[8]

The English-language word "peace," however, is too limited a concept
to carry all the weight of dismantling the heavy burden of brokenness and
"setting things right with the world." For this reason, it will be fruitful for

---

5. Isa 9:6–7; italics mine. Verse 7 continues: "Of the increase of his government and
peace there will be no end."

6. Luke 2:8–14.

7. Matt 5:9.

8. Rom 5:1–2; Eph 2:13–18.

our reflection to examine the Hebrew term often rendered "peace" in English translations of the Bible. That term is the word *shalom*. The noun *shalom* occurs some 235 times in the Old Testament and more than 100 times in its Greek translation, *eirēnē*, in the New Testament. *Shalom* is a very broad concept, and that is of course a good thing, because, as the biblical Scriptures insist repeatedly, the world is in serious crisis and faced with a very "broad" dilemma.

In fact, as we shall see, there is no single word in the English language that captures the full meaning of the Hebrew word *shalom*. Perry B. Yoder, in his 1987 book on this matter, draws our attention to the term's complexity in the title he chooses for his work, *Shalom: The Bible's Word for Salvation, Justice and Peace*. Yoder goes on to explain that in addition to these three words, "salvation," "justice," and "peace," the term *shalom* is also used in various passages of Scripture to describe a state of "health" and "righteousness," but also of "well-being," "security," "wholeness," "integrity," "abundance," "intactness," "honesty," "prosperity," "right relationships," "protection," "life-giving-ness," "harmony," "straightforwardness," "reconciliation," "blame-lessness," "rightness," and "good accord."[9] Sometimes in the biblical text these terms would appear to be covering a wide range of unrelated realities. Elsewhere they seem to be used differently in their Old and New Testament contexts. But, in general, there is a clear sense of continuity and connected-ness between them. The overlapping and interrelated meanings of the many and wide-ranging terms signifying *shalom* allow us to make a number of observations about them:

1. *These terms are central to God's peace-making initiative.* The Scriptures emphasize that God has stepped forward and provided a comprehensive response to a comprehensive problem. When sin, rebellion, brokenness, and alienation characterize every aspect of the human experience, then peace, healing, salvation and wholeness must equally be present at all levels as well. And this is precisely, according to the biblical message, what God's multi-dimensional *shalom*-making project intends to offer.

2. *These terms are about relationships.* Shalom addresses the problem of broken relationships in whatever form they come—relationships between people, between people and nature, between people and God. "*All things* in heaven and earth will be brought together in Christ," says the Apostle Paul, all things personal and social, physical and spiritual,

9. Biblical references to these various terms can be found in chapter 2 of Yoder 1987, 10–23. More expansive treatments of this matter are available in: Mauser 1992; Schertz and Friesen 2003; Swartley 2006; and Yoder and Swartley 2001.

emotional and ecological.[10] Wherever broken relationships can be found—inward, outward, or upward—healing, help, and hope are envisioned and provided by the God who wants to "set things right."

3. *These terms belong together.* To obtain the full picture of God's *shalom*-making plan, the many and varied descriptor-words used to define it must be held together. These words, we have noted, are closely interrelated, "all branches growing from a single tree," as biblical scholar Ulrich Mauser says (1992, 33). Each of these terms adds needed color and deeper meaning for gaining a full understanding of God's reconciling initiative. Keeping the terms together means, among other things, that we cannot strive for "prosperity" at the expense of "justice." Neither can we acquire "abundance" while losing our "integrity," nor seek "security" and sacrifice "peace." God's gift of *shalom* is not offered as a kind of smorgasbord with selectable options; it is an integrated set of components which together "make for peace" in God's vision for a reconciled world.

4. *These terms depict the way things ought to be.* God's *shalom* is not simply the absence of armed conflict. It is an all-encompassing vision of the way things ought to be at every level of our existence if and when God's will and ways are fully embraced and faithfully practiced. *Shalom* is not a negative concept, but a positive one. It is a plan for the transformation of human life and relationships under God's leadership where "old things are passing away" and "all things are becoming new."

Jesus, the Messiah, is at the center of God's shalom-making initiative

All of the New Testament texts that describe God's intentions to "set things right" with the world place Jesus, the Messiah, at the very heart of the plan.

> *Col 1:19–20*: For God was pleased to have all his fullness dwell in [Messiah], and through him to reconcile to himself all things, whether things on earth or things in heaven, by making peace through his blood, shed on the cross.

10. References to God's intentions to reconcile "all things" (*ta panta*, in Greek) can be found in Col 1:20 and Eph 1:10. The cosmic scope of "all things" is described by Westcott as signifying all things in their unity, the sum of all things, seen and unseen, in the heavens and upon the earth, whatever their sphere of being, their mode of existence, or their relation of dependence upon God (see his commentary on the book of Ephesians, 1909, 187).

Eph 1:10: And [God] made known to us the mystery of his will according to his good pleasure, which he purposed in Christ [Messiah], to be put into effect when the times will have reached their fulfillment—to bring all things in heaven and on earth together under one head, even Christ [Messiah].

Eph 2:14-17: For [Christ Jesus] himself is our peace, who has made the two one [Jews and Gentiles] and has destroyed the barrier, the dividing wall of hostility, by abolishing in his flesh the law with its commandments and regulations. His purpose was to create in himself one new man out of the two, thus making peace, and in this one body to reconcile both of them to God through the cross, by which he put to death their hostility. He came and preached peace to you who were far away and peace to those who were near.

Jesus the Messiah, according to these and other New Testament texts is the one God has designated as his primary *Shalom*-Maker. Followers of Jesus believe, therefore, it is in Jesus' life and ministry that we obtain the clearest picture of God's project to make peace with the universe. And that is why Jesus the Messiah becomes the barometer, standard, and point of reference by which all else in the universe must be interpreted, understood, and judged.

When we become overwhelmed with the violence, wars, and conflict in our world, we ask, "How are we to understand these events in relation to God's initiative in Jesus to make peace with the world?" When there are parts of God's written Word, particularly in the Old Testament, we find difficult to understand, we ask, "What light and truth does Jesus, God's primary *Shalom*-Maker, shed on this matter?" When the church, as the professed followers of Jesus, miss the mark by resorting to violence, crusades, and war, thus falling short of the model and message Jesus has provided, we ask, "What would it take to work and walk more faithfully as disciples of the Prince of Peace?"

Following Jesus means joining God in the Shalom-making project

We began this chapter with the statement that the Holy Scriptures we call the Bible is a book comprised of many shorter books with *one* primary and pervading theme: God's purposes and activity in redeeming the world through a chosen people, called out to be a blessing to all peoples of the world as a model and messenger of God's will and ways. This theme takes on its fullest meaning in the New Testament with the coming of the Messiah and the central role he plays in carrying out God's reconciling plan. The Apostle Paul puts it this way when writing to the believers in Corinth:

> Therefore, if anyone is in Christ [the Messiah], he is a new creation; the old has gone, the new has come! All this is from God, who reconciled us to himself through Christ and *gave us the ministry of reconciliation*: That God was reconciling the world to himself in Christ, not counting men's sins against them. *And he has committed to us the message of reconciliation. We are therefore Christ's ambassadors, as though God were making his appeal through us.* We implore you on Christ's behalf: Be reconciled to God. (2 Cor 5:17–20; italics mine)

The Apostle declares here that God is not only making peace with the world through the Messiah, God is further inviting all those who have embraced his offer of peace to become ambassadors of the Messiah as models and messengers of God's reconciling initiative. This then becomes the primary identity and activity of the Messiah's people, to embody God's peace project and to extend its healing effects through word and deed to the world. When God's people are faithful to their calling, "the old will go and the new will come." When they fail, they recognize and repent of their shortcoming, receive anew God's peacemaking offer to them in Jesus, and recommit themselves to the *shalom*-promoting ministry to which they have been called.

An early Christian hymn exhorts believers: Imitate the Messiah, God's Shalom-Maker!

There is no distinguishable collection of hymns in the New Testament comparable to the Psalter, the book of Psalms, in the Old Testament. There are however, in the view of most scholars, a number of early hymns embedded at various points throughout the text.[11] One such hymn is found in Phil 2:6–11. Here early followers of the Messiah are counseled to imitate their leader and have the same humble and servant-like attitude as "that of Christ Jesus" (v. 5):

> Who, being in very nature God,
> did not consider equality with God something to be grasped,
> but made himself nothing,

---

11. Some of those most frequently cited are: Phil 2:6–11; Col 1:15–20; 1 Tim 3:16; 6:15–16; 2 Tim 2:11–13; Titus 3:4–7; Heb 1:3–4: and Rev 15:3–4. Other doxologies can be seen in Rev 1:6-8; 4:11; 5:9–13; 11:15–18; and 12:10–12.

taking the very nature of a servant,

being made in human likeness

And being found in appearance as a man,

He humbled Himself

And became obedient to death

even death on a cross.

Jesus' servant-like ministry and consequent death are, according to this hymn, *not* the proof of failure. Quite to the contrary and rather astonishingly, they are the very way God has chosen to bring about his saving, reconciling purposes in the world. We know this, according to the Apostle Paul, because God rewarded the Messiah's faithful obedience by giving him a name and place above all others. The hymn declares:

Therefore God exalted Him to the highest place

And gave Him the name that is above every name

That at the name of Jesus every knee should bow

In heaven and on earth and under the earth

And every tongue confess that Jesus Christ is Lord,

To the glory of God the Father.

On the Road to Dialogue and Peacebuilding

Can this approach to *shalom* in the Bible be fruitful in furthering peaceful conversations and building bridges of reconciliation between Christians and Muslims? Some may feel that emphasizing the centrality of the Messiah in God's peacemaking efforts is not the most obvious or helpful place to begin such conversations. Yet, as South African writer, David Bosch, has stated, "Dialogue means witnessing to our deepest convictions, whilst listening to those of our neighbors" (1991, 484). This kind of passionate and transparent truth-telling can and should characterize people of faith on both sides of the exchange, be they Muslim or Christian. For as the participants at the World Council of Churches gathering in San Antonio expressed it: "We affirm that witness does not *preclude dialogue* but *invites* it, and that dialogue does not *preclude witness* but *extends* and *deepens* it" (see Wilson 1990, Section I.27, 32; my italics).An authentic recounting of the Christian faith cannot, according to Bosch, "surrender the conviction that God, in sending Jesus Christ into our midst, has taken a definitive and eschatological course of action and is extending to human beings forgiveness, justification, and a new life of joy and servanthood" (1991, 488). This is at the core of God's peacemaking initiative as it is and has been experienced by the Christian community for now over 2,000 years.

What Christians have sometimes failed to remember and practice, however, is that the *methods* of God's Peace-Maker, the Messiah, must be consistent with his peace-proclaiming *message*. True followers of the Messiah, the Prince of Peace, will thus come to the table of dialogue "not as judges or lawyers, but as witnesses; not as soldiers, but as envoys of peace; not as high-pressure salespersons, but as ambassadors of the Servant Lord" (Bosch 1991, 489). It is in this spirit that all Christians should welcome the conversations with our Muslim brothers and sisters such as those modeled and experienced in the presentations and fraternal gatherings that have been an integral part of compiling the reflections found in this volume.

Next Steps Forward?

There are many hopeful signposts scattered throughout the chapters of this volume that provide directional clues for Muslims and Christians in moving forward in a fruitful way toward peace and reconciliation between our communities.

Dr. King in her introductory chapter notes the changing climate in recent years among scholars of various academic fields in demonstrating more openness to recognizing the important contribution religion can make in building bridges of understanding in our fractured world. "Rather than looking only at the ways religion can and does promote violence," King writes, "scholars and practitioners have turned to studying ways in which religion can be a positive influence."[12] People of religious persuasion—and most notably those committed to working for reconciliation—should join enthusiastically in this conversation, recording and recounting stories of peacemaking that grow out of their various traditions. Many such stories do exist, of course, though they are *not*, unfortunately, widely known or told.

Dr. Syamsuddin in his important chapter[13] reminds us that we need to revisit our sacred texts and do the hard work of identifying the key themes and values of our communities, rather than being sidetracked and distracted by more marginal "proof-texts" or misinterpretations that often shape popular opinion and practice. Syamsuddin models this when he states that, "one of the main purposes of Islam is to establish peace for human beings." The word "peace" or *salām*, he says, is closely related to "mercy" and "rec-

12. See King, "Introduction," above.

13. See Syamsuddin, "A Peaceful Message beyond the Permission of Warfare (Jihad)," below.

onciliation." These two words and concepts "are mentioned explicitly in many Qur'anic verses and speak of peace firstly between God and human beings and also among human beings."[14] If Syamsuddin's assertions here are correct, then Christians—who might well wish to make the same claims about their own faith—should have plenty about which to engage in fruitful conversation with Muslim sisters and brothers concerning God's ultimate will and desire for the human family.

In the chapter by Father Doctor Akiki[15] we are directed to the various starting points where Christians and Muslims can begin constructing bridges of understanding between our religious communities. Some of these that he references from his context in Lebanon include: (1) common themes and values in the Sacred Books; (2) vibrant spirituality and strong rituals of prayer and worship; (3) Arabic spiritual and popular songs; and (4) common beliefs in the Muslim and Christian faiths.[16] Starting with what we share in common and moving to what is more problematic or complicated is wise counsel that various writers propose throughout this volume.

Along these same lines, Jared Holton's chapter (chapter 6) should be highlighted for the helpful, practical "schematic" tool he offers as "Steps to Peacebuilding through Music."[17] Holton identifies five—potentially six—such steps representing levels of engagement in the music-making process: (1) shared listening; (2) performing music for the Other; (3) learning music from the Other; (4) playing together; (5) shared performance; and eventually (6) joint composition. While these steps can be viewed descriptively as levels of engagement happening simultaneously in music-making with "the Other," they can also be experienced as steps in a gradual progression of ever deeper involvement with a musical culture other than one's own.

Holton's schematic brings to mind a similar tool developed by the Roman Catholic Dominican priest, Father Yves Congar, who served as a key architect in the early 1960s for the Vatican II Council that did so much to open the door to conversations with the Church's Protestant "separated brethren." Congar identified five modalités d'engagement ("ways of engaging") with people of differing faith beliefs or practices.[18] These included:

14. Ibid.

15. See Akiki, "Music for Peace and Reconciliation from Lebanon," below.

16. Ibid.

17. See Holton, "Performing Towards Peace," below.

18. I am unaware of whether or not Father Congar ever referenced this list in any of his publications. But it did serve as an outline for a course I was privileged to take under his tutelage in the winter of 1977 at the Catholic Institute in Paris. The course was entitled "Le défi de l'écuménisme: Conversations entre Catholiques, Orthodoxes et Protestants" and the student group was composed entirely of non-Catholics—Greek

- **Personal relations**—friendships, hospitality, one-to-one relationships, meal sharing, informal small gatherings, fostering fun and camaraderie, etc.

- **Projects**—group activities, fund-raisers, work teams, mobilizing for common causes like eradicating poverty, homelessness, or infectious diseases, etc.

- **Piety**—spiritual disciplines, rites and rituals, formalized liturgical recitations or musical compositions, silent or directed retreats, etc.

- **Prayer**—corporate worship, common liturgy, exhortation, singing, reading portions of Sacred Books, etc.

- **Propositions**—conversations about doctrine, confessions of faith, belief systems, theological statements and creeds, etc.[19]

Congar, like Holton, offered these activities as possible "ways of engaging"—one activity at a time or by practicing several of these activities simultaneously with one or multiple groups of people holding differing faith perspectives. Congar also insisted, however, that there exists a progression here from "personal relations" to "projects" and on to "piety," "prayer," and "propositions" in a hierarchy of ever-increasing complexity and challenge. As one moves from simple physical or social activities to worship and theological reflection, the level of commitment to serious dialogue and authentic encounter intensifies, requiring an ever-deeper understanding and appreciation of both one's own tradition and that of the "Other's" in the process.

This is precisely, however, that to which Christians are called. In the words of Miroslav Volf, cited by Dr. King in her introductory reflections above,[20] the bold claim is made that

> living with the other in peace is an expression of our God-given *humanity*. We are created not to isolate ourselves from others but to engage them, indeed, to contribute to their flourishing, as we nurture our own identity and attend to our own well-being (Volf 2005, 12–13).

Orthodox, Reformed, Lutherans, Mennonites, and others. Father Congar was the only Roman Catholic in the group and he did a masterful job of modeling what he gave his life to promoting—sensitive, respectful dialogue with people whose views and traditions were significantly different from his own.

19. The five categories offered here were Congar's, albeit in French: *Relations personnelles, projets, piété, prière, and propositions*. The examples given here to more fully illustrate the five activities are my own, based on illustrations that Father Congar himself provided at the time.

20. See King, "Musical Gateways," below.

FOR DISCUSSION

1. Create a diagram or pictorial graph representing the semantic range of shalom as examined in this chapter. How does *shalom*'s linguistic domain differ from the word for "peace" in your own language?

2. Krabill states that Christian peacemaking from a biblical perspective centers on Jesus, the Messiah. How might this help and hinder dialogue between Muslims and Christians?

3. A famous saying goes, "Show me your songs, and I will tell you your theology." Do you agree or disagree with this statement? Consider Krabill's discussion of Phil 2:6–11 and other early Christian song texts cited in the footnotes.

4. PROJECT: Analyze the remarks on "dialogue" in the concluding comments of the chapter. Evaluate these perspectives in light of your own religious, moral, and/or ethical convictions. Write a personal statement of religious dialogue that will guide you in pursuing peacebuilding in your context. Share with your class or study group, and amend your statement after receiving feedback.

References cited

Blair, Edward P. 1975. *Abingdon Bible Handbook*. New York: Abingdon.

Bosch, David J. 1991. *Transforming Mission: Paradigm Shifts in Theology of Mission.* Maryknoll, NY: Orbis.

Charles, J. Robert. 2005. *Opening the Bible: Essays by Howard H. Charles.* Elkhart, IN: Institute of Mennonite Studies.

Krabill, James R. 2005. *Is It Insensitive to Share Your Faith?* Intercourse, PA: Good.

Mauser, Ulrich. 1992. *The Gospel of Peace: A Scriptural Message for Today's World.* Louisville: Westminster John Knox.

Rogerson, John. 1972. *William Barclay Introduces the Bible.* Oxford: Bible Reading Fellowship.

Schertz, Mary H., and Ivan Friesen. 2003. *Beautiful Upon the Mountains: Biblical Essays on Mission, Peace, and the Reign of God.* Elkhart, IN: Institute of Mennonite Studies.

Schroeder, David. 1966. *Learning to Know the Bible.* Newton, KS: Faith and Life.

Swartley, Willard M. 2006. *Covenant of Peace: The Missing Peace in New Testament Theology and Ethics.* Grand Rapids: Eerdmans.

Volf, Miroslav. 2005. "Living with the 'Other.'" In *Christian Reflections on Peace: Divine and Human Dimensions,* edited by J. Dudley Woodberry et al., 3–22. Lanham, MD: University Press of America.

Westcott, B. F. 1909. *Saint Paul's Epistle to the Ephesians.* New York: Macmillan.

Wilson, F. R. 1990. *The San Antonio Report Geneva: World Council of Churches.*

Yoder, Perry B. 1987. *Shalom: The Bible's Word for Salvation, Justice and Peace.* Nappanee, IN: Evangel.

Yoder, Perry B., and Willard M. Swartley. 2001. *The Meaning of Peace.* 2nd ed. Elkhart, IN: Institute of Mennonite Studies.

Yoder Neufeld, Tom, and David Neufeld. 2009. "Jesus and the Bible," in *Jesus Matters: Good News for the 21st Century*, edited by James R. Krabill and David W. Shenk, 49–62. Scottdale, PA: Herald.

CHAPTER 4

A Peaceful Message beyond
the Permission of Warfare (Jihād)

An Interpretation of Qur'an 22:39–40

by Sahiron Syamsuddin

Introduction

The Qur'an deals, on the one hand, with peace (and reconciliation) and, on the other, with "justified" conflict and violence. There are some verses that articulate the establishment of peace and reconciliation and other verses that speak about punishment for infidels and *jihād* in the sense of "justified" war. This seemingly contradictory phenomenon is closely related to the existence of what the Qur'an (chapter 3:7) calls *muḥkamāt* ("clear") and *mutashābihāt* ("ambiguous"/"unclear") verses. Muslim scholars have defined these two terms in different ways that I will not explain in detail in this paper.[1] However, I would like to express my position in this case. The verses whose "direct" meanings are in line with moral ideas and messages are called *muḥkamāt* (clear) verses, whereas those that seemingly contradict moral ideas are called *mutashābihāt* (unclear) verses. On this basis, one can say that verses on peace and reconciliation are *muḥkamāt*, whereas verses on "punishment-stories" and on "justified" war (*jihād*) are *mutashābihāt*.

This brings us to the methical question: How do we understand these verses? For purposes of this paper, two approaches are used. First, the hermeneutical method known as the quasi-objectivist modernist method

---

1. For the different opinions on the definition of muḥkamāt and mutashābihāt, see Syamsuddin 2009, 80–81).

will be applied to the interpretation of Qur'anic verses on war. Second, because there are a large number of "sword" verses, this chapter focuses solely on the interpretation of Qur'an 22:39–40, the verses that, according to Islamic tradition, constitute the first verses on war that were revealed to Prophet Muhammad. There are at least two reasons for choosing these verses. First, by paying attention to these verses, the main reasons why the Prophet and his followers went to war can be understood. Second, all other verses on war should be understood with reference to these two verses. Otherwise, they could be misinterpreted and misunderstood.

Method of Interpretation

According to the quasi-objectivist modernist method, the Qur'an is understood and interpreted by paying attention to its textual and historical contexts, grasping its moral values, and applying it in accordance with these moral values. The methodical strategy goes beyond understanding the literal meaning of the Qur'anic text. Scholars such as Fazlur Rahman (1982), Mohammed Talbi (1992), and Nasr Hamid Abu Zayd (1995), who use this method, focus on the universal moral intentions (*maqāṣid*) of the verses. They maintain that the universality of the Qur'an lies in Talbi's concept of *maqāṣid* (universal moral intentions), Rahman's *rationes legis*, and Abu Zayd's *maghzá* (significance). In order to understand the central message of the Qur'anic verse, both traditional and modern methods of interpretation are to be used.

Rahman, who is familiar with the hermeneutics of Emilio Betti and Hans-Georg Gadamer, proposes the idea of a "double movement" and explains that "the process of interpretation proposed here consists of a double movement, from the present situation to Qur'anic times, then back to the present" (Rahman 1982, 5). According to this theory, one must first understand the meaning of a certain Qur'anic passage(s) by paying attention to its historical situation or specific problem to which it was the response. In this step the macro-situation in terms of society, religion, customs, institutions, and the life of the Arab community as a whole at that time has to be considered. Second, one must extrapolate a certain moral principle from the historical understanding of the Qur'anic passage. Finally, this moral principle that constitutes the main message of the text, is then applied to the present context.

A similar idea is suggested by Mohammed Talbi who proposes a "*maqāṣid* -oriented reading" (*qirā'ah maqāṣidīyah*), in which the orientation of a text (*taḥlīl ittijāhī*) is to be examined by using historical, anthropological, and intention-based analyses (Talbi 1992, 118). However, a point to note is that these scholars do not provide a detailed explanation as to the "significance" of these verses leaving the following question unclear: Is the main message the one that was understood in the time of the prophet Muhammad or the one that is defined during the moment of interpretation?

In my opinion, there are two types of "significance": the phenomenal and the ideal. The former proposes that the main message be understood and applied according to the needs of the community during that particular timeframe, beginning from the period of Prophet Muhammad until today (the moment of interpretation). From this definition, there are two types of significance, the historical-phenomenal and the dynamically-developed type. The historical one is the main message of the Qur'an which is understood and applied at the time of revelation, while the other (i.e., the dynamically-developed one) is the main message that is understood and defined during the time of interpretation. In order to understand the historical one, it is necessary to understand the historical context of the macro and micro socioreligious communities at the time of revelation. The historical information contained in *asbāb al-nuzūl* becomes very important. Meanwhile, understanding the dynamically-developed significance requires the development of thinking and the understanding of the *Zeitgeist* ("spirit of the time") of the interpretation. This kind of interpretation represents a combination between objectivity and subjectivity, past and present, and divinity and humanity.

The second type of significance, the ideal one, refers to the accumulation of human insights regarding the main message of the verse. However, in my opinion, the ideal significance is not that relevant because, regardless of the wisdom of human insights, absolute truths can only be known by Allah and will only be revealed at the end of human civilization.

Verses on Peace and War: Muḥkamāt and Mutashābihāt

Let us turn to address the types and priorities of verses in relation to peace and war and then consider the interpretative issues surrounding the term *jihād*.

Understanding and Interpretation of the Verses

In the introduction I mentioned the existence of "clear" (*muḥkamāt* and "unclear" (*mutashābihāt*) verses and that the verses on peace be included in the category of *muḥkamāt* ("clear") verses because they are evidently in line with moral principles. On the contrary, verses on the justification of war/conflict are *mutashābihāt* ("unclear") verses. There are different ways to approach *muḥkamāt* and *mutashābihāt* verses, particularly if the verses seem contradictory to each other. In this respect, al-Zamakhshari's opinion in *al-Kashshaf,* that *mutashābihāt* verses are secondary to *muḥkamāt* verses, is pertinent. He advocates *tuḥmalu al- mutashābihāt ʿalayhā wa turaddu ilayhā*, that "the *mutashābihāt* should be understood in light of the *muḥkamāt* ones and with reference to them" (See al-Zamakhshari 1998, 1:528). In other words, the level of the *mutashābihāt* verses is considered to be lower than that of the *muḥkamāt*. On this basis, if there are verses in the Qur'an that seem to be contradictory and are difficult to reconcile, the priority and authority lies first with *muḥkamāt* verses. The best method of interpretation understands the verses in their own textual and historical contexts.

One of the main purposes of Islam is to establish peace for human beings. Semantically, the word "peace" or *salām* or *silm* in Arabic, is closely related to "mercy" (*raḥmah*) and "reconciliation" (*ṣulḥ* and *iṣlāḥ baynahum*). These words and concepts are mentioned explicitly in many Qur'anic verses and speak of peace firstly between God and human beings and also among human beings. For example, it is clearly stated in Qur'an 21:107 that the Prophet Muhammad was sent as "a mercy to the world" because "he brought teachings that can make the people of the world happy, if they follow him" (ibid., 4:170). This happiness can be achieved in this world and in the world thereafter.

Peace is also mentioned in the context of the Qur'anic revelation (Qur'an 97:1–5):

> We have indeed revealed this (Message) in the Night of Power:
> And what will explain to thee what the night of power is? The
> Night of Power is better than a thousand months. Therein come
> down the angels and the Spirit by Allah's permission, on every
> errand: Peace! This until the rise of morn!

Qur'an 6:125–27 mentions that God gives a peace to the true believers and welcomes them to paradise. God also greets all the Prophets with peace.[2] The word *iṣlāḥ* (reconciliation) is mentioned, for example, in Qur'an 49:10: "The believers are but a single brotherhood: So make peace and reconciliation between your two (contending) brothers; and fear Allah, that ye may receive Mercy."

---

2. Qur'an 37:79, 84, 109, 120, 130, and 180.

Notably, all the verses that speak of establishing peace and reconciliation are *muḥkamāt* verses because they are considered easy to understand
and their literal meaning is accompanied by a moral principle, that is, peace.
On this basis, we can conclude that, for Muslims, peace is a fundamental
component of Islam (See Waugh 2004, 33–35). As such, Muslims are to apply this theological concept of peace in their lives.

A stirring example is that of Prophet Muhammad. The notion of peace
played a role in his interactions with the community. Muslim historians
mention that it was a difficult task for the Prophet to deal with the Arabs
in Mecca at that time. Yet he maintained a peaceable attitude toward them.
There are verses in the Qur'an where Prophet Muhammad was ordered to be
patient with infidels.[3] The Prophet's forgiveness can be seen, for instance, in
Qur'an 2:109; 5:13; 15:85; 43:89; 45:14; 60:8–9; 64:14. He also tolerated them
as much as he could (Qur'an 2:62, 256; 5:69; 3:19; and 5:82). His peaceful
preaching and debates with them are mentioned in Qur'an 3:64; 4:63; 16:64,
125; 29:46; 41:34. There are also some Qur'anic verses (2:208; 4:90; 8:61;
3:28; 47:35) that refer to treaties with infidels that promoted peacemaking.
In short, during the early period of his career in Mecca, Prophet Muhammad avoided conflict with unbelievers, preferring to deal peaceably with
them. It was only in the later Meccan period when he no longer could find
any peaceful means for dealing with non-believers, that he responded with
violence and finally adopted the military aspect of *jihād* during the Medi-
nan period (see Landau-Tasseron 2003, 40).

The Meaning of the Word Jihād in the Qur'an

The term *jihād* in the Qur'an is a polysemious word, that is, a word that
contains multiple meanings. As such, there is a need to pay attention to
the context of its use in order to know the intended meaning of a certain
verse. Harun ibn Musa (d. at the end of the second year of *Hijrah*), for
example, mentions in his *al-Wujuh wa al-Naza'ir* that the word *jihād* has
three possible meanings (see ibn Musa 1998, 319). First, it means *al- jihād
bi-l-qawl* or jihad-by-oral-statement (Qur'an 25:52; and 9:73). The statement *wa-jāhidhum bi-hi jihādan kabīran* in Qur'an 25:52 is interpreted by
Ibn Musa as an order for the Prophet Muhammad to preach the Qur'an
to the unbelievers. Other interpreters who agree with this understanding

---

3. Qur'an 2:139; 3:20, 111; 4:80–81; 5:99, 105; 6:66, 69, 70, 104; 7:180, 199; 10:99,
108–9; 11:121–22; 13:40; 15:3, 94–95; 16:82; 17:54; 19:84; 20:130; 22:68; 23:54; 24:54;
25:43; 27:92; 29:50; 30:60; 31:23; 32:30; 33:48; 34:25; 35:23; 37:174; 38:70; 39:15; 40:55,
77; 42:6, 48; 43:83; 44:59; 46:35; 50:45; 51:54; 52:31, 45, 48; 53:29; 54:6; 68:44, 48; 70:5,
42; 73:10–11; 4:11; 76:24; and 88:22

are al-Tabari (see Ibn Jarir al-Tabari 2001, 17:470) and al-Zamakhshari (see Al-Zamakhshari 1998, 4:362–63). Second, it also means *al-qitāl bi-al-silāh* or war, such as in Qur'an 4:95. This theme will be explored further later. Third, it means *al-'amal*, hard work (Qur'an 29:6, 69; and 22:78). The statement *wa-man jāhada fa-innamā yujāhidu li-nafsihi* (and whoever strives hard, he strives only for his own soul) in Qur'an 29:6 is interpreted by Ibn Musa as *man 'amila al-khayra fa-innamā ya'malu li-nafsihi wa la-hu naf'u dhālika* (those who do good things actually do good things for themselves and they will receive the benefit of the things). Al-Zamakhshari's *Kashshaf* has a similar interpretation (see Al-Zamakhshari 1998 4:535–36).[4] In the case of the polyvalent nature of the word *jihād*, Ella Landou-Tasseron makes four guidelines, by which one recognizes that the term denotes warfare: (1) when the word comes together with military idioms, such as "shirkers" (*mukhallafūn, qā'idūn*; Qur'an 4:95; 9:81, 86), or to "go on raids" (*infirū*; Qur'an 9:41); (2) when the verse deals with a military action, such as Qur'an 5:54, in which a linkage between harshness toward unbelievers, fearlessness and *jihād* appears; (3) when the textual context of a verse refers to a military significance, such as Qur'an 9:44; and (4) "when *j-h-d* in the third form is followed by a direct object," such as in Quran 9:73; 66:9. On the basis of these criteria, she points out that there are only ten verses in which the word *jihād* means warfare (Landau-Tasseron 2003, 36).In contemporary Muslim society however, the word *jihād* is often used with reference to warfare. This reduction in meaning has systemically been taking place throughout history by Muslim scholars of Islamic law. Almost all the classical books on Islamic law contain one chapter on war, and the term used here is *jihād*. However, it is important to note that, in terms of the application of *jihād* in the sense of war, Muslim scholars in the past have been very careful, applying "war" only in very limited situations, such as if they are defending their country from imperialists. However, this attitude was adopted by a vast majority of Muslims before the September 11, 2001 terrorist attacks in New York City. As such, the usage of the concept of *jihād* by some Muslims presently as a basis for terror and for attacking unbelievers in several countries seems unfounded and can be seen as "false." It is important to reiterate at this point that the Qur'anic verses on war must be understood correctly by paying attention to their historical and textual contexts in order to grasp the main message of the text.

4. In this case, al-Tabari has a different interpretation. He mentions that the word *jihād* in the verse refers to war against the polytheists. See Ibn Jarir al-Tabari 2001, 18:361.

The Interpretation of Qur'an 22:39–40

Next we investigate more specifically the first direct Qur'anic verses on warfare via their historical context and linguistic analysis with a view to coming to their central message.

Historical Context of the Verses

If we look at the chronology of the revelation of Qur'anic verses on war, we will find that the first verses to be revealed are Qur'an 22:39–40 (See Ibn Jarir al-Tabari 2001, 16:576). It reads:

> Permission (to fight) is given to those upon whom war is made because they are oppressed, and most surely Allah is well able to assist them. Those who have been expelled from their homes without a just cause except that they say: Our Lord is Allah. And had there not been Allah's repelling some people by others, certainly there would have been pulled down cloisters and churches and synagogues and mosques in which Allah's name is much remembered; and surely Allah will help him who helps His cause; most surely Allah is Strong, Mighty.

These verses were revealed in Medina after the Prophet and his Companions were expelled from Mecca and subsequently migrated to Medina. Al-Tabari interprets Qur'an 22:39 in *Jami' al-Bayan,* as follows: "God gave permission to the believers who fought against the polytheists, because the latter oppressed the former by fighting them" (ibid., 16:571). Similarly, al-Zamakhshari mentions in his *al-Kashshaf* that the Meccan polytheists had inflicted serious harm to the believers and had come to the Prophet with the intent purpose of hurting him. However the Prophet still chose the way of peace and said to his followers, "Be patient! I am not ordered yet to go to war" (Al-Zamakhshari 1998, 4:199). The same account is also found in al-Razi's *Mafatih al-Ghayb* (al-Razi 1981, 23:40). Both al-Zamakhshari and al-Razi also insist that fighting was finally permitted in this verse only after war had been forbidden in more than seventy verses (Al-Zamakhshari 1998 4:199; al-Razi 1981, 23:40). Al-Tabari quoted, among others, Ibn Zayd's statement: "This permission was granted after the Prophet and his companions had practiced forgiveness on the polytheists for a period ten years" (Ibn Jarir Al-Tabari 2001, 16:575). It is evident that this indicates that all possible avenues of peace with the Meccan polytheists who had inflicted violence on Prophet Muhammad and his followers have been exhausted. Attempts to avoid violence, including practicing patience, forgiveness, and leaving the polytheists alone, were unsuccessful as the polytheists consistently treated the believers violently and cruelly to the extent that they did not permit the Muslims to enter Mecca in order to perform the pilgrimage.

Linguistic Analysis

The verses comprise some words and idioms that clearly refer to specific conditions when war is permitted and that indicate the main message of the verses. The words and idioms are as follow:

1. *Udhina li-lladhīna yuqātalūna bi-annahum ẓulimū* (Qur'an 22:39).

In order to gain an accurate understanding of this verse, we should note that the statement translates as, "Permission (to fight) is given to those upon whom war is made because they are oppressed," which requires us to pay attention to two important words: *udhina* ("permission [to fight] is given") and *ẓulimū* (they are oppressed). The word *udhina* is the passive form of the word *adhina*, the active form. Ibn Manzur in *Lisan al-'Arab* points out that the words *adhina lahu fi l-shay'i* have the same meaning as *abahahu lahu* (one permits something to someone else) (Ibn Manzur n.d., 1:52). The subject of *udhina* in Qur'an 22:39 is *al-ḍamīr al-mustatir* and refers to a particular historical war engaged by Prophet Muhammad and his companions. In that context, the companions asked the Prophet regarding the permissibility of conducting war against polytheists. The word *udhina* used indicates that war is only permitted on the condition that all other avenues for peace have been exhausted. The paraphrases *li-lladhīna yuqātalūna* ("to those upon whom war is made") and *bi-annahum ẓulimū* ("because they are oppressed") denote that war is permitted only under certain conditions. In this case it is because of oppression.

Again, in terms of legal implications, the "permission-structure" for war, that occurs for example in Qur'an 22:39, is often regarded as lower in the quality of conduct than the "instruction-structure" of other verses, such as *qātilū* ("fight!") in Qur'an 2:190, 244; 3:167; 4:76; and *infirū* ("go in raids!") in Qur'an 9:38–41. However, in my opinion, the "instruction-structure" should be understood as under the shadow of the "permission-structure," and not on the contrary, because the former (i.e., the "instruction-structure") comes after the wars had transpired. In other words, the main message of permission for going to war should always be kept in mind, when the "sword verses" are being applied. The main message of Qur'an 22:39–40 will be mentioned in the next section.

2. *Alladhīna ukhrijū min diyārihim bi-ghayri haqqin illā an yaqūlū rabbunā llāhu* (Qur'an 22:40a).

The inference from this statement, translated, "those who have been expelled from their homes without a just cause except that they say: Our Lord is Allah," infers that a legitimate reason to go to war is the unjust behavior of their enemies who have driven Muslim believers from their homes without an acceptable reason. This is likened to the oppression mentioned in Qur'an 22:39. The latter part of the verse "*illā an yaqūlū rabbunā llāhu*" ("except that they say: Our Lord is Allah") informs us that there was no religious freedom at that time and the reason for their expulsion from Mecca was that they believed in the one and only Allah. The Meccan infidels forced every person to subscribe to their polytheistic beliefs and if anyone were to refuse and become a Muslim, they would be punished or even killed.

3. *wa-lawlā daf'u Llāhi n-nāsa ba'dahum bi-ba'din la-huddimat ṣawā mi'u wa-biya'un wa-ṣalawātun wa-masājidu yudhkaru fī-hā smu Llāhi kathīran* (Qur'an 22:40b).

This statement translates to: "Did not Allah check one set of people by means of another, there would surely have been pulled-down monasteries, churches, synagogues, and mosques, in which the name of Allah is commemorated in abundant measure. Allah will certainly aid those who aid his (cause)." Another legitimate reason to go to war was the lack of religious freedom at that time. This verse suggests that if the Prophet and his companions had not gone to war, the Meccan infidels would have destroyed all places of worship, such as monasteries, churches, synagogues, and mosques. Interpreting the above statement, al-Zamakhshari states:

> Allah gives power to the Muslims over the infidels through war.
> If not, the polytheists would have seized the followers of different religions in their times and taken over their places of worship and then destroyed them. They would not have left Christians churches, Christian monks, monasteries, Jews synagogues or Muslim mosques alone. (Al-Zamakhshari 1998, 4:199)

The Central Message of Q. 22:39–40: the Abolishment of Oppression, the Establishment of Religious Freedom and of Peace

An analysis of the textual and historical contexts of Qur'an 22:39–40 was required in order to provide an accurate understanding of why permission for war was granted to the Prophet and his companions. This analysis revealed

that the central message of these verses is threefold: the abolishment of oppression, the establishment of religious freedom, and of peace. Going to war
is thus not the central issue but rather a means to achieve a moral and ethical
end. This suggests that war is to be avoided as long as there are any remaining possible nonviolent ways to achieve this moral end. This conclusion is
reiterated by Muhammad Shahrur's *Tajfif Manabi' al-Irhab*. He asserts:

> Indeed, the peaceful *jihād* on the way of Allah might only be
> followed by warfare in situations of the highest necessity in
> order that all human beings have freedom of choice (*hurriyat
> al-ikhtiyar*) and this includes freedom of religious belief and
> expression, freedom to establish the religious symbols of all reli-
> gions and sects, justice and equality. (Shahrur 2008, 138)

Following this, strict guidelines and restrictions as to who can be killed
in battle are laid out. The Prophet and his companions were commanded in
Qur'an 2:190 not to kill non-combatants and those who cannot offer resistance such as women, children, old people, the handicapped, and their likes.
Ibn 'Abbas provides this useful interpretation, "Do not kill women, children,
old people and those who submit themselves to you peacefully" (see Ibn
Jarir al-Tabari 2001, 3:291). This clear prohibition of killing applies (1) only
to those who engage in violence and oppression over Muslim believers, (2)
to those who do not accept religious pluralism, and (3) to those who do not
want to make peace. It thus suggests that the act of killing is not the main
purpose of war. A discussion of the purposes of war follows:

1. The Abolishment of Oppression

Oppression or *zulm* in Arabic is considered morally wrong in Islam.
Lexically, the word *zulm* means *wad' al-shay'i fi ghayri mah allihi* (to put
something in a place that is not correct) (Ibn Manzur n.d., 4:2756). When
used in the Qur'an, it connotes that this is an attitude that is against God's
law. The most negative type of oppression is *shirk* or polytheism (Qur'an
6:82; and 31:13). Another meaning of the word *zulm* is to act with the intention of hurting a person or violating a person's rights or property. I submit
that this is the most relevant meaning for Qur'an 22:39: *udhina li-lladhina
yuqātalūna bi-annahum zulimū* ("Permission [to fight] is given to those
upon whom war is made because they are oppressed"). On another level,
zulm refers to the act of expelling people from their land, as mentioned in
Q. 22:40. Drawing from these meanings, we can infer that this verse communicates that Allah hates oppression. As such, Muslim believers are allowed to take neccessary action, even war, to prevent themselves from such
a predicament. However, war is indeed the last recourse and is only to be

used when all possible means of a peaceful resolution have been sought and exhausted.

2. The Establishment of Religious Freedom

The second main message is regarding religious freedom. The Qur'an stresses the importance of human choice and freedom of belief. Qur'an 2:256 mentions that force should not be used where religious beliefs are concerned (see Syamsuddin 2010, 49–60). Permission for war during the time of Prophet Muhammad was granted in order to establish this religious freedom, a principle that the Meccan infidels did not uphold, as indicated in Qur'an 22:40. However, in order to establish religious freedom, peaceful ways should be explored first and Prophet Muhammad set this very example. It is reported that in the sixth year of Hijrah, when the Hudaybiya treaty was agreed upon, the Prophet and his Companions wanted to perform the 'umrah, but the polytheists prevented them to do so. After some "diplomatic" communication, both sides came to an agreement that Muslims were allowed to perform the religious ritual every seventh year (see Ibn Jarir al-Tabari 2001, 3:304–5).

3. The Establishment of Peace

The third aspect is the goal of establishing peace and this suggests that peace is an important tenet in Islam. Islam promotes living peaceably with all human beings regardless of their religious affiliations or cultural roots. This attitude of peacemaking was practiced by Prophet Muhammad and his followers in Medina where they lived in harmony together with Jews and Christians. As mentioned earlier, there are also Qur'anic verses that command Muslims to preserve peace in their community. On this basis, it can be inferred that the focus of Qur'an 22:39–40 is not on going to war but that of establishing peace. As long as human beings who are in conflict can achieve peace without the act of physical war, war is not permitted.

Concluding Remarks

From the above discussion, I submit that radical and terrorist Muslims have misunderstood the Qur'anic verses on war. Their misunderstanding arises because, first, they have positioned the verses on war on the same level as the Qur'anic verses on peace. In my opinion, the Qur'anic verses on war must be placed under the shadow of the Qur'anic verses on peace, and that war and sword verses have to be considered in light of the Qur'anic verses on peace. Second, these verses on war have been understood literally and their textual and historical contexts ignored.

In this article, I have interpreted Qur'an 22: 39–40 by paying attention to their textual and historical contexts. The exegetical result is that the central message of these verses where permission for war was revealed for the first time is not that of war in and of itself. Instead it contains a message that upholds strong moral and ethical values: the abolishment of oppression, the establishment of religious freedom, and the establishment of peace. This has to be applied at all times and in all places. Warfare can only be conducted if all possible aveneus of peacemaking have been explored, applied, and exhausted. This strongly advocates for all avenues toward peacemaking and peacebuilding to be explored and applied in conflict situations.

FOR DISCUSSION

1. Syamsuddin employs historical context to shed light on textual interpretation. Describe the historical context of Qur'an 22:39–40.

2. Distinguish the differences between perspectives of jihad as "permission-structure" and "instruction-structure."

3. In what situations does Syamsuddin suggest, from Qur'anic verses, that *jihād* as warfare is to be utilized by Muslims? Examine various contemporary contexts of violence done in the name of Islam. In your opinion, are they justified by these principles? Discuss your evaluations with the class or study group.

4. PROJECT: Find a copy of the Treaty of Hudaybiya, a diplomatic communiqué between the Muslim community from Medina and a group from Mecca. Read the text and analyze the agreement as well as the historical context. How might this situation illustrate the concept of *jihād* from Qur'an 22:39–40, as interpreted in this chapter?

References cited

Abu Zayd, Nasr Hamid. 1995. *An-Nass, as-Sultah, al-Haqiqah.* Beirut: al-Markaz al-Thaqafi al-'Arabi.

Ibn Jarir al-Tabari, Muhammad. 2001. *Jami' al-Bayan.* Vols. 3, 16, 17, and 18. Edited by 'Abd Allah ibn 'Abd al-Muhsin al-Turki. Cairo: Hajar.

Ibn Manzur. N.d. *Lisan al-'Arab.* Vols. 1 and 4. Cairo: Dar al-Ma'arif.

Ibn Musa, Harun. 1988. *Al-Wujuh wa al-Naza'ir fi al-Qur'an al-Karim.* Edited by Hatim Salih al-Damin. Baghdad: Wizarat al-Thaqafa wa al-I'lam.

Landau-Tasseron, Ella. 2003. "Jihad." In *Encyclopaedia of the Qur'an,* edited by Jane D. McAuliffe, 3:35–43. Leiden: Brill.

Rahman, Fazlur. 1982. *Islam and Modernity.* Chicago: University of Chicago Press.

Al-Razi, Fakhr al-Dir. 1981. *Mafatih al-Ghayb.* Vol. 23. Beirut: Dar al-Fikr.

Shahrur, Muhammad. 2008. *Tajfif Manabi' al-Irhab.* Damascus: al-Ahali.

Syamsuddin, Sahiron. 2009. *Die Koranhermeneutik Muhammad Sahrurs und ihre Beurteilung aus der Sicht muslimischer Autoren.* Würzburg: Ergon.

———. 2010. "Foundations for Freedom and Religious Freedom in the Qur'an." In *Freedom and Responsibility: Christian and Muslim Explorations,* edited by Simone Sinn and Martin L. Sinaga, 49–60. Minneapolis: Lutheran University Press.

Talbi, Mohammed. 1992. *'Iyal Allah.* Tunis: Saras li-n-Nashr.

Waugh, Earle H. 2004. "Peace." In *Encyclopaedia of the Qur'an,* edited by Jane D. McAuliffe, 4:33–35. Leiden: Brill.

al-Zamakhshari, Mahmud ibn 'Umar. 1998. *Al-Kashshaf.* 6 vols. Cairo: Maktabat al-'Abikan.

CHAPTER 5

Cantillation as a Convergence Point of the Musical Traditions of the Abrahamic Religions

by Nidaa Abou Mrad

translated from the French by Kirk-Evan Billet

The solemn reading of sacred texts and prayers by melodic means holds a central place in the Abrahamic monotheistic religions. This practice of melodic reading, known as cantillation, is indeed at the heart of Jewish, Christian, and Muslim ceremonies; appointed celebrants assume responsibility for it. Other ritual elements having more apparent musical content are organized around it, these being undertaken by cantors or by the gathered faithful. On the periphery and bordering on the secular are these parareligious chants, often of a laudatory, jubilant, or offertory character. Transcending both doctrinal differences and differences in musical style, cantillation constitutes an important convergence point of traditional musical practices related to worship in the Mediterranean region, in line with the perspective of divine transcendence and prophetic revelation. Cantillation gives priority to theologal[1] communication channels between the divine and the human, just as it subjugates μέλος (melos)[2] to Λόγος (Logos).[3] This chapter puts forward

1. "Theologal" refers to the quality of having God as object or being directed toward God.

2. *Melos* originates with ancient Greek ideas about music: "Music in [the] sense of a performing art was called *melos*." "[P]erfect *melos* . . . consisted not only of the melody and the text (including its inherent elements of rhythm and diction) but also highly stylized dance movement" (Mathiesen 2001, 327–48).

3. *Logos*: "the divine wisdom manifest in the creation, government, and redemption of the world and often identified with the second person of the Trinity" (www.merriam-webster.com/dictionary/logos [accessed July 29, 2011]).

a synthetic approach to these questions and sketches a correlative reflection on the prospects for a musical catalysis of interreligious encounter.

Logos and Melos

The important ritual function of music means that this art, along with the dialectical relationship between *Logos* and *melos,* has been subjected since antiquity in the Mediterranean region to cultural tremors inherent in the confrontation between two antithetical worldviews.

The first cosmology is based on immanence—that is, the union of the divine and a world emanating from the divine—and is concerned with both religious practices called "pagan" and also pantheistic or monistic beliefs and philosophies current in the ancient world. These confer on music full (ontological) autonomy and also its position beside *Logos*. For example, it is Pythagorean thought that makes music and the proportions of its melodic intervals the paradigmatic model for divine symbolic numerology.[4] Thus ideological reinforcement of the occult power of music further consolidates its role as the inducer of ritual trance.

The Abrahamic religions present a completely different view: God creates the universe *ex nihilo* by an act of proclamation[5] and transcends it. He reveals himself through his *Logos,*[6] which shows humanity the way of salvation. No worldly reality is divine in and of itself, even though all realities are called to sanctification by God. This cosmology confers no divine attribute on music as such, much less on the rational or numerological nature of the world. In order to make sense of this, the musical act is called to bear the divine *Logos*, to be logophoric[7] and therefore theophoric,[8] and to do so, above all, by means of stylized and melodious enhancement of the recitation of

---

4. Pythagorean cosmogony (the body of myths describing the birth of the universe) relies upon the monochord and the quantification of intervals by means of superparticular relations ($n+1 \div n$) of the lengths of vibrating strings in order to describe the construction of the spirit of the world in *Timaeus* 34b, a neo-Pythagorean work of Plato.

5. The utterance of the divine creative Word or *Logos*: "Esto!" "Fiat!" "Kun!"

6. While prophets reveal the divine word for all three religions, Christianity distinguishes itself from Judaism and Islam in that it sees the divine Word (*Logos*) as the second divine Trinitarian hypostasis, the Son, who is incarnate and made man in order that humans should be deified.

7. The philosophical sense of "logophore" (the idea as bearer of the spoken essence) does not apply here, but rather its literal sense: music bears the Word. However, in Christology, the two meanings are blended.

8. "Theophory" refers to "bearing" or "carrying" God.

sacred prose. Put another way, cantillation is the ascetic basis of a liturgical music that serves the same function as preaching.[9]

Music derives its spiritual legitimacy from its integration into religious rituals and from its full compliance with the traditional theologal requirements of monotheisms. At the same time, a legalistic, literal Islam recognizes only with great difficulty the reality of a music underlying the recitation of Qur'anic verses. It advises against or even prohibits music and listening as being likely to distract the faithful from devotional duties or to lead them into trance states having strong hints of heterodoxy, if not paganism. Likewise, the sacredness of liturgical music is subjected to drastic conditions within traditional Judaism and Christianity and within mystical Islam (Sunni Sufism and Shiite Gnosticism) (During 1988).

The first aim of cantillation is to contribute to the anchoring of prayer, preaching, and teaching in the revealed divine message. Rejecting the worldly character of an orator's tone—whether that of politician or philosopher—the teaching reciter favors melodic reading, thus protecting the utterance of the divine *Logos* through a traditional stylization of melodic intervals. Consequently, the cantillation is totally bound to the divine Word.

According to Solange Corbin (1961, 3), the approach is one "in which the word will have predominance over the music, but in which the latter plays an obvious role of regulator and clothes the word in solemnity." For cantillation in an Abrahamic context, this leads to the tacit rejection of certain musical procedures (10–11), as described below. The first two address texture, while the last two are systemic:

1. Polyphony is absent.

2. Instrumental accompaniment is proscribed.

3. Measured or periodic rhythm is set aside in favor of a rhythmic delivery reflecting the intrinsic meter of the language.

4. Any fixing of musical phrasing by means of precomposition or notation[10] is excluded; given the absolute preeminence of the sacred text in relation to melody, the latter must remain ephemeral and fluctuating, and therefore improvised.

Solemn recitation is the province of the unaccompanied voice of a solo reciter who cultivates a certain musical asceticism, avoiding any vocal

9. "Liturgical music must, by definition, serve preaching, and therefore it must have a theologal purpose" (Lossky 2003, 32).

10. Even though certain traditions (Greek, Latin, Syriac, Hebrew) make use of notation (generally ekphonetic) for intonation and punctuation formulas, the exhaustive or precise notation of cantillation is neither possible nor meaningful.

sensuality or egotism. Stillness, solitude, silence: these three characteristic traits of mystical ecstasy transpose themselves onto the plane of the cantillation, which can induce calm, internalized states of spiritual rapture in the hearer. On the other hand, formulation of musical phrasing is modeled principally on the phonetics of the recited text and on its rhythmic and melodic "outcroppings." Thus, the duration of sounds is determined by syllable values, more or less long or short, in the text,[11] and the variation in pitch around a reciting tone follows the curves of accents and vowel colors. Further, formulas of melodic expansion, characterized as either neumatic[12] or melismatic,[13] appear only on long syllables and generally subscribe to a logical punctuation of the text. Particularly among Eastern traditions, these serve to underline meaning and *Logos*.

Cantillation both symbolizes and delineates ritual musical practices that emphasize *melos* in acts of worship that give priority to communicative channels running from the human pole to its divine counterpart. Ritual uses of music range from refinement (music as purifier) to praise or jubilation (music as sacrificial act [Quasten 1983, 15–19]) to trance in its various manifestations (Rouget 1989). This range extends also to paraliturgical practices arising as expressions of the Abrahamic religions, such as communal trances induced by music in Protestant Afro-American communities, Catholic charismatic movements, and Sufi rituals.

An anthropologically contextualized approach to metric models for the rhythm of musical statements in the traditions of the Mediterranean basin gives rise to three stylistic schemata, which I designate as follows: a cantillatory schema, a ritornello schema, and a hymnic schema. In the cantillatory schema, a musical utterance has a rhythm that mimics the verbal meter. Its melodic contour is consistent with the profiles of vowel formants and prosodic intonation and also with traditional modal formulas, which are polarized by reciting tones and stay far away from any compositional fixity. Cantillation, in its original pure form as unmeasured recitation of sacred prose, aligns with an anthropological perspective that is theologal (Lossky 2003) and "melophobic" (Molino 2007, 1155–60)—or at least wary of *melos* and inclined to subjugate it to revealed *Logos*, as is characteristic in the monotheistic religions.

---

11. In general, a syllable is long if followed by two consonants and short if followed by one. Cantillatory rules for the Arabic language go further, to the extent that the relative value of a long syllable depends on its precise composition.

12. A neume (from the Greek πνεῦμα, meaning "spirit" or "breath") is a short melodic formula. This name is likewise applied in the medieval Latin ecclesiastical tradition to the graphic symbols, which allow notation of such formulas.

13. A melisma serves to fill a long syllable with consecutive neumes.

In the ritornello schema, a reiterative musical statement has a rhythm that traces the periodic rhythm of gesture (for example, march or dance [Chailley 1996, 17–18]). Its melodic contour is independent of the text, which can accommodate melisma. When the music is not strictly instrumental, the ritornello aligns with an anthropological perspective that embraces mystery,[14] with a Dionysian connotation (Molino 2007) whose intensification can lead to trance.

In the hymnic schema, a reiterative musical statement has a rhythm, which reflects both the prosodic meter of verses (set to music according to strophic logic) and also the periodic meter of regular gesture. Its melodic contour, independent of phonological characteristics of the text (because of the strophic nature of the setting), adopts a formulaic modal logic polarized by the final tone of the mode. The hymn aligns with an anthropological perspective that is musical and has a sapiential or Sufi component with an Apollonian connotation (Molino 2007).

Musical Lineage

Although many world religions have recognized cantillation practices (and although certain non-religious musical traditions employ procedures analogous to recitation [Picard 2008]), only the Abrahamic religions place cantillation at the center of their worship and make it the prototype of their ritual musical practices—given that, as Nicolas Lossky (2003) states, it symbolizes hearing the divine voice.

This prototype can be traced back to first-century synagogue chant, a worship practice clearly centered on public reading of the Bible.[15] Cantillation of prose consists in the introduction of modal melody into recitation in a way that respects prosodic metric delivery. The cantillatory phrasing for each verse is introduced by an intonation formula, in order to center it on a reciting tone (predominant note of modal phrasing) and to punctuate it with clausulas and cadences.[16] Moreover, the psalms are cantillated *a cappella* and antiphonally (by two alternating choirs) or responsorially (in

14. Mystery is related to a ritual path of initiation and salvation in some religions of antiquity.

15. "Temple music was transcendental in nature: in the same way as a sacrifice, it offered itself to the eternal. A contrario, synagogue chant assumes a functional role above all else. In a simple and spare style, it aims to unite the congregation around a body of common texts. Music, then, is in the service of the word: serving as carrier and memory aid" (Roten 1998, 30).

16. The formulas known as teamim have been noted according to an ekphonetic procedure (a mnemonic procedure for the notation of formulas without specifying pitch) since the middle of the first millennium.

alternation between verses by the officiant and responses by the assembly) (Adler 1968, 473; Roten 1998, 30).

Christian liturgical music is linked directly with its origins in the synagogue tradition, from which it preserved and adapted numerous elements (Hoppin 1978, 30; Corbin 2000, 63; Shiloah 2005, 363; Sieger 2000, 21). Principally, scriptural cantillation[17] and psalmody were preserved, along with the Jewish Passover ritual, which contains some elements taken up in the eucharistic celebration. Reshaped elements include prayers and declarations cantillated by the officiating priest, responsorial litanies (such as the *Kyrie eleison*), and the psalmody of canticles (such as the *Magnificat*).

If we contrast verbal rhythm with measured (gestural or periodic [Chailley 1996, 17–18]) rhythm, prose cantillation aligns with the verbal side, while psalmody and poetry lean in the direction of periodic rhythm by respecting prosodic meter. Periodic rhythm is apparent in the strophic[18] character of hymns,[19] a practice with pagan and heterodox gnostic origins, and one that was integrated into paraliturgical (and later liturgical) settings in Maronite, Greek Orthodox, and Syriac Orthodox Christian contexts in the wake of St. Ephrem of Nisibis and St. Ambrose of Milan (Corbin 2000; Hage 1999, 65).

Basically, the original service of the Mass, like synagogue worship, rests on three broad prototypes of liturgical music according to a ternary dialectic that brings into play rhythmic aspects governed by the aesthetic dynamics of worship and theology (Abou Mrad 2007, 97). The first of these prototypes, cantillation, represents the fundamental category of liturgical music and has a theologal function. The second prototype consists of psalms or reiterative hymns, which assume the essential laudatory or jubilatory function (as in the Apollonian schema) and are secondary in the traditional Abrahamic liturgical sense. Lastly, a responsorial prototype results from a synthesis of the first two, to the extent that alternation between the officiant's voice (representing symbolically the divine pole) and those of the assembly (proceeding from the human pole) allows integration of

17. This ecclesiastical cantillation was done principally in Greek, the universal Christian liturgical language of its first three centuries, and later in the liturgical languages of local churches.

18. Strophic chant consists in the reiteration of the same melody for a series of verses or strophes.

19. Strictly speaking, a hymn is a strophic piece "without refrain, its strophes sung by means of a single melody, the consistent meter of verses facilitating exact reproduction of the melody" (Corbin 2000, 133). This form, in complete opposition to that of biblical songs of praise (psalms, canticles, and pseudo-hymns), which are devoid of all metric versification (isosyllabic or by syllable count) and all rhyme, appears in reaction to exogenous intrusions.

the irresistible tendency to communal extroversion into a rigorous liturgical economy, coming close to the Dionysian schema.

Along with this ritual component, manifesting itself rhythmically according to these prototypes, there is a cultural melodic component. This consists in the imprint left by melodic characteristics proper to the Near East on the modal systems of Hebraic musical traditions, on their ancient and medieval ecclesiastical counterparts, and on the corresponding medieval Islamic elements. The central characteristic of this melodic component is the Zalzalian framework, which emphasizes the melodic intervals of the neutral second[20] and the major second (Idelsohn 1992; Abou Mrad 2005).

The last third of the first millennium witnessed the maturation of ecclesiastical musical traditions in the East as in the West. This was also the birth period of Arab art music in the context of the Umayyad caliphate in Damascus and Medina and the Abbasid caliphate in Baghdad. This tradition proceeded from popular urban counterparts of Mecca and Medina (in the western Arabian peninsula) as a consequence of confrontation with the artistic musical traditions of the cultures of conquered regions—principally Syriac, Byzantine, Egyptian, and Persian. More particularly, the ecclesiastical musical tradition of Syria, notably through its modal composition, seems to have strongly influenced music at the newly established Umayyad court and its Abbasid successor (Abou Mrad 2008, 92–93).

The religious musical traditions of Islam are related, from the melodic standpoint, to their secular counterparts from the same cultural territories (and also to Christian religious counterparts throughout the Near East), while showing distinctive rhythmic, structural, and stylistic features related to their ritual functions. More especially, cantillation of the Qur'an, in its elaborated or melismatic manifestation, known since the eighteenth century by the generic term *tajwīd* (in its musical sense), represents, according to Frédéric Lagrange (2008, 27–28), an updated form of the medieval notion of *qirā'ah bi-l-alḥān* (melodic reading). From the time of its origin, this type of solemn reading has proceeded, on the rhythmic level, from strict orthoepy according to the rules of *tajwīd* (in the linguistic, technical, and canonical sense of the term) and from quantitative syllabic prosodic meter. The aim has been to maximize the intelligibility of the divine Word while at the same time distinguishing solemn reading clearly from measured secular song. Though the melodic component of cantillation is wholly based on the common scalar modality of the Mediterranean region, its modal formulation is a product of particularized stylistic norms.

---

20. The neutral second is an interval between a minor second and a major second, corresponding to a flexible notion of three-quarters of a tone (around 150 cents).

Outline of a Typology of Styles in Religious Cantillation

Mediterranean traditions of religious cantillation from the first millennium converge, adhering to a set of systemic and ascetic norms:

1. Cantillation is strictly monodic in texture, unaccompanied, and generally performed by a solo reciter.

2. Melodic patterns arise from a modality characterized by predominance of a Zalzalian framework (including in the Christian West until the schism of 1054 [Abou Mrad 2008]); melodic patterns also demonstrate formularity, principally by relying on reciting tones.

3. Unmeasured verbal rhythm predominates.

4. Melodic content is primarily improvised, within the strict boundaries of the tradition, and without the slightest sign of pre-composition or full notation.

Beyond these commonalities, and in addition to specificities inherent in the various languages, differing formulaic expression and differing melodic organization can be observed in cantillation throughout the region, sometimes even within a single religious body. Michel Brenet documents this stylistic variation as early as 1926: "Cantillation is a form of religious melody, primitive in construction and closer to declamation than to song as such, though susceptible to being interwoven with vocalises."[21] This notion that vocalises or melismas can be interpolated in an unpredictable manner within cantillation is indeed the principal element in observable stylistic differences. In general, three styles of syllabic-melodic presentation may be distinguished:

1. syllabic: syllable receives only one note;

2. neumatic: syllable receives a short formula (neume), combining two or three notes;

3. melismatic: syllable is expanded copiously with notes, creating a melisma (often built of a succession of neumes).

The belated prescriptive notation[22] of formulas used for solemn recitation, as preserved in the medieval Latin ecclesiastical tradition, documents a syllabic style that Solange Corbin (1961, 11) characterizes as purified, confirming the tendency to relegate cantillation to the background relative to chant proper, and to place it effectively between spoken and sung. In this

---

21. Michel Brenet, *Dictionnaire pratique et historique de la musique*, s.v. "cantillation."

22. In square notation on four lines, such as appears in the books prepared by the monks at the Abbaye Saint-Pierre de Solesmes.

instance, two dialectics, assumed to be homologous, are juxtaposed: recitation vs. chant, and syllabic style vs. melismatic style.

Extrapolating to other cultural contexts, François Picard (2008, 19) conveys the notion of simplification of phrasing, inherent in recitation—in addition to the use of syllabic style—by recourse to processes foreign to the usual notion of chant: "the pitch instability of voices, glissandi, the use of pitches foreign to the scale." He gives as examples, in the Chinese context, the Buddhist cantillation *fanbai* as distinct from sung *gezan* hymns, and, in the context of traditional Corsican polyphony, a recited psalm verse ("sung without singing") as opposed to a sung antiphon (Picard 2008, 12, 18–20).

Nothing attests, however, that neumatic—or even melismatic—cantillation practices did not develop alongside presumed syllabic practices in the Latin medieval context, as in the living traditions of Eastern churches. Eastern ecclesiastical cantillatory traditions, like their Islamic counterparts, do not mark out the difference between cantillation and chant by systematically allocating a syllabic style to the former, but according to the four systemic norms described above. Certainly, some types of Eastern cantillation are syllabic, or are even sometimes performed *recto tono*, but practices in these cases are dictated by certain constraints, for example:

1. rapid recitation during Eastern Christian monastic offices;

2. teaching the Qur'an through the syllabic style of didactic *tartīl*;

3. the recent practice of some Arab media of resorting to syllabic style, out of context, in order to avoid offending Salafist sensibilities, taking care to attenuate the musical component of Qur'anic cantillation.

The other distinction among types of cantillation concerns the modal organization of melody around pivot degrees or reciting tones. The Hebrew and Latin traditions generally use a single reciting tone, a predominating modal degree, on which the cantillation concludes (modal final). In such a case of unipolar modality, there is a single pivot degree (or "mother-tone," according to the lexicon of Dom Jean Claire [1962 and 1975]).[23] Eastern ecclesiastical traditions stay close to this principle while favoring melismatic style to the extent that time and the abilities of the cantor allow. However, many Orthodox reciters from Mediterranean patriarchates make use of a tripolar modality, in which more than one reciting tone is employed as pivot degree, in addition to the modal final. They also integrate passing alterations to the modal scales into their phrasing, in the spirit of a temporary "modulation." Finally, it must be noted that a process of shifting the reciting

23. The extension of this approach to non-Latin Mediterranean traditions is systematized in Abou Mrad 2008.

tone is observed in several contexts, including the Latin tradition (Corbin 1961, 29–30).

As for Qur'anic cantillation, its highest musical manifestation—*tajwīd*—according to twentieth-century Egyptian norms analyzed by Frédéric Lagrange (2008), is resolutely melismatic and multipolar. It constitutes a consummate art that marries the systematic improvisation of Eastern modality to the rigorous observance of the meter of the Arabic language. It is the most developed form of religious cantillation, from the musical standpoint, in the Mediterranean region. Insofar as *tajwīd* challenges the validity of characterizations such as "primitive" (Brenet), "purified" (Corbin), or "between spoken and sung" (Picard) that are attributed to some forms of cantillation, it shows that these characterizations can in no case be generalized, unless *tajwīd* were to be considered as something other than cantillation—an absurd proposition, given that it completely respects the norms of cantillation outlined above.

In fact, melismatic Qur'anic cantillation constitutes a perfect example of religious art in which musical creativity stretches to infinity while remaining bound to and inspired by *Logos*. It is in this spirit that ascetic or negative rules of cantillation (no instruments, no polyphony, no measured rhythm, no composition, no notation), rather than desiccating its musical basis, refocus it on the essence of the principle and not on anything "primitive." Asceticism is therefore only the catalyst for a transcendence that arises from a creative model centered on the quintessence of Eastern modality and Arabic meter. This attitude extends to the deepest expressions of the Arab art music tradition of the Near East—to be precise, secular musical forms that remain bound to a majority of the ascetic norms of cantillation. The two primary examples are the cantillation of classical Arabic poetry, whether measured or unmeasured, and instrumental improvisation adhering to the metric paradigms of cantillation, which is designated by the generic term *taqsīm*. These musical practices generally associated with the secular cultural realm, if the original ascetic or mystical spirit of cantillation is respected, preserve its imprint and testify to its theophoric character in a land of exile.

The aspiration to an infinite melismatic expansion of the sonorous clothing and prolongation of vowels corresponds precisely to the polysemy of a Greek term highly valued by the Fathers of the church: epectasy.[24] Melismatic cantillation's quality of epectasis is basically a manifestation of the straining of the human toward God, as expressed by St. Gregory of Nyssa in

---

24. "The term επεκτασις / epektasis in classical Greek means "extension, prolongation," particularly in philology: it indicates the lengthening of a short vowel" (http://www.epectase.com/ [accessed February 20, 2009]).

his "dorsal (Mosaic) vision of God" or by St. John Climacus with his "Ladder." It would be as if logophoric melismas, by throwing themselves into the passionate abyss of the vowels, were climbing up the ladder of sounds and straining toward the infinite without attaining it, integrating a form of the infinite in themselves and bearing witness.

Coda: Cantillation as Musical Catalyst of Interreligious Encounter

The systemic ascetic norms of cantillation have always existed to protect prayer from worldly drift and to anchor it in *Logos*. But beyond this asceticism, which would be stifling if it were ceded to a Pharisaic autarchy, cantillation proceeds from a mystical tension, particularly in its melismatic manifestation. It is the theophoric character of music bearing and totally bound to *Logos* that integrates it into an economy of sanctification by epectasy and that renders it almost epiphanic. Even when it no longer explicitly bears sacred text, vocal or instrumental music that is still in line with the ascetic and mystical logic of cantillation retains the imprint of *Logos* in its ontological depth and manifests its meaning.

In light of this dynamic of theologal communication oriented from God toward humans, the communal and jubilatory portion of the Abrahamic musical traditions—oriented from humans toward God and fellow humans—has intensified at various times in history. The first factor in this intensification is competition from paganisms and other heresies (ancient and modern) that engender syncretisms on the hymnic model of St. Ephrem of Nisibis, St. Ambrose of Milan, and popular Sufism. Another factor encompasses the modernist ruptures with tradition, as in the Protestant Reformation, Vatican II, and the charismatic movements.

The last third of the twentieth century was marked by a rise in aspiration for Muslim-Christian dialogue and interreligious encounter. The importance of music as a ritual vector and as a predominant communication medium within the present globalized civilization means that it is indispensable to this aspiration. A response might follow one of two antithetical paths according to whether the reference model takes up the theologal perspective or its communal reciprocal.

The latter path is convivial and syncretic. It gives priority to the encounter, avoiding the pitfalls of doctrinal differences and heightening communal musical expression, far from any reference to music's vital theologal function. These are largely attempts at mixing or recombining made among musicians and musics of diverse religious origins, and generally result in products belonging to the mainstream and "world music."

The former path leads back to the initial meaning of music's rituality in the Abrahamic context. Though verses of the Bible and the Qur'an diverge on numerous points, the gesture that consists in making melody the favored vector of the divine Word as it plunges deep into the hearts of the faithful is the same in the framework of both religions. Cantillation, as a traditional hermeneutic act that is both spiritual and musical, is at the center of this process.

It is difficult to contemplate an interreligious encounter of depth without placing at the forefront the deep meaning of the religious phenomenon and the essence of Abrahamic religious aspiration. In the final analysis, it is a mystical project: to plunge God deep into humans in order to sanctify them. The authenticity of Christian and Muslim religious experience cannot be assessed except by the measure of this project's realization. Far from any modernist aspiration, only a hermeneutic traditionalism on the spiritual plane can come to terms with this path. Only the mutual harmonizing of mystical paths and the sharing of spiritual experiences can open the way to a true interreligious encounter.

If music is to be the expression of this aspiration, it must follow the traditional theologal path. Mutual listening to musical traditions with a mystical dimension, and in this case with a strong cantillatory component, is alone capable of catalyzing the convergence in a relevant manner. It is certainly not the superficial musical recombinations and anecdotal concurrences (dervishes whirling in a chapel or *qawālī* singing spirituals) that will be able to make progress toward Muslim-Christian convergence, but rather the plunging of believers into their spiritual traditions in the pursuit of sanctification.

Postlude: A Personal Testimony

In response to Dr. Roberta King's kind request, I would like to share a personal experience, lived as both participant and witness, which will serve as an active fulfillment of the propositions in the coda of this chapter. This musical, human, and spiritual experience is that of the Classical Arabic Music Ensemble since it's founding in Lebanon in 1998. I assigned a central objective to this ensemble: to make known the Arab art music tradition of the *Mashriq* (the eastern Mediterranean region of the Arab world) according to the authentic stylistic and systemic norms that are too often sidelined by interpreters of this repertoire. But very soon, I felt the necessity of offering concerts centered on encounters between the religious and mystical texts belonging to Christianity and Islam, with the texts presented in musical contexts following this tradition and those related, such as the Antiochian Orthodox and Syro-Maronite traditions. This undertaking corresponded not only to my spiritual aspiration at that time to highlight the convergences among the mystical journeys at the heart of both of these religions, but also to the interreligious nature of the ensemble's membership.

The first major project of this endeavor appeared in 1999 in the form of "The Annunciation to Mary," a concert and CD built upon a mystical Muslim and Christian understanding of the Annunciation. Such an approach is in keeping with the two religions' close agreement on the narrative of the Annunciation and above all on the sanctification of the Virgin Mary. Cantillation of Bible and Qur'an verses and also mystical poems stood at the center of this work, in acknowledgment of cantillation's place as the ideal musical vehicle for mystical religious utterance. Later, I entrusted the cantillation of St. Paul's hymn to love to a *shaykh* (person respected for special religious knowledge in Islam). Other programs of mystical and musical convergence met with the approval of audiences in Lebanon, Syria, Tunisia, France, Italy, Belgium, and Germany.

In 2009 at the Antonine University, I offered a new version called "The Annunciation: An Islamic/Christian Mystical Oratorio" both in concert and on CD. This time, the work involved the participation of a *shaykh* along with cantors and instrumentalists from the four major religious communities in Lebanon. The audience was equally diverse, and, together, we experienced a strong spiritual and musical conviviality. This event also contributed to a dynamic within Lebanese society that led to the 2010 government decision to make the feast of the Annunciation (March 25) a national Muslim and Christian holiday.

When Dr. King asked me to give a concert during the Beirut segment of Songs of Peace and Reconciliation, I presented "Songs of Divine Love," the event she describes so kindly in the prologue of this book. In experiences such as these, the cantillation of sacred texts, done in accordance with the musical traditions strongly allied to them, provides means of expressing the quest for encounter among those who love God. The encounter takes place without doctrinal syncretism, but in affirmation of both the beauty of mystical traditions and also the efficacy of musical traditions as channels for fulfilling human-divine love.[25]

---

25. This chapter evolved from a paper given at Songs of Peace and Reconciliation Colloquium, Beirut, April 2–5, 2009, the revision of an article published in French in 2009: Abou Mrad 2009.

FOR DISCUSSION

1. What is the theological framework for cantillation, as represented in the Mediterranean region?

2. Reflect on Abou Mrad's theocentric ("theophoric") position on interreligious encounter versus Kraybill's Christocentric position in Christian peacemaking. Identify the advantages and disadvantages of each position, and evaluate your own position.

3. Abou Mrad describes cantillation as a "hermeneutic act that is both spiritual and musical." As the area of hermeneutics deals with the art of interpretation, discuss the difference between text-based encounter and music-based encounter within Muslim-Christian dialogue. How might this influence the purpose of such dialogues?

4. Reread the "postlude" section of this chapter. How might mysticism function in Muslim-Christian encounters? What is the purpose of such encounters, according to Abou Mrad?

5. PROJECT: Log on to the website: http://www.songsforpeaceproject.org/ and view the cantillation performance led by Nidaa Abou Mrad and recorded live from the Common Sounds Symposium in Beirut, Lebanon. The musicians are Muslims and Christians. Record your reactions to the performance. Reflect on the ways music was used as a convergence point for a Muslim-Christian encounter. How might this experience be meaningful both for the musicians and the audience? In your opinion, would this be a successful encounter in your context? Why or why not?

References Cited

Abou Mrad, Nidaa. 2005. "Échelles mélodiques et identité culturelle en Orient arabe." In *Musiques: une encyclopédie pour le XXIe siècle*. Vol. 3, *Musiques et cultures*, edited by Jean-Jacques Nattiez, 756–95. Arles: Actes Sud.

———. 2007. "Compatibilité des systèmes et syncrétismes musicaux: une mise en perspective historique de la mondialisation musicale de la Méditerranée jusqu'en 1932." *Filigrane* 5 (*Musique et globalisation*): 93–120.

———. 2008. "Prolégomènes à une approche vectorielle neumatique de la modalité." *Revue des traditions musicales des mondes arabe et méditerranéen* 2 (*Musicologie des traditions religieuses*): 90–128.

————. 2009. "Quelques réflexions sur la cantillation religieuse en Méditerranée." *La pensée de midi* 2, no. 28: 53–64.

Adler, Israël. 1968 . "Histoire de la musique religieuse juive." In *Encyclopédie des musiques sacrées*, 1:469–93. Paris: Labergerie.

Brenet, Michel. 1926. *Dictionnaire historique et pratique de la musique*. Paris: Colin.

Chailley, Jacques. 1996. *La musique et son langage*. Paris: Zurfluh.

Claire, Jean. 1962. "L'évolution modale dans les répertoires liturgiques occidentaux." *Revue grégorienne* 40: 196–211; 229–245.

————. 1975. "Les répertoires liturgiques latins avant l'octœchos: I. L'office férial romano-franc." *Études grégoriennes* 15: 5–192.

Corbin, Solange. 2000. *L'église à la conquête de sa musique*. Kaslik, Lebanon: Université Saint-Esprit de Kaslik.

————. 1961. "La cantillation des rituels chrétiens." *Revue de musicologie* 47, no. 123: 3.

During, Jean. 1988. *Musique et extase: l'audition mystique dans la tradition soufie*. Paris: Michel.

Hage, Louis. 1999. *Précis de chant maronite*. Kaslik, Lebanon: Bibliothèque de l'Université Saint-Esprit de Kaslik.

Hoppin, Richard. 1978. *Medieval Music*. New York: Norton.

Idelsohn, Abraham. 1992. *Jewish Music in Its Historical Development*. New York: Dover.

Lagrange, Frédéric. 2008. "Réflexions sur quelques enregistrements de cantillation coranique en Égypte (de l'ère du disque 78 tours à l'époque moderne)." *Revue des traditions musicales des mondes arabe et méditerranéen* 2 (*Musicologie des traditions religieuses*): 25–56.

Lossky, Nicolas. 2003. *Essai sur une théologie de la musique liturgique: Perspective orthodoxe*. Paris: Cerf.

Mathiesen, Thomas J. 2001. "Greece, §I: Ancient." In *New Grove Dictionary of Music and Musicians*, edited by Stanley Sadie and John Tyrrell, 327–48. London: Macmillan.

Molino, Jean. 2007. "Du plaisir à l'esthétique: les multiples formes de l'expérience musicale." In *Musiques: une encyclopédie pour le XXIe siècle*, edited by Jean-Jacques Nattiez, 5:1154–96. Arles: Actes Sud.

Picard, François. 2008. "Parole, déclamation, récitation, cantillation, psalmodie, chant." *Revue des traditions musicales des mondes arabe et méditerranéen* 2 (*Musicologie des traditions religieuses*): 9–24.

Quasten, Johannes. 1983. *Music and Worship in Pagan and Christian Antiquity*. Translated by Boniface Ramsey. Washington: National Association of Pastoral Musicians.

Roten, Hervé. 1998. *Musiques liturgiques juives: parcours et escales*. Arles: Actes Sud.

Rouget, Gilbert. 1989. *La musique et la transe, esquisse d'une théorie générale des relations de la musique et de la possession*. Paris: Gallimard.

Shiloah, Amnon. 2005. "Judaïsme et islam: Les monothéismes face à la musique." In *Musiques: une encyclopédie pour le XXIe siècle*, edited by Jean-Jacques Nattiez, 3:358–85. Arles: Actes Sud.

Siegert, Folker. 2000. "Les judaïsmes au Ier siècle." In *Aux origines du christianisme*, edited by Pierre Geoltrain, 11–28. Paris, Gallimard.

PART THREE

Multi-Disciplinary Explorations

CHAPTER 6

Musical Gateways to Peace and Reconciliation

*The Dynamics of Imagined Worlds[1] of Spirituality
at the Fes Festival of World Sacred Music[2]*

By Roberta R. King

*In an age of heightened globalization and recurring conflicts,
festivals of world sacred music are emerging as safe places where
musicians and participants from varying faiths are coming
together in new ways. For brief moments in time, people experience imagined worlds of spirituality, moving from encountering
the "other"[3] to experiencing "one another" in emerging configurations of global community. Serving as musical gateways to
peace, festivals foster recognition, respect, and appreciation for
one another. Focusing on the social spaces of imagined worlds*

1. See Appadurai 1999, 220–30.

2. An annual festival established in 1994 at the time of the first Gulf War with the purpose to gather the "great musical traditions of the sacred, the spiritual music and the world music" (Kabbaj 2009), at that time a totally new concept in the East and in the Arab world where festivals of sacred music were focused on western sacred music.

3. I am cognizant of postcolonial discussions on the negative use of the term, "other" (see Said 1979; and Ashcroft, Griffiths, and Tiffin 1998, 167–73). Yet, one of the implicit purposes of the Fes Festival is to breakdown pejorative stereotypes of the "other" that many attendees unconsciously carry with them as will be noted in the in-terviews presented here. Thus, I have chosen to use this term as a means to interact with such attitudes and to discuss possible changes away from misplaced perceptions.

*of spirituality in relationship to festival musicians and partici-
pants, this chapter identifies and explores communication dynamics of peacebuilding through music. (See Appadurai 2009)*

Figure 5: Entry gate to Fes, Morocco's Ancient City: the *Madīnah*.

As the *petit taxi* approaches the *Bab El Makina*, my North American
mind is trying to sort out the significance of the Arabic word *bāb*. *Bāb*-s,
beautifully ornate Moorish doors or gates, seem to appear almost everywhere around Fes. The *Bab El Makina*, a massive gate built in 1886 as an
entry into the Royal Palace, rises up before me. Awash with festive lights and
ancient thick walls that contain two smaller entry *bāb*-s, each with security
X-ray machines, I negotiate my way through them to the first *mechouar*,
or ceremonial square.[4] The opening ceremony of the 14th edition of the Fes
Festival with its theme of "Paths of Creation" (*Les voies de la création*) is
about to begin. But I am held up by men in tuxes and women in long black
evening gowns wearing extremely long dangling earrings, plus, wait-a-min-
ute . . . what are those military-like men in white formal attire brandishing
sabers doing here? What is happening? I find myself within a restricted area,
unable to move, and trying to be patient. Something formal is happening,
certainly, but I have no idea what. Here I am, out of my comfort zone and
in a nation reportedly 98.7 percent Muslim, 1.1 percent Christian, and 0.2

4. Program notes for the 14th edition of Fes Musiques Sacrées du Monde, 2008, 23.

percent Jewish.[5] I'm grateful at least to speak French, but wishing I knew colloquial Moroccan Arabic.

Finally, we are allowed to move into the second major square, an open-air auditorium with its vast numbers of chairs marked by boundaries for the elite and the less expensive areas. We are ushered forward to the front area, gladly enjoying the chairs with soft, velvet red padding. A beautiful and gracious upper-class Moroccan woman elegantly dressed in a very fashionable white pantsuit looks over toward me and begins to comment on the evening. As we are talking, the royal princess of Morocco arrives and takes her place. Ah! That is what the military honors were for. It is indeed a dazzling "gala" event complete with princess and loyal following. Hospitality is abundant; Moroccan mint tea is served to anyone who reaches out for the proffered glass.

The setting is magnificent with its immense open-air auditorium seating at least 6,000 people defined by a backdrop of immense multiple *bāb*-s opening in graduated sequence in grand Moorish architectural style. The world-class performers emerge through this sequence of portals to perform on a vast stage.

Surprised, I find myself listening to Western sacred music and American gospel proclaiming the Christian faith.[6] Yet, I am seated outdoors in Morocco, a Muslim nation known for its religious tolerance and currently celebrating 1200 years as a kingdom. I thought I would hear North African and Middle Eastern music. However, I am listening to African-American gospel[7] in a North African setting with the princess in attendance. Seated among the local elite and government officials from Europe and North Africa, this is not the Morocco I imagined. My stereotypes are awash.

I set up my video camera, begin filming and taking ethnographic field notes. I am doing participant-observation and at the same time enjoying the good music, surprisingly, of my own heritage. Then, it happens, Jessye Norman sings "Swing Low, Sweet Chariot," "Amazing Grace," and Duke Ellington's "Lord's Prayer," all well-known, standard gospel repertoire. The phrase

5. Central Intelligence Agency, "The World Factbook," https://www.cia.gov/library/publications/the-world-factbook/geos/mo.html (accessed 9/27/09).

6. Jessye Norman, the African-American classical singer, was the featured artist with the West-coast American Rachael Worby conducting the L'Orchestre Lyrique Régional Avignon-Provence.

7. The program included: the Allegretto from Beethoven's Symphony no. 7, Bach's Magnificat, Handel's "He Shall Feed His Flock," John Williams's theme-music from the movie *Schindler's List*, Duke Ellington's "Lord's Prayer" and "Come Sunday," plus a collection of spirituals.

"that saved a wretch like me," from Amazing Grace strikes and touches the inner depths of my very being in a powerful way. I find myself suspended between two realms. Is it true? Am I hearing the Christian gospel sung in the middle of a predominantly Muslim setting? My emotions are profoundly touched; I find myself silently weeping. Here I sit, hearing my faith tradition sung before a religiously diverse audience. I experience a paradigm shift; not all peoples who follow Islam are as the American media present it. I've always known this in my head, but I have never experienced it before. Now, that truth moves to the heart dimension in a profound way. I am profoundly moved as I sit among peoples of multiple faiths while my own faith is given voice in the presence of "others."

The performance of gospel music with full orchestra has honored those who follow Christianity, a minority group in Morocco, through the practice of hospitality in presenting western sacred music first. I turn to speak to my neighbors about the music, and then I remember. "Oh, they do not speak English. I wonder what they understand?" Yet, as Jessye Norman sings Handel's "He Shall Feed His Flock," members of the audience link arms with one another. What is going on here? There is a glimmer of hope within my soul that we as peoples of differing faiths indeed have more in common than I have previously known. A previously unimagined expanse has opened out before me.

Imagined Worlds of Spirituality: Performing Sacred Musics

The dynamics experienced at the *Bab El Makina's* musical space speaks into profound longings and desires for global communities of peace, the overarching purpose of the Festival originally established in response to the first Gulf War in 1994 (Kabbaj 2009). Founded on "a universal mission of peace and establishment of cordial relations between peoples," (Sadiqi 2008, 9) music, chants, dances, voices, and gestures of the great traditions of the sacred world religions encounter one another, seeking to foster mutual respect and dialogue "in order to build a world of hope and peace" (ibid.). Thus, on one level, a sense of "imagined communities" (Anderson 2006, 6) begins to emerge. Anderson argues that a "contemporaneous community" can be formed around poetry and song forms. Indeed, at the Fes Festival, a contemporaneous sense of coming together occurs as people experience the poetry and sacred musical repertoires from major world religions. The western sacred music performed at the opening event, for example, with its assumed musical universalism fostered commercially through the promotion of "world music," belongs to a global repertoire and is produced for a global cohort of people who share socioeconomic and educational backgrounds. Although originally written in reference to nationalism, Anderson's position also resonates true for Fes's transnational event. He claims,

> there is in this singing an experience of simultaneity. At precisely such moments, people wholly unknown to each other utter the same verses to the same melody. The image: unisonance ... the echoed physical realization of the imagined community. (Anderson 2006, 145)

Thus, in brief encounters of experiencing simultaneity through music and the arts, there exist liminal moments of being together in a commonness of humanity that evoke unisonance and the experience of a longed-for imagined community where people peacefully live together as neighbors. We must, however, question how much is understood and to what degree community is formed. "Imagined" community is significant in that even though the audience has experienced a sense of *contemporaneous community*, individual members of the audience will never know most of those with whom they have shared their experience. A sense of vital connection exists between members of the audience even though they "have no idea who they may be" (145), nor what they have understood from the musical sound and lyrics.

Appadurai's extension of Anderson's imagined communities to include "imagined worlds" contributes to a further understanding of Fes's transnational character where multiple worlds "are constituted by the historically situated imaginations of persons and groups spread around the globe" (Appadurai 1999, 222). The fluidity of current world travel fosters peoples living in "imagined worlds," ones that are dependent on individualized experiences and the original communities to which they belong. In this way, the notion that "every human society is an enterprise of world-building" (Berger 1967, 3) continues to ring true in a global age of heightened interaction between multiple societies. New aesthetic forms of global imagination arise as "an emergent way of capturing the present historical moment and the total reconfiguration of space and cultural identity characterizing societies around the globe" (Erlmann 1996, 468). They are forms that evoke implications for the intersection of music and peacebuilding.

The official program of the festival[8] is oriented toward a fluid, global audience, made up of international elite classes, local and international

8. This is the original program of the festival. Tickets for the festival include the full ten-days of concerts (about $500); costs for most local residents are prohibitive. Thus, festival leadership has added a concurrent, no-charge "Festival in the City" that

government dignitaries—especially from the Francophone world—intellectuals, and a growing international tourist, leisure class on quests for authentic experiences (MacCannell 1999). The Spirit of Fes Foundation, the organization behind the festival, considers it "an opportunity to promote tourism and bring people together through culture and spiritual dialogue,"[9] which sets the scene for religious and interfaith dialogue via music and the arts. Thus, the transnational event fosters imagined worlds of people coming together and further delimits its parameters to spiritual and religious interactions resulting in what I am calling "imagined worlds of spirituality." In this chapter, I suggest that festival attendees and participants who follow the events of the official festival program encounter and experience "imagined worlds of spirituality" that allow for dynamic interaction with peoples of differing religions, ideological creeds, forms of spirituality, and national backgrounds via sacred musics and the performing arts.

My purpose here is to explore "imagined worlds of spirituality" embodied through performing the sacred in music as it relates to dynamic peacebuilding. Significantly, peacebuilding scholars recognize the important role of the imagination in seeking to transform peoples' attitudes toward one another. They assert "that imagination is the key to these artistic acts by which new things come into existence, old things are reshaped, and our ways of seeing, hearing, feeling, thinking and so forth are transformed" (Johnson 1993, 212). In such reconfigured spaces the newly transformed relationships are engendered and address the overarching goals of peacebuilding (Huda 2007, 691). Thus, I address communication dynamics and issues in peacebuilding among religious peoples, in particular among Christians and Muslims, by investigating the role music festivals play in bringing about understanding of the "other" in ways that foster transformed attitudes and behavior toward one another. Based on a synchronic ethnographic study,[10]

---

allows local city residents to participate through its own set of concerts and activities. Research in this chapter is focused mainly on the official program, but includes one event from the "Festival in the City."

9. Fatima Sadiqi, Message from the General Director of the Fes Festival program book, 9.

10. Based on ethnographic research at the 14th edition of the Fes Festival for World Sacred Music, June 6–12, 2008, this is a synchronic study. Although the festival venues numbered five in total, I focused on three musical arenas, those of the official festival program and one Festival in the City venue. In total, I attended, filmed, and did participant-observation at four Fes meeting lectures and seventeen concerts: eight concerts at the Bab Makina, five concerts at the Musée Bathe, and four concerts at the Dar Tazi. Interviews were conducted at the Bab Makina, the Musée Bathe, and two restaurants in the city.

I focus on social spaces, locations, and arenas of interrelational dynamics generated between and among performers and their audiences as entryways into peaceful relations among religious peoples.

Gateways to Spirituality: Musical Spaces

Building on its long history, part of the genius of the Fes festival is its multiple locations centered around the ancient *madīnah*—a heritage site made up of Mosques and mausoleums of great Muslim personages, narrow cobble-stone alley ways, arts and crafts, tantalizingly wonderful Moroccan food stuffs and restaurants, spiritual places of study and higher learning, and ways of life that contrast greatly with twenty-first-century global entities. Entrance to the *madīnah* is demarcated by various *bāb-s* located around its periphery. Each *bāb*, distinctively unique and representative of its historical period, serves as a gateway to the richly, thriving life found within its borders. As one enters, newcomers find themselves encountering "another" world and ways of life unique to this region of North Africa.

Similar to the *bāb-s* of the Fes *madīnah*, each of the festival venues serves as a musical gateway into religious dimensions via its musical offerings, providing social spaces for relational interaction. In reference to peacebuilding and any desire for constructive social change, such spaces often "refer to the locations of interaction among people who are not like-minded . . . and not like-situated across the social divisions and levels of leadership within the setting" (Lederach 2005, 183). With attendees coming from multiple religious traditions, the common factor is their focus on music and the sacred. In the following, I consider three musical spaces and reflect on the interactive dynamics located both on stage and among individuals in the audience.

The Bab El Makina: Grand Formal Spaces

The Bab El Makina, the largest and most festive venue of the festival, offers the grandest concerts with the most renowned world-class musicians performing in a formal setting. With the stage at a great distance from the majority of people in the audience, both local, sacred musical practices and interreligious musical experiments are on display. Two primary purposes are achieved in this venue.

Figure 6: Fes, Morocco: the Bab El Makina as Grand Formal Space.

First, major sacred music traditions are given voice. Sufi whirling dervishes and Pakistani *qawālī* songs represent Muslim sacred traditions, while Greek Byzantine choirs and gospel singers make their Christian statements. A wide range of relational interaction takes place among audience members. Seated among peoples of different religious persuasions, there is a mutual longing for the "other" to understand one's own religious tradition and to engage in the highly emotional expressions contained within music traditions of the Middle East (Nettl 2008; Racy 2003). For example, Majida El Roumi, whose concert was billed as "A Call for Peace by the Peace Star," sang a highly moving song in Arabic about her beloved Lebanon. Observing the local attendee's deep level of intense, emotional involvement in the song, I commented to my Moroccan neighbors, "That was a powerful song!" Turning toward me, they asked with great passion, "Did you understand what the song was saying?" Even though I appreciated the music produced, I had to admit I could not understand the song lyrics. Their disappointment was obvious. While experiencing "simultaneity" in the music performance with its immense affective impact, major gaps in mutually knowing the "other" remained.

Second, newly emerging configurations of musical religious dialogue, perhaps the most daring, innovative, and risky elements of the festival, took place through the attempted fusions of sacred musical traditions. One concert, for example, brought two totally distinct religious musical forms,

American Gospel and *Qawālī*[11] Sufi songs from Pakistan, onto the same stage.[12] Each group had opportunity to play their own music. Then, drawing from the improvisational aspects inherent in each of their traditions,[13] they attempted "to call the public to engage with the Muslim and Christian text in a simultaneous moment of intimate experience, looking at the most powerful emotions" (Biétry-Rivierre 2008, 32). In actuality, the event became one of "cautious approaches into one another's music" creating an "encounter of two musical universes" with a certain awkwardness developing between the two groups. In this setting, two highly developed music cultures, each with their distinctive set of rules for music making, were asked to fuse their "worlds" together. As *Le Figaro* reported, "Certainly improvisation created great risk. But the attempt, in the end, did not bear a great amount of fruit" (32).

Similarly, the following evening's concert saw the Al Kindi Ensemble with Sheikh Hamza Shakour and the Munshidins (whirling devishes)[14] of the Damascus Mosque share the stage with the Tropos Byzantine Choir of Athens. The contrast of totally immobile singing with the circular whirling of the dervishes is striking. How can these two groups come together musically? Once again, the attempt at fusion and symbolic integration met with a certain awkwardness that derived from expert musicians specializing to a high degree in their own musical performances seeking to stretch themselves into new musical universes. Such fabrication of events, as rightly argued by Laurent Aubert, are not altogether convincing.[15] In the attempt to find common aspects of each other's musical universe, a certain amount of glossing occurred resulting in sometimes moving to the lowest common denominator rather than allowing highly trained musicians to soar to their level of expertise. Aubert provides a sharp critique when he notes:

11. A Muslim Sufi form found in Pakistan and India.

12. The specific performing groups were Craig Adams and the Voices of New Orleans and Faiz Ali Faiz with his ensemble from Pakistan.

13. Nettl notes that "One of the central features of Middle Eastern music is improvisation, the creation of music in the course of performance . . . memorized and handed down through oral tradition" (Nettl 2008, 75).

14. Sufism is a mystical branch of Islam wherein followers "believe that one may attain union with God here and now if one follows a proper spiritual practice" (Marcus 2007, 43). Furthermore, "Sufism, as a category, in and of itself, stripped of local practice and the meanings conveyed through the individualized genealogies descended from specific sheikhs, has taken a place in the global imagination as a world religion. As a religion effaced of local meaning, Sufism has been forced to represent a postmodern otherness" (Bohlman 1997, 62).

15. Laurent Aubert, Interview by author, Fes, Morocco, 11 June 2010.

> I think that (musical) encounters are truly interesting in rela-
> tion to the amount one sufficiently understands of the person's
> music with whom one is dialoguing. It was a bit as if they were
> people with different languages pretending to dialogue, each
> one speaking their own (musical) language . . . But, the intention
> of the evening was good and worthy of praise.[16]

Certainly, the dialogue between music and dances of religious character are fraught with multiple difficulties and criticisms. Perils such as mere
simulation, the profaning or desacralization of sacred traditions, and in-
sidious cultural voyeurism abound as sacred genres are removed from their
original contexts. "Pretending to dialogue" speaks strongly of the level of
not understanding one another and raises questions about the "ritual's relation with the sacred and the way this relation appears when out of context"
(Aubert 2007, 29–30), plus additional concerns surrounding "decontextu-
alization" and "recontextualization" of ritual musics (Kapchan 2008, 480).

Yet, responses in the audience elicit a wide range of reactions within
individuals. One Western journalist's multivalent responses, for example,
included 1) sudden, unexpected weeping at hearing a familiar religious
song (the sevenfold Amen); 2) reactionary remembrances of her Catholic
background while listening to the Byzantine Orthodox music; 3) affronts
on her spirituality in observing with confusion the whirling dervishes of
Damascus; and 4) eventually finding that the musical experience helped her
to *bridge* into approaching the "other" relationally. In spite of her professional role, she found herself increasingly engaging with *imagined worlds of
spirituality* that shifted her paradigms. Going yet further, another participant explained:

> To me, singing together is a way to have peace . . . inside my-
> self. It brings different parts of myself together. I feel that in my
> body when I see a Muslim choir and a Christian choir singing
> together, moving together. It brings a fulness and an intercon-
> nection, everything in myself together.[17]

Thus, the symbolic significance of experiencing two religious traditions attempting to perform together on stage provided an integrative function that created new combinations of cognitive processing and offered a
personal inner hope and interconnections that suggested the possibilities of
peace between religious groups.

---

16. Ibid.

17. Interplay Woman 2, Interview by author, Fes, Morocco, 10 June, 2008.

Batha Museum: Mid-size Formal Spaces

The *Batha* Museum,[18] the former palatial home used for royal audiences during the summer months in the late nineteenth and early twentieth century, provides an intimate setting for contemplating the sacred through music. Here, after entering through two sets of *bāb*, the large patio is transformed into a stage located under an ancient Barbery oak tree with branches fully extending over the stage and filled with the sound of local birds adding their unique musical motifs. Both the Fes Encounters, philosophical discussions on Art and the Sacred in the morning[19] and afternoon concerts, take place here. Limited in seating, Arabic rugs cover the stage and floor of the front area providing opportunity for the audience to sit on the ground just a foot from the stage, up close and personal. Seating is limited to about 500 people. It is here that the dynamics shift. Just as one may feel distant from the performers on stage at the *Bab El Makina,* so the *Batha* Museum setting affords more intimacy, not only with the music and its performers, but also among people in the audience. A new set of sacred music experiences is striking and brings additional dynamics to the event by offering both "presentational music performance" and "participatory performance styles" (Turino 2008).

The Impact of Presentational Music

Ghada Shbeir is representative of performing solo music in a presentational style where a performer or group of artists "prepare and provide music for another group, the audience, who do not participate in making the music or dancing" (26). Accompanied simply on the traditional, Middle Eastern *qānūn*, Shbeir's singing is recognized for taking "the audience to the spiritual spheres of meditation and inner silence" (Fés Program, 33). Shbeir, a Lebanese professor at Kaslik Lebanese University of Saint Esprit, sings a repertoire of songs from the second century in Syriac, considered by many to be the Aramaic language spoken by Jesus. Shbeir is focused not only on the performance of sacred music, but pursues transmitting a message. In her performance, the spirituality of Lebanon's early Maronite church emerges.

18. Built between 1873 and 1893, this royal home was turned into a museum in 1915. In French, it is referred to as Musée Bathe.

19. The Fes Encounters are constituted predominantly of an encapsulated group of intellectuals, philosophers, art historians, Islamic art scholars, painters, poets, ethnomusicologists, composers, screen writers, journalists, linguists, and theologians whose agenda is to discuss philosophical issues found in sacred music that challenge their worldview and belief systems.

The texts, according to the daily Moroccan newspaper, *Au Fait*, "evoke the Holy Week during which Jesus was crucified. They speak of the suffering of Mary and Jesus when he was on the cross" (June 10, 2008). As Shbeir sings she feels

> the mystery. There is something hidden that I cannot under-
> stand. Sometimes I imagine in the past times, a mixture of
> persons who lived with Jesus and I see the same passages and
> human experiences. Its a language that is connected with the
> church, when one sings, one senses direct (immediate) tran-
> scendence, in conversation with God himself. (*Au Fait*, Mardi
> 10 juin 2008)

Here, Shbeir highlights what many are searching for as they partici-
pate in "imagined worlds of spirituality," that of spiritual transcendence. As one woman explains, "I hope I can talk without breaking down because I've been so, . . . my heart has been so open these last few days. . . . For me the first afternoon performance—the Lebanese woman singing the early Christian songs was incredibly beautiful and moving."[20] Even though she could not understand the language of the songs, she sensed a spiritual depth. Shbeir's pure vocal quality has communicated deeply to many in the audience, especially the spirituality seekers, who are listening for and seeking inner spiritual peace.

Significantly, the political tensions of Lebanon partially motivate Sh-
beir's participation at the festival. Through music she desires to contribute to the well being of her country by pursuing peace via her musical mission.

> Because when one is outside of one's country, we do not often
> speak of the politicians or those who are killing each other,
> but we speak above all about the values of one's country, the
> philosophers, the artists and musicians. In order to pass on
> our message, it requires the foundation of music to approach
> one another, to be more friendly and more brotherly. (*Au Fait*,
> Mardi 10 juin 2008)

Within Shbeir's world of spirituality, the festival's musical performanc-
es offer opportunities to consider values and deeper issues of life, and above all to approach the unapproachable, and to enter into friendly and brotherly relationship. Within this aesthetic space, people have opportunity to engage in longed-for and desirable peaceful behavior.

---

20. Interplay Woman 3, Interview by author, Fes, Morocco, June 10, 2008.

The Interrelational Dynamics of Participatory Music

While the *Bathe* Museum provides opportunities for personal contemplation via presentational one-way music, its intimate setting also fosters more dynamic, interactive participatory music. Participatory music is "a special type of artistic practice in which there are no artist-audience distinctions, only participants and potential participants performing different roles, and the primary goal is to involve the maximum number of people in some performance role" (Turino 2008, 26). The Tartit Women's Ensemble from Mali, whose Tuareg singing tradition is inherently participatory, has transformed its Tuareg exotic African format to that of a stage presentation. Yet, after some solo work and ensemble playing, as they begin to dance, the performance cannot help but begin to "slip off the stage" where audience members who know and understand the tradition are more than eager, even longing to join in the dance. Among them are Tuareg university students currently living in Fes. The students, dressed in their finest long gowns and white head scarfs with just their eyes exposed, what is perceived as "exotic" and "authentic" by the global audience members seated among them, do not hesitate to join in the dance. They are pleased to be recognized and "seen" through the dancing of their culture. One of the students excitedly explains:

> It's magnificent because today we feel at home. It is our music, our songs, and our dance. We hope that people could know our music because it is something from our country, even if it is not very much . . . The fact that people have known (seen) our culture means a lot to us. It is inseparable to our culture.[21]

The joy of traditional "small voices" fairly and equitably represented alongside "big voices" of other nations through cultural music and dance has touched them profoundly. They are delighted to be recognized and afforded respect through their cultural customs that are essential to their identity.

Meanwhile, a Malawian tour-leader from the United States who spontaneously danced with the Tuareg student exclaims that

> there was a generosity because I don't know the full extent of how they dance, I mean I kind of have an idea, and it is the generosity of spirit, of coming to dance with me, and no judgment, no lets do it like this. Just, again, an interplay . . . following and leading.[22]

21. Tuareg Etudiant 3, Interview by author, Fes, Morocco, 8 June, 2008.
22. Massa Kobanda, Interview by author, Fes, Morocco, 10 June 2008.

This "heightened social interaction" (Turino 2008, 28) focuses on the sonic and kinesic interaction between the participants and prioritizes *doing and creating* together, resulting in strong social bonding as an outsider enters into a people's musical heritage. The impact of such music-making is important for relational peacebuilding. Sociologist Barbara Kirschblatt-Gimbel argues:

> A hallmark of heritage productions--perhaps their defining feature--is the foreignness of the "tradition" to its context of presentation. This estrangement produces an effect more Brechtian than mimetic and makes the interface a critical site for the production of meanings other than the "heritage" message. Messages of reconciliation, or multiculturalism or biculturalism, or of development are likely to be encoded in the interface. (1995, 374)

Indeed, when the line between performers and audience melted away as the danced performance slipped off the stage, relational barriers were jumped over as interactive participation fostered through artistic dialogues spontaneously occurred. Participatory music created a momentary opportunity to simply skip over existing socioreligious barriers and to enter into "traditional music's timeless character, by the fact that it seems to transcend the limitations of time and culture in order to reach the most intimate regions of the human soul" (Aubert 2007, 17).

Dar Tazi: Smaller Informal Spaces

The final *bāb* is a small, almost non-descript, dark, wooden gate forcing one to stoop low as one enters into the courtyard of the *Dar Tazi*. Built in 1900 AD, the open lawn area provides a place for the non-formal setting of the Sufi nights, where the musicians from the formal *Bab El Makina* concerts perform for local residents. Participatory music has priority over presentational. As one enters, the place is teeming with life and excitement of another sort. The dynamics have shifted yet again; this is a local family event as the people of the city come out to enjoy their musical heritage of "Sufi nights" in a setting that conjures up community life. A Muslim religious music event drawn from the Sufi traditions, the festival version creates a community atmosphere and *ambience* as the music is performed. Local families and outside guests seated on the lawn have opportunity to engage with each other, including mutual enjoyment of the children. The setting provides one of the rare opportunities not only to sit together in a music event, but also to interact with both local and global audience members, and where international tourists experience local peoples within their own personhood and context. The event and its setting fosters breaking out of the "encapsulation" mode where social groups stay within their designated program. Tourist attendees rush to find a place on the grass where they can experience the truly, if somewhat artificially staged, authenticity of Moroccan Sufi practice. People come with varied expectations, some with a desire to go deeper in spiritual reflection, others seeking to experience trance, while many of the local people have come to socialize and encounter the visitors. It is a type of social-relational and aesthetic space where tourists are allowed not only to peek into the tradition (MacCannell 1999), but also to participate in it.

Communication Dynamics: Affective Space

What, then, are the communication dynamics impacting people? In each of the three venues discussed above, from large formal to small informal settings, participants have revealed openness toward approaching the "other" by exploring socioreligious differences through expressive cultural and sacred musics. Not only do people broaden their horizons but they are experiencing new music cultures. This experience moves one from direct cognitive processing of differences to affective and emotional engagement with one's self and with those one is seated among in the audience. Scholars are coming to see the arts as "a special form of communication that has an integrative function" (Turino 2008, 3): one that not only integrates social groups but also individual selves become more integrated within their own internal spaces of imagined worlds.

Communicatively, music functions within three main dimensions: affective, cognitive, and behavioral (see Figure 7 below).

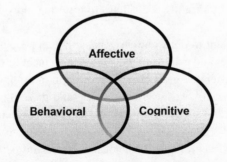

Figure 7: Three Dimensions in Music and Song (King 2009, 166).

Scholars and philosophers have a long history of identifying the strong link between affect, emotion, and music. As Langer successfully argued, "Music is a tonal analogue of emotive life" (Langer 1951, 27). Likewise, more current researchers, such as Gary David have maintained, "music and emotion are so similar that it is difficult to distinguish where one starts and the other leaves off" (David 2005). This is particularly true within many of the Arab music traditions performed at the Fes Festival. In an excellent study on *Making Music in the Arab World*, Racy argues, "Today, the direct association between music and emotional transformation pervades the performers' and listeners' world. Modern Arab musicians and musical connoisseurs stress that above all, Arab music must engage the listener emotionally" (2003, 4). Thus, the festival occurs with additional high expectations of musical performance to incite the transformation of emotions through extended interaction.

In the case of song, the cognitive dimension often takes initial precedence and dominates the musical experience through its sung text. Yet, when well wed to a particular music cultural style, it is the affective dimension that stirs the soul and brings a depth of experiential meaning to both individuals and cultural cohorts. In multireligious and multicultural settings, differing cohorts within the audience assign meaning to the music based on the depth or lack of understanding that one brings to the music. If one understands both the text and the music tradition, meaning is generated in both the cognitive and affective domains. However, if an outsider to a music tradition engages mainly in musical sound as a result of neither knowing the language nor understanding the sung text, the affective realm comes to the fore and becomes the main arena of engagement. With a pluralism of multiple sacred musics performed at the festival, where people come open to differences and experiencing the sacred, yet do not understand music traditions on deep levels, the affective dimension of music dominates and significantly contributes to fostering individuals' *imagined worlds of spirituality.*

It is important to note, however, that although people may be seated next to each other and exhibit a predisposed movement toward the "other," they still each generate a great deal of variation in meaning assigned to the musical experience. As scholars note, "affect and meaning through music is derived from the social, historical and cultural contexts in which the music is situated" (Gray 2008, 64), leading each listener to respond to and interpret musics according to their local contexts and personal histories. Yet, in the musical spaces at the festival we have repeatedly seen high levels of affective "simultaneity" through music, with individuals achieving a musical liminality and simultaneously experiencing a sense of Turnerian *communitas* (Turner 1969) in spite of the extent of divergent histories and religious backgrounds. In this way, the affective dimension of music carries a profound influence in opening diverse peoples and their belief systems to one another. Thus, in spite of a lack of deep understanding of music traditions, an "affective exchange" (Kapchan 2008, 470), or what could be called an "affective dialogue," occurs that facilitates recognizing and approaching the "other." As Laurent Aubert notes,

> in relation to perception and appreciation of music, of the music of the other, of music of another culture, such appreciation generates an emotion, an entrance to resonating in a specific manner. This allows many barriers to be jumped . . . And I think that music is perhaps one of the purest instruments of dialogue between cultures in that one touches the essence of life, one touches the emotional in ways that go beyond the mental aspects.[23]

This interaction is taken further and elucidated by Becker who discusses expanded notions of possible relationships between music events and listening participants. She argues:

> Performers and listeners find themselves in a relationship in which they define each other through continuous, interactive, ever-evolving musical structures and listener responses. Meaning resides in the mutual relationship established at any given moment in time between particular listeners and music events. A group of listeners develops a "community of interpretation" [Fish 1980], not necessarily uniform, but overlapping in some salient features. (Becker 2010, 128)

This, then, becomes the musical gateway, an entry portal to another way of life that fosters recognizing new dimensions about a people's humanity through musical interaction. More significantly, the meaning of a musical act lies in not only the sound generated, but also in, among, and between the people taking part in the musical performance, both performers and audience-participants alike. Mutual participation creates a

> metaphor for ideal relationships as the participants in the performance imagine them to be: relationships between person and person, between individual and society, between humanity and the natural world and even perhaps the supernatural world. (Small 1998, 13, quoted in Urbain 2008, 15)

---

23. Laurent Aubert, Interview by author, Fes, Morocco, 11 June 2008.

Multidimensional in essence, musical spaces facilitate experiences that access affective domains with possibilities for transformational impact that functions simultaneously on two levels: the social group and the individual level.

Conclusion: Musical Gateways to Peace and Reconciliation

Global festivals bring together peoples of various socioeconomic backgrounds, differing religious faiths, and multiple national and cultural heritages who would not otherwise choose to meet together. For brief moments in time, people from around the globe, whether seeking spirituality, self-revelation, the exotic, and/or novel vacations, find themselves coming together at the Fes Festival of World Sacred Music and discover themselves experiencing their unique *imagined worlds of spirituality.* Located within the multiple safe spaces of the festival for encountering the "other" through the musical arts, many distinctively different from their own, attendees of the festival find themselves shifting from observing the "other" to experiencing "one another" in momentary configurations of community.

Over a period of ten days, people encounter one another on a regular basis in the social spaces of sacred music performance. As they venture through the various musical entryways, or *bāb-s,* they begin to interact with one another. Paradigm shifts in attitude toward the "other" begin to take place; for many, barriers are jumped as jaded and negative stereotypes of the "other" are transcended and seem to melt away. Thus, a festival can move one from cognitive processing of differences to affective and emotional engagement, finding a common ground in music with the significant benefit of relating with the various peoples mutually involved in the event. Through the vehicle of music, participants at the festival are given tools for recognizing each other's basic humanity, for attributing dignity, for growing in mutual respect, for giving voice to "hidden" peoples who hail from exotic or highly inaccessible places, and for experiencing coexistence on a common, human level, in spite of political or religious tensions.

As an ethnomusicologist who has worked in sub-Saharan Africa for more than two decades, I am aware of the multiple levels of interaction that occur at any musical event that have not been addressed in this study. I have attempted to consider the Fes festival from a self-reflexive position of an outsider encountering a new world of music and spirituality. The study is not exhaustive; many questions remain. For example, what would be the global audience response if they were able to speak Arabic or understand the languages of the songs performed on stage? To what degree could or would

this interfere with transcendent affective responses of assuming commonality among various peoples? In spite of the Festival in the City program, the
local Moroccan community is often not directly involved with the events
of the official program developed for international attendees. What are local perceptions of outsiders temporarily invading their homeland? Are they
mostly concerned with the economical side of the festival? What relational
impact between religions does the festival create for them? Do they also
experience attitudinal shifts in viewing the "other"? To what extent is the local Muslim population concerned about the broadening of the sacred music
traditions to including the sacred musics of Buddhism and Hinduism? At
what points do differences of worldview and cultural perceptions diverge
between the strong French-Moroccan organizational collaboration? In spite
of a united front, one wonders about the interpersonal dynamics between
musician performers back stage when they are out of the spot light. These
are all areas that have yet to be further investigated.

However, it remains that at transnational festivals, such as Fes, we have
seen that music and musical spaces can serve as dynamic instruments of
peace.[24] As Aubert notes, "Music can play a role in developing a chemical
mix, that is music transmits a state, a reality that obviously surpasses that of
words."[25] Furthermore, music and the arts

> are a realm where the impossible or nonexistent or the ideal
> is imagined and made possible, and new possibilities leading
> to new lived realities are brought into existence in perceivable
> forms. (Turino 2008, 18)

The Fes Festival creates multiple opportunities to imagine new possibilities for living together in a global world. It offers accessing what for many
appears inaccessible in a world caught up in strife and conflict. It consciously
and subconsciously communicates on multiple levels as it exposes various
audiences to differing religious worlds, i.e., Muslim history and spiritual
contexts such as Fes, constant and gracious hospitality, the repeated opportunities to engage with both local and international people, and a model
of coexistence through the inclusion of several sacred music traditions. A
continuum of engagement exists, where some are encountering the "other"
for the first time while some people enter with linked arms, walking further down the spiritual path of seeking deeper understanding of themselves
while also remaining open to the "other." Most significantly, the focal point

---

24. It can also serve as an instrument of war and conflict.
25. Laurent Aubert, Interview by Author, Fes, Morocco, 11 June 2010.

is the vehicle of music where critical shifts in attitude toward one another are processed internally in individual attendees via social engagement.

Thus, music and the arts provide spaces to engage in perceiving *imagined worlds of spirituality* where people have opportunity to "approach one another, to be more friendly and more brotherly."[26] Through repeated musical dialogues between contrasting sacred music cultures,[27] people sense new possibilities for relating with each other and bestowing dignity on one another.

An Australian journalist and playwright living in Fes captures well the paradigm shifts in attitude and perspectives that can take place:

> I think that the impact of the festival as a media event to foster [political] peace is probably limited. But I think that individuals who are drawn here, experience something which they take away and then talk about ... I don't think that great social movements start with festivals. They start with individuals. And all of the political and religious experience that history has taught us, shows this is personal, experiential. And I think that is an important thing that the festival does. I know it's worked for me. My feelings towards Islam—towards the "other"—is now at a stage where I know I will never understand. But I will feel comfortable in not understanding because I trust that the connections I have are heart connections, which my intellect can't quite grasp. And to try and grasp would be futile. So to exist in it, is possible.[28]

The hope of mutual coexistence built on relational trust is highly significant in an era longing for peace. Experiences of previously unimagined peaceable coexistence, ones that can create a longing to maintain openness to others, regardless of their culture or religion, forge new visions for the future. Although sustaining dynamic peace is complex and beyond the means of one festival, the musical gateways of the Fes Festival offer significant first steps in a long process toward peacebuilding and reconciliation allowing people to incrementally move, and sometimes significantly, along a continuum from exclusion toward embracing one another as neighbors (see Volf 1996).

---

26. Ghada Shbeir June 10, 2008.

27. Even though the musical fusion is a bit awkward.

28. Interview with Sandy McCutcheon, July 11, 2008.

FOR DISCUSSION

1. Have you ever experienced paradigm shifts in your emotional or affective self at a music event? Review King's personal responses at the Fes Festival and reflect on your own responses. Write about these experiences, and remember to focus more on affective reactions than cognitive reactions.

2. Distinguish between presentational and participatory performance. For each one, reflect upon the influences of such performances, both for the individual and community.

3. King quotes Laurent Aubert as saying the following: "[M]usic is perhaps one of the purest instruments of dialogue between cultures in that one . . . touches the emotional in ways that go beyond the mental aspects." Agree or disagree, and discuss with your class or study group.

4. PROJECT: Attend a musical event that seeks to bring together different (and potentially conflicting) cultural and/or religious identities. As a participant observer, record the affective responses from various audience members, including yourself. Interview at least three individuals after the event. Next, analyze your results, utilizing King's "Three Dimensions in Music and Song" (Figure 7). In your opinion, were affective responses able to bridge perceived cognitive dissonances (e.g., differing belief systems, conflicting ethnic groups) in the audience? Share your findings in a study group.

References Cited

Anderson, Benedict. 2006. *Imagined Communities: Reflections on the Origin and Spread of Nationalism.* New York: Verso.

Appadurai, Arjun. 1999. "Disjuncture and Difference in the Global Cultural Economy." In *The Cultural Studies Reader,* edited by Simon During, 220–30. 2nd ed. New York: Routledge, 1999.

Ashcroft, Bill, Gareth Giffiths, and Helen Tiffin. 1998. *Key Concepts in Post-colonial Studies.* London: Routledge.

Aubert, Laurent. 2007. *The Music of the Other: New Challenges for Ethnomusicology in a Global Age.* Translated by Carla Ribeiro. Burlington, VT: Ashgate.

Becker, Judith. 2010. "Exploring the Habitus of Listening: Anthropological Perspectives." In *Handbook of Music and Emotion: Theory, Research, Applications,* edited by Patrick N. and John A. Sloboda Juslin, 127–58. Oxford: Oxford University Press.

Berger, Peter L. 1967. *The Sacred Canopy: Elements of a Sociological Theory of Religion.* New York: Anchor.

Biétry-Rivierre, Eric. 10 June 2008. "Quand les chants maronites, pakistanais et gospels se rencountrent." *Le Figaro*: 32.

Bohlman, Philip V. 1997. "World Musics and World Religions: Whose World?" In *Enchanting Powers: Music in the World's Religions*, edited by Lawrence E. Sullivan, 61–90. Cambridge, MA: Harvard University Press.

David, Gary. 2005. "Vamp 'Til Ready: Musings on Music and Emotion." http://www. philosphere.com/article61.html?&MMN_position=61.61. Accessed February 2009.

Erlmann, Veit. 1996. "The Aesthetics of the Global Imagination: Reflections on World Music in the 1990s." *Public Culture* 8: 467–87.

Fish, Stanley. 1980. *Is There A Text In This Class? The Authority Of Interpreting Communities.* Cambridge, MA: Harvard University Press.

Gray, Anne-Marie. 2008. "Music as Tool of Reconciliation in South Africa." In *Music and Conflict Transformation: Harmonies and Dissonances in Geopolitics*, edited by Olivier Urbain, 63–77. London: Tauris.

Huda, Qamar-ul. 2007. "Memory, Performance, and Poetic Peacemaking in Qawwali." *Muslim World* 97, no. 4: 678–700.

Johnson, Mark. 1993. *Moral Imagination: Implications of Cognitive Science for Ethics.* Chicago: University of Chicago Press.

Kabbaj, Mohammed. 2009. "History of Fes Festival of World Sacred Music." Casablanca Travel and Tours [cited September 21 2009].

Kapchan, Deborah A. 2008. "The Promise of Sonic Translation: Performing the Festive Sacred in Morocco." *American Anthropologist* 110, no. 4: 467–83.

King, Roberta R. 2009. *Pathways in Christian Music Communication : The Case of the Senufo of Cote d'Ivoire.* American Society of Missiology Monograph. Eugene, OR: Pickwick.

Kirschenblatt-Gimblett, Barbara. 1995. "Theorizing Heritage." *Ethnomusicology: Journal of the Society for Ethnomusicology* 39, no. 3: 367–79.

Langer, S. K. 1951. *Philosophy In A New Key: A Study In The Symbolism Of Reason, Rite, And Art.* Cambridge, MA: Harvard University Press.

Lederach, John Paul. 2005. *The Moral Imagination: the Art and Soul of Building Peace.* Oxford: Oxford University Press.

MacCannell, Dean. 1999. *The Tourist: A New Theory of the Leisure Class.* Berkeley: University of California Press.

Marcus, Scott. 2007. *Music in Egypt.* New York: Oxford University Press.

Nettl, Bruno. 2008. *"Music of the Middle East" in Excursions in World Music.* 5th ed. Upper Saddle River, NJ: Prentice-Hall.

Racy, A. J. 2003. *Making Music In The Arab World: The Culture and Artistry Of Tarab.* Cambridge: Cambridge University Press.

Sadiqi, Fatima. 2008. "Paths to Creation: Message from the General Director." In *Programme du Festival de Fès des Musiques Sacrés du Monde*, 8. Morocco: Fondation Esprit de Fès.

Turino, Thomas. 2008. *Music as Social Life: The Politics of Participation.* Chicago: University of Chicago Press.

Turner, Victor. 1969. *The Ritual Process: Structure and Anti-Structure.* Chicago: Aldine.

Urbain, Olivier. 2008. *Music and Conflict Transformation: Harmonies and Dissonances in Geopolitics.* Edited by Majid Tehranian. Toda Institute Book Series on Global Peace and Policy. London: Tauris.

Volf, Miroslav. 1996. *Exclusion and Embrace: A Theological Exploration of Identity, Otherness, and Reconciliation.* Nashville: Abingdon.

CHAPTER 7

Performing toward Peace

Investigations into the Process of Peacebuilding through Shared Music in Libya[1]

by Jared Holton

Music is a resource . . . for world building.

—DeNora 2000, 44

The concert's finale of a cherished local folk song drew instant applause from a mixed audience of over two hundred people, mainly Libyan. The recognizable *īqāʿ* (rhythmic mode) on piano and interweaving, repetitive violin melody was a fitting way to end the Tripolitanian concert, which largely represented works from the Western Classical music tradition. And yet, it may not have been the music that the audience was cheering. The Libyan violinist and I stood quite proudly on stage finding it difficult to understand the significance of our concert; after all, we had witnessed in the span of one week our originally small-scale musical evening at his local university grow to a formal event at the top concert venue in Tripoli, the capital of Libya. Later, we were informed that this was the first time within living memory that an American and a Libyan had performed music together publicly, and in recognition of the recently improving relationship

1. The research, experiences, and conferences discussed in this paper were conducted before the historic political upheavals of the so-called "Arab Spring" in 2011.

158

between the two countries following four decades of sordid history, the music that evening had a power of its own encapsulated in the relationship of its musician-creators.[2]

That night we encountered a profound function of music in the human experience: music is a vehicle for deepening mutual understanding and building peace between individuals and communities of different cultures and faiths.[3] The function of music has similarly been described as a "template" by music sociologist Tia DeNora, "against which feeling, perception, representation and social situation are created and sustained" (2000, 44), as well as a "social force" and a "resource" for transformation by ethnomusicologist Thomas Turino (2008). Such definitions may feel intuitively true but beg further analysis: What are the steps to developing mutual understanding in a musical context? How is the "social situation" of peace realized between musicians and among their communities?

After three years of teaching music professionally in an international school in Tripoli, as well as participating in music within the Libyan community, I reflect here on the many experiences and performances I had as a musician and academic practitioner within Libya in order to gain an awareness about these relational dynamics inherent in musical practices and the possibilities of peacebuilding.[4] The aim of this paper is to suggest a reflective tool whereby musicians use their artistic talents to challenge contextual conflicts with a view toward building mutual trust and peace between parties. The suggested schematic will assume that conflict is present in a given musical context—whether physical, ethnic, interreligious, interpersonal, or psychological. The contextual conflict of my research in Libya dealt with psychological misperceptions of ethnicity (as an American) and religion (as a Christian). It is our human responsibility to curb this tendency toward misperceptions in relationships and communities, and to use conflicts as "motors of change," as Lederach proposes (2003, 5), to transform a given context into one of mutuality and generosity in perceptions. As this publication asserts, music stands as a meaningful medium for such change, and

2. In using "power" I am referring to Bohlman's discussion of the inherent "aesthetic power" within music to transform (2002,13). This paper will extend his brief discussion of music's power to transform through performance into sociological realms where commodities of peace, trust, and understanding are forged as embodied values among musicians, sometimes extending to audiences.

3. For a brief introductory discussion of the complexities involving the use of the arts towards cultural criticism, see Phillips 2004.

4. In this sense my approach is based in phenomenological and experiential research rather than in empiricism. Thus, my proposals are "suggestive rather than definitive." See Stone 2008, 167.

this paper calls the musician to the responsibility of engaging his/her art to this end.

Before introducing the schematic, it is necessary to describe briefly the context of conflict used in this study. Indeed, the greatest potential in peace-building through music originated exactly from my role as an American Christian musician living in a Libyan Muslim environment.

The Context: Layers of Conflict: Political, Religious, Cultural

The infamously sordid political relationship between Libya and America was a backdrop for my daily encounters in life and work. Many would be surprised that the largest military base outside of America during the 1960s was the Wheelus Air Force base in Tripoli. However, one of the political effects of the 1969 Revolution was the evacuation of foreign service from Libyan soil, including an emptying of America's Tripolitanian base. Through the 1980s, Libya was deemed responsible for several bomb attacks including a Berlin discotheque in 1986, the 1986 Lockerbie disaster, and the French UTA flight in 1987. The US engaged Libya by bombing Tripoli in 1986, and instigating sanctions against the country. After a decade of icy relations, diplomatic engagement began with negotiations to settle the Lockerbie incident, and the new century brought an easing of the economic sanctions in 2004, and even an official visit from US Secretary of State Condolezza Rice in 2008.

Misperceptions between Americans and Libyans are not simply political, but also interreligious. Based upon the assumption that Arabs are homogeneously Islamic, both culturally and religiously, many Libyans perceive Christianity in the same way. From this view, all Americans are born into the culture and religion of Christianity and called "Christians." Culturally, it follows then that the American media as a global phenomenon, under the banner of "Hollywood," represents the values and lifestyles of Christians—a belief quite prevalent in the Arab world—summed up by violence, greed, drunkenness, deceitfulness, promiscuity and otherwise immodest behavior. These religious misperceptions of Christianity are only counter-balanced by a common American misperception that Islam is a violent religion and Muslims are terrorists. In both cases, misperceptions become stereotypes and widen the relational gap between self-professed Christians and Muslims, domestically and abroad.[5]

---

5. I am aware of the discussion of "essentialism," whereby an identity as a complex whole is reduced to a few accentuated parts and these taken as basic or "essential" to the entire. In my paper, identity tags such as "Christian" and "Muslim" are used as such based upon those who designate themselves in this way. In actuality, it is because of the

Additionally, the role of a professional musician in Libya has an ambiguous place within the local Islamic framework. While other Muslim majority countries may not see any ambiguities within the relationship between music and Islam, I can only comment on the Libyan context. By using historical texts in the Qur'ān, Ḥadīth, and Sunnah, and contemporary experiences in Egypt as a student of *tajwīd*, Kristina Nelson posits that there are two general Muslim positions on the polemic: those who reject music unconditionally, and those who accept music conditionally (1985, 50; cf. Marcus 2007, 89–95). The Libyans whom I encountered (musicians and non-musicians) fit into the second of the two positions. There are specialized Libyan musicians, but few have made a full-time profession of music.[6] As has been explained to me, some locals believe it is not an honorable profession and can be perceived as leading to "loose" living (e.g., illicit sexuality, alcohol, and drug abuse), a perception demonstrated by A. J. Racy's research into the *ṭarab* musicians of the Arab world (2003, 47–51). More culturally acceptable is to have a day-job and play music in the evening with friends, as many Libyan musicians have chosen to do. This is the context of *Al-Fajr al-Jadīd*, a state-sponsored music center in Tripoli for rehearsal, performance, and recording.

Misperceptions can be overcome with political rhetoric and religious dialogue, and yet, building trust and fostering mutual understanding that leads to peace is a work of the heart and lends itself to the role of music at the hands of competent and learned musicians. Therefore, I propose a schematic for how peacebuilding and deeper mutual trust are possible within the faculties of music listening, learning, and performing.

The Schematic

The schematic (figure 8) represents the development of peace and mutual understanding within five key activities in music. In nearly every level of the schematic, I have utilized Thomas Turino's helpful analysis and distinction between participatory and presentational musics (2008). In brief, participatory music represents music that is "refashioned" each performance by choosing from a selection of available musical resources, referring both to performers and instrumentation. The musical elements of such a performance often include repetitive and open forms, dense textures, few dynamic

---

complexities within each of these named identities that misperceptions and conflicts arise.

6. On account of this, Brandily labels Libyan musicians as "semi-professionals," since they participate in society via other vocations, and receive payment almost incidentally for their musical service (2001, 651).

contrasts, unaltered rhythms, and improvisation within a regular structure. On the other hand, presentational music is a "set item" performance, often predictable according to form and requiring extensive rehearsal. Rather than the open and more simplistic style of participatory music, the musical elements of presentational music include clear and regulated textures (e.g., a string quartet normally comprises two violins, one viola, and one cello), contrastive dynamics and rhythms, and a leaning toward individual virtuosity. This distinction between forms of music-making aids the analysis of various musical activities in noting how performing musicians form social bonds. In particular, participatory music will be a featured category in the following schematic since its process of music-making is perhaps more intensive relationally owing to its open forms and improvisatory style, all of which imply more direct communication between musicians.

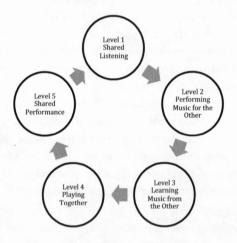

Figure 8: Steps to Peacebuilding through Music (Holton 2011)

Among the many ways to describe this process, I have identified five levels to tease out the dynamic of peacebuilding evident between musicians, and at times including audiences, within a given context. In this manner, the schematic should not be used as a prescriptive linear, methodical model in gaining mutual trust; rather, it is a cyclical and evolving model that can be entered at any level and repeated numerous times as greater degrees of trust are established. My Libyan musician colleagues and I formed cross-cultural relationships via the initial stages of the schematic simply as we became introduced to one another's music and made conversation. Even as we operated in levels three and four, we often returned naturally to levels one and two in our relationships. This process substantiates the developing trust in one another as humans and musicians.

Additionally, the schematic presupposes participatory skills in per-formance between two music cultures. While each level has the possibility of an "audience," the schematic assumes a one-to-one relationship between at least two musicians (as defined in his/her own culture) from different cultures or faiths. Relationality is a key feature in the music-making process, and often leads to significant emotional bonds between musicians (Woody and McPherson 2010, 404–6; Titon 2008, 25–41; Small 1998,10, 140).[7] Without such relational bonds, the foundation for reciprocal trust and un-derstanding is lost. Furthermore, in relying on these bonds between musi-cians, the audience becomes a formal, active agent within the peacebuilding process of levels two and five. Essentially, the schematic helps to document explicitly the implicit transformation occurring between musicians from conflicted contexts throughout the music-making process.

Level 1: Shared Listening

At the most basic level, the faculty of listening begins to establish respect and understanding between musicians. The ear—one of the musician's greatest assets in music-making—also functions as a gateway to the heart. In conducting an empirical study on ways of listening to short musical and non-musical sound samples, Nicola Dibben verified that people tend to make decisions on what they hear based not on acoustic features but on culturally and physically defined traits of sound. Listening involves "hearing meanings" above hearing acoustic and structural attributes of the sounds (2003, 198). As musical meaning is socially constructed, shared listening between musicians provides an opportunity to open relational space for constructing new social bonds and associations. Thus, most important to the process of shared listening, is the *shared* aspect of the event. Music per-ception can often be varied and dissonant from musician to musician; yet the moment of shared listening attunes us to the same sounds and provides an opportunity to deepen relationship.

This music perception, or the process of becoming aware of sounds and their combinations, has normally been explained in a cognitive,

7. According to the late Anthony Storr, a British psychiatrist and music connois-seur, if Vico, Rousseau, and Blacking are correct in theorizing that music preceded verbal language and is, thus, essential to humankind and our socializations, then "we can perceive that language and music were originally more closely joined, and that it makes sense to think of music as deriving from a subjective, emotional need for com-munication with other human beings" (1992, 16). The complexities of the connections between music-making and emotion theory cannot be expounded here. Research in this area began with the foundational study conducted by Meyer, *Emotion and Meaning in Music* (1956). For a discussion on the latest research, consult the erudite handbook edited by Juslin and Sloboda (2010).

rational way using an information-processing approach. One becomes aware of "music" in a series of stages, beginning from the recognition of simple sounds to the more complex recognition of tonality, meter, and even aesthetic value (Clarke 2005,13). However, one can also recognize more complex structures of sounds without being able to identify its simpler structures. For example, one could correctly identify sound patterns as "jazz" without being able to articulate the rhythmic triplet patterns or timbre combinations characteristic of the genre. As a critical response to the information-processing approach theory, Eric Clarke's ecological approach is helpful in explaining how humans perceive music and attribute meaning. As ecology seeks to describe the relationship between organisms and their environment (including to each other), this approach describes the perception of music based on what the music *affords* the listener. For example, a chair, as an object, affords sitting in one context, but may afford protection in another if used as a weapon. The idea that music "excites," "touches," or "moves" someone is an example of music's affordances via a perceiver's way of listening (Clarke 2005, 36–38).[8] For our purposes, shared listening viewed from an ecological approach focuses on how meaning is formed from the physical and social contexts where music is heard. This approach suggests that in the act of listening, perceivers can relate and quite possibly connect interpersonally based on a shared event. A shared listening event between musicians allows a moment of what Clarke calls "mutualism" (2005, 56–57), in which each musician benefits from hearing about the meanings attributed to the particular music sample, however different they are. Shared listening engages our identities in relationship. More familiar music to one listener affirms a sense of self, and less familiar music to another allows a transformation of the self through exploration and discovery (148). Sharing this process of identity detection and formation bonds listeners and builds deeper connections of relationality.

In receiving musical hospitality, I was often touched when my Muslim hosts tuned the radio station to music deriving from Western art forms in honor of my presence, whether that was Mozart's *Eine Kleine Nachtmusik* or Bryan Adam's "All for One." These musical forms are more a part of my own musical culture than that of my host culture. However, in the moment of "mutualism," when we listened together and discussed the music, opportunities to understand new meanings in the sounds opened and allowed us to appreciate and learn from each other. Yanni's eclectic Mediterranean-style blend, a local favorite, was a frequent point of conversation with my Libyan

---

8. The definition of object "affordances" was first proposed by the American psychologist and philosopher James Gibson.

colleagues; and although I cringed based upon my proclivity toward Gin-astera, Prokofiev, and Beethoven, I participated in the shared moments of listening in order to connect and sustain our beginning attempts at relating.

Likewise, when I listened to my hosts' musics, both recorded and live, the listening act showed an acceptance and appreciation of who my hosts were and their willingness to share. One of my relationships was built solely from cruising Tripoli's streets for hours listening to Arabic popular music and discussing the improvisation of Andalusian Flamenco jazz guitarist Paco de Lucia. Once Ibrāhīm al-Sāfī's '"Aiūnik Jasār" (n.d.) hit the Libyan music shelves, it was played non-stop from car to market to villa and one of my Libyan friends taught me the words of the chorus. We still sing it together as an act of reliving this shared memory. Berber music from the Jādū Music Festival (October 2008), Tuareg women drumming from the Ghadames Music Festival (October 2008), and the perennial Tripolitanian *zukrah* wedding music exemplify excellent opportunities for initial relationship building with other musicians in context as listening affirms their humanity and culture through appreciation of their music. Mutual understanding starts with the musician's ear.

Level 2: Performing Music for the Other

In this level musicians share music that is mainly presentational in style, although that may change according to the cultures involved. For example, although participatory music does not emphasize the virtuosic soloist, improvisation within the group does have elements of presentation. When one performs music for another, whether informally within a home context or formally in a concert hall, the performer presents a piece of the inner self, which finds a positive or negative connection to the listeners. A social bond is created, and deep connections with others are formed that are basic and indispensable to social survival (Turino 2008, 3–4). The inherent vulnerability in music performance is magnified in cross-cultural situations where the listeners are not from the same music culture as the performer. Great care must be taken in selecting music for the other; and in listening to the other's music one must expand the range of the ear to appreciate a genre potentially very different than one's own.

My first performance for a Libyan musician was Scott Joplin's *Maple Leaf Rag*, an American jazz standard for piano. The reception was positive. The harmonic progressions, triplet patterns, and "catchy" melodies seemed to fit well with popular music in the Arab context, and the clear and cleverly shaped melodies connected with Libyan musical tastes. A year later in preparation for a public solo performance in Zāwiah celebrating the life and work of Libyan poet ʿAlī Sidqī ʿAbd al-Qādr, I chose two piano pieces from the Western Classical music tradition: Chopin's posthumously published "Nocturne in C-Sharp Minor, no. 20" and Schubert's "Impromptu no. 3 in Eb Major." I treasure these pieces and also thought the melancholic mood of the first and uninhibited melodies of the second would communicate with my Libyan audience. Indeed, as I shared these pieces in performance, several sang along to Chopin's surging melodies and many enjoyed the musical drama of Schubert. Open and sincere conversations during a communal meal after the concert, proved that new relationships had been forged during my short musical performance. Poet to musician, we exchanged artistic symbols that initiated a developing trust and mutuality.

Relationships also became more substantive as my friends performed music for me: a university-trained violinist performed a saucy Arabic version of Johannes Brahms's "Hungarian Dance no. 5" with flair and extended rubato; another musician friend invited me to his performance where he was playing backup acoustic guitar for an outdoor concert with Libyan pop-idol Aīman al-Hūnī; on a subsequent occasion I sat in a room with a family of musicians during the Maulid al-Nabī,[9] listening to an a cappella performance of traditional stories and poetry set to local melodies. Each of these performances built a fundamentally deeper relationship between myself and the other musicians that extended beyond a mere sharing of CDs and MP3s.

At this point in the schematic the audience can also act as a formal participant in the peacebuilding process by experiencing reciprocity and growing trust through the vicarious sharing of music. As a guest at a Libyan *maʾlūf* [10] concert, audience members made overt attempts to make me (the visitor) feel comfortable through words of welcome and insistence that I take a seat of honor. They then shared their cultural music through their own local performers. Afterwards, audience and performers alike elicited my opinion as they sought response to their overtures. My acceptance of their performed music created interpersonal connections not previously present. Likewise, when musician friends would invite me to perform, the audience relied on my colleagues' trust in me as they accepted and wel-

9. "The Birthday of the Prophet" is an annual celebration during the third Islamic month, Rabīʿ al-Awwal.

10. Maʾlūf music is the traditional music of North Africa believed to have been transported across the region by fleeing Andalusian refugees beginning in the tenth century CE. The Umayyad and Abbasid capitals of Damascus and Baghdad, respectively, consolidated this "Arabo-Persian" influenced music in the early Islamic caliphate. See Davis 2004, vi.

comed me to the stage. In the act of performance from one music culture to another, the musicians can demonstrate to a wider audience the potential for peace. A further discussion of this point will come in the "shared performance" of level five.

Of course, at this level a rejection of the other's music may cause more conflict than gains in peacebuilding. Research suggests that careful music selection will influence an emotional response based on culture-specific preferences regarding consonance and dissonance (Thompson and Balkwill 2010). In cross-cultural relationships sensitivity, openness, kindness, and musical intelligence are necessary ingredients to foster peace, especially when musical tastes differ.

Level 3: Learning Music from the Other

Four weeks after arriving in Libya in 2008, I found myself walking down the streets of Tripoli's Old City, hitting a *bes* drum in rhythm with other Libyans singing and playing in celebration of the Maulid al-Nabī. I had intended only to listen and observe the festival, enjoying a unique musical experience of a new culture. However, my musician friends were eager to share their culture; and, in their opinion, the best way was to participate. It took little skill to beat the *bes* drum in time as they showed me; but my willingness to take part delighted the throng of men, and communicated my posture of goodwill.

Later that year, I was invited to attend evening *ma'lūf* rehearsals in *Al-Fajr al-Jadīd*, a center in Tripoli for Libyan traditional music. Weekly, I visited these rehearsals and watched singers and instrumentalists perfect the art of this Libyan genre. The ensemble introduced me to ancient Arabic words central to their history and faith, and oral histories from the people's origin. It was a privileged experience that deepened my understanding of the Libyan people and music, based in Arabian lore. With excitement, they taught me traditional *īqā'āt* (rhythmic modes) such as *Murābah* and *Falāhī*, and asked me to bring a keyboard with Arabic tunings so I could join the ensemble, thus moving fluidly from a level two (their presentation of *ma'lūf*) to a level three exchange (my participation in rehearsals).

Playing the piano in Libyan musical idioms was appreciated, but when I began to learn their own instrumentation, Libyans expressed profound approval. Taking a locally purchased *'ūd* (akin to the Spanish lute), I went to my first lesson at the beginning of July 2008, excited and hopeful. The one to two hour lessons were demanding and often comical, as my tutor's family would listen in to the American attempting a Fairouz song or a one-octave rendition of *maqām al-Ḥijāz*. I was hopeless with the *rīshah* (plectrum), and watched my teacher shake his head in despair at my tremolo; however, my efforts to learn a new musical culture did not go unnoticed. After two months of lessons, my teacher appreciatively commented that I truly was a musician—just not in the Arabic style yet. Despite my slow progress, learning Arabic music on the *ʿūd* grounded me to the place and people of Libya.

This newfound knowledge in the Arabian musical world of quartertones, *maqāmāt*, and *īqāʿāt* allowed me greater access into Libyan music. I began to listen to local *taqāsīm* (improvisation) with open ears and to hear arabesque and melodic beauty I had not heard before. More importantly, I began to dialogue with local musicians about their own music. Based on these exchanges made possible by my increased musical understanding, trust and camaraderie developed.

Reciprocally, local musicians have also pursued my own musical tradition. At the request of a Libyan musician colleague, I ordered a score of Paganini's "Twenty-Four Caprices" for solo violin. Despite Libyan folk music and traditional improvisational technique remaining his strength, he showed me his Paganini skills one month later with a serious attempt to play one of the caprices. I was touched with his honest attempt to learn a different musical tradition, which I knew well. Despite the difficulties in learning music from the other culture, it is a step toward peace that requires investment of time and hard work, and is a commitment that requires the extension of self into unfamiliar realms. The great effort necessary to learn a new musical language creates more substantial interconnections between musicians during the learning process and subsequent performances than simply listening to and/or sharing music. And in turn, developing skills in another music culture opens the door to participating musically within that culture as level four indicates.

Level 4: Playing Together

"We need to make a concert," many of the Libyan musicians said within my first weeks in the country. As we played together, first informally (level four) and then publicly (level five), I witnessed the relationships growing significantly in mutual understanding and respect, due as much to increased time together as to performance pressure and shared musical experience in the participatory music style. Participatory music, as a flexible and unpredictable style, is particularly powerful because of the communal dimensions of playing in sync as self-identities or projections of the self are actualized in the act of music-making within group participation. Turino suggests that this type of music "connects people more intimately and powerfully because of shared interactive engagement among all participants in the actual doing of the activities with each other" (2008, 61–62). As musicians weave together parts and interplay voices, the self-conscious musician is absorbed into the activity as a whole of creating combined music, which often leads to, in the most positive sense, a special type of trust and social bonding.

In a similar way, rehearsing presentational music builds and deepens social bonds between musicians. In preparation for a performance at a public music festival, a Libyan guitarist and I organized a simple chord structure for the piano to accompany his improvisations in "gypsy jazz" style. Although the chord progression derived from a common harmonic movement in European-based music theory (i.e., I–vi–IV–V7), his improvisation was most certainly from a North African traditional melodic genre, with many *rīshah* techniques for the *'ūd* transferred to a guitar in Western tuning. Likewise, rehearsals for a violin-piano concert represented a mixture of Bach counterpoint, Mozart melodies, and Libyan rhythms along with the use of an Arabized solfege system. In these experiences we were working together to fuse our musics and represent both cultures. The trust in our relationships was enhanced during the rehearsals as we made mutual decisions about the performances that put our reputations on the line.

Symbolically, then, one can note the more intimate meeting of cultures at this level as musicians work to honor each other in producing and presenting music. Cross-cultural jam sessions are challenging because representatives from two cultures are searching for common ground minute by minute in order to make participatory music. However, when music is made and new fusions emerge, relationships are greatly strengthened through the process, and mutual understanding is intensified. Bringing this music to the stage in performance (level five) continues to intensify trust and understanding, and opens new vistas for challenging misperceptions and advocating peace in a wider arena.

Level 5: Shared Performance

The opportunity for peacebuilding between musicians and with the local community is at its greatest potential when "formal" performance is achieved. In this bracketed time of public music-making, advances in peacemaking are possible in exponential degrees due to the increased number of participants, i.e., the audience. In public performance, the musician-to-musician relationship is the archetype that showcases new relational possibilities. According to Small, musical performances do not just present these archetypal relationships but teach audiences about the values associated with them. The performance, then, "allows those taking part [the audience] to try them on, to see how they fit, to experience them without having to commit themselves to them," and thus incorporates new values into their understanding through affirmation, both cognitively and emotionally (1998, 183). In so doing, audience members are given opportunities to reinterpret misperceptions and stereotypes, and participate in the musical event where opportunities for knowing and enjoying "the other" exist.

When music is performed by artists representing conflicted groups, there is the possibility of imagining mutual understanding and reconciliation on a larger public scale based upon the deepened relationship between the musicians. The trust forged between the musicians becomes a bridge that the audience may utilize. By viewing the shared performance of musicians that have found a deeper harmony and peace in relationship, audience members can participate in these realities. Musicians in shared performance are the "fulcrum" that challenges the audience to expand their understanding of the other and adjust their perceptions (Turino 2008, 62). When audiences participate in the peacebuilding process in this way, it provides the possibility of exposing others within the wider cultural cohort to reconciliation, thus broadening the base of peacebuilding in a realm of conflict.

At such an event, referred to in level four, 200–300 Libyan-Berber male faces stared at us as we performed a short improvised piece using a Western chord progression. It was 2:00 am at the Jādū Music Festival (October 2008), and, in an attempt to liven up the crowd, we accelerated the tempo and used as many syncopated music riffs as possible. Playing on an old but treasured village keyboard, I improvised music with my Libyan guitarist friend with joy and excitement. With an announcement that an American was playing, an array of cell phones appeared to document the occasion. For a brief musical moment, there seemed to be no conflict between America and Libya. The local guitarist's trust in me was accepted by the audience as a sign that I was trustworthy, and our collaboration was a visible symbol of the burgeoning peace between us, and to some degree our nations and faiths.

Weeks after the Jādū Music Festival, a shopkeeper in my neighborhood of Tripoli exclaimed, "I saw you at the Jādū Music Festival!" Since Jādū is a two-hour drive south into the nearest mountain range from Tripoli, I was shocked. Although I had not seen this man in Jādū, and knew that he himself was not a musician, we still met in peace: Libyan to American, Muslim to Christian. Music was the basis for our association, and the association was made as a result of the bridge created by the relationships with my Libyan musician colleagues.

The introductory story to this chapter narrates the concert on March 15, 2009, when a Libyan musician colleague and I performed in the austere Corinthia Hotel venue, as advertised in the local Tripolitanian newspaper,

Awīa. The first question of the Libyan TV crew after the concert, "How did you start playing with a Libyan musician?" expressed surprise and curiosity at the unusual spectacle of a Libyan and American musical pair. Indeed selections of the concert were repeatedly aired on the television news station *Al-Libya* in the "highlights of the week" program, and the story was covered in the three other national media networks (Agha 2010). Significantly, the networks focused their coverage on the finale—a popular Libyan piece— much to the appreciation of local Libyans. Whole families (including women who rarely attend such live performances) watched the news as I beat out their own rhythms on the piano. Thus, through these media channels, the audience expanded from those actually present in the concert to those who vicariously participated through the media events. Since the airing of the news, I have shaken numerous Libyans' hands who saw the program and emotionally connected to the memorable performance between an American and Libyan.

In each of these formal performances, the relationship between the Libyan performer and myself was authentic, originating through the vehicle of music, and developed by the performance process that exacted mutual respect, cooperation, and vulnerability. Performances, in particular, have a relational dynamic that shapes, challenges, and quite possibly transforms: "Something has changed between the participants through the fact of having undergone the performance together. Who [they] are has changed, has evolved a little, either through [their] having been confirmed in our concepts of ideal relationships and of who [they] are or through having had them challenged" (Small 1998, 140). As our understanding of each other's musical traditions grew through listening, sharing, and performing, our relationship (culturally defined by the "polarities" of American-Libyan, Christian-Muslim) deepened and solidified. The peacebuilding journey progressed exponentially as real and perceived cultural boundaries were crossed by the communal sharing of music, solidarity formed, and new possibilities appeared to replace misperceptions.

Implications

The most widely publicized examples of peacebuilding through music are the mega events covered by the media, such as performances of Daniel Barenboim and the late Edward Said's West-Eastern Divan Orchestra,[11] or the "Roads to You" tour directed by Zade Dirani and sponsored by Her

11. "Innovators: Peacemakers," *Time*, July 28, 2010, p. 48. Cf. Barenboim and Said 2002, 11, 60.

Majesty Queen Noor of Jordan (Zade Foundation 2009). While such events touch thousands of people at one given time, as well as present courageous artistic solutions to political problems, the importance of music-making at the grassroots level should not be underestimated as musical catalysts seek to transform conflict into peace utilizing music.[12] As mentioned earlier, it was the evolving relationship between Libyan musicians and myself that allowed others, namely audiences, to participate in the peacebuilding dynamic. Music is a gateway to the heart and mind, and as Finnegan describes, it represents a "human resource through which people can enact their lives with inextricably entwined feeling, thought and imagination" (2003, 188). Substantive relationships, musician to musician, are not superficial and have the power to transform misperceptions of wider groups through performance.

During the 2009 SOPR Beirut conference one of the scholars asked why composition as a musical practice had not been used in the peacemaking process for this investigation, and although I did not practice musical composition with any Libyan musicians, I concur with my colleague. Composition may be a level six in the peacebuilding schemata as this process involves a consistent and committed effort over a presumably longer period of time. The benefits in completing a joint composition in coordination with its subsequent performances offer a unique opportunity for building peace with a variety of audiences. Performing these types of joint compositions in further locations with similar conflict is worth further exploration and analysis.

The traditional ethnomusicologist, hitherto, is one who enters a given musical culture to explore, document, and synthesize a particular style or genre of created and organized sound. This process normally results in the publication of a specialized book, article, or dissertation contributing to our human understanding of world musics. This schematic asks a further research question of the musicology specialist: Can ethnomusicologists be peacebuilders? My experiences summon deeper reflections on how the role

---

12. Arguably, transformation within society can be possible by employing humanly created and organized sound. It is important to note that using music in this way may differ from the opinion of some ethnomusicologists, namely the late John Blacking: "Music cannot change societies . . . It cannot make people act unless they are already socially and culturally disposed to act. It cannot instill brotherhood . . . or any other state or social value. If it can do anything to people, the best that it can do is to confirm situations that already exist. It cannot in itself generate thoughts that may benefit or harm mankind…but it can make people more aware of feelings that they have experienced, or partly experienced, by reinforcing, narrowing or expanding their consciousness in a variety of ways" (1973, 107–8). Thus, I will suggest an expansion of the role of the ethnomusicologist in a musical context.

of an ethnomusicologist can be expanded to peacemaker by more direct and dynamic participation in the musical culture, suggesting an extension to the traditional boundaries of the participant-observation model.[13] This developed role of the ethnomusicologist is understandably challenging in its ethics, raising concerns about power relationships and motivation between the musicians. The "Statement on Ethical Considerations" published in 1998 by the Board of the Society for Ethnomusicology offers guidance in not only understanding that an appropriate "cultivation of relationships" is a natural part of the research process, but also that ethnomusicology will "often involve a *long-term commitment* to the rights and concerns of field consultants and their communities" (Society for Ethnomusicology 1998; italics mine). Thus, the process of "performing toward peace" may unfold within the working musicians' relationships. The ethnomusicological peacemaker is a demanding role, but one that could offer conflicted areas of the world hope and relational interaction through music and performance.

The Continuing Conversation

The proposed schematic is a tool for developing peace and mutual trust through musical skills and performance. The following connections to select chapters within this book highlight the application of these levels to achievements of peace in other contexts of conflict.

In her reflections on the 2008 Sacred World Music Festival in Fes, Morocco, Dr. Roberta King comments on the process of "experiencing one another" through public performances with mass appeal. Although she reflects more on the festival audiences ("imagined worlds of spirituality") rather than the dynamic of the performing musicians, Dr. King explains how peacebuilding can be realized by moving conflict from cognitive to affective dimensions utilizing music. This supports the schematic generally, and builds upon our understanding of the audience in level five, specifically. Her proposed extensions of drawing upon the cognitive and affective connections to promote behavioral change in support of peace (thus, *unisonance*) are constructive reflections and illustrate the power of public performance to build communal trust and understanding.

---

13. From the perspective of anthropology and, more specifically, ethnography, cf. Spradley 1980. From the perspective of ethnomusicology, cf. Stone 2008, 12–13. Titon's "ethnomusicology in the public interest" (2008, 179) calls for an active approach to ethnomusicology, combining engagement with the culture, reflection, inscription, and empathy—the latter introducing subjectivities of feeling, which I am connecting to the activities of developing trust and mutual understanding through music.

In the same way, Dr. Sooi-Ling Tan uses the dimensions of cognition, affection, and action[14] and describes youth performances in Indonesia. This is another example of how public performances—specifically, levels two and five—lend themselves to multifaceted peacebuilding where there are conflicts and barriers to interpersonal communion. She consistently reflects on the element of "self" in the music-making process, which raises interesting and pertinent issues of intrapersonal communion in the act of peacebuilding. As also in many levels of the schematic, a musician's conception of identity is continually engaged from moments of mutualism in shared listening, to accepting the transformation inherent in learning a different music culture, to publicly presenting music in performance. Music is a symbol for behavioral change, as Dr. Tan summarizes, and could be utilized in peace education within troubled world regions.

Mustafa Said brings a detailed perspective on how music-making leads performers to greater degrees of relationality and cooperation in performance. Although the *munshid* (soloist) and the *biṭānah* (singing group) in the *tawshīḥ* tradition are presumably from the same culture and religion, this analysis is helpful in allowing one to see the dependence of musicians on each other in practicing and presenting certain musical forms, and how performers deepen relationally through performance. Moreover, the suggestion of the ethnomusicologist as potential peacemaker finds a viable place in Dr. Marcel Akiki and Irwansyah Harahap's writing. In both cases, the musician-peacemaker was a vital and compelling force for fostering peace in each musical context.

Conclusion

Is it possible, through music, to turn the tide of a long-established misperception of "the other," or even divert the dash to warfare and violent confrontation created by victims and perpetrators alike, through music? Could this schematic be used as a "roadmap for peace," not in the hands of politicians or sectarian leaders but musicians?

The purpose of this chapter is to provoke reflection (and eventually action) that would utilize music in conflicted areas of the world for peacebuilding. As demonstrated through my experiences and the experiences and writing of my colleagues contained in this volume, music offers opportunities in building strong interpersonal connections between peoples in conflict. Where such conflict exists between Christians and Muslims, music

14. See also King, "Musical Gateways to Peace and Reconciliation," above.

is an avenue to explore toward realizing peace and deepening understanding of the other.

The schematic represents a guide for performing musicians within a cross-cultural or intercultural context. It is a tool that is useful for understanding and interpreting a variety of musical encounters between musicians of different cultures and/or religions. Through these five levels of musical engagement, deeper mutual understanding, and peacebuilding are pursued through relationality, a key feature if peacebuilding is a goal of the musical process. Music remains a vehicle whereby trust is established and continually deepened through various musical activities. As I reflect as an American Christian living and working in a Libyan Muslim context, music has been the vital catalyst for gaining respect and trust from my hosts, and in turn developing my affection for them as we seek to live in peace.

FOR DISCUSSION

1. Reflect on your music-making with other musicians. Which types of musical activities have led to deeper relationships? Synthesize your experiences with the schematic and reflect on the cyclical nature of the levels.

2. Musical performances focusing on building peace and trust are a common occurrence today. Search the internet for two local and two global events. Reflect on some of these events covered by the media and place them on the schematic. Do you think musical events occurring at higher levels are more effective in peacemaking than events at lower levels?

3. "The ethnomusicologist is a peacemaker." Agree or disagree with this statement, noting the advantages and disadvantages of this role in a cross-cultural context.

4. PROJECT: Using the schematic as an analytical lens, classify the examples of musical activity and/or performance as described within another chapter from the book's Part III Multi-Disciplinary Explorations. Are there correlations between the author's research in your chosen chapter and the effectiveness of the schematic levels? Why or why not? How might the schematic help develop and implement music events within the process of conflict transformation in your context?

References Cited

Agha, 'Isām. November 7, 2010. Interview with the author.

Barenboim, Daniel, and Edward W. Said. 2002. *Parallels and Paradoxes: Explorations in Music and Society*. New York: Vintage.

Blacking, John. 1973. *How Musical is Man?* Seattle: University of Washington Press.

Bohlman, Philip. 2002. *World Music: A Very Short Introduction*. Oxford: Oxford University Press.

Brandily, Monique. 2001. "Libya." In *The New Grove Dictionary of Music and Musicians*, edited by Stanley Sadie, 14:649–51. 2nd ed. New York: Grove's Dictionaries.

Clarke, Eric F. 2005. *Ways of Listening: An Ecological Approach to the Perception of Musical Meaning*. New York: Oxford University Press.

Davis, Ruth. 2004. *Ma'lūf: Reflections on the Arab Andalusian music of Tunisia*. Lanham, MD: Scarecrow Press.

DeNora, Tia. 2000. *Music in Everyday Life*. Cambridge: Cambridge University Press.

Dibben, Nicola. 2003. "Musical Materials, Perception, and Listening." In *The Cultural Study of Music: A Critical Introduction*, edited by Martin Clayton et al., 193–203. New York: Routledge.

Finnegan, Ruth. 2003. "Music, Experience, and the Anthropology of Emotion." In *The Cultural Study of Music: A Critical Introduction*, edited by Martin Clayton et al., 181–92. New York: Routledge.

"Innovators: Peacemakers." *Time*, July 28, 2010, 48.

Juslin, Patrik N., and John A. Sloboda. 2010. *Handbook of Music and Emotion: Theory, Research, Applications*. Oxford: Oxford University Press.

Lederach, John Paul. 2005. *The Little Book of Conflict Transformation*. Intercourse, PA: Good.

Marcus, Scott. 2007. *Music in Egypt*. New York: Oxford University Press.

Meyer, Leonard B. 1956. *Emotion and Meaning in Music*. Chicago: University of Chicago Press.

Nelson, Kristina. 1985. *The Art of Reciting the Qur'an*. Cairo: American University of Cairo Press.

Phillips, Gerald L. 2004. "Can There Be 'Music For Peace'?" *International Journal on World Peace* 21, no. 2: 63–73.

Racy, A. J. 2003. *Making Music in the Arab World: The Culture and Artistry of Tarab*. Cambridge: Cambridge University Press.

Al-Sāfī, Ibrāhīm. n.d. "'Aiūnik Jasār." *Yūm Al-Sāfir*. Tripoli, Libya. n.d.

Society for Ethnomusicology. 1998. "Statement on Ethical Considerations." http://webdb.iu.edu/sem/scripts/aboutus/aboutethnomusicology/ethical_considerations.cfm.

Spradley, James. 1980. *Participant Observation*. Belmont, CA: Wadsworth.

Stone, Ruth. 2008. *Theory for Ethnomusicology*. Upper Saddle Rive, NJ: Prentice-Hall.

Storr, Anthony. 1992. *Music And The Mind*. New York: Ballantine.

Thompson, William Forde, and Laura-Lee Balkwill. 2010. "Cross-Cultural Similarities and Differences." In *Handbook of Music and Emotion: Theory, Research, Applications*, edited by Patrik N. Juslin and John A. Sloboda, 755–88. Oxford: Oxford University Press.

Titon, Jeff Todd. 2003. "Textual Analysis or Thick Description?" In *The Cultural Study of Music: A Critical Introduction*, edited by Martin Clayton et al., 171–80. New York: Routledge.

————. 2008. "Knowing Fieldwork." In *Shadows in the Field: New perspectives for fieldwork in ethnomusicology*, edited by by Gregory Barz and Timothy J. Cooley, 25–41. New York: Oxford University Press.

Turino, Thomas. 2008. *Music as Social Life: The Politics of Participation*. Chicago: University of Chicago Press.

Woody, Robert H., and Gary E. McPherson. 2010. "Emotion and Motivation in the Lives of Performers." In *Handbook of Music and Emotion: Theory, Research, Applications*, edited by Patrik N. Juslin and John A. Sloboda, 401–24. Oxford: Oxford University Press.

Zade Foundation. 2009. "Roads to You: Celebration of One World." No pages. Online: http://roadstoyou.com (accessed April 19, 2009).

CHAPTER 8

The Art of *Tawshīḥ*

Reflections on Cooperation in Sufi Music

by Mustafa Said

The vocal performance genre known as *tawshīḥ*, is an important part of *inshād* (a broad category of Islamic hymnody), and also figures prominently in the Sufi parareligious Islamic music tradition of the eastern Arab world. It is based on responsorial dialogue between the *munshid*, a vocal soloist with an improvisatory role, and the *biṭānah*, a group of singers. The latter perform the main pre-composed musical phrases of the *tawshīḥ*, providing a framework within which the *munshid* builds improvisations that refer to these pre-composed phrases.

The nature of this interaction between *munshid* and *biṭānah* raises compelling questions of practice. How do the two performing entities organize their collaboration? Is there a *miftāḥ* (key) or secret code that exists between the *munshid* and the *biṭānah* that regulates the wholly unrehearsed actions of stopping, starting, repeating, and silence? How and when can the *munshid* cause the *biṭānah* to pause without disturbing the flow of cooperation? What is the signal given by the *munshid* to the *biṭānah* when he wants them to repeat? And what clue do they take from him when they continue? To go even further, on what levels might this spirit of teamwork be a model for cooperation and acceptance of others in life outside *tawshīḥ* performance?

At certain points in a *tawshīḥ*, the *munshid* cuts the *biṭānah* off in order to begin an improvisatory passage; at other moments, the *biṭānah* continues or repeats phrases. A mysterious connection appears to link them with each other, determining how they receive each other and how they proceed together. For example, to create an opening for improvisation, the *munshid* brings about a pause in the *biṭānah* by one of several means, generally before the beginning of a verse. Similarly, to move the *tawshīḥ* forward, he may allude to the next phrase or even remain silent. In this way, improvisation is linked to cooperation in performance; each aspect of the relationship between *munshid* and *biṭānah* is an example of cooperation. In order to reveal the essence of this cooperation, including the signals that make up a kind of secret communication between the two performing entities, a practical approach is required. My procedure here is first to examine the social and historical context of *inshad*, next to classify the types of improvisation present, and then to analyze the musical interaction that goes into *tawshīḥ*—in particular, the *biṭānah* parts that respond to signals from the *munshid*. Finally, I will address the implications of this model of musical interaction for interreligious understanding, based upon my own experiences.

Figure 9: Beirut: Mustafa Said Performing on the *'ūd*

A Brief History of Inshād and the Mashāyikh Field

Religious and parareligious melodic practice in Islam, outside Qur'an recitation, can be traced back to the migration of the Prophet Muḥammad from Mecca to Yathrib, known after his settling there as al-Madīnat al-Munawwarah (the lighted city). When he reached the town, the people welcomed him with the singing of poetic lines. It is said that they sang "Ṭalaʿa l-badru ʿalaynā"[1] ("the full moon shined on us") as a group hymn (Farmer 1929).

The *adhān* (call to prayer) may be the true foundation stone of *inshād*. The Prophet chose to give the *adhān* to Bilāl ibn Rabāḥ to raise because he had the best qualified voice—not because he was loudest. Over the centuries from that time to the present, the *adhān* itself has been a domain of melodic creativity. During the Ottoman era, and maybe even before, every *adhān* was raised from a specific *maqām* (melodic mode), meaning that five *adhān*-s were heard in five different *maqām*-s each day. This tradition is still practiced in Turkey and in some parts of other Islamic countries today.

With the dawn of the Abbasid era (132–656 AH, 750–1258 CE), Sufi spiritual fraternities began to flourish; music was a rich source of inspiration in their practices. The Mawlawī (Mevlevi) order, which appeared during the thirteenth century and was founded by Jalāl al-Dīn al-Rūmī(d. 1273 CE), was the broadest in terms of incorporating music, including certain musical instruments. In particular, the *nāy* (end-blown flute) has long been considered a holy instrument through which a human can reach high levels of spirituality. Other Sufi orders focused more on the human voice than on instruments. Though music in Sufi orders remained primarily within the order's practice, beginning with the sixteenth century, Mawlawī music had a direct influence on the classical music of the Ottoman court (Feldman 1996).

The Nahḍah, an Arab cultural renaissance period occurring between approximately 1798 and 1939,[2] reached an important phase for music in Egypt during the second half of the nineteenth century with the work of ʿAbduh al-Ḥamūlī (1843–1901) and Muḥammad ʿUthmān (1855–1900), who were major figures in the spread of the forms and formulas of *inšād* to secular art music. During the age of the Nahḍah, *inshād* steadily found its way outside the Sufi orders. Before this, music in religious ceremonies and events had been a type of popular or folkloric music, such as hymns allowing general participation and the folkloric type of *inshād* practiced outside Sufi orders known as *madḥ*. Though Ibrāhīm al-Muwayliḥī (1902, 406) referred to *inshād* in his writings as *ghinā' awlād al-layālī* ("songs of the nights' sons," i.e., the repertoire of singers for occasions), this designation applies properly only to the *madḥ*. Often, *munshid*-s were given the title

1. اِنْ يَلَعْ رُدَبْلَا عَلَيْنَ طَلَعْ

2. For further discussion of the Nahḍah, see Lagrange 1994; Lagrange 1996; Racy 1976; Abou Mrad 2003; Rizq 1936–1939; al-Khulaʿī (1904) 1993; Hourani 1962.

shaykh, a term recognizing special knowledge of religious concepts and practices. The term *mashāyikh*, a plural form of *shaykh*, refers generally to these respected persons. Some were naturally touched by the musical renaissance that took place in the secular realm and that was supported by the Khedive of Egypt himself. Some, for example *shaykh* Salāma Ḥigāzī, even left the *inshād* field during the Nahḍah, becoming secular singers; others, like *shaykh* Yūsuf al-Manyalāwī, continued in both secular and Sufi practice.

A third way, however, was not only to remain in the *inshād* field but also to carry the tradition to the world outside the various Sufi orders. *Munshid*-s following this path developed the *inshād* from the inside, presenting it in its best light, until elements of *inshād* and of secular music merged more fully and gained equal footing. The main figures in this respect are the *mashāyikh*: in particular, Aḥmad Nadā and Ismā'īl Sukkar from the second half of the nineteenth century, and *shaykh* 'Alī Maḥmūd from the first half of the twentieth.

Inshād evolved to a position as an art of social and religious events, such as Ramaḍān nights, the Prophet's birthday, birthdays of Sufi imams, weddings, and condolences. At these events, a number (usually three) of performance sequences or suites, called *waṣlah* (plural, *waṣlāt*) would be given, each one of them in a specific *maqām*. These *waṣlāt inshādīyah*, then, are the primary performance context for the art of the *munshid* or *shaykh*.

Living Sources

During my childhood, between 1987 and 1993, I was actively involved in the art of *tawshīḥ* as a student of this school. It was transmitted to me through the *mashāyikh* of the Aḥmadī mosque of Tanta, named after the imam Aḥmad al-Badawī (d. 1274). This mosque, according to the *mashāyikh*, contained for centuries the best and most famous school of *inshād*. It reached its end as a school of *inshād* around 1995 after being incorporated into the academic system of al-Azhar.[3] The Aḥmadī school included *mashāyikh* from Tanta, though others used to come as visitors from time to time from several cities in Egypt. It is also said that the school drew both *mashāyikh* coming to teach and students coming to study from outside Egypt before today's national borders were drawn. A few of the *mashāyikh* teachers at this school during its final period were *shaykh* Aḥmad Ḥijāb, *shaykh* 'Abd al-Jalīl al-Tantāwī, *shaykh* Muḥammad 'Imrān, and *shaykh* Ṣāber. My elucidation of the art of

3. Al-Azhar is the name of a mosque established by Al-Mu'izz Lidīn il-Lāh al-Fāṭimī, the first Fatimid caliph. During the twentieth century it became a series of Islamic schools in a religious academic system in Egypt.

tawshī]ḥ builds on personal training and practice and is amplified by interviews with leading expert *mashāyikh*[4].

The Science of Music from the Point of View of the Mashāyikh

'Ilm al-samā' (the science of listening) or *'ilm al-nagham* (the science of music), in the *mashāyikh* point of view, is divided into three parts. The first two of these are often symbolized by reference to pairs like night and day, sun and moon, earth and heavens, etc. The first is *wazn*, which can be understood as the rhythmic system; the second is *nagham*, corresponding to the system of melodic modes. These two facets are not just obtainable but truly indispensable for any person who is to recite the Qur'an, or enter the field of Sufi *inshād*, or both. They are transmitted through study with an expert in this field—from a mind to a mind and from a heart to a heart. Even if the precepts were to be written down—they are not—a person would never learn them except through direct communication between *murshid* (the instructor and initiator) and *murīd* (the student or initiated one). *Wazn* and *nagham* are considered together to form a technical catalyst that leads to the third part of the science of music: *wuṣūl*. This last part may be understood as accomplishment: its other names are *ibdā'* (creativity) and, in colloquial Egyptian, *qiwālah*—that is, "saying" in the sense of speaking through music. *Wuṣūl* is not imparted by any teacher or other person on earth. According to tradition, it is not attainable except by those gifted enough to reach a state of *wuṣūl* by themselves through a divine gift bestowed only on those pure enough to receive the spirit of the Creator and serve as his messenger. An artist thus blessed must be committed to the proper use of such a prized spiritual gift and must avoid all misuse of or damage to it.

The rhythmic system of the school of the *mashāyikh* rests on the first level of classical Arabic language articulation rules, especially Qur'anic recitation rules (*qawā'id al-tilāwah*), as well as on the Arabic poetic meters known as the Khalilian meters (*al-awzān al-Khalīlīyah, al-buḥūr al-Khalīlīyah*). In the science of *al-'arūḍ*, half of each verse is measured to the word *fa'ala* and its variant patterns (with prefixes, infixes, or suffixes) in a process known as *taf'īlah*. The practical application of these rules means that the student must learn how to begin an improvised phrase in ways that conform to the patterns inherent in the prevailing meter.

4. I interviewed shaykh Muḥammad al-Helbawi (December 24, 2007), shaykh Walid Shahīn (December 25, 2007), and shaykh Ihab Yunes (December 26, 2007; also in an online session June 8, 2009).

The system is initially taught through a model melody such as "Lāzimat al-Burdah," which is related to a famous poem written in the thirteenth century by the imam al-Buṣayrī as a tribute to the Prophet Muḥammad, or "Lāzimat al-'Awādhil," which is related to the introductory section of a famous nineteenth-century *dawr*[5] that was used in both Sufi and secular music traditions (al-Jindi 1895; Lagrange 1994, 304; Abou Mrad 2004). The *munshid* may, in his improvisation, choose to stay close to the melody, building his improvisations from its spirit, or he may set it aside, creating from the essence of the mode itself.

The unmeasured improvised cantillation[6] of poetry or prose is not far from Qur'an recitation, but it differs in that the strict articulation rules of the Qur'an (*qawāʿid al-tilāwah*) are not present and there is more opportunity to give emphasis to musical and lyrical priorities. The melodic modes of *inshād* are the same as those used in reciting the Qur'an. Furthermore, a true *munshid* is one who first studies Qur'an recitation and the Arabic language along with music, so that a *munshid* is often also a *muqri'* (reciter)—likewise the reverse. The theory regarding music is the same on both levels.

A brief introduction to the modal system is in order here. In this system, an octave (*dīwān*) is divided into seven main notes or scale degrees (*darajah*-s) called *al-sabʿah al-sulṭānī*: *yakkāh*,[7] *dūkāh*, *sīkāh*, *jahārkāh*, *banjkāh*, *shāshkāh*, and *haftkāh*. Considered to be the principal or "pure" scale degrees, these seven may be thought of as the equivalent of C, D, E half-flat,[8] F, G, A, and B half-flat, relative to the Western scale.

There are also seven main *maqām*-s, which are divided into two categories: *aṣīl* (authentic or principal), and *muwallad* (generated or derived). The three "authentic" modes—Rāst, Bayyātī, and Sīkāh—are those that embody the Zalzalian framework (Abou Mrad 2008) with its inclusion of neutral seconds, each more or less three-quarters of a tone. In this framework, the interval of a fourth is divided into a major second and two neutral seconds. The other four modes (Baladī, ʿUshshāq, Ṣabā, and Ḥijāz) are considered to be derived from the three principal modes. The *mashāyikh* recognize that

5. A vocal genre on a colloquial text, comprising pre-composed sections, but also providing space for vocal improvisation.

6. For further discussion of cantillation, see Abou Mrad, "Cantillation as Convergence Point," 117–31 in this volume.

7. The name of each darajah is a compound word formed of two Persian words: for example, yakāh or yekgāh derives from yek, which means one or first, and kāh (pronounced gāh in Persian), which means degree or mode.

8. Generally conceived as a quarter-tone higher than E-flat and a quarter-tone lower than E. In actual musical practice, significantly more subtlety of intonation is present than this simplification implies.

the *maqām* has a direct influence on both the performer and the listener. Authentic *maqām*-s reflect positivity or neutrality: it is sometimes said that Rāst reflects happiness, Bayyātī reflects purity, and Sīkāh reflects joyfulness. On the other hand, the process of appropriation (*al-ḥarakat al-qabḍīyah*) that generates the derived modes registers negativity of mood. For example, Jahārkāh and Ṣabā reflect sadness, ʿUshshāq reflects nervousness, and Ḥijāz reflects memories of the past, especially passionate ones.

Becoming a Munshid

A person who wants to practice this art must advance through many stages before becoming a *munshid* or *shaykh*. The first stage in the learning process is a series of organized non-academic classes that traditionally occur in the mosque around a column, where the teaching *shaykh* sits leaning his back. His *murīd*-s (students) sit around him, mainly listening, with no papers or pens in their hands except in very rare circumstances. A student in these sessions memorizes the Qur'an and learns the rules of Qur'an recitation, Arabic language and grammar (*naḥw*), poetry and intonation (*ṣarf*), linguistic rhythmic rules (*wazn*), rhythmic rules for poetry (*ʿarūḍ*), and also history, mathematics, and Islamic liturgy. Special emphasis is given in separate sessions to *ʿilm al-samāʿ*.

During the learning process, a student goes with his *shaykh* almost everywhere he performs. In the beginning, the student is only a listener sitting in the front row; later he is a member of the group, known as the *biṭānah*, that accompanies the *munshid*. After a period of time that varies from one student to another, and according to the instructor's guidance, a student chooses his path: to become a performing *munshid* himself, or to become exclusively a teacher or a *muqri'*, or even to leave the field entirely.

In the end, the *qawāʿid* (rules, theories) put forth for both the melodic and the rhythmic systems are only for educational purposes and have no real impact on the practicing field. The student is repeatedly reminded that the two systems are like a book he should memorize in order to forget—after the understanding permeates his spirit, becoming a part of him. As the Arabic proverb says, "Whose master is his book in perpetuity, his mistakes are more than his ingenuity"[9] (al-Miṣrī 1975, 50). Confirming this attitude is the story of Abū Nuwās, a famous poet of the first Abbasid era. His instructor, al-Khalaf, began by asking him to go to a Bedouin site and learn ten thousand lines of Arabic poetry. When Abū Nuwās returned to his instructor happy with what he had memorized, al-Khalaf then asked

مَن كان اُستاذه كتابه وَاتصالاً هذا كتابه، كثُر خَطأه وقلّ صَوابه .9

him to stay for some years in a far-off monastery in order to forget all of the verses he had memorized. Only after Abū Nuwās returned from his years of forgetting in the monastery did al-Khalaf finally permit him to write poetry (al-Miṣrī 1975).

Proceeding from this example, a short time after the student completes his studies, the instructor's emphasis is less on the student's ability to define a *maqām* or a *ḍarb* (rhythmic unit or period) than on his ability to recognize a *maqām* or a *ḍarb* and create in it.[10] To be a *munshid* or a *muqri'*—that is, to receive the *ijāzah*, the guild license to practice—the student has to pass a very serious—though non-academic—examination of his artistic capabilities of creativity and originality. For this test, the student must demonstrate before a jury of *mashāyikh* his mastery of the modal and rhythmic systems by performing seven *waṣlah*-s in the seven modes, including both measured and non-measured improvisations.

The Art of Tawshīḥ

Tawshīḥ is the main pillar of the *waṣlat inshādīyah,* a kind of improvisatory suite or sequence of pieces in one *maqām.* The normal position of *tawshīḥ* is at the end of the *waṣlah*; however, most *waṣlah*-s include more than one. Some variation in terminology regarding *tawshīḥ* should be mentioned. In the book documenting the 1932 Cairo Congress of Arab Music, the term *dārij* is used for *tawshīḥ* (*Recueil* 1934, 164–67), even though record company catalogs and disc labels, along with many *munshid*-s, had used the term *tawshīḥ* for a number of years before the conference. At that time, *dārij* referred to a composed poem chanted by a group, their leader stopping them after every line to sing half of that line to a different melody. It may be that *dārij* was then a synonymous term that later disappeared from use.

As a literary form, *tawshīḥ* encompasses any poem that carries religious or Sufi meaning. It also can take on other literary forms, such as the *muwashshaḥ,* which appeared in Spain during the ninth century, or even be a multirhymed poem. Musically speaking, *tawshīḥ* may be the most free form in the entire Arabic classical music tradition: it does not use a refrain structure, and there is complete freedom regarding choice of mode or rhythmic cycle for the *tawshīḥ.*

As a musical form, *tawshīḥ* centers on the group singing of the *biṭānah.* For each line of poetry, there is a corresponding musical phrase. For example, if the *tawshīḥ* lyrics comprise eight verses, there will be eight musical phrases, including introduction, climax, and conclusion. A composer may

10. See also During 1994.

end a musical phrase on the final note of the *maqām* of the *tawshīḥ* or on another note that imparts a sense of partial conclusion: for example, under some circumstances, the top note of the second tetrachord of the *maqām* may function as a cadential note. A composer may even take a phrase into another melodic mode or sub-mode; however, at the end, the *tawshīḥ* returns to its main mode except in rare cases. Phrases that visit another *maqām* are generally not found in the introduction but only later, during the climax of the *tawshīḥ* and toward the conclusion. After any such modulation, phrases gradually return to the main *maqām* of the *tawshīḥ*.

The essence of the *tawshīḥ* depends upon the self-contained nature of these rather short phrases, because a *tawshīḥ* is never performed as a continuous unit. After nearly every phrase, there is a pause for the *munshid* to interject an improvisatory solo, known as *tafrīd*, or even several on the same line of poetry. To each *tafrīd*, the *biṭānah* responds with the same pre-composed phrase (called *iʿādah*). Sometimes, especially in the beginning or near the end, and always according to the *munshid's* mood, the *biṭānah* may continue to the next pre-composed phrase immediately, with no improvising break in between.

Classifying Improvisation in the Tawshīḥ

There are three main ways a *munshid* may address the *tawshīḥ* text when building a *tafrīd* between any two pre-composed phrases. These three approaches are essentially types of improvisation distinguished from one another in terms of the relation to the text. The first type may be thought of as untexted, since in this case the *munshid* uses no text at all—only a non-lexical syllable such as "ah." In this way, he treats his voice as though it were an instrument. Untexted improvisation usually occurs in the beginning and near the end of the *tawshīḥ*.

I refer to the other two types of improvisation as "internal-textual" and "external-textual." In the case of internal-textual improvisation, the *munshid* takes up either part or all of the text just sung by the *biṭānah*. If the *munshid* wants the *biṭānah* to respond by repeating the phrase, he builds his *tafrīd* on the entire text of the phrase. On the other hand, if he wants the *biṭānah* to respond by going on to the next phrase, he creates a short phrase using only the final two or three words of the line. The last of the three approaches to text in improvisation, the external-textual type, occurs only rarely. In this case, the *munshid* turns to a text or poem having no relation to the *tawshīḥ* in question. Special circumstances, such as Ramaḍān celebrations or a memorial to an imam, may provide an appropriate context

for this type of improvisation, which in any case never occurs in the beginning of the *tawshīḥ* but only at the end of the middle section or—even more
likely—near the end.

From the musical standpoint, there are two main approaches taken by
the *munshid* in creating *tafrīd*-s. But before discussing these, I would like to
consider an important type of cooperative improvisation that is largely the
province of the *biṭānah*.

The pre-composed musical phrases in a *tawshīḥ* are never merely
sung in their original form, but are subject to spontaneous decoration by
individual singers. This may occur when the *munshid* joins the *biṭānah* in
singing one of the pre-composed phrases, but it is also a significant feature
within the *biṭānah* itself. As an individual singer in the group deviates from
the melody a little by introducing subtle ornamentation, the result is simultaneous slightly different versions of the melody—a phenomenon defined
as heterophony. It is important to note that this type of improvisation does
not add new melodic content to the performance but rather embellishes
the melody already present. Because of this absence of additional melodic
content, this practice has been called monomodular improvisation (Lortat-
Jacob 1987; Abou Mrad 2004).

As mentioned above, the *munshid* may make these heterophonic or-
namentations, but it is often individual members of the *biṭānah* who do
so. Attentive listening to each other, not previous preparation, is what allows spontaneous ornamentation to be effective in performance. Members
of the *biṭānah* take care not to crowd a phrase with too many ornaments;
they also avoid conflicts between ornaments. When the group senses that
one singer is embarking on an embellishment, they assist by keeping to the
melody, thereby allowing each spontaneous ornament its space. A spirit of
cooperation, far from any individual display or competition, characterizes
this type of localized improvisation.

Returning to the *munshid*, there is an observable distinction between
two main musical approaches to improvisation on the basis of measured or
unmeasured music. Underlying measured improvisation is a regular pulse
like that felt in musical meter. In a *tawshīḥ* composed on a specific rhythmic
cycle, the *munshid* may adhere to this cycle in his improvisation. A *munshid* may perform measured improvisation throughout the entire *tawshīḥ*;
however, more often it is limited to brief passages that either fill in gaps in
long pre-composed phrases or act as transitional material. Recordings from
the beginning of the twentieth century show that some of the *mashāyikh*
of the past did occasionally adhere to a rhythmic cycle throughout the entire *tawshīḥ*; oral history from the interviews I conducted confirms this

tendency as an option. Regarding the *tawshīḥ* text, it should be noted that external-textual improvisation, taking poetry outside the lyrics of the *tawshīḥ*, is not employed in measured improvisation.

The most common musical approach to improvisation among the *mashāyikh,* especially in the modern period, is unmeasured cantillatory improvisation. In this type, the *munshid* moves in unmeasured musical time outside any rhythmic cycle. Unmeasured improvisation may occur whenever and wherever the *munshid* chooses during the *tawshīḥ*. Some later *munshid*-s even dispense with the measured type altogether, performing cantillatory improvisation all the way through the *tawshīḥ*. As for the text, the *munshid* may call upon the untexted, internal-textual, or external-textual types of improvisation as he sees fit, observing the lyrical metrics in all cases.

Signals between the Munshid and the Biṭānah

As is clear from the discussion above, improvisation is the central component in *tawshīḥ,* while pre-composed phrases provide crucial context. In performance, these two strands of the *tawshīḥ* come together as a unified form by means of signals passed between the *munshid* and the *biṭānah.* Two general categories of signals are necessary in achieving a cooperative, organized dialogue between the two entities. Signals of the first category govern the choice of the *munshid* either to begin an improvisatory passage or not, and, if he does improvise, whether this occurs in the middle of the pre-composed phrase or at its end. Signals of the second category govern the choice between repeating a pre-composed phrase or moving on to the next.

When the *biṭānah* finishes any phrase of the *tawshīḥ,* a cue signaling how the performance will proceed is necessary. At this point, the *munshid* decides whether to perform a *tafrīd* or to continue to the next phrase of the *tawshīḥ.* As mentioned above, phrases of the *tawshīḥ* are not linked; they are usually separated by pauses. If the *munshid* decides to improvise, he starts his *tafrīd* during the pause. He cannot wait until after the pause, or the *biṭānah* would go on to the next phrase, causing an undesirable clash. Similarly, the *munshid* does not begin his *tafrīd* at the end of the pause; on the contrary, he starts as early as appropriate in order to make it easier for the *biṭānah* to understand his choice. On the other hand, if the *munshid* simply wishes to proceed to the next phrase without improvisation, he only has to leave the pause unfilled and the *biṭānah* will understand that they should go on.

Some long pre-composed phrases of *tawshīḥ* include a small gap in the middle, allowing for a breath. In this case also, the *munshid* is free to fill in the gap or simply allow the silence. If he chooses to impose a brief impro-visatory passage over such a gap, most often he uses non-lexical syllables; rarely, he might use one or two words of the text.

Another juncture where signals become important occurs near the end of each *tafrīd*. Here, the signal given by the *munshid* actually functions as two cues in one. The first allows the *biṭānah* to recognize that the *tafrīd* is concluding; the second clarifies whether the *munshid* wants to repeat the phrase or proceed to the next. In bringing his improvisation to a close, the *munshid* indicates the *waḥdah* (beat) by the speed of his movement in order for the *biṭānah* to continue safely. If the *munshid* wants the *biṭānah* to repeat the previous phrase, he ends his *tafrīd* on the modal aspect of that phrase. If he wants to go on, he touches on the aspect of the next phrase as a signal to proceed. In this respect, it should be noted that adjacent phrases in a *tawshīḥ* normally bring out contrasting aspects of the mode.

In *tawshīḥ* performance, responsibility for these cues rests upon both the *biṭānah* and the *munshid*. For *biṭānah* members, it is important to main-tain awareness of the signals. Their group concentration, teamwork, and cooperative spirit form the true gateway to effective group improvisation, though on a practical level all of these are also necessary for interpreting signals from the *munshid* in order to assure correct entry into each phrase. The *munshid*, for his part, must be able to concentrate deeply and move with authority through the *tawshīḥ*, taking care to provide clear signals to his *biṭānah*. In his *tafrīd*-s, he must always find ways to create something new without repeating himself. Above all, the chanting *shaykh* must avoid actions that show off, that cause listeners to lose interest, or that diminish the mystical, sacred atmosphere of *tawshīḥ*.

The Endeavor of Cooperation in the Inshād Field

As previously noted, the melodic and rhythmic rules of the school of the *mashāyikh* are primarily for educational purposes. In actual practice, rules are not the true controller of the relationship between *munshid* and *biṭānah*. Understanding others, positive energy, and the desire for high-quality work are the active forces in this relationship.

Throughout the history of performance, there are examples of appar-ently individualistic performers whose work reveals true cooperation. Such dynamic partnerships are apparent in concerts given all over Egypt, even in religious ceremonies, and are documented in recordings. One fine example

is the collaboration of two famous musicians of the Naḥḍah: *shaykh* Ali
Mahmoud (1878–1946), a prominent Egyptian *munshid* of the first half of
the twentieth century, and Sami Chawa (1889–1965), the celebrated Syri-
an-Egyptian violinist. Regardless of the difference in religion between Ali
Mahmoud, who was Muslim, and Sami Chawa, who was Christian, these
two men made great recordings together that continue to be important references for all musicians of the eastern Arabic music tradition. The pair also
left behind moral examples that are useful standards of human behavior for
any true musician of today's world. A contemporary example is the well-
known Raymond, who, though he is Christian, has been a member of many
biṭānah of the *mashāyikh* in Egypt simply because of his love of the art of
tawshīḥ.

Conclusion

Practical cooperation, grounded in a deep musical and spiritual connection,
is a major contributor to the mystical and sacred atmosphere of *inshād*. The
connection between improvisation and cooperation is something I internalized during my training as I walked with the *mashāyikh* and performed
with them. Building the essence of cooperation in improvisatory contexts is
a way for the performer to leave ego behind, to be immersed in give-and-
take with others. In the *tawshīḥ*, even though the *munshid* has a special role
as soloist, the interaction between the *munshid* and the *biṭānah* does not
promote the attitude of a hierarchy. The overriding concern is a spirit of
cooperation. For me, this spirit can be applied in all types of Arabic music
and also in many musical traditions around the world; it plants something
in the human soul that gives peace and a desire to produce the best possible
work. Now I am striving to apply this spirit in Ensemble *Aṣīl*, the group I
formed in 2003 as a way of developing Arabic classical music anew, always
based on this principle of collaborative work.

If we return to the internal meaning of the practice of *inshād*, which
was carried as a flag from one generation to another, regardless of religion
or ethnicity, we can avoid seeing our own ego as the source of development. If we return to those practices and develop them from the inside,
reviving and finding the new there, we can avoid the continual search for
the new based on zero, in ignorance of what came before. To benefit truly
from others' experiences—avoiding the common practice of simply copying
them—it is necessary to look to the spirit and methods and not simply the
results. This perspective is applicable to other parts of life beyond musical

performance. Is it not better to dive deeper into a sea of peace than to take from the surface thinking that this will lead us to reconciliation?

Earlier, I posed the question of how the spirit of teamwork in the art of *tawshīḥ* could serve as a model for cooperation and acceptance in other contexts. The musician who possesses this cooperative spirit in music has no choice but to carry it outside of music also. It is not a matter of accepting the other but rather a kind of melting into the other and receiving the other into one's self, just as the performers in *tawshīḥ* are attuned to each other through a deep spiritual and musical connection, allowing multiple types of improvisation to come together in beauty. The mystical and sacred atmosphere of *inshād* can take us beyond religious differences, which have nothing to do with the divinity of music. If such differences are allowed to stand as obstacles, then spiritual music cannot succeed in its capacity to purify people's souls

FOR DISCUSSION

1. In considering the real cooperation and relational interaction between the *munshid* (soloist) and the *biṭānah* (singing group) in the *tawshīḥ* tradition, extend this concept to musical collaboration in your own tradition. Describe these traditions in detail and analyze types of cooperation between musicians.

2. Improvisation in *tawshīḥ* is a balance of both freedom and control between performers. How might this exemplify peacebuilding in contexts outside of these performances?

3. Mustafa Said is a gifted composer and brilliant Egyptian Muslim-trained performer. He can perform in multiple situations and for different purposes. Go to YouTube and listen to Mustafa performing one of his own compositions in concert in Europe: http://www.youtube.com/watch?v=6xQC2DoODsk. Discuss the impact and function of the performance in light of music for peacebuilding.

4. PROJECT: *For musicians*: Play music with other musicians in a genre that allows improvisation and some freedom in musical expression. What sort of discussion is necessary before performing together? After rehearsing and/or performing your music, how successful were you in cooperating with other musicians? How does this experience combined with Said's perspective in *tawshīḥ* music influence your awareness as a musician? *For non-musicians*: Interview several musicians from the same musical ensemble, which has a regular repertoire of improvisatory pieces. Ask about their cooperation with one another in performance and how they fostered this type of interaction. If possible, watch them perform and notice these relationships. Relate your research to Said's perspective in *tawshīḥ* music performance.

References Cited

Abou Mrad, Nidaa. 2003. "*Al-faqīh wa-l-murannim: al-'iṣlāḥ min ad-dākhil.*" [The imam and the singer: the endogenous reform.] In *Music in Arab Renaissance*, edited by Nidaa Abou Mrad, n.p. Amman: Arab Academy of Music.

———. 2004. "Formes vocales et instrumentales de la tradition musicale savante issue de la Renaissance de l'Orient arabe." *Cahiers de musiques traditionnelles* 17, 183–215.

——. 2008. "Prolégomènes à une approche vectorielle neumatique de la modalité." *Revue des traditions musicales des mondes arabe et méditerranéen* 2: 89–128.

During, Jean. 1994. *Quelque chose se passe: Le sens de la tradition dans l'Orient musical.* Paris: Verdier.

Farmer, Henry George. 1929. *A History of Arabian Music to the XIIIth Century.* London: Luzac.

Feldman, Walter. 1996. *Music of the Ottoman Court: Makam, Composition and the Early Ottoman Instrumental Repertoire.* Berlin: Wissenschaft und Bildung.

Hourani, Albert. 1962. *Arabic Thought in the Liberal Age 1796-1939.* London: Oxford University Press.

al-Jindi, ʿUthmān Muḥammad. 1895. *Rawḍ al-Masarrāt fī ʿilm an-naghamāt.* [Gardens of joyfulness in the science of music.] Cairo: Maṭbaʿat al-Gumhūriyya.

al-Khulaʾī, Muḥammad Kāmil. (1904) 1993. *Kitāb al-mūsīqī al-sharqī.* [The book of Eastern music.] Cairo: Maktabat al-dār al-ʿarabīyah li-l-kitāb.

Lagrange, Frédéric. 1994. "Musiciens et poètes en Égypte au temps de la Nahda." Doctoral thesis, Université de Paris VIII, Saint-Denis.

——. 1996. *Musiques d'Egypte.* Paris: Cité de la Musique/Actes Sud.

Lortat-Jacob, Bernard. 1987. "Improvisation: le modèle et ses réalisations." In *L'improvisation dans les musiques de tradition orale,* edited by Bernard Lortat-Jacob, 45–59. Paris: SELAF.

al-Miṣrī, Ibn Manẓūr. 1975. *Abū Nuwās fī tārīkhihī wa-shiʿrihī.* Beirut: Dar al-Jil.

al-Muwayliḥī, Ibrāhīm. 1902. "ʿAbduh al-Ḥamūlī." In Jurjī Zaydān, *Tarājim mashāhīr al-qarn al-tāsiʿ ʿashar.* [Biographies of famous nineteenth-century figures.] Beirut: Manshūrāt Dār Maktabat al-Ḥayāt, 406.

Racy, Ali Jihad. 1976. "Record Industry and Egyptian Traditional Music: 1904–1932." *Ethnomusicology* 20, no. 1: 23–48.

Recueil des travaux du Congrès de musique arabe qui s'est tenu au Caire en 1932. 1934. Cairo: Imprimerie nationale, Boulac.

Rizq, Qusṭandī. 1936–1939. *Al-Mūsiqá al-Sharqīyah wa-l-ghinā' al-ʿarabī* [Eastern music and Arabic singing], parts 1 and 2. Cairo: Al-Maṭbaʿah al-ʿaṣriyah.

CHAPTER 9

Music for Peace and Reconciliation from Lebanon

by Marcel Akiki

Introduction

When I initially heard about the project, "Songs of Peace and Reconciliation between Muslims and Christians," I thought the venture seemed rather ambivalent in terms of its nature and purpose. First, the topic "songs" is rather broad in scope and involves multiple disciplines ranging from the academic and artistic to the spiritual spheres. Second, the subject of "peace" is not only academic in nature but also encompasses a spiritual component. Third, the title itself suggests there are conflicts occurring between Muslims and Christians and as such, efforts have to be made to bring about peace and reconciliation. However, from my perspective neither of these two communities in Lebanon will acknowledge that there are any deep religious or spiritual conflicts. When asked about the matter, Muslims and Christians will quickly respond that they are not in conflict with the other. Sadly, both communities are also aware of the political agenda that has unfortunately engendered aggression or conflict in Lebanon.

Since the beginning of the Lebanese war in 1975, it has been my deep conviction that peace or rather coexistence and mutual understanding between Muslims and Christians can be enhanced in Lebanon by discovering our mutual cultural identities particularly through Lebanese traditional and popular music. Because of this, I decided to devote my academic life focus on ethnomusicological research and the teaching of Lebanese traditional-popular music. With this in mind I began a PhD program at the Sorbonne University, Paris, in 1982. As fears of war between Palestine and Israel in

Lebanon escalated in the period thereafter, I decided to conduct musicological research in southern Lebanon in order to collect information on the popular and traditional music of that region. Despite the prevailing dangers and tensions, I managed to visit about fifty Druze, Christian, and Muslim villages where I was always well received. The villagers granted permission to record their music. A few years later, I managed to visit more than two hundred villages in Lebanon in order to collect more songs. Although Lebanese musical traditions are fast disappearing, the village elders were still able to provide fragments of musical memories that I could record, collate, and later analyze.

In this chapter, drawing heavily from my own personal experience as a musician, priest, and peace catalyst, I will first discuss the vital role of music peace catalysts in peace building and, second, several ways by which songs and music have been used instrumentally in fostering peace and reconciliation in Lebanon.

The Socio-Religious Context and Peace Initiatives

Since the formation of modern Lebanon, the nation has experienced much instability and violence. Economic, political, and demographic divisions within Lebanon finally escalated into a protracted civil war that lasted from 1975 to 1992. My colleague Dr. Jon Hoover has elaborated on the complex intricacies of the political and religious landscape in Lebanon that has fueled this instability.[1] This prolonged conflict, current instability, and ongoing volatility has resulted in the loss of lives and economic disruption, severely damaging familial and societal life in Lebanon.

On the positive side however, despite the decades of hardship and conflict, there have been growing alternative movements of peace in Lebanon that demonstrate the Lebanese desire to live peaceably with one another. One such example is that Christians and Muslims attend each other's respective religious festivals. During these important occasions, politicians and clerics from Muslim and Christian communities deliberately visit the church or mosque, thus making these venues an important space where communities can mutually recognize and respect the practices and identities of the other. Similarly in the rural villages of Lebanon, Druze and Christian Maronite communities participate together in wedding and funeral ceremonies. Furthermore, Muslims and Christians share common pilgrimages. For over three decades, thousands of Muslims and Christians

---

1. See Hoover, "Muslim-Christian Relations and Peacemaking in the Arab World," 51–70 in this volume.

have made pilgrimages of prayer to several Christian holy shrines and sanctuaries dedicated to the Virgin Mary. One such pilgrimage is to Our Lady of Harissa (See Harissa.Info. "The Lady of Lebanon"), over the bay of Jounieh on the Mediterannean Sea, and the other to Our Lady of Bechuat, in Bekaa (AsiaNews.it. "Lebanese Christians, Muslims Celebrate Annunciation Together"). Furthermore, peace projects such as "Caux: Initiatives of Change," an international movement committed to "building relationships of trust across the world's divides," also contribute toward peacebuilding.[2] Established during the 1980s when Lebanon was at war, members of this group have dedicated their lives to living a life of integrity and love. Their goal is to act as reconcilers between the Muslim and Christian factions and communities.

With such peace initiatives taking place, let us now focus on the contribution of music and song toward peace and reconciliation.

Musical Catalysts for Peace

Although initiatives and programs for peace are important, it is my conviction that the most potent force for peacebuilding lies in persons who take on intermediary roles as peacebuilders. Let me share first my own experience as a music educator, and, second, highlight the role of popular Lebanese music icons such as Fairouz and the Rahbanni brothers as peace catalysts.

2. See Caux: Initiatives of Change.

Music Educator: Father Marcel Akiki

I will begin with my personal experience of using music education projects in promoting peace. From my journey, I have discovered that music education projects are effective peacebuilding tools. Through dynamic teaching methods in music education such as the Orff method as well as the implementation of musical workshops, children learn to engage with diversity. Together with that, the formation of choirs and musical ensembles that comprise youths and children from diverse religious affiliations and social backgrounds allows for greater interaction and engagement with the other. Let me highlight two such instances.

First, upon completion of my first doctoral degree in June 1985, I returned to Lebanon and found a country at war. The academic infrastructure, particularly the graduate music schools, were in a state of disrepair. Consequently, it was fairly impossible to undertake any ethnomusicological research on the Lebanese musical traditions that I was particularly interested in. Subsequently, I decided that my priority should shift from research to caring for the Lebanese people. During the war, the most important question was that of survival and healing from the devastating effects of war. I became increasingly convinced that music could help bring healing on a psychosociological, cultural, and spiritual level. As such, I started a musical movement called "Lebanon-Hope-Music," primarily for Lebanese children and youth. This project included setting up a music school and establishing children's choirs and instrumental ensembles, which ultimately involved over two hundred people. The participants were mainly Christians who were victims of war and had suffered displacement, loss of families, and loss of their homes. The goal of this group was to sing about peace, particularly building peace between the different factions in Lebanon: Druze, Christians, Palestinians, and foreigners. Some of the activities included visiting schools, hospitals, senior homes, orphanages, implementing Orff Instrumentarium Workshops, and holding television interviews. Eventually, when the military situation permitted, the choir embarked on concert tours.

The themes of the choirs' repertoire reflected diversity and focused mainly on patriotic, humanistic, and spiritual values. One of the most appreciated songs was a French song written to address children who were victims of war atrocities and violence. The poignant words of hope in this song echo:

Children of my country, beautiful flowers of innocence
Sing your song, sow your hope
Children of my country, little heart of suffering
Sing your song, sow your hope
Don't close your heart and open your house,
Love will defeat the hate and will be your song.

Later, the student choir "The Hope Makers" of the Antonine Sisters' School, a well-known Lebanese private school, recorded this song as part of a CD that they produced. Unfortunately, this musical movement came to a grinding halt in 1989 when increasing armed hostilities and tensions prevented any further activities. In that same year, I made a major decision to become a priest.

The second instance occurred between 1997 and 2004 when I had another opportunity to participate in a musical project with students from the Lebanese University of Beirut. As part of the Orff Instrumentarium combined with singing workshops, I gathered Muslim, Druze, and Christian students together. These students came from different regions implicated in the civil war of 1975–1990, and they were considered to be in enmity with the other. These workshops provided wonderful opportunities for interaction where students learned to engage and work with the other, thus contributing a vital link toward peacebuilding.

Popular Musical Icons: Fairuz and the Rahbani Brothers

The renowned singer throughout the Middle East and beyond, Fairuz, or Nuhad Hadda, was born in the village of Dbayye-al-Chouf in Mount Lebanon and eventually moved to Zqaq el Blat in the city of Beirut. She began her music career as a chorus member for the Lebanese Radio Station in 1947. By the 1950s, singing songs written by the Rahbani brothers, she established herself in Lebanon as a talented singer with a splendid voice. Her fame spread worldwide through her many artistic productions such as the annual Baalbeck Festivals, the global dissemination of her songs, musical plays, Lebanese operetta and films, and eventually gaining recognition not only in the Arab world but also in Europe and in North America.

Fairuz worked primarily with the Rahbani brothers, Assi and Mansour, and later with her son Ziad Rahbani. Together they were a team, with Mansour writing the lyrics, and Assi, her former husband, composing the melodies, arranging the music, and providing a global vision. Fairuz's songs incorporated western and/or Arab scales, instruments, and technique, and drew on Arab and Lebanese folk music genres. This together with nationalistic, religious, and moral themes in their songs helped create a Lebanese identity.

For example, the song, *"Bayti Ana Baytak"* (My house is yours, I have nobody to help me), has a deeply religious theme calling on the mother of Jesus to bless and protect Lebanon while simultaneously reflecting a Lebanese nationalism and a deep love for the country. These themes of religion and nationalism that feature strongly in Fairuz's repertoire of songs have an immense formative impact in Lebanese society as they draw from the cultural roots of rural life in Lebanese villages, stir a nationalistic vision of freedom and independence, contain political themes, and depict human and moral values, all of which are pertinent to Lebanese. It is not surprising that Fairuz is considered a legend in Lebanon and a musical symbol of Lebanese identity. Her singing of peace, despite the internal political turmoil in Lebanon, communicates strongly a message of peace to the people of Lebanon.

Implementing Music for Peace and Reconciliation

The invaluable work of the above music catalysts of peace bring to attention two approaches to implementing songs of peace and reconciliation in Lebanon: the spiritual-musicological and the anthropological-musicological approach. Both approaches share the musicological aspect that includes the use of traditional, neo-traditional, and popular genres of Lebanese music.

Spiritual-Musicological Approach

Pursuing peace and reconciliation begins from a spiritual place and flows out of a vital relationship with the God of peace attained through the reading of the sacred books and in prayer and worship. The initial and necessary step toward peacemaking begins with inculcating an inner peace with God and within the self. Out of this, peace with others can be sincerely sought. As such, the true seeker of peace, whether Christian or Muslim, focuses first on growing in spiritual authenticity and second on creating deeper understanding and building bridges between diverse and conflicting communities. These bridges include shared spiritual and moral values, theology, and songs that serve as common ground from which relationships can be enhanced.

Common Themes and Values in the Sacred Books

The Qur'an and the Bible share several similar tenets calling on believers to love God and to love others and provides a strong premise for peacemaking. In the Qur'an Allah advises: "Hold to forgiveness, command what is right and turn away from the ignorant."[3] Other verses extol the virtue of pardoning the other person who has wronged you, citing that Allah is "Ever-Forgiving, Most Merciful."[4] Furthermore, "if someone pardons and puts things right, his reward is with Allah."[5] From the Bible, in Proverbs 19:11, human beings are exhorted to "overlook an offense," and to be "humble, gentle, patient with one another in love." Psalm 51:1 is a prayer asking mercy from the tenderness of God.[6] Similarly in the New Testament, the Christian community is advised to "bear with each other and forgive whatever grievances you may have against one another. Forgive as the Lord forgave you."[7] These sacred texts that uphold the values of forgiveness, repentance, love, and reconciling with enemies are consistently reflected in the prayers, songs, and worship of Christians and Muslims and form a wonderful premise for peacemaking.

Common Spirituality

A vibrant spirituality courses through the veins of both Islam and Christianity as both have strong rituals of prayer and worship. Muslims observe the ṣalāh (Islamic ritual prayer) five times a day, and engage in du'ā', prayers of supplication that are more spontaneous and personal. These prayers are conducted in the adherent's own language and call upon Allah for help, guidance, and strength in specific situations.[8] Christians too have their own worship and prayer rituals on both communal and personal levels.

Aside from this, there is also the pursuit of mystical life. In Islam within the Sunni tradition, Sufism[9] or *Taṣawwuf*, a mystical movement, seeks to find divine love and knowledge through a direct personal experience of God. *'Irfān* (Yazdi 1997), a Shiite confession, pursues a spiritual road

3 Qur'an 7:199.

4. Qur'an 24:22: "They should rather pardon and overlook. Would you not love Allah to forgive you? Allah is Ever-Forgiving, Most Merciful."

5. Qur'an 42:40: "The repayment of a bad action is one equivalent to it. But if someone pardons and puts things right, his reward is with Allah."

6. Ps 51:1: "Have mercy upon me, O God, according to thy loving kindness."

7. Col 3:13. For other verses, see Eph 4:32; Matt 6:14.

8. Examples of these can be found in the Qu'ran and the Sunnah.

9. Sufism or *Taṣawwuf* consists of a variety of mystical paths that are designed to ascertain the nature of humankind and God and to facilitate the experience of divine love and wisdom in the world. The practices of contemporary Sufi orders and suborders vary, but most include the recitation of the name of God (Schimmel 1997).

that leads to gnosis (See Mutahhari 2012). Music plays a large part in these movements. Mystic Sufi music is represented by the music of Sufi *inshād* religious singing in Arab and Muslim countries. The lyrics are drawn from either Qur'anic verses or from poetic spiritual texts composed by famous Sufi figures such as al-Ḥallāj or ibn 'Arabī or Al Ghazali.[10]

Interestingly, Sufism and the great mystics in Christian spirituality share several beliefs as both spiritualities uphold high and moral virtues, agree on the concept of sanctification. Furthermore, the mystical experience of the kindness and tenderness of God of the saints in the Catholic Church parallels that of the Sufi experience. Although Sufis are a small minority in Lebanon and have no official social impact or influence on the Muslim Sunni community, their influence is significant as they are a source of inspiration to a large number of musicians, artists, and philosophers in the world (Lings, 1999). The Arab Sufi music of Nidaa Abou Mrad and his Classical Arabic Music Ensembles is one such example. Their album, "Wiṣāl: An Arab Sufi Concert," as the title suggests, draws from the notion of human-divine union or wiṣāl. The songs are the result of a unique collaboration between the texts drawn from the master mystics of Islam such as Zayn al-Abidīn, Alī ibn Husayn Zayn al-Abidīn, Rābia al-Adawiyya, al-Husayn ibn Mansur al-Hallaj, Shaykh Muhyi al-Din Ibn 'Arabī, and the music created by Nidaa Abou Mrad, a devout Orthodox Christian (Abou Mrad, 2010).[11]

Common Beliefs in the Muslim and Christian Faith
Islam and Christianity share numerous dogmas that can gather their communities together. These include the monotheist conception of God, the figure of Abraham as the father of believers,[12] and a large number of prophets such as Moses. A shared narrative is that of Mary and the birth of Jesus. Found in Qur'an 19, Surat Maryam or verses about Mary chronicles the miraculous birth of John, the annunciation to Mary and the birth of Jesus, and the belief in life after death and paradise.

10. See Aquol 2006.

11 . See also a Muslim spiritual song for repentance, "Rabbaah" (Oh Lord) sung by a well-known Egyptian singer, Mohammad Abdo, lyrics by the poet At-Taaher Zamakhshare, and music by Said Abu Khashabe.

12. Qur'an 6:74.

Figure 11: Downtown Beirut: Mosque and Orthodox Church

As many research institutions seek to find all possible ways of dialogue between Muslims and Christians (e.g., "A Common Word"), the use of songs based on these common topics can be a relevant approach. In Lebanon, venues for these songs include interreligious artistic musical initiatives such as concerts and choirs. As these shared beliefs are affirmed during these concerts, the ensuing camaraderie allows controversial and often divisive issues—for example, the divinity of Christ, the incarnation, and the crucifixion—to be accepted.

Arabic Spiritual and Popular Songs:
Lebanon possesses a vast repertoire of Arabic spiritual songs that contain themes of peace, love, and forgiveness. A striking example is the song-prayer of St. Francis of Assissi, "O Lord use me for your peace,"[13] which has been translated into Arabic and sung by both Muslims and Christians. This song is not merely a passive prayer for peace but actively advocates for cultivating peace in adversarial situations.

Lebanese also appreciate Lebanese folk and popular songs and these songs that have religious themes are popular. In this respect, Fairuz sets a striking example. Her songs such as "*Ya Umm al Lah*" (Oh mother of

---

13. For lyrics of the song, see http://www.catholic.org/prayers/prayer.php?p=134.

God) and *"Baytī anā Baytak"* (My Home is yours, I am helpless) are deeply felt invocations to Mary and God. She also sings about love and charity in *"Al Mahabā"* (Love), taken from the writings of Khalil Gibran, a renowned Lebanese writer, poet, and philosopher.

Anthropological-Musicological Approach

Lebanon has rich cultural and musical traditions spanning hundreds of years from Mount Lebanon that value peace and reconciliation. In a story, Fenghali reported in 1935:

> A bride in the Christian village of Fghal in the region of Batroun (north) doesn't enter the nuptial house, but stays outside on her horse, if she knows that two persons need to be reconciled. She used to ask for their immediate reconciliation in front of her and the entire village. The author reported that once a bride in this same village stayed on a horse for more than four hours waiting for this reconciliation before proceeding with the ceremony. (1935, 84)

This story demonstrates the high value given to peacemaking between conflicting parties in the Lebanese community. These sociocultural values and musical traditions are vital areas that the Lebanese can draw from for peacemaking.

Opportunities for Reconciliation of the Past
A traditional practice of reconciliation between two parties in conflict is for victims to encounter their perpetrators personally or, if that is not possible, in symbolic ways and to make peace with them. I have personally experienced this tradition of brotherhood and reconciliation among my students. As a professor teaching "Popular Traditional Lebanese Music" in the Lebanese University of Beirut, Muslim, Christian, and Druze students are given a research assignment where they are to return to their villages and discover and collect their musical traditions that remain in the memory of their elders. These students are children of those involved in the Lebanese war, children of victims and of their attackers, former enemies. These students now sit side by side in class in an atmosphere of brotherhood and mutual acceptance. In many cases, these former "enemies" have journeyed together to their respective villages in order to collect and record Lebanese musical traditions and are always welcomed by both sides. Christian students who have experienced atrocities in war through violence, murder of their parents, relatives or friends, and massacre in their villagers still courageously

returned to the very places where these destructive acts were perpetrated. In spite of their traumatic memories, some were even able to visit the homes of their attackers and conduct interviews regarding their musical traditions.

Sharing Common Popular Traditional Lebanese Songs and Festivals

Common popular, traditional Lebanese songs in Mount Lebanon facilitate an atmosphere of brotherhood between Muslim, Druze, and Christian communities (Akiki 2010). Below are two examples of wedding songs from the Druze and Christian communities in Mount Lebanon. The first is a wedding procession song for men, the Hida, and the second is a wedding ritournelle for the bride on her way to her new home.

Hidā - ʿArīsinā šaihi š-šabāb

عريسنا شيخ الشباب

1 عريسنا شيخ الشباب	شيخ الشباب عريسنا
2 زحلة عروس مزينة	ومزينة برجالها
3 ويا ربي تكبر مهرتي	وبصير انا خيالها
4 دار العريس دار الفرح	عريسنا شيخ الشباب
5 عريسنا شيخ الشباب	شيخ الشباب عريسنا

Our bridegroom is the bravest of all	The bravest of all is our bridegroom
Zahlé is a embellished bride	She is embellished by her brave fighters
Oh Lord, may my mule grow	That may I become her rider
Then the bridegroom's home	is the joy's home
Our bridegroom is the bravest of all	The bravest of all is our bridegroom.

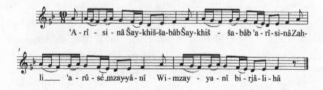

Figure 12: Hidā-ʿArīsinā šaihi š–šabāb

Hillī wi-fraḥī yā dār (Baskinta)

هلّي وافرحي يا دار عالعميّم

جبنا عبلا لعنتر   هلّي وافرحي يا دار   1

فتّح عا خدودك زرار...   والورد الجوري يا عريس   2

1- Rejoice O my Home   We have brought 'Ablā to 'Antar

2- And your red roses of   Have grown and colored your cheeks
      bridegroom

Hil - lî__wif-ra - hî yâ dâr__ Jib-nâ 'Ab-lâ la-'An - tar__

Figure 13: Hillī wi-fraḥī yā dār (Baskinta)

These songs, sung by Lebanese from all walks of life contain commonly shared themes pertaining to beauty of love, commitment, and marriage and enable involvement by all who are present at the wedding. Participating in the wedding ceremonies enhances good relationships and foster camaraderie.

The Popular Neo-traditional Repertoire

The middle and later part of the twentieth century saw an emergence of neo-traditional songs that are now considered as part of the Lebanese musical tradition. Composers and singers such as the Rahbani brothers, Fairuz, Nasri Chamse d-Din, Wadi el Safi, and Zakī Nassif have made significant contributions to this genre. These songs capture the character of the changing Lebanese society, with its dialectic between the old and the new and the local with the global. What is pertinent here are the embedded themes that contain views, longings and aspirations shared by all Lebanese.

For example, all Lebanese identify completely with Fairuz as she sings poignantly, "I love you Lebanon, my country." This profound love for Lebanon is felt deeply by Lebanese from all walks of life and religions. This song expresses the stark realities of a land previously made up of festivals and celebrations, but now torn asunder. However, it provides a hope and a new vision of Lebanon that will be reborn anew with dignity. These emotional associations allow Lebanese to identify with the songs and express their deep griefs and also fervent hopes.

In another song, A'tini nal-Nay (Give me the flute), the dominant symbol of the nāy (flute) in Khalil Gibran's poem is a powerful one. This song carries the listener to old times when Lebanon was peaceful. Although the notes of the flute lament and continue to lament, they also sing out a prayer and hope that, despite calamity and death, there will be a return to better times when the warmth of love will pervade instead.

Songs such as these reiterate common concerns and yet aspirations that resonate deeply with Lebanese. Using the poetry of a beloved son of Lebanon, Khalil Gibran, the symbol of the nāy, the imagery of the enduring mountains of Lebanon together with the magnificent voice of Fairuz evokes a deep emotion and response within Lebanese. They are urged not to be weary but to return to Lebanon. Furthermore, there is also a revisioning of a new Lebanon, a place for all Lebanese that captures their imagination.

This potent combination of Arabic-Western musical styles capturing the spirit of the old and the new, and lyrical themes and images that Lebanese identify deeply with, such as love for Lebanon, sacrifice for the nation, the eternal cedar as the symbol of Lebanon, the ancient Lebanese village life, hospitality, and the fight for liberty, justice, freedom, and independence, contribute greatly to the formation of a dynamic Lebanese national and cultural identity. Through song, these core values enable a revisioning of a peaceful Lebanon in contemporary times to be expressed, internalized, and ultimately to become embedded in the imagination of the Lebanese people.

The Poetic and Musical Practice of Zajal

The well-known zajal, a traditional form of oral strophic poetry practice, is a type of traditional and popular Lebanese poetic and musical improvisation. There are a large number of zajal troupes in Lebanon with the majority being found in Mount Lebanon. During a performance, a troupe of four poet-singers use poetic, melodic improvisation to express various themes, problematic issues, and arguments in competition form. What is unique is that each troupe can comprise members from diverse ethnicities and religions. With that, this traditional musical practice is representative of the possibility of a peaceful and working coexistence among Muslims, Christians, and Druze.

Conclusion

In conclusion, we are left with the salient question: Can music and songs improve relations between Muslims and Christians? My definitive answer is yes. I have demonstrated that Muslims and Christians in Lebanon share a repertoire of songs: popular Lebanese traditional, neo-traditional, and even religious songs that help bring about mutual understanding and enable coexistence. The performance of songs and also musical research activities enable dialogue between these differing groups. Furthermore, there are common themes and topics that Christians and Muslims share. From their respective sacred books, both religions espouse the values of love, peace, and forgiveness in the face of conflict and their enemies. We can draw on these values in times of conflict. Finally, what needs to be emphasized here is the potent role of human intermediaries who can act as musical catalysts of peace and reconciliation. Their mediatory role enables continuing dialogue between groups in conflict.

As a caution, it is important also to acknowledge that there are complexities that prevent or hinder peace and reconciliation. One of them is indulging in "extremism" in religion and politics. Another is the issue of justice. This is an all-important issue that cannot be sidestepped. It is pointless singing for peace and reconciliation if injustice is being perpetrated and human rights are being trampled. This only breeds ongoing deep anger, hatred, and bitterness. Connected with this, perhaps songs that champion social justice, truth, and human rights need to be prioritized. Songs that identify with the suffering faced by our community also aid in rebuilding. In my opinion, once there is justice, any song will be a real celebration and dance for life.

Finally, until the day when complete justice is accomplished, peacemakers have to ask heaven for strength, consolation, and inner peace within themselves and for their communities. What is needed is also courage to face the challenges ahead in this increasingly complex world, and always holding on to the words in the prayer of St. Francis of Assisi who advocates that we be the instruments of peace and goodwill to all humankind.

FOR DISCUSSION

1. In both his introduction and conclusion, Akiki states that peace-builders themselves are the "most potent force" in developing peace. What is your perspective on the role of the peacebuilder working within conflicted communities?

2. Label all the musical genres that were used in peacemaking from this chapter (e.g., popular musics). Classify song texts, poems, or other musical forms from your own experience in peacemaking that fit these genres. What other musical genres can be used to build peace in communities?

3. Akiki argues that the spirituality of the peacebuilder is important in the process. In your opinion, what is the role of spirituality in peacebuilding? For further extension, relate your ideas to Leder-ach's concept of the "moral imagination," as described in the intro-duction of this book.

4. Martin Luther King Jr. famously said, "Without justice, there can be no peace." Akiki discusses his perspective of this idea in the conclu-sion, adding the dynamic of music. How does music interface with and between justice and peace? In which order are/should they be developed? Use experiences from your class or study group to evi-dence your conclusions.

5. PROJECT: Akiki gives numerous names of websites and organiza-tions that are or have been active in peacemaking in the Lebanese context. Choose one of these organizations and analyze their ap-proach to peacemaking using music. Outline this approach in a way that can be used in contexts other than Lebanon. Write up the analysis and present to your class.

References Cited

Abou Mrad, Nidaa. 2010. "*Wiṣāl: An Arab Sufi Concert.*" Beirut, Lebanon: Forward Music, compact disc.

Akiki, Marcel. 1985. *Les chants populaires traditionnels de mariage au Liban. Les chants qarradi.* Thèse de doctorat en musicologie, Sorbonne, Paris IV.

———. 2010. *Les chants syllabiques de mariage au Mont-Liban.* Thèse de doctorat nouveau régime en ethnomusicologie, Paris X, Nanterre.

Anawati, Georges C., and Louis Gardet. 1976. *Mystique musulmane: Aspects et tendances, expériences et techniques.* Études Musulmanes. Paris: Vrin.

Aquol. 2006. "Pop Inshaad: the Rise of Islamic singers." http://www.aqoul.com/archives/2006/03/popinshaad_the.php

AsiaNews.it. March 24, 2009. "Lebanese Christians, Muslims Celebrate Annunciation Together." http://catholickey.blogspot.com/2009/03/lebanese-christians-muslims-celebrate.html.

Boulous, Sargon. "Origins of a Legend." http://almashriq.hiof.no/lebanon/700/780/fairuz/legend/biography.html. Accessed June 25, 2014.

Boullata, Kamal, and Sargon Boulous, eds. 1981. *Fairouz: Legend and Legacy.* Forum for International Art and Culture. Chicago: Maqam.

Caux: Initiatives of Change. http://www.caux.iofc.org/en/taxonomy/term/561. Accessed June 25, 2014.

"A Common Word." A Common Word between Us and You. http://www.acommonword.com/. Accessed June 24, 2014.

Corbin, Henry. 1983. *Face de Dieu, Face de l'homme, Herméneutique et soufisme,* Flammarion, Paris.

Feghali, Michel. 1935. *Contes, légendes, et coutumes populaires du Liban et Syrie,* Librairie d'Amérique et d'Orient. 1. Paris : Adrien-Maisonneuve.

Francis of Assissi. http://www.americancatholic.org/Features/Francis/peaceprayer.asp

Harissa.Info. "The Lady of Lebanon." http://www.harissa.info/.

Lings, Martin. 1993. *What is Sufism?* Cambridge: Islamic Texts Society.

Massignon, Louis. 1975. *La Passion de Hallâj, martyr mystique de l'Islam.* Paris, Gallimard.

Mutahhari, Murtadha, et al. 2012. "Light Within Me." http://www.al-islam.org/light-within-me-mutahhari-tabatabai-khomeini.

Obeid, J. 1998. *The Prayer In The Songs Of Fairuz* (in Arabic). Beyrouth, Lebanon: University of Kaslik.

Salibi, Kamal. 1993. *A House of Many Mansions: The History of Lebanon Reconsidered.* London: Tauris.

Schimmel, Annemarie. 1975. Sufism: The Mystical Dimensions of Islam. Chapel Hill, NC: University of North Carolina Press.

———. 1996. *Le Soufisme ou Les Dimensions mystiques de l'Islam,* Paris: Cerf.

Veinstein, G. 1998. "Les voies de la sainteté dans l'islam et le christianisme: Présentation." *Revue de l'histoire des religions* 251, no. 1: 5–16.

Yazdi, Muhammad Taqi Misbah. 1997. *Islamic Gnosis (Irfan) and Wisdom (Hikmat).* E-book published by al-Tawhid Islamic Journal 14, no. 3.

INDONESIA

CHAPTER 10

Voices of Peace and Reconciliation in Contemporary
Islamic Music

The Kyai Kanjeng and Suarasama Ensembles

by Rithaony Hutajulu

*The significant feature of musical communication is not that
it is untranslatable and irreducible to the verbal mode but
that its generality and multiplicity of possible messages and
interpretations brings out a special kind of "feelingful" activity
and engagement on the part of the listener, a form of pleasure
that unites the material and the mental dimensions of musical
experiences as fully embodied.*

—KEIL AND FELD 1994, 91

This chapter explores approaches towards peace and reconciliation expressed through Islamic music in Indonesia.[1] It focuses on two Muslim
bands and their musician leaders in Indonesia; namely the Kyai Kanjeng
Sepuh band led by Emha Ainun Nadjib from Jogjakarta and the Suarasama
band led by Irwansyah Harahap from Medan. In particular, I will focus on

1. My research was drawn from my personal experience in Suarasama as a vocalist
and co-founder of the group and my preliminary research on Kyai Kanjeng in Jogjakarta. Data used in this paper was gained through gathering information from personal
interviews with both groups and leader, books, compact discs and the internet.

the background, thoughts and perspectives of the leaders of these ensembles regarding peace and reconciliation as expressed through their music performance and music making.

By examining their philosophical ideas, the process of music making, song-lyrics, and musical sound expressed in their performance, I will demonstrate first, how (two Muslim) musicians communicate messages of peace and reconciliation and second, how the process of peace building is realized through musical interaction and communication not only among the performers but also with their audience. Finally, the power of music performance in enhancing interfaith dialogue between Christians and Muslims is analyzed.

Kyai Kanjeng and Emha Ainun Najib

Kyai Kanjeng is a Muslim band in Indonesia consisting of twenty-five musicians and singers. Formed in 1997 by a famous Indonesian Muslim leader, Emha Ainun Najib, the group[2] comprises members who are mostly drawn from the conservatory of music and the Indonesian Institute of the Arts (*Sekolah Tinggi Seni Indonesia*), and as such possess basic training in Javanese traditional music and theater. As for the name Kyai Kanjeng, the word "Kyai" in Javanese means an "Islamic expert or scholar," and "Kanjeng" is a name of an important character in a play created by Emha known as "Pak Enjeng" (Mr. Kanjeng). Recently, another word "*sepuh*," which means "elder," was added to their name.

Emha Ainun Nadjib is known in Indonesia for his many gifts: as a writer, a poet, a social critic, and also as a religious spokesperson. Affectionately known as "Cak Nun," Emha studied in a *pesantren*[3] (school of Islamic teaching). Subsequently, he learned the art of poetry from a renowned teacher, Umbu Landi Paranggi, an Indonesian Sufi poet who had a strong influence on Emha's life. His training in theater included attending theater workshops in the Philippines (1984), an International Writing Program at Iowa University, USA (1984), the International Poetry Festival in Rotterdam in Holland (1984), and Festival Horizonte III in West Berlin, Germany (1985). To this day, he has created eight plays for theater, sixteen books of poetry, and more than thirty other publications.

2. Novi Budianto originally led Kyai Kanjeng with a membership of around eleven persons. They were often asked by Emha Ainun Nadjib to accompany his poetry or to accompany his theater performances. The first time they collaborated with Emha was during the Gedongombo case where Emha was helping the village community face the government to stand up for their rights. Since then their collaboration with Emha has continued until today.

3. In Indonesia, *pesantren* are schools of Islamic teaching.

Emha is considered a controversial figure by the mainstream Indonesian community as well as by the Islamic community because his provoking opinions articulated in his performances and writings, often contain political and religious critiques of the government and religious authorities. He is a member of Nahdatul Ulama[4] a religious, social, and political organization that was led by the late Abdulrahman Wahid (Gus Dur), an Islamic intellectual and former president of Indonesia who initiated or promoted inter-religious dialogue especially among Christians and Muslims.

The musical style used by Emha Ainun Nadjib and Kyai Kanjeng[5] is *campur sari*,[6] a type of *gamelan* fusion[7] ensemble that includes Western musical instruments, such as the electric guitar, bass guitar, drums, and keyboards as well as the gamelan instruments. Described by scholars as "a product of musical interaction between one or more cultures, with a wide rand of forms, this musical hybrid consists of the elements of *keroncong*, Javenese gamelan, *dangdut*, and popular music is extremely popular among the Javenese" (Suppangah 2003, 10). The diversity of instruments, such as *saron* instruments, *suling* flute tuned to the Arabic scale, violin, electric bass, keyboard, Arab *'ūd* and *qānūn*, *dangdut* drums, *rebana* frame drums, Javenese *kendang* and drum kit, and language with Javanese Islamic *shawalat*[8] songs, sung in Arabic, Indonesian, and Javanese reflect the plurality, openness, and depth of intercultural flexibility of the group.

4. Nahdatul Ulama (NU) is a religious, social and political organization that was formed in 1926 by several ulamas who wanted to preserve Islamic religious culture and promote the spirit of nationalism in response to the encroaching influences of modernization and colonialism. According to their website, they are the largest Muslim organization in Indonesia with an estimated 30 million followers. From 1984 to1989, Abdurrahman Wahid (also known as Gus Dur), the grandson of the first NU founder Hasyim Asy'ari, led NU. Abdurrahman Wahid was the President of Indonesia for two years (1999–2000). See http://www.nu.or.id/page.php?lang=en (accessed April 10, 2011).

5. Emha Ainun Nadjib and Kyai Kanjeng Sepuh have released three noteworthy cassette albums which are successful among Indonesian youth. These cassette tapes contain "Muhammad's Gift", 1998; "Wirid Padang Bulan" (Padang Bulan Recitation) 1999; and "Maiyah Tanah Air" (Togetherness of Our Country) 2001." (Barendregt and Zanten Popular Music In Indonesia, 79.)

6. Supanggah 2003, 10. Rahayu Supanggah has described campur sari as a product of musical interaction between one or more cultures, with a wide range of forms. Campur sari is a mixture of karawitan and keroncong, with langgam and dangdut music, and (to a certain extent) rock music.

7. See also Barendregt and van Zanten 2002, 79–80, for an analysis on Kyai Kanjeng Music.

8. In the 1990s they became famous with Indonesian audiences for their first album "Kado Muhammad" with the hit song titled, "Tombo Ati," which contained a religious message.

Suarasama and Irwansyah Harahap

Formed in 1995 by Irwansyah Harahap and Rithaony Hutajulu in Medan, North Sumatra, Suarasama's ensemble consists of five to nine musicians who are mostly students and graduates of the department of ethnomusicology, Universitas Sumatra Utara (University of North Sumatra). They have produced three music albums, the first being *Fajar di Atas Awan* ("Dawn Above Clouds"). The title song from that album, *Fajar di Atas Awan*, was compiled in *Music of Indonesia Vol. 20*, produced by the Smithsonian (1999). In August 2008 this album was reissued by Dragcity of Chicago, USA in both CD and vinyl and was distributed in several countries all over the world (USA, Canada, Europe, Australia, Japan, Singapore, etc). The second album, *Rites of Passages* (2002), and *Lebah* ("Bee"; 2008) are indie albums.

As with Kyai Kanjeng, Suarasama is also extremely diverse. In terms of instrumentation, Suarasama draws from the rich plethora of ethnic musical instruments predominantly from Asian cultures. For example, in their first album, the group incorporated instruments such as the Malay *gambus* (a lute influenced by Arabic and particularly Yemeni traditions), the Persian *daff*, and Indian *tabla* and *sruti* box. In Suarasama's other albums, "*Rites of Passage*" and "*Lebah*," instruments such as the Turkish *saz*, electric *sitar* (an adaptation of the Indian instrument), African *djembe*, and Toba Batak *hasapi* were used. Furthermore, the group does not project itself as an exclusively Muslim ensemble performing only Islamic music. Instead, musicians from all faiths are recruited and, at any given performance, there are Muslims and Christians collaborating together. The ensemble is also a mix of the old and the new with young and upcoming students performing with the more experienced performers who have been with the ensemble since its inception. Indeed, Suarasama is more like a music community.

Figure 14: Suarasama: Irwansyah Harahap (co-founder and director)
performs with wife, Rithaony Hutajulu (co-founder)

As the main composer for Suarasama, Irwansyah Harahap is particularly well versed in the Toba Batak gondang music and skilled in the Malay *gambus*. During his studies in the University of Washington, he studied under several musicians from different cultures such as Nusrat Ali Fateh Khan (Pakistan), Silvestre Randafison (Madagascar), Sujat Hussein Khan and Akhram Khan (India), and Darius Talai (Iran). With exposure to such rich and wide influences, Irwansyah's musical compositions are based on various musical concepts and aesthetics of world musics, such as African, Middle Eastern, Indian, Pakistani Sufi, Eastern European, Southeast Asian, as well as North Sumatran music (Batak and Malay) traditions. In Indonesia, Suarasama falls within the category of "world music" since they perform mostly in the context of world music and jazz music festivals.

Aside from his diverse musical orientation, Irwansyah Harahap as a Muslim creates music that flows from his personal interpretations of love and hope toward God. There are also songs whose themes are related to peace and humanity. "Fajar di Atas Awan" (Dawn above the Clouds) is "an example of many of Irwansyah's songs concerned with religion, here the peace that comes when faith reasserts itself after a period of doubt and distance from God. The composer . . . notes that 'spiritually, textually, and musically' the song is influenced by Nusrat Fateh Ali Khan, (a world renowned Pakistani musician) and *qawālī*, the devotional music of the Sufis" (Smithsonian Folkway Recordings 1999).

Figure 15: Suarasama Ensemble Members Performing

Many of his musical compositions are basically in the form of instrumental music, sometimes adding vocal humming; there are also some lyrical songs. Irwansyah himself believes that "the nature of music is 'in sounds itself,' [musical] texts could only deliver (the) messages, not (the) meanings."[9]

Peacebuilding through Socioreligious Gatherings

Emha Ainun Najib, along with Kyai Kanjeng, has initiated many approaches to peacebuilding in the form of Islamic socioreligious gatherings (*Shawalatan*). The first religious gathering he conducted was at Padang Bulan, a monthly gathering at the Jombang area in East Java in the mid-1980s. Subsequently in 1990, *Kenduri Cinta*, a forum for cultural friendship and humanity, was initiated at Taman Ismail Marzuki (TIM) in Jakarta. This forum, or "performed discourse" as Rasmussen (1998, 198) aptly calls it, is conducted in a very open, non-partisan, and lighthearted way and embraces a cross-genre approach to the arts. In Jogjakarta in Central Java, another gathering called Maiyayah/ Macapat Syafaat—*maiyah* means meeting; *macapat* refers to a Javanese six-line verse form; while *syafaat* means religious meditation—was formed and included a monthly Qur'anic recitation. Each of these community forums involved hundreds of participants who would come and listen to music, poetry, and religious sermons and also participate in sociocultural discussions.

In the last few years, the gatherings focused on establishing discussion forums that brought together not only students and religious leaders from varying Islamic affiliations but those from Catholic and Protestant communities in Indonesia. During *Kenduri Cinta*—*Kenduri* means a ritual gathering that involves a common meal; *Cinta* means "love"—authorities from various religious bodies in Indonesia are invited to discuss pressing social and political issues particularly on the issue of interreligious tolerance in Indonesia. This socioreligious gathering has become a venue for various groups, for political actors, religious figures, and popular artists to interact with each other under the basic commonality of love and has become a routine gathering attended by hundreds of participants from various communities. On its impact, Rasmussen asserts, "conflict resolution or at the very least communal catharsis occurs predictably during the course of any given evening, as Nadjib honors the diversity of local voices, by sharing music, entertaining questions and contributions from the audience, reading poetry or discussing local issues" (2010, 199).

9. Harahap August 11, 2010.

Emha has consistently promoted peace among interfaith communities by using music as a vehicle toward this goal. Evidence of this is seen when he has been invited to speak during Christmas celebrations in churches in the vicinity of Jogjakarta. Because of the inclusive nature of his performances, he and his band Kyai Kanjeng Sepuh have also been invited to perform in several countries abroad since 2005: Australia, Holland, and several Arab countries.[10] They are known in Indonesia for their ability to mediate and facilitate cross-cultural, -ethnic, and -religious dialogues using the arts.

The process of music making in Kyai Kanjeng is centered around Emha's ideas and creativity. For the musical arrangements, the members usually try to interpret Emha's suggestions. A Kyai Kanjeng performance involves the combination of narration or sermon and poetry with the accompaniment of, or alternating with, musical performance. Emha's creativity lies more in the realm of the textual, where music becomes an accompaniment and strengthens the message of Emha's narrations and orations.

Peacebuilding through the Process of Music Making

The underlying philosophy behind Suarasama's musical compositions and performance can be analyzed through the name of the group. Suarasama[11] is compound of two words, "suara" and "sama," both of which have multiple meanings. In the Indonesian language, the term "suara" means "voice, sounds, opinion" or "thought." At the same time, suara is derived from the Sanskrit word "svara" which means "melody." The word sama in Indonesian language means "equal" or "togetherness" and has its roots in Arabic where samāʿī means "listening with a deep soul" and also "proportion." As Irwansyah is deeply influenced by many Sufi traditional musical cultures, the word samāʿ, as in the Sufi tradition, means "a hearing with the 'ear of the heart,' an attitude of reverently listening to music and/or the singing of mystical poetry with the intent of increasing awareness and understanding of the divine object described; it is a type of meditation focusing on musical melody, by use of instruments, mystical songs or combining both"

10. In October 2008 Emha Ainun Najib with his ensemble was invited by Prostentante Kerk Netherlands (Protestant Church Council) to perform in several cities in Holland for three weeks. During the stay he had chances to speak with several religious authorities in Holland like Driss el-Boujoufi representing the Dutch Islamic community and Awraham Soetendorp representing the Dutch Jewish community, as well as other Protestant and Catholic leaders. See http://www.padhangmbulan.com/info/4-berita/131-deklarasi-damai-islam-yahudi-kristen.html.

11. Irwansyah and Rithaohny studied various concepts and aesthetics of music cultures of the world through their studies in ethnomusicology at the University of North Sumatra since the 1980s and at the University of Washington from 1990 to 1995.

(Lewisohn 1997, 4). Regarding the significance of the choice of the name, Irwansyah explains further the name's significance as an "attempt to create understanding between people (by means of music) without setting some up as superior to others" (Smithsonian Folkway Recordings 1999).

This underlying philosophical name of Suarasama is also applied and manifested in the process of music making among the group. With Suarasama, music making emphasizes communication among the musicians, the practice of listening to each other, and learning how to make music in proportion and harmony with the other musicians. For example, in Suarasama's musical arrangements, the sounds are multilayered and every instrument has a defined part and time to play. Not all instruments are played throughout the composition where, for example, a performer sometimes only plays the cymbal at the beginning and at the end of a particular composition with another musician playing drone notes using the Indian *sruti* box. Additionally, while one musician keeps particular repetitive drumming patterns, the others will play in interlocking patterns and rhythmic improvisations. Or, some of Irwansyah's music compositions oftentimes begin with free improvisations of a solo melodic instrument for several minutes before other instruments and voices are added texturally to the piece.

During a Suarasama music rehearsal Irwansyah usually begins by explaining the basic concepts of the piece that will be played. As the practice proceeds, musicians who are not having their parts rehearsed will sit and listen. For Irwansyah, it is vital that every musician knows all the musical parts that are being played and the performer has to exercise his or her ability to the other musicians in relation to his/her own. Through this method of musical practice, Irwansyah believes that "everyone will learn to understand something outside or beyond selfness."[12]

Another way in which the process of "peace building" is implemented in Suarasama's music is through the use of tempos that tend to be relatively slow and repetitive. According to Irwansyah, persons who play in this tempo practice the value of "patience." He is of the opinion that "if a person cannot practice patience he/she will never understand "the feeling of peace."

Interfaith Dialogue through Music

Both Emha and Irwansyah use music and performance as a means of interfaith dialogue effectively. The following are two examples.

12. Harahap August 11, 2010.

Silent Night in *Shawalat*[13] *Badr* Words: Kyai Kanjeng

In events that involve communities from varying religious[14] backgrounds, especially from the Christian communities, Emha specifically chooses relevant musical repertoires and arrangements to suit the participants. One piece that is quite often performed by Kyai Kanjeng is *"Silent Night* using *Shawalat Words,"* in which Emha and Kyai Kanjeng sing the Christian melody of "Silent Night" with Indonesian Muslim *Shawalat Badr* devotional texts. This is appropriate in that, on the one hand, the song phrases or *shawalat,* are common to Indonesian Muslims as a type of religious poetry denoting "praise for the prophet Muhammad" and, on the other hand, "Silent Night" (translated, *Malam Kudus*) is a Catholic and Protestant carol. Both "Silent Night" and *"Shawalat Badr"* melodies and lyrics are to a certain degree already familiar to all Indonesians regardless of their religious backgrounds, with the *shawalat* being heard especially during the Ramaḍān[15] season and "Silent Night" universally heard during Christmas. *Shawalat* as the form used is also appropriate, as it is known as "music for everyone." It is participatory in nature and is a "kind of music making by the group and for the group." Interestingly, while the texts are devotionals, the function of shawalat is primarily social (Rasmussen 2010, 180). The following is an example of a *Shawalat Badr* text:

> Shalatullah Salamullah
>
> Alla Toha Rasullilah
>
> Shalattullah Sallamullah
>
> Alla Yasin Habibillah
>
> Tawassalna Bibismillah
>
> Wabil Hadi Rasulillah
>
> Wakulli Mujahidilillah
>
> Bi Ahlil Badri Ya Allah

13. Shalawat are religious songs, usually in praise of praise of the Prophet Muhammad often in the Arabic language.

14. The relationship between Islam and Christianity in Indonesia can be viewed as a "silent dispute," although the degree of this feeling varies among different communities. However, under the Pancasila ideology that has been implemented since the New Order era, the five official religions that are officially recognized by the Indonesian government (Islam, Protestantism, Catholicism, Hinduism, and Buddhism [and now Confucianism]) can live side by side and practice their respective faiths, and many efforts have been made to foster peacebuilding and harmony between Muslim and Christian communities.

15. Ramaḍān is the month in the Islamic tradition during which Muslims conduct a fasting ritual throughout the course of the month.

Shalatullah Salamullah

Alla Toha Rasullilah

Shalattullah Sallamullah

Alla Yasin Habibillah

God's grace and salvation

May he always remain a prophet, a messenger of God

God's grace and salvation

May he remain *yassin*,[16] a beloved prophet of God

We testify to the blessing of the name of God

And by the prophet who shows [the truth], [he then] is the messenger of God

And all those who fight for God

Blessed are the companions of *badar*,[17] O God.

Therefore, Emha and Kyai Kanjeng use "*Silent Night* in *Shawalat Words*" as a symbol or a form of expression of religious tolerance (Rambitan 2003, 46)[18] and reconciliation between Christian and Muslim communities. In performing the song, Emha often begins by asking the Christian group of singers (the church choir) to sing "*Malam Kudus*" ("Silent Night") accompanied by the Kyai *Kanjeng* ensemble. Following that, he and the ensemble continue singing the same tune (of "Silent Night") using *Shawalat Badr* lyrics. This is a demonstration of a form of interreligious dialogue through music performance whereby Muslim and Christian musicians can perform and share the same stage, singing side by side and in collaboration. "*Shawalat Badr* in *Silent Night*" has become Kyai Kanjeng's most important piece in promoting interreligious dialogue and they have performed this piece in many places in Indonesia, on their European tour, in Malaysia, and in Arabic countries.

As shown in a Kyai Kanjeng video documentary, Emha seems to exercise caution as he demonstrates the *Shawalat Badr* using the melodic phrases of "Silent Night." He says, "I would like to apologize to my Muslim

16. *Yassin* is a name of one chapter in Al Qur'an (Islamic holy book).

17. *Badar* is the name of a major war that prophet Muhammad himself fought together with his followers.

18. Rev. Rambitan explains that the relationship is somewhat of a "'dispute' between Christianity and Islam in Indonesia. This is especially due to the ways in which the two religions perceive Jesus within the purview of their respective religions. He elaborates on the need to understand Jesus as portrayed in the Bible, Jesus in the Qu'ran and finally the ways to introduce and communicate Jesus in the Indonesian Christian and Muslim community."

friends. This is for my Christian friends." He then goes on to explain that "Muslims should not sing "Silent Night" using the original words but they can still collaborate in the performance while on the same stage. As he says humorously albeit accurately, "If you are a goat, be a goat. If you are a buffalo, be a buffalo. But you can't mix a goat and a buffalo. So let everybody be who they are, but let them live in harmony in the same place."[19] The impressions of the audience, both Muslim and Christian, as they hear this song, cannot be fully explored in this paper. However, one initial observation is that through the use of the song, Emha attempts to break previous narrow assumptions regarding the song. Dr. Krabill, during the Songs of Peace and Reconciliation consultation in Jogjakarta, 2010, mentioned that the melody of certain songs such as "Silent Night" possess definite associations with Christianity. In my opinion, this is the very reason why Emha chose this particular song and the music. As Indonesians have already internalized these lyrics describing the birth of Jesus Christ and have only associated it with Christianity, Emha attempts to challenge or break this narrow perception of the use of the song. As he said after demonstrating this piece in front of an audience in Aceh, "There are no so-called Christian songs, there are no so-called Muslim songs. I am doing *shawalat*."

Shalawat to the Prophets: Suarasama

Aside from performing and using music as a tool to practice "peace" and "equality" within all musical cultures, Irwansyah has composed some songs that reflect interfaith dialogue. The third Suarasama album, *Lebah* ("Bee") aptly demonstrates this. On the record jacket, Irwansyah articulates that the album is "an interpretation of the mystery of the long journey/history of civilization (*sebuah tafsir tentang misteri perjalanan sebuah peradaban*." In this album Irwansyah composed three pieces that represent three icons or prophetic figures of the Abrahamic religions (Islam, Christianity, and Judaism) with songs titled, *Ibrahim Alaihissalam* (*Abraham Peace Be upon Him*), *Isa Alaihissalam* (*Jesus Peace Be upon Him*), and *Habibullah: Muhammad Shallallahu Alihiwassalam* (*Muhammad Peace Be upon Him*). The lyrics of these songs are basically "praise to the prophets." The following are the texts of the songs mentioned above[20]:

Ibrahim Alaisalam (Abraham, Peace Be upon Him)

It has long waited, my heart's passion longing

19. See Milovanovic 31 May 2010.
20. See Jogyakarta concert at the French Cultural Center footage.

To pray to my Lord, in total willingness

You give promise, to give with heart and soul

In my loneliness, I bow down to God

Yea Illahi, Allahu Rabbi, I surrender to You Rabbi [my Lord]

Yea Illahi, Allahu Rabbi, I give thanks to You Rabbi [my Lord]

Months become years, times becomes a guide

Two descended of the same family, the origin of all human beings

He becomes a sign, of the greatness of his God

Two who are brothers, born of the mercy of two mothers

He becomes a story, the Prophet of God the Creator

His heart has been tested, pious to his God

He has been greeted by all of humankind

His grave has been exalted, his name has been praised

Yea, Abraham, peace be upon him, Yea Abraham, peace be upon him

Yea, Abraham, peace be upon him, Yea Abraham, peace be upon him

(Yea Rabbi, Yea Rabbi, Yea Rabbi)

Isa Alaihissalam (Jesus, Peace Be upon Him)

Nun stars twinkle, white clouds spread out

Birds are singing, welcoming the arrival of the Beloved

Yea Jesus, peace be upon him Yea Jesus, peace be upon him (2X)

Yea Jesus, peace be upon him, Yea Prophet, peace be upon him

When he was born, the power was given

He was ordered, to bring the message of praise

Yea Jesus, peace be upon him Yea Jesus, peace be upon him (2X)

Yea Jesus, peace be upon him, Yea Prophet, peace be upon him

He teaches love, affection and hope

He reminds us that sin can be exchanged for salvation

Yea Jesus, peace be upon him Yea Jesus, peace be upon him (2X)

Yea Jesus, peace be upon him, Yea Prophet, peace be upon him

He was predestined to be the lighter of the way

He was resurrected, to bring a message of praise

Yea Jesus, peace be upon him Yea Jesus, peace be upon him (2X)

Yea Jesus, peace be upon him, Yea Prophet, peace be upon him

Habibullah, Muhammad Ya Rasullulah
(Beloved of God, Muhammad Apostle of God)

Beloved of God . . . Yea apostle of God

Yea Muhammad, honored Prophet

Salawat and peace to you . . . oh, Prophet

The promise of God upon his beloved

Yea Muhammad, God's mercy upon the universe

A gift from above for the life of the guide that brings his followers to him

Yea . . . apostle of God . . . Yea apostle of God

Yea . . . apostle of God . . . Yea Beloved of God

According to Irwansyah Harahap, through these three songs he tries to represent the historical interpretation of the Abrahamic religions in which all of the three different religions are derived from the same roots. All of them bring "peace" (*salām*) to the earth and human beings and it is a peace that originates from God. Furthermore he points out that interestingly, all the three prophetic figures are prominent within the scriptural texts of Christians and Muslims.[21] However, in my observation, Jesus (in Christianity) or Isa (in Islam) is almost never included in *shawalat* or praise to the prophet among Muslims in Indonesia. To this point, Irwansyah comments, "this is an attempt to renegotiate the legacy of Islam and Christianity which basically come from the same roots." He continues, "Scriptures can be interpreted differently and religion can be an ideological subject. However, faith and truth is something that you find within yourself."[22]

The Power of Music to Communicate Peace

Having discussed each ensemble, this section discusses the power of music to communicate peace through Emha Ainun Najib's and Irwansyah Harahap's experiences with their ensembles. The focus will be on how these messages are delivered through music and conveyed and communicated to audiences and listeners.

Kyai Kanjeng's music has fused many songs from various genres ranging from Arabic sounds to Javanese traditional music and music of the Western world in such a way that it can be presented through Kyai Kanjeng's *gamelan* ensemble. Emha brings to his listeners a music that adopts many styles of music and combines them to create a new form. Besides the "Silent Night" adaptation, Kyai Kanjeng has also adopted songs like "Imagine" from

21. Dr. William Hodges, one of the Songs of Peace Reconciliation consultation participants who is an ethnomusicologist as well as theologian, in his interview with a Kompas newspaper reporter said that Islam and Christianity, in fact, share many similarities including the prophets.

22. Harahap August 11, 2010.

John Lennon and "Sailing" by Rod Stewart. In terms of musical characteristics, and their openness to sounds from outside their local cultural milieu, what Kyai Kanjeng has done is not something new but their music has contributed to the development of *campur sari* in Java. It emphasizes creativity and flexibility as Rahayu Supanggah notes:

> *Campur sari* reflects the degree of pluralism in artistic taste, aesthetic understanding, and application of ethical norms in the Javanese community today. The inclusion of various styles of regional music (including Western music) also reflects the openness and depth of cultural relations, both national and international, by Javanese society. (2003, 15)

This chosen style and repertoire is significant as it is a living representation of the discourse between local Javanese society and the global world. Creating a performance using such diverse elements and cultural styles also involves a lively set of group dynamics of cultural interaction that involve dissonance, adaptation, dialogue, and openness, all of which are elements that contribute to peacebuilding. Furthermore, this incorporation of diverse musical elements has provided Emha with opportunities to interact with others outside of his religious community:

> With Kyai Kanjeng music I traveled around seven cities in Holland, October 2008, entered Protestant and Catholic Churches, entered a synagogue as well as mosques. We met with leaders from other religions. One result was the birth of "Peace Declaration" among Muslim, Christians and Jews from all over Holland that was launched on January 8th, 2009. ("Deklarasi Damai Islam-Yahudi-Kristen." 2009)[23]

Another interesting point is the ability of the Kyai Kanjeng performance to create a discourse around music. According to his blog "Musik dan Jagad Politik Republik 2009" (Music and Republic Political Discourse 2009), Emha recounts how Kyai Kanjeng's performance in London opened up an important discussion with Yusuf Islam (Cat Stevens) regarding the topic of the permissibility of music in Islam. Emha's point is as follows:

> There is nothing wrong for Muslims to drive cars, use airplanes, refrigerators and mobile phones although Muslims created none of these. From Indonesia, we bring the Kyai Kanjeng *gamelan*

23. This declaration was agreed upon between the Muslims of the Government of Netherlands, the Council of Churches in the Neterlands and Awraham Soetendorp of the Dutch Union of Progressive Judaism. This agreement was conveyed to the Al-Azhar University, Cairo. http://www.facebook.com/note.php?note_id=43005343457

and it is the same thing as you driving your car. All these are only vehicles. What is wrong for a Muslim regarding music are two things: First, bringing music inside the mosque, playing music to accompany prayer, and mixing other *ibadah mhdloh* [everything that related to faith] with music. The second problem is when a Muslim does not place God above everything else, hurts other people and takes something that does not belong to him. (Nadjib 2009)

Suarasama's music, particularly the album *Fajar di Atas Awan* (Dawn above the Clouds) has been described as quiet, evocative, and beautiful. The music crosses language and cultural barriers and effectively evokes intended rich imagery within the hearer. Audience reviews of Suarasama's albums reveal how music communicates peace with one particular thread pointing out how music inculcates inner peace within the listener. From the album, *Fajar di Atas Awan* (Dawn above the Clouds) produced in 1998, comes this pertinent comment:

The album title translates to "dawn over clouds," and the music does reflect that heavenly (or, more broadly, spiritual) imagery. With compositions that rarely fall short of the seven-minute mark, and one that runs twice that, the group's songs are given room to stretch and breathe, achieving a certain inner peace that overcomes whatever cultural or language barriers might keep people from connecting with them. (Klein 2008)

Suarasama's music, described as "patient music, never in a hurry to get anywhere in particular, yet all the more impactful when it reaches its destination," allows the listener to slow down and be absorbed in the affective power of the music and the meditative mood it evokes. Another comment echoes this:

When listening to the title track on Suarasama's first ever vinyl release, you don't need to know that *Fajar di Atas Awan* translates to Dawn Over the Clouds in order to picture a slow rising sun over mist and mountains. That's the beauty of this quiet, evocative album. Even if you don't understand a word of Indonesian, you'll still be captivated by the diverse instrumentation and meditative mood. (Pearson 2008)

Elaborating on how music evokes inner peace, another commentator describes this piece as a "composition above the sky that penetrates the veil of the heart." The strength of the piece is in its lyrical content that contains textual meaning and also "the repetitive rhythms that imitate heart beats that communicates a feeling of calm and peace."[24] When this is accomplished, cultural or language barriers are broken down leaving the audience ready to connect more deeply with the music.

The strong element of faith and spirituality deeply embedded in Suarasama's performances also contributes to peacebuilding. "At its core, this is devotional music, with melodic and rhythmic arrangements that—besides evoking mist-covered mountains—communicate themes of faith and spiritual ecstasy" (Pearson 2008). From two other comments on the album we note the spiritual intonations:

> This really fine-sounding music, really beautiful expression of the soul. The songs and singing derive from Muslim devotionals, and the holy air spreads through every room that the music comes into . . . faith is a theme of the lyrics, which even when not translated or understood, convey their essences with a meditative, prayerful approach, often using multi-part harmonies that indicate at (and create in the listener) higher ecstasies . . . While any epiphanies are ultimately in the ear of the beholder, there's no question that the group is reaching for something bigger than itself, searching beyond borders in all directions and dimensions for spiritual truth by way of melody. (Klein 2008)

With deepening spirituality through music, a greater awareness of others and the interrelated world we live in is engendered. Indeed, "the world grows closer and smaller, but no less wonderful and exciting; the sound of its people and the impulses within them still an exotic treasure. As walls come down and our neighbors come closer, Suarasama seeks to bring us the song inside us all" (Norman Records n.d.). Clearly, peacebuilding is enhanced because spirituality causes barriers to be broken and crossed and enables a greater sensitivity and tolerance to other religions and cultures.

Thus, we see that music can be interpreted in many different ways depending on the listener but one common thread is that it can communicate feelings of peace and reconciliation. Irwansyah believes that music is able to build awareness of interrelationships that surround us individually and communally. As a result, we learn about each other and mutual understanding is built. Music transcends ideology and dogma and is a vehicle that delivers meaning that can be interpreted freely and subjectively. For, as Irwansyah notes, music is fully intertwined with what he calls, "the meaning of life itself."[25]

---

24. Patricia Angelica, Comment about Youtube video of Suarasama, "Fajar di Atas Awan," on Facebook, August 3rd, 2010. (Original comment is in Indonesian.)

25. Harahap August 11, 2010.

Conclusion

In light of the above discussion, it is evident that music has been used as a vehicle to foster peace and reconciliation. The above approaches show some similarities and differences as to how this is achieved. It is interesting that in both these cases music is used to convey ideas and feelings of peace and reconciliation. On the one hand, Kyai Kanjeng focuses on the power of narration and the religious message through the music that they present. Suarasama, on the other hand, lets the music itself "speak" the message of peace and reconciliation. In terms of musical sounds, Kyai Kanjeng takes elements of music that are the most popular and the most accessible to the ear of their listeners. Suarasama chooses genres of music that have long histories and traditions using them as symbols to remind the listener to return to the rich heritage of music and religious traditions in the world. In order to create a symbol of oneness through music, both Suarasama and Kyai Kanjeng desire to find a "common sound" that is the point of commonality and a bridge for people of all religions of the world. These two cases point to two Indonesian Islamic perspectives regarding the relationship with Christianity in view of the inherent differences that have arisen since these two religions were brought to Indonesia.

Finally, let me end with these two apt quotations that summarize the philosophy of these two groups regarding peace:

> "*Salam* means reconciliation, Islam means to create freedom toward reconciliation, Islam means working towards a peaceful life for all human beings."[26] (Emha Ainun Nadjib)

> "We share the same world, We share the same sun,
> We share the same air, All of it come from the One."
> (Irwansyah Harahap)[27]

---

26. Nadjib 18 February 2012.

27. Excerpt of Irwansyah Harahap's song lyrics, "We Share," a song commissioned for the Jogyakarta Songs of Peace and Reconciliation consultation, April 2010.

FOR DISCUSSION

1. Create a chart that will compare and contrast Kyai Kanjeng and Suarasama within these categories: instruments, genres, performers, influences.

2. Both music groups use theologically rich song texts. What might be the advantages and disadvantages of using theological texts in fostering peace between Muslim and Christian communities? How do Emha Ainun Nadjib and Irwansyah Harahap deal with these disadvantages?

3. From the examples within this chapter, we see that peace and transformation within communities are developed by the power of music and the power within music. Contrast these two perspectives of music as utilized by Kyai Kanjeng and Suarasama.

4. Using Jared Holton's schematic from the previous section of this book, classify the peacemaking efforts through music illustrated in this chapter.

5. PROJECT: Choose one of the two music groups to research. Go to the official website of either Kyai Kanjeng (www.caknun.com) or Suarasama (www.suarasama.or.id) and explore the information, recent news, and discography presented. Choose five songs from past albums and listen to them without taking notes. Afterwards, record your reactions and reflections. Listen to these songs again and record further reflections as you listen. How do the song texts (get a translation if necessary), style of singing, and instrumentation, melody, and rhythm come together for the purposes of peacemaking? How do these reflections extend your understanding of how music can be utilized in peacebuilding efforts?

References Cited:

Barendregt, Bart, and Wim Van Zanten. 2002. "Popular Music In Indonesia Since 1998, In Particular Fusion, Indie And Islamic Music on Video Compact Discs And The Internet." *Year Book For Traditional Music* 34: 66–113.

Betts, Ian L. 2006. *Jalan Sunyi Emha*. Jakarta: Penerbit Budaya Kompas.

Gehr, Richard. 2008. "Suarasama's Tour of Indonesia. The Village Voice." http://www.villagevoice.com/2008-08-12/music/suarasama-s-tour-of-indonesia/.

Harahap, Irwansyah. Interview by author. Medan, Indonesia. August 11, 2010.

Harnish, David D., and Anne K. Rasmussen. 2011. *Divine Inspirations: Music and Islam In Indonesia*. New York: Oxford University Press.

Keil, Charles, and Steven Feld. 2003. *Music Grooves: Essays And Dialogues*. Chicago: University of Chicago Press.

Klein, Joshua. 2008. "Suarasama: Fajar di Atas Awan." http://pitchfork.com/reviews/albums/12218-fajar-di-atas-awan/. Accessed April 11, 2011.

Lewisohn, Leonard. 1997. "The Sacred Music of Islam: Sama' in the Persian Sufi Tradition." *British Journal of Ethnomusicology* 6: 1–33.

Milovanovic, Selma. 31 May 2010. "Indonesian Singer Tapping into Fame to Deliver a Message of Peace." http://www.theage.com.au/world/indonesian-singer-tapping-into-fame-to-deliver-a-message-of-peace-20100530-wnfe.html.

Nadjib, Emha Ainun. 2009. "The Silent Pilgrimage." http://www.thesilentpilgrimage.blogspot.com/.

———. 2009. "Musik dan Jagat Politik Republic." http://media.isnet.org/sufi/Etc/Musik.html.

———. 18 February 2012. "*Islam adalah*" (Islam is). http://caknunartikel.blogspot.com/2012/02/islam-adalah-cakn-nun.html.

Norman Records. N.d. "Suarasama: Fajar di Atas Awan." http://www.normanrecords.com/cd/101019-suarasama-fajar-di-atas-awan.

O'Connell, John M., and Salwa El Shawan Castelo-Branco. 2010. *Music and Conflict*. Chicago: University of Illinois Press.

Pearson, Laura. 2008. *Suarasama: Fajar Di Atas Awan (Drag City)*. http://www.venuszine.com/articles/music/sounds/4128/Suarasama-28k.

Rambitan, Rev. Stanley R. 2003. "Jesus in Islamic Context of Indonesia." *Rec Focus* 3, no. 2: 38–48.

Rasmussen, Anne K. 2010. *Women, the Recited Qur'an, and Islamic Music in Indonesia*. Berkeley: University of California Press.

Smithsonian Folkways. 1999. "Music of Indonesia, Vol. 20: Indonesian Guitars." *Smithsonian Folkway Recordings*. http://media.smithsonianfolkways.org/liner_notes/smithsonian_folkways/SFW40447.pdf.

Supanggah, Rahayu. 2003. "Campur Sari: A Reflection." *Asian Music: An Indonesian Issue* 34, no. 2: 1–20.

CHAPTER 11

A *Samanic* Messenger

Interfaith Dialogue through Art Performance[1]

by Irwansyah Harahap

Peace is about consciousness. If we make it narrow, it'll be narrower; if we make it wide, it'll be wider.

—MARZUKI HASAN

Introduction

Music performances and performers have a unique ability to transcend cultural and religious barriers, to bridge differences, and to create solidarity. This paper highlights the *saman* traditional art performance of Aceh as one such example and Marzuki Hasan, a widely acclaimed master artist of the *saman* tradition, as one such performer.

Peacebuilding and healing of and from conflict are two vital areas for the peoples of Aceh, a land that has borne the brunt of a civil war that began in 1976 between the Indonesian government and the Free Aceh Movement (GAM), and the massive natural disaster of the tsunami on 26 December 2004 in which 200,000 people died (Kartomi 2009). In the aftermath of the

1. This paper was written for a consultation forum "Songs of Peace and Reconciliation: A Comparative Study of Music, Worship and the Arts among Muslims and Christians." The first forum was held in Beirut, Lebanon, April 1–5, 2009; and the second forum was held in Jogjakarta, Indonesia, March 31–April 3, 2010. I would like to thank Dr. Tan Sooi Ling for assisting me in the process of constructing this paper.

tsunami, although a peace accord was struck ending the civil conflict, many survivors had already suffered significant trauma. In the process of rebuilding Aceh, I had the opportunity to collaborate with Hasan on "Rising above the Tsunami: Restoration and Recovery through Reviving the Acehnese Intangible Cultural Heritage," a field project conducted by Sacred Bridge Foundation Jakarta in collaboration with UNESCO whose goal was to bring healing and restoration through the arts. During the three-month duration of this program, from January to March 2006 in Banda Aceh, Nanggroe Aceh Darussalam (NAD) province, Indonesia, I had the opportunity to observe Hasan as he taught, performed, and helped bring healing through the arts. As I engaged in intimate informal conversations with him, I was intrigued by how he has inculcated peace in his life and with others through his varied experiences as a widely acclaimed performer, both locally and globally, and as a teacher at Institut Kesenian Jakarta (Jakarta Arts Institute).[2]

This paper addresses how interfaith dialogue is promoted and how peace is fostered through the traditional art performance of *saman* in Indonesia. It focuses on an individual, Marzuki Hasan,[3] who has shaped and adapted this traditional art form to align with the multicultural and multireligious Indonesian society to the extent that *saman* is now regarded as both a traditional and a modern art performance. I argue that, by knowing and understanding the individual (Barnouw, cited by Kottak 2008, 10)[4] artist's experiences, we can learn how *saman* as an art expression and a way of communication can increase mutual understanding among diversities of cultures and becomes the language of peace and reconciliation.

This discussion comprises three sections. First, a description of the *saman* performance will be elucidated. In particular, this section highlights the use and functions of the *saman*, its aesthetics, undergirding philosophical and religious beliefs as it pertains to peacebuilding. Second, a biography of Hasan as a *samanic* artist is enumerated. Following this will be a discussion

2 I later had a chance to interact with him quite frequently in 2007–2008 during the "Rhythm Salad" collaborative music clinic and workshop by Sacred Bridge Foundation in Jakarta, where we both were artists-instructors.

3. From my interactions with Hasan during the two projects, "Rising from the Tsunami" and "Rhythm Salad," I decided that Hasan's life experiences would be an appropriate topic to share in this colloquium.

4. I use the word "individual" here in projecting Hasan's personal views as related to the term "personality," which means "a more or less enduring organization of forces within the individual associated with a complex of fairly consistent attitudes, values, modes of perception which account in part for the individual's consistency of behavior." Kottak continued by saying, "The consistency of an individual's personality reveals itself in varied settings—work, rest, play, creative activities, and interaction with others. Thus, we can think of personality as an individual's characteristic ways of thinking and acting" (262).

on how one individual's, in this case Hasan's, experiences, attitudes, and actions impact a community toward peace as differences are bridged across cultures and religions and intercultural relationships forged. Some critical questions asked include: What are the philosophical beliefs undergirding *saman* that enhance peace? What are the social rules and aesthetic expressions of *saman* as it is performed in its cultural contexts that foster solidarity? How does an individual's worldviews and religious beliefs impact other performers and communities and help shape a healthy perspective toward plurality of cultures and religions?

The Samanic Performing Art

Saman is an Acehnese traditional performing art form from the area of Gayo in the south-western part of Aceh. More locally known as *tarian duduk* (sitting dance), or in the Acehnese language as *rateb meusekat* (for women's performance) and *saman* (for men's performance), it is an integrative art expression that combines *syair* (poetry), *nyanyian* (singing), and *tarian* (dancing). In this section I will describe the *saman* tradition highlighting three characteristics that contribute toward solidarity and community.

Saman in Community Ritual Life

Woven into the social and religious life of Acehnese society, *saman* is usually performed during Islamic celebrations such as Mawlid Nabi Muhammad SAW (Celebrating the Birth of the Prophet Muhammad, Peace be upon him) and the ʿĪd al-Fiṭr celebration that takes place after the Ramaḍān fasting ritual. Apart from that, *saman* is also performed during rituals such as weddings, circumcision or death ceremonies. Traditionally, it is an artistic form of "competition" (*saman jalu*) that takes place between two or more groups that are assembled from different villages, with each *saman* group consisting of fifteen to thirty people. The use of *saman* during festivals and special occasions provide space for the community to gather and to interact. Today, the *saman* (*Tari Saman*) is also performed outside the Acehnese contexts as a cultural performance and involves only a single group performance.

Saman: Cooperation and Competition

A *saman* performance is a perfect picture of harmony in song and motion. In any given performance, fifteen or more men or women kneel in a tight row and perform a combination of *syair* (sung poetry), hand gestures, and

torso movements. There are no accompanying instruments and the performance is carried melodically by voice and the rhythm kept rigorously by
handclaps, finger snaps, and hand slaps on the chest and thigh. In a compelling description of *saman*, Margeret Kartomi underscores this theme of
unity:

> In 1982 and in 2004–2009, I attended several all-night Sufi
> gatherings of brotherhoods in village heads' homes, *meunasah*
> or mosques. The men sat in circles singing praises of Allah,
> Muhammad and other prophets to their own frame-drum ac-
> companiment, or sang unaccompanied from the Dala'il Khairat
> book of supplications in soaring unison, led by a local *teungku*
> or *ulama*. As the men sang and prayed, some swayed from side
> to side and sometimes clapped together rhythmically. (2010, 90)

The need for precision and tight synchronization of movements in *saman* requires close cooperation among the members of the performance
group. Each person in the group has a designated and unique role to play
in contributing to the cohesiveness of the group performance. Situated in
the middle of the line is the *pengangkat* (raiser) who is the primary leader
of the group (*Syekh*). He is the central figure responsible for choosing the
themes of the *syairs* to be sung as a response to rival competitors, the melodic formulas that are often created spontaneously, and the choreography
of movements to be presented by the group. Second, there is the *pengapit*
(locker) who functions as a co-leader and is responsible for aiding the *pengangkat* in rendering the song or executing the types of dance movements.
Third, the *penupang* (holders) are the dancers on the extreme right and left
of the line of dancers. Their role is to ensure that the dancers are in position and the line remains tight and straight. Following an Achenese analogy,
their importance is likened to a *penamat kerpe jejerun* (holding the *jejerun*),
the *jejerun* being a type of grass with very strong roots that are difficult to
uproot. Finally, the *penyepit* (the ones who "act" in between) are the regular dancers who support the dance movements under the direction of the
pengapit (locker).[5] Close cooperation among performers is demonstrated as
each execution of the individual's performance is always done in relation to
other performers.

A *saman jalu* performance also thrives on the relational tension between cooperation and competition. Each village has its own repertory of
traditional, named gestures,[6] with the basic gesture (*lagu selalu*) being

5. "Deskripsi Tari Saman" (Saman Dance Description).

6. Over 130 gestures have been documented and more are being created. *New Grove
Dictionary of Music and Musicians*, s.v. "Saman."

placing the right hand on the left thigh, shifting it to the right thigh and back again, then striking the chest three times. On top of that, "each group develops its own *lagu gerriyet* (virtuoso gestures) in their ongoing efforts to confound their competitors" (Sadie and Tyrell 2002, 349). The criteria of a good *saman jalu* performance are how well and creative the *syair* is presented and how diverse and tight the body movements are. *Saman* cultural performances that feature a single group performance are judged mainly by the aesthetics of the dance performance. Whatever the case, the close cooperation required within each *saman* group and the friendly tensions elicited during intergroup competition contribute toward healthy group dynamics and foster solidarity.

In light of the above, it is clear that the nature of *saman* contains an underlying basic philosophical concept of social life and relationships. During the *saman* rehearsals, Hasan points out, "we learn to discipline ourselves toward *kebersamaan* (togetherness); *kemufakatan* (social consensus), *membina kerukunan* (social balance and solidarity), *kekompakan* (friendship), and *kesatuan masyarakat* (unity within society)."[7] In other words, *saman* is a way of practicing personal as well as social behavior emphasizing the values of togetherness, social consensus, social solidarity, friendship, and unity. In Marzuki's poignant words, "*saman* is a way in which we sensibly present ourselves among others."[8]

Saman and Islam

Like almost all types of Acehnese performing arts, *saman* is based on Islamic teachings and traditions. It is not clear as to how the *saman* tradition began in Gayo, Aceh. Some local artists claim that it was brought by a religious leader, Syekh Saman who introduced Islam to Aceh, while others say that *saman* is related to the teachings of the *Samaniah* Sufi order. Kartomi attributes the introduction of *saman* to Muhammad Sammān, "whose teachings resulted in the creation of the *Sammāniyah* brotherhood at Medina in the first half of the eighteenth century" (2010, 92). She further elaborates that "Sammān composed the words and laid down the rules of the body movements and accompanying postures of this form of *ratéb*. After members of the Acehnese Sufi brotherhoods had become adept performers of the communal liturgy (*liké*), some artists among them apparently developed the religious sitting dance (*ratéb duek*), with participants kneeling close together

---

7. See "Deskripsi Tari Saman" (Saman Dance Description), for a more comprehensive description of saman.

8. Marzuki, Personal Interview. Banda Aceh. January 2006.

in rows or circles as they sang *diké* while swaying from side to side and performing simple body percussion" (92–93)

Hasan explains that, "in the view of the religious perspective, *saman* [like other types of Acehnese traditional performing arts such as *seudati* (standing vocal-dancing), *ratoh*, and *liki angguk* (dikr/remembrance to God)] is meant 'to bring one closer to God'" (Hasan 2006). He asserts that all the movements in *saman* are drawn from the *sholat* (Islamic ritual prayer—see pictures below). However, he also points out that the *saman* incorporates more elaborate movements as compared to the *sholat* ritual due to *saman's* application of a set of more artistic values.

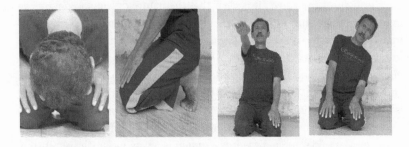

Figure 16: Some Basic Movements of the *Saman* Tradition

A strong element in *saman* is *syair*, textual-poetry messages that are expressed in a call and response vocal singing style. *Syair* combines the teaching of the Qur'anic Book of Islam, Hadith (the Book of jurisprudence source of Islamic teaching) and the teaching of *Taṣawwuf* (Sufism), which often contains *kisah* (historical teaching), *dakwah* (religious-moral teaching) and social critiques. One example of *syair* in *saman* performance can be seen below:

> *Hei . . .*
> *bintang*
> *Jalla We . . .*
> *Wetimu . . .*

Translated, *Bintang Wetimu* means "East Star"; *Jalla We*, One of God's Name; *Jalali wa Ikram*, which means "Is Most Bountiful."[9] According to Hasan, this anonymous traditional folk Acehnese poem reflects the teaching of Sufism, in that it upholds the value of humility. One should realize

9. See Qur'an Sūrat Al-'Alaq, 96:3.

that "only God is most bountiful" no matter how high a person rises or how much a person has achieved. Hasan's statement is basically drawn from the Qur'an, *Sūrat Al-'Alaq* (96:3), which says, "Proclaim! And Thy Lord Is Most Bountiful."

As one of the functions of the *saman* is *dakwah* (religious teaching), the songs and texts of the *saman* transmit the teachings and values of Islam regarding beauty, love, and brotherhood. Furthermore, Hasan asserts that singing poetry (*pantun, syair*) in a spontaneous way has traditionally been used to neutralize conflicts that exist within and between Acehnese societies (Hasan 2006). Traditionally, *saman* functioned as a public venue that Acehnese use to address current social and religious issues within their society. As such, *saman* artists have the opportunity to present social critiques as well as religious messages through their rendition of spontaneous sung poetry. The beauty of this, as Hasan explains, is "not in scriptural dogmatic ways such as most Muslim *ulamas* do, but in a more social dialectic and rhetorical way."[10]

Marzuki Hasan: A Samanic Messenger of Aceh

Kent brings out the critical issue that "music is peaceful or unpeaceful not because of the inherent character of music itself but because of the way that it is used" (Kent, quoted in Urbain 2008, 104) and because of that an important variable in peacebuilding is the performer who uses the arts. Marzuki is one such example of a performer who aptly uses the arts for peacebuilding.

Born in Meudang Ara Rumoh Baro village, Blang Pidie, Southwest Aceh, Nanggroe Aceh Darussalam (NAD), Indonesia on May 3, 1943, Hasan grew up in a *sufi*-Muslim family and was trained in the art of Acehnese *syair* (poetry) tradition from youth. Hasan elaborates, "Since childhood, I have studied and was trained in traditional Acehnese arts. As I grew up, I became familiar with *dhikr* ["remembrance and ways of reciting the names of Allah"], *seni baca al-Qur'an* [the art of reciting the Qur'an], and other types of Acehnese-Islamic traditions. I always listened to my parents reciting various types of *dhikr–Lailahaillallah kalimah toyibah kukaetkan*."[11] In the 1960s,

---

10. Although this is a traditional Acehnese practice, it is currently increasingly difficult to locate *saman* artists who have this ability to carry these messages through spontaneous sung poetry. This loss can be attributed to the repression of traditional arts during the political regime of Suharto (1965–1998) where all forms of traditional arts that contained political and social critiques were prohibited in Indonesia. Suharto's regime believed that these "critiques" would create social disorder. As a result, *saman* is presently used for entertainment.

11. Hasan, Marzuki. Personal Interview. February 2011

he moved to Jogjakarta in Java to continue his studies, not in the arts but in sports at Sekolah Guru Olah Raga (Sports School for Teachers), graduating in 1970.

After a short stint as a sports teacher in Jogjakarta, Hasan decided to return to the *saman* tradition, which was, as he said "my destiny/gift in this world." He recalls his parents reciting the *dhikr*—"*Lailahaillallah kalimah toyibah kukaetkan matee, qullu la 'et dikata lidah, Allah Allah ingat dalam hatee*" (translated: "There is no god but Allah, the ultimate sentence to remember until we die")—and "this remains etched in my memory throughout my life." In 1975 he was invited to join the teaching staff in the Lembaga Pendidikan Kesenian Jakarta/LPKJ (now the Institut Kesenian Jakarta/IKJ, the "Jakarta Arts Institute.") where he has worked as a lecturer and instructor in Acehnese music and dance.

It was in IKJ that Hasan's world began to expand as he worked with many artists-colleagues from different cultural, artistic, as well as religious backgrounds. These interactions opened him toward diversity and helped shape his views on how to present himself among diverse peoples and religions. However, he admits that this journey has not been easy. Marzuki recalls his mono-cultural/-religious upbringing, "When I was young and living in Aceh, I was surrounded by Muslim artists and Islamic traditions. My activities were solely related with the realm of Acehnese culture." However when he moved to Jakarta in 1971, he became involved in projects with different artists from varying cultural and religious backgrounds. "I often engaged in collaborative art projects, for instance, with the late I Wayan Dia, a famous Balinese artist who was also a dance lecturer in IKJ, Jakarta and a Balinese Hindu. I found that there are no barriers at all." In terms of attitudes toward those from other religions, Hasan holds the view that religion is personal and separates people, and that "Islam has taught me that my religion is my religion and your religion is yours."[12] He notes that, while this separation is true in terms of religious beliefs, there are no divisions where the arts is concerned. In fact, collaboration with artists from differing cultures and religions can be "mutually enriching as long as we are able to get away from our pre-existing conceptions and prejudices."[13]

Hasan has performed around the world: in the United States, Europe, the Middle East, Japan, as well as other countries. The experiences gleaned from performing, practicing, and living in other social environments have helped shape his thoughts and feelings about "the other." For example, when he was performing in many places in the U.S. in the 1990s, he lived mostly

12. Hasan. Personal Interview, February 2011
13. Ibid.

with American Christian families and he found them to be "friendly" and "respectful" even though they knew that he is a Muslim. Such attitudes of welcome and embrace accorded to him have been formative in his views regarding others. As he aptly puts it, "If they [the other] are so kind to you, you should give them also kindnesses. Life should be like that."[14].

As part of a cultural exchange program by the Asian-African Conference in Namibia (southern Africa) in 2007, Hasan was involved in a collaborative *saman* performance with Catholic school children in Namibia in 2007. Over forty-five days from July to August 2007, he taught Namibian students how to perform the *rateb meusekat*. He describes his experience:

> Before I teach them [Namibian school children] to sing and dance, I first introduce them to the *saman* tradition. I tell them honestly that *saman* is part of the Acehnese arts that reflect the Islamic tradition. The songs and dance movements derive expressly from Islamic teaching and practices. As such I tell them at the onset the meaning behind the *saman* movements and songs and from then on, we are able to practice without having any pretensions. What surprised me was that they really listened to me.[15]

At the end of the conference Hasan and his students performed this collaborative *rateb meusekat* before the delegates of the Asian-African Conference, who received it extremely well. Looking back on this experience, he says, "I am glad that I had this opportunity to teach young students because when they grow up, they will definitely remember this cultural moment positively."[16] Indeed, these cultural moments where participants from different religions and cultures learn to perform together is a good peacebuilding model.

Another aspect of Hasan's peace efforts is his involvement in the popular arts educational projects, the *Forum Apresiasi Seni Pertunjukan/ASP* (Performing Arts Appreciation Forum).[17] Initiated by Dewan Kesenian

14. Interview with author, February 2011. During the Song of Peace and Reconciliation consultation forum in Yogyakarta, March 30–April 3, 2010, Habib Chirzin, in his paper "Peace, Forgiveness and Compassion That Sung In The Quran" (2010) described one sūrah (chapter) related to the perspective of Islam toward peace, "If they seek peace, then seek you peace. And trust in God for He is the One that heareth and knoweth all things [8:61]. In my view, Marzuki Hasan's perspective about human relations has been influenced by this thought.

15. Hasan. Personal Interview, February 2010.

16. Ibid.

17. Hasan has been involved in Forum Apresiasi Seni Pertunjukan/ASP (Performing Arts Appreciation Forum) initiated by Dewan Kesenian Jakarta (The Jakarta Arts

Jakarta (The Jakarta Arts Countil), the project serves to introduce traditional arts to public high schools in Jakarta. Master artists of Indonesian traditional arts are invited and young students are given the opportunity to interact and to learn the various art traditions. During these projects, Hasan accepts the opportunity to introduce *saman* to students of varying social, cultural, and religious backgrounds. For example, he taught a group of students from a Catholic high school in Jakarta, and had the opportunity to interact with foreign students from other nationalities: Japanese, Dutch, Swiss, French, and American. Hasan comments, "My students who live in the Netherlands and Switzerland already have their own *saman* groups in their countries. Every year they come to visit me and they always want to learn *saman* in a deeper and more comprehensive way."[18]

Based on Islamic teachings and his life experiences as a *saman* artist, Hasan has developed a salient philosophy for relating with others. First, he acknowledges that differences are a natural part of human existence. Differences can become volatile points of conflict if approached wrongly. The proposal is to relate across cultures and religions with a sense of *ikhlāṣ* (true-honesty)[19], a word that embodies three important traits: honesty, integrity, and lack of pretension.[20] His view is that if one relates to the other without pretension, this neutralizes suspicion and bias.

Marzuki recounts an ideological debate he had with some of the Acehnese *ulama* (Islamic religious leaders) in Aceh, who claimed that singing and dancing was *ḥarām* (prohibited) in Islam. This issue is a contentious one, as Kartomi establishes: "[The Acehnese] assert that the pre-Islamic genre are *sumbang* ("wrong, off track") and dismiss as *mistik* (mystical) such genres as the *ulak* ("water flowing backward") dance . . . They do not, however, reject those non-Islamic genres to which Muslim phrases or songs of praise have been added . . . [such as] *puji pade Tuhan ilahi Rabbi . . . Assalamualaikum* ("peace be with you")" (2005, 30). However, opinions vary widely among Acehnese religious leaders regarding the permissibility of the arts in Islam. In line with this, during this debate, Hasan told the Islamic leaders "that art is not expressly prohibited in Islam but it is excesses in worldly matters that is." Furthermore, he vehemently stated, "While it is true that arts can be a vehicle used to destroy people, it also can be used to

Council) in Jakarta for many years. This forum basically reflects a popular movement in the traditional arts of Indonesia by way of introducing and bringing some traditional artists into public high schools in Jakarta.

18. Hasan. Personal Interview, February 2010.

19 Ikhlāṣ ("Honest feeling') is a term used in Islamic teaching to denote an attitude of giving and receiving something without any pretension.

20 Hasan. Personal Interview, February 2010.

create love and peace."[21] Finally, Marzuki holds the conviction that Islam can be shared and understood through performing arts. He believes that in Islam Allah [God] does not prohibit one from interacting with other peoples. As such, his position is that, "as a Muslim, I serve as a saman artist; that is my destiny. With that I try to give something to people; for me that is part of *ibadah* (to serve good deeds to people)."[22]

The Samanic Artist and Peacebuilding: A Discussion

Drawing from the above discussion on *saman* as a performing art that possesses properties that foster peace, and Marzuki, a *samanic* artist who has used *saman* to build bridges of peace, let us further explore three peacebuilding elements: inculcating peace within, practicing peace with others, and communicating peace through religion (Islam) and the arts. Here the discussion draws upon Michael Jackson's (1998) theory of intersubjectivity: that reality is relational, single selves are part of a commonalty, and that there is a dialectic between the particular and the universal. Jackson posits:

> How the particular is related to the universal is one of the most ubiquitous and persistent questions in human life . . . The question of the relationship between particular and universal domains thus dissolves into a set of questions about how we give and take of *intersubjective* life in all its modes and mediations—the physical and metaphysical, conscious and unconscious, passive and active, kind and unkind, serious and ludic, dyadic and collective, symmetrical and asymmetrical, inclusive and exclusive, emphatic and antagonistic—which prefigures and configures more discursive and categorical forms of relationship. (Jackson 1998, 2–4)[23]

Drawing from the above, we can infer that the particular inevitably impacts the universal and the local impinges upon the global. As such, stories of the local conflict and disaster from Aceh have affected both local and global society. No one can forget the sounds and sights from photographs and video feeds pictorially describing the utter destruction of Aceh in the aftermath of the tsunami and this remains seared in the consciousness not

21. Ibid.

22. Ibid.

23. Jackson explains that "we must not misconstrue intersubjectivity as a synonym for shared experience, emphatic understanding or fellow-feeling. For my purposes, intersubjectivity embraces centripetal and centrifugal forces and constructive and destructive extremes without prejudice."

only of the Acehnese but also of the world. The curfews, economic instability and loss of lives as a result of civil conflict leave a society displaced and suffering. The repression of the arts and artists during conflict disrupting the ritual life of village communities impacts the national and global arts community.

Conversely, the consciousness of peace building using music and performance through a single person, Marzuki, has a positive ripple-effect impact on Acehnese and Indonesian society. For example, Kartomi attests, "following the tsunami, west-coast Acehnese singers Hasan of the Jakarta Arts Institute, and the popular singer Rafly, of Studio Kande, sang the tragic, high-pitched west-coast laments on the national media, especially Metro TV. Their involvement in Aceh's recovery was to extend far beyond their immediate audiences and the pockets of potential donors. They and many other artists took part in efforts to alleviate the trauma of the tsunami survivors through music" (2009). In other words, Hasan's life is a demonstration of how positive peace can be inculcated and sustained.

Inculcating Peace within

Peacebuilding begins with the individual. In Hasan's life, his positive attitude toward others flows from a deep Islamic spirituality that is enhanced and enriched during *saman* performances. During the "Uncommon Sounds" concert in Yogyakarta,[24] Dr. William Hodges notes the integral role of spirituality in peacebuilding, "One should reconcile with God first before trying to reconcile with others." Hasan possesses such spirituality and has contributed to peacebuilding on several levels.

On one level, Hasan as an individual, or in Jackson's terms "the particular," adopts a posture of humility that is shaped by his own personal religious experiences as well as his Sufi upbringing. This attitude enables him to cross barriers and to build relationships interculturally with others (the universal). On another level, Hasan's spirituality enables him to absorb the various experiences he is exposed to from other cultures. This has broadened his thoughts about the "meaning" of relationships. Based on Jackson's argument, Hasan possesses the ability to consciously maintain an "intersubjective" relational dialogue with others.

In the area of "faith" and the potential divisiveness of dogmatic religious ideology, Hasan's approach is that faith is something very personal, or in his words, "an individual's effort to understand God," and is to be

---

24. This concert was held on March 1, 2010, in conjunction with the Songs of Peace and Reconciliation Consultation in Yogyakarta (March 30–April 2, 2010).

respected. This undergirds his openness toward others who are from other religious faiths that he encounters in his work and travels. Hasan's debate experience with the Acehnese *ulama* (Islamic religious leaders) regarding the use of music in Islam, demonstrates his ability to transcend the confines of dogma by acknowledging the dangers of excesses in music and yet articulating the potential of music to enhance spirituality, harmony, and peace.

Practicing Peace with Others

During his interactions with others, Hasan practices peace by responding to conflicting situations with honesty, integrity, and without pretension. His debate with the *ulamas* is one such example. His honesty with his students about the Islamic underpinnings of *saman* enables trust and relationships to be built. In a sense, he practices peace[25] that is not devoid of conflict or challenges.

Communicating Peace through Religion (Islam) and Arts

As an artist, Hasan has succeeded in imparting the knowledge of Islam to non-Muslims through the *saman* performance. Islamic ritual and moral teachings clearly reflected in the performance have become familiar to other non-Muslim performers. As Hasan says, "most of the Islamic expressions which are found in *saman* performance have been practiced by all of my students, either Muslims or non Muslims; such as the phrase '*Assalamualaikum*' ('May God give peace upon you') or the *dhikr* ('remembrance') and other ritual expressions."[26] What he communicates is an Islam that values harmony, beauty, and peace. The manner by which he communicates to his students is a suitable model of "peacebuilding" across cultures and religions. Through the artistic values of the *saman* performance, social interactions are facilitated and interfaith dialogue promoted. In other words, Hasan has successfully lived and imparted his knowledge of, in Galtung's words, positive peace[27] to others.

---

25. *Webster's Encyclopedic Unabridged Dictionary of the English Language* (1989, 1060) explains that peace can be understood as "a state of mutual harmony between people or groups, especially in personal relations; ... freedom of the mind from annoyance, distraction, anxiety, an obsession, etc; tranquility; serenity; a state of tranquility or serenity."

26. Hassan. Personal Interview, February 2010.

27. John Galtung argues that there are two types of peace: negative and positive. "Negative peace" is a situation in which there is suspension of open rivalry between enemies, but without the creation of a lasting process of harmonious coexistence.

During his presentation in the consultation "Songs of Peace and Reconciliation" in Yogyakarta, March 30–April 3, 2010, Dr. Habib Chirzin reiterated, "Islam per se is a religion of peace (*Salam*)." Muslims greet one another daily with the use of the word *salām* or "*Assalammualaikum.*" One of the most common prayers reflects a hope for ultimate peace: "*Allahumma Anta as-Salam, wa Minka as-Salam*" (Allah Lord, You are the Highest Peace, and the Source of Peace belongs to You). The knowledge of "peace," in fact, has to be practiced and challenged in order for it to be meaningful. Marzuki indeed practices peace even as he performs *saman* globally.

Conclusion

Saman is a performance that requires close cooperation and reflects harmony and solidarity. Performed during special celebrations and rituals, it is the focal point of community gatherings. The message of the poetry communicates a spirituality that is characterized by humility and love. The strong collective and relational aspects of the performance provide a good platform for peacebuilding. However, it is important to note that any art form has the capacity to reinforce either peace or violence. Much is dependent on how the art is used and who uses them.

Marzuki Hasan is a performer who has used *saman* as a platform to create peace, setting an example of how performers can use the arts for peacemaking. He does this by, first, possessing a deep Islamic spirituality that impacts his attitudes toward others. Second, out of this, his humility toward God and subsequently toward others, his honesty and integrity when working with diverse communities, and his unpretentiousness while dealing with conflicting issues all enable him to establish positive peace. Furthermore, the message of Islam as a religion of peace and harmony is communicated each time he performs the *saman*, breaking stereotypical notions of Islam as a religion of war.

Indeed, a performer carries this responsibility of using the arts to be a messenger of either peace or violence. In this case, Hasan chose to be a messenger of peace and is an example to be emulated. As he poignantly says, "Peace is about consciousness. If we make it narrow, it'll be narrower; if we make it wide, it'll be wider."

"Positive peace" is the prevalence of both understanding and peaceful coexistence between people. Here, there is no animosity, exploitation of the other, or hidden hatred. Positive peace, therefore, would encourage human cooperation and integration for the benefit of all. (Galtung in Meme 2008.)

FOR DISCUSSION

1. As with Marcel Akiki in the previous section of this book, Harahap agrees that the ethics and inner spirituality of the peacebuilder is critical to peacemaking: "Any art form has the capacity to reinforce either peace or violence. Much is dependent on how the art is used and who uses them"; and thus, the peacebuilder is a "messenger of either peace or violence." Discuss the validity of these statements. Do you agree or disagree with this perspective? Support your evaluations.

2. Hasan's debate with the Acehnese ulama demonstrates that interfaith dialogue often requires intrafaith dialogue. Explain this statement in your own words and evaluate the usefulness of intrafaith dialogue.

3. In the discussion section, Harahap gives a threefold methodology for those leading peacemaking efforts. How could this methodology be used in your own context to assist peacemakers?

4. PROJECT: Go online to Youtube and type in "saman performance." View several different saman performances in various contexts (Note: many of these performances have been removed from their original Indonesian contexts, as described in this chapter.). In your own words, how might the technique, artistry, and musicality of saman foster peace?

References Cited

Aryo Ardhianto. August 20, 2010. "Acehnese Art, Islamic Spiritualism, and Marzuki Hasan." Foreword of the 9th Session of Listen to the World Series, August 20, 2010, Namarina Studio, Jakarta.

Vladimir I. Braginsky. 1993. "Universe-Man-Text: The Sufi Concept of Literature (with special reference to Malay Sufism)." *Bijdragen tot de Taal-, Land-en Volkenkunde* 149, no. 2: 201–25.

Deskripsi Tari Saman ("Saman Dance Description"). 1991/1992. Departemen Pendidikan dan Kebudayaan Kantor Wilayah Propinsi Daerah Istimewa Aceh, Proyek Pembinaan Kesenian Daerah Istimewa Aceh.

Meme, Kinoti D. 2008. "The Missing Piece in Peace building: The Role of the Church in Interethnic Relations in the 21st Century City." PhD diss., Fuller Theological Seminary.

Hasan, Marzuki. January 2006. "Raising Above Tsunami." Lecture given at Sacred Bridge Foundation, Banda Aceh.

———. February 2010. Personal Interview with Irwansyah Harahap by the author.

Helen Myers, ed. 1992. *Ethnomusicology: An Introduction.* New York: Norton.

The Holy Qur-an: English Translation of the Meanings and Commentary. Al-Madinah Al-Munawarah: King Fahd Holy Qur-an Printng complex.

Jackson, Michael. 1998. *Minima Ethnographica: Intersubjectivity and The Anthropological Project.* Chicago: University of Chicago Press.

———. 2006. *The Politics of Storytelling: Violence, Transgression and Intersubjectivity.* Copenhagen: Museum Tusculanum Press.

Kartomi, Margeret. 2005. "On Metaphor and Analogy in the Concepts and Classification of Musical Instruments in Aceh." *Yearbook of Traditional Music* 37: 25–57.

———. 2009. "Surviving Conflict," *Inside Indonesia* 96. http://www.insideindonesia.org/edition-97/surviving-conflict.

———. 2010. "The development of the Acehnese sitting song-dances and frame-drum genres as part of religious conversion and continuing piety." *Bijdragen tot de Taal-, Land-en Volkenkunde* 166, no.1: 83–106.

Kottak, Conrad Phillip. 2008. *Cultural Anthropology: Appreciating Cultural Diversity.* 13th ed. New York: McGraw-Hill.

Sodikin, Amir. August 13, 2008. "Marzuki dan Kesetiaan pada Saman." Kompas. http://otomotif.kompas.com/read/2008/08/13/22533919/marzuki.dan.kesetiaan.pada.samanSamanic.

Sadie, Stanley, and John Tyrell. 2002. *The New Grove Dictionary of Music and Musicians.* Vol. 24. 2nd ed. London: Grove.

Shepherd, John. 1991. *Music as Social Texts.* Cambridge: Blackwell.

M. Quraish Shihab. 2006. *Wawasan Al-Qur'an tentang Zikir & Doa.* Jakarta: Lentera Hati.

Urbain, Olivier. 2008. *Music and Conflict Transformation: Harmonies and Dissonances in Geopolitics.* London: Tauris.

CHAPTER 12

Peacesongs

Forging a Musical Peace Communitas
among the Youth in Indonesia

by Sooi Ling Tan

> There were no boundaries that night. Regardless of ethnicity, culture or religion, young musicians cheered each other on vociferously as they performed for peace during the Rock the Peace concert in Bandung, Indonesia on April 24, 2010. Whether it was rock, popular or fusion of world and traditional Sundanese music, the audience applauded and swung to it, appreciating every inflection, every riff, and every effort. As the sounds of music rocked the Ciwalk open-air mall, camaraderie transpired and by the end of the night, a liminal musical peace *communitas* emerged among the musicians, the audience, the organizers and support staff. This was, to me, a foretaste of peace.

This scene offers a strong contrast to incidences of ethnic, religious, and political conflict that have plagued Indonesia historically. Between 1997 and 2002, at least 10,000 people have been killed in ethnic violence throughout the archipelago (Bertrand 2004, 1). In 1996–1997 and 2001, two waves of violent clashes between the Dayaks and Maduerese in West and Central Kalimantan led to the deaths of at least 1,000 people. In Maluku at least 5,000 people were killed in a war between Christians and Muslims between 1999 and 2002 (ibid.). As recently as June 2010, Muslim-Christian religious tensions erupted in Bekasi over alleged "Christianization" practices. The somber reality of these incidences highlight the urgency for peacebuilding efforts in Indonesia to go beyond surface overtures and move toward what Teun E. van Dijk calls "a complete idealogical reorientation" (quoted in Skyllstad 2000) and, according to Elise Boulding (2000),[1] toward a "culture of peace," a culture that promotes peaceable diversity.[2] Building a culture of peace among the youth of Indonesia represents the very aspirations held by a young Muslim, Irfan Amalee, and a Christian, Eric Lincoln, when they birthed Peace Generation, a peace educational program in Bandung, Indonesia in 2006. Following Galtung (2004), undergirding Peace Generation are the tenets of peace education that seeks to develop in each person a capacity to transform conflicts with empathy, creativity and non-violence. As part of their programs, music and songs have been used as peace tools. Using Peace Generation as a case study, this paper seeks to understand how music and music events, working closely together with peace educational programs, facilitates and sustains a peace culture particularly among the youth of Indonesia. From the findings of lyrical analysis on Peace Generation songs and ethnographic research on two music events, "Breaking the Walls" and "Rock the Peace" concerts, this chapter discusses, first, on an individual level, music's intrinsic ability to transform and internalize peace values and, second, on a collective level, the transformational dynamics in music events that contribute to the formation of a musical peace *communitas*.

A Case Study: Peace Generation, Bandung, Indonesia

Within the persistent context of resurgent unrest in Indonesia, Amalee and Lincoln saw the vital need to spread and implant the values of peace within a new generation of Indonesians: the youth. They chose a media that appealed to young people: interactive comic books containing twelve modules on peace values.[3] What is distinctive is the core philosophy of seeking peace development at a holistic level that addresses the development of the whole

1. Elise Boulding is Professor Emeritus of Sociology at Dartmouth College. In her book *Cultures of Peace: The Hidden Side of History* (2000), she examines stories about women, children, the Two-Thirds world, indigenous peoples, and marginalized voices and asserts that there are cultures of peace existing alongside the dominant culture of violence in the world. Much of everyday living—the nurturing, families, the celebration of events, human creativity—represents examples of peace culture hidden from official view.

2. Boulding, *Cultures of Peace.* This implies a culture that holds shared meanings and values and diversity between different peoples of the world. The emphasis is on how to deal with differences.

3. Students will study each book for a month. There are six stories in a book and each can be studied per week. In a year, peace education is accomplished.

person, body, mind, and spirit in the context of community. With this as a goal, students are led through lessons that enable them to: (a) have a proper view of self, (b) have a proper view of others, and (c) forge relationships and overcome conflict by rejecting violence and embracing diversity (Lincoln and Amalee 2007).[4] Since its inception until 2009, more than one thousand teachers have been trained to teach these modules with more than twenty-three thousand students in various regions of Indonesia such as Aceh, Bandung, Jakarta, and Banjermasin.

Music in Peace Generation: A Description

Increasingly, music and songs are being used as tools for peacebuilding in Peace Generation. A peace hymn is sung as students pledge their commitment to peace. In a peace education program, "Breaking the Walls," two groups of students from differing schools and cultures were brought together and songs were used as icebreakers. Following this, a Peacesongs mini-album (1) was produced that featured two songs written by students from this program. The album consists of five songs wherein two of these tracks are in the form of music videos, a form that resonates with the young participants. Finally, on 24 March 2010, Peace Generation organized a concert, Rock the Peace, attended by approximately a thousand people.

Peace Hymn. Written by Irfan Amale, this hymn is sung upon completion of the peace education modules. The lyrics appropriately affirm diversity and call for differences to be appreciated and honored.

> *Peace Hymn*
>
> *Damai di dunia mulai dari diri kita* (Peace in the world begins from within us)
>
> *Semua yang kita miliki, kita syukuri* (All that we possess, we are grateful for)
>
> *Itulah kunci berdamai dengan diri* (That is the key to peace with ourselves)
>
> *lihatlah sahabat, secara lebih dekat* (Friend, look more closely)
>
> *hingga tak ada , prasangka atau curiga* (Until there is no prejudice and suspicion)

---

4. An example of having a proper view of self is: a person with low self-esteem often resorts to use of drugs, sex, violence and vandalism; too much high self-esteem leads to arrogance and isolation. An example of having a proper view of others: viewing others too lowly leads to discrimination and oppression; and viewing others too highly leads to fear, being a minder, and unhealthy relationships.

Itulah kunci kedamaian abadi (That is the key to lasting peace)

More importantly, the lyrics affirm that peace in the world begins with the individual and urge for the breaking down of walls of prejudice and suspicion. Indeed, as the lyrics, are sung, students with heart-felt emotion accept the solemn responsibility of being peacemakers in their community.

Breaking Down the Walls. On 6 February 2008, two diverse groups of students, Christian students from the Bandung International Alliance School and Muslim students from SD Darul Arqam, Garut, met for a day at the Islamic boarding school in Garut. Although initially separated by walls of ethnicity and religious and social backgrounds, these students spent the day together, engaged in group activities, and even played a basketball game that was watched by 650 people—teachers, religious leaders, students, and outsiders.

Interestingly, songs emerged as one of the binding factors. Christian students from the International school wrote and performed a song entitled "*Bebas* (Free)," especially for that occasion. This sparked off the beginning of a musical conversation between the two groups. After this event, Muslim students from SD Darul Arqam Garut reciprocated by forming a band known as the Ma'had. Together with Irfan Amalee, they wrote and performed a song called "*Kalau Gentlemen Nggak Usah Ngegeng*" (If you are a gentleman you don't need to join a gang). This ongoing conversation has been taken to another level as both Tim Lewis (a student from Bandung International Alliance School) and the Ma'had have collaborated in producing a mini-album, *Peacesongs Mini Album (1)*. In this instance, music and song became a catalyst for discourse and dialogue between two diverse communities.

As the day concluded, the students from the two schools were exchanging contact information. Perceptions of the "other" had undergone a change. "Well I thought they would be insensitive and proud. But it turns out they are really kind," says a Muslim student.[5] "People are more friendly than I thought they would be," says a student from Bandung Alliance School.[6] Walls of separation dissolved between Muslim and Christian students.

Rock the Peace. There was a buzz, an excitement that morning of Rock the Peace concert at Ciwalk, Bandung. Musicians, mostly high school students, arrived for their sound check greeted by sound engineers and crew who had spent the early morning setting up the stage and equipment. As

5. Interview, Breaking Down the Walls.
6. Ibid.

North of Here (NOH),[7] a band from Savannah, Georgia, USA went through their sound check, six members of Te.O.Pe from SMKN Bandung Jurusan Seni Musik (SMKN Bandung, Department of Music and Arts) arrived carrying their instruments—excited and yet tentative. They were the winners of the auditions held where ten bands vied for the coveted spot as the opening act for the concert. Next, a girls' choir from SMP Muhammadiyah 8, Antapari Bandung, practiced the "Peace Hymn" on stage with their *angklung*.[8] Soon the polyrhythmic sounds of percussion and drums filled the open space when the group Lisan took the stage. Their adviser, who is both the group's music director and the school's vice principal told me that they are from Pondok Pesantren At–Tajdid Muhammadiyah Singaparna, Tasikmalaya. The group would perform songs that incorporate traditional, popular, and world music genres. The *Mahad* were the last to arrive. This was certainly an intriguing preview of the night's concert. I held my breath at the range of diversity: there were Christian musicians from the United States, Muslim high school students from Bandung and the surrounding areas, genres of music that spanned from rock music to the Sundanese sounds of the *angklung* and world music, the use of Western instruments and traditional Javanese instruments, all of which could very well be a recipe for either intercultural strife and misunderstanding or bonding. However, there were two binding elements: their common love for music and the cause of peace.

Meanwhile Peace Generation volunteers began setting up tents opposite the stage with Peace Generation paraphernalia. T-shirts, jackets, badges, bags, pins, and write-ups on Peace Generation were going to be sold. As this was a maiden event, there was some measure of uncertainty organizationally. However differences of opinion were set aside as everyone worked intently for one purpose: to make this occasion a success and to make a strong expression for peace in Indonesia.

In the afternoon, gasps of joy erupted as Amalee appears with a huge poster board that was promptly mounted at the side of the stage. The poster board featured photographs of world peace activists: Dalai Lama, Nelson Mandela, John Lennon, Mahatma Gandhi, Martin Luther King Jr., and

---

7. North of Here (NOH) is an indie pop/rock band from Savannah, GA.

8. *Angklung* is an Indonesian musical instrument consisting of two to four bamboo tubes suspended in a bamboo frame, bound with rattan cords. The tubes are carefully whittled and cut by a master craftsperson to produce certain notes when the bamboo frame is shaken or tapped. Each *angklung* produces a single note, so several players must collaborate in order to play melodies.

Ahmad Shafii Maari. Lennon's poignant invitation from the song "Imagine," to pursue peace so that the world will live in unity, was prominent.

The organizers informed me that they wanted to ensure that this was not merely an entertainment event but that peace themes were clearly and overtly communicated. Because of that the music program would be interspersed with publicity regarding peace and the work of Peace Generation. Awareness of the goal of the event was furthered with Young Peace Maker awards given out to four recipients, honored for their work with Peace Generation.

As the evening approached, the concert was preceded by a bike show that drew some curious onlookers. As I looked around, there were several categories of participants. There were the musicians, their support group of teacher advisers and also fellow students, close supporters of Peace Generation, and shoppers. As this was held in an open air space in the middle of a busy shopping complex in Bandung, shoppers stopped by to observe the event. Some stayed and others paused for a while. Albeit, by the end of the evening, the organizers estimated that there were over 1,000 people at the event.

The nine-member group *Lisan* opened the show with their fusion of contemporary, world, and Sundanese music. Their interlocking rhythms in the percussion coupled with the use of local instruments such as *kaluak, lok lok*, together with three African *djembes* provided a riveting rhythmic pulse. The sound of the double recorder, keyboard, and vocal harmonies provided the melodic contours comprising both diatonic and pentatonic scales in harmony. Their song, "*Rindu Damai*" (Longing for Peace) written by Yusef Rafiki (a member of *Lisan*) stood out as well and expressed their conviction that engaging in conflict is not a solution to any problem. On the contrary, responding with non-violence engenders peace. Following this was the girls' choir and *angklung* band from SMP Muhammadiyah 8, Antapari Bandung, performing the Peace Hymn. The audience responded in support by singing along with them whenever possible.

The stage was now set for the next three rock bands. Te.O.Pe, a five-piece band comprising drums, lead guitar, bass guitar, keyboard and a lead vocalist playing rock and hard rock music, soon got the crowd involved through the charismatic lead vocalist's call and response. They gave a highly energetic performance. Their composition, "*Perdamaian*" (Peace) expressed this dilemma that, although many people love peace, yet wars abound more and more. Their repeated chorus, *Bingung, bingung, ku memikirnya* (I am confused when I think about it) sung in a dramatic mock confusion style, aptly expressed this baffling predicament.

Figure 17: Te.O.Pe: Performing at Rock the Peace Concert,
Bandung, Indonesia. 2010

When the Ma'had began their set, the crowd had already gathered and filled the open space. They rocked the space with their raw energy and uninhibited performance as a band. Finally, North of Here rounded up the evening with their polished and yet dynamic performance. When they invited the recorder[9] player from Lisan to collaborate with them for the last piece, it was a moment that encapsulated the openness and musical collaboration among musicians that spread ultimately to the audience that night. When Te.O.Pe and Ma'had took the stage, NOH Band members immediately rushed forward to the front of the stage, cheering them on voraciously. Similarly, when NOH performed, the other band members stayed behind and supported. That night, every musician was part of the other's performance and if they were not playing they were fully supporting. It was as if "your success is my success, your failure, mine." Indeed I mused, "Where were the walls? Where were the differences?"

Movements toward a Musical Peace Communitas

The above three examples demonstrate how music is used as a peace tool in Peace Generation. Notably, the events began with participants as strangers to

9. The recorder is a "wind instrument of the fipple, or whistle, flute class closely related to the flageolet." See http://www.britannica.com/EBchecked/topic/493798/recorder, for a further description.

each other with the initial lurking suspicions and unhealthy presumptions. As the events unfolded, relationships were enhanced and what evolved was a spontaneous musical *communitas* for peace. The question is, "What then are the dynamics of this movement toward embracing the other?"

Undoubtedly any movement toward peace begins with the individual. However as Indonesia is a group-oriented society that values societal harmony, relationships, and social responsibilities, any sustainable peace efforts have to move beyond the personal to the collective. This section discusses how music impacts the individual and also carries this transformation to a collective level with the formation of a spontaneous musical peace *communitas*, a peace culture in community. At this stage, let me clarify that the use of the word *communitas* is deliberate. Translated, *communitas* is an Indonesian word meaning "community" and connotes a group of people that have some level of belonging, social ties, and responsibilities. In ritual studies, *communitas* is used by Victor Turner (1969) to refer to the spirit of community (Turner 1969, 96)[10] that is characterized by an essential and human bond, transcends social status, and, in the case of Peace Generation, religious affiliations. This liminal community is characterized by openness, lack of pretension, togetherness, and comradeship (St. John 2008), which are the very qualities that are the building blocks of desired communities of peace.

On an Individual Level

As school children sing the peace hymn, they are moved deeply. Lincoln elaborates, "There is a singing and a hearing, and this makes people say that this is what I want to be a part of."[11] An internal change toward the goal of peace was occurring and here are some dynamics:

Confronting Prejudicial Attitudes. Lincoln astutely notes, "Music is the thing that moves the message from the intellect to the heart, feeling and desire."[12] This touches on music's remarkable ability to penetrate emotional defenses and impact a person on the affective level. This is vital for transformation as prejudicial attitudes often rest on emotional rather than cognitive grounds. Through song, discriminatory attitudes are challenged and a person comes into a greater self-awareness, an important precursor to change. Through the singing of the peace hymn, the profound impact rests

10. Turner describes this as undifferentiated community or a communion of equal individuals. Communitas designates a feeling of immediate community that may involve the sharing of special knowledge and understanding.

11. Conversation with Lincoln, Bandung. January 20 2009.

12. Ibid.

on the intersection and integration of three factors: the affective (through song), the cognitive (through peace lessons), and an open and accessible environment of peace learning that the Peace Generation modules create.[13]

Implanting and Internalizing Peace Values. Irfan Amalee adds that music or song "enables students to internalize and memorize what they've learnt."[14] Song "enables them to recall what they have already learnt and touches their heart."[15] The use of song as an implanting and internalization tool has been widely used in religious and political circles in Indonesia, and in the Muslim and Christian worlds. For example, music and songs have been used to promote nationalism and to reinforce identity in Indonesia. One such song, "Indonesia Raya," was written for a youth congress in 1928 and expressed the national aspirations of one nation, one people, and one language (Lockard 1988, 61). This song later became the national anthem when Indonesia achieved independence from the Dutch in 1950. In Amalee's organization, Muhammadiyah, anthems such as the march, "Mars Sang Surya" (The Sun), composed by Djarnawi Hadikusumo, are sung to promote solidarity during local and national meetings. Similarly in the Christian tradition, hymns have accompanied the growth of Christian movements. For example, in the Wesleyan Methodist movement, hymns had both pedagogical and transformative functions. "The secret of the Methodists lies in the admirable adaptation of their music and hymns to produce effect; they strike at once at the heart, and the moment we hear their animated, thrilling choruses, we are electrified" (Scott, quoted in Mouw and Noll 2004, 5). Because Peace Generation recognizes the profound effectiveness of music, Amalee points out that professional musicians are hired to arrange and produce the music in order to ensure the quality of the songs.

Shaping New Attitudes. The focus on youth, a critical period in human development, is also another dynamic that enhances effective peace education. Studies reveal that ages ten to fourteen are critical formative years in a human being and it is during these years that a "child may either develop positively towards openness or stiffen into stereotypical attitudes and negative patterns of behavior" (Skyllstad, quoted in Urbain 2008, 173). Additionally once prejudicial attitudes have been internalized, they are extremely difficult to change. Robert Lifton elaborates that by the time a child reaches thirteen, his or her desire to understand and grapple with ethical

---

13. See King, "Musical Gateways to Peace and Reconciliation," in this volume.

14. Conversation with Amalee, March 11, 2010.

15. Ibid.

and moral dilemmas may be at its height (Harris and Morrison 2003,158). As such, adolescence is a pivotal time because, while there are struggles with issues of identity, there is also energy present to grapple with ideologies and values (ibid.).

Muthiah Umar, the principal of the SD Muhammadiyah Antapani school, where Peace Education is taught, supports this notion of educating peace to the young. She asserts, "It is our desire that they (students) understand that the way to solve problems is not necessarily through violence."[16] She notes that this is contrary to the prevailing culture of violence that school children in Indonesia are exposed to. Under her leadership, about one thousand students take Peace Studies as a subject for two hours a week. A total of fifty-three teachers in SD and SMP are prepared through specialized training.

In summary, the discussion above illustrates the role of songs and music events in breaking down internal bias within individuals enabling healthy new values and attitudes to be implanted. This internal change is a precursor to genuine collective change.

On a Collective Level

At the onset of "Bridging the Walls," there were two distinct and separate communities: Muslim school children from an Islamic Boarding School in the outlying area of Bandung and International School Students from the city of Bandung who were mostly Christians. At the onset of "Rock the Peace," there were also diverse communities gathering for a common cause. As the events progressed, and through what Christopher Small terms "musicking" (1998, 9),[17] I witnessed how music wove her charms and threaded these communities together to become a musical peace *communitas*.

An Equal Space. Music events such as *Breaking the Walls* and *Rock the Peace* are able to draw a group of people together into a liminal space that create ideal conditions for transformation. "I like the songs the bands were

16. In Bandung, Indonesia, Mutiah Umar, the principal of the Muhammadiyah Antapani Elementary School strongly advocates the teaching of peace education to her elementary school children in order to counter the climate of conflict and violence experienced by her students. Under her leadership, about 1,000 students take Peace Studies as a subject for two hours a week. A total of fifty-three teachers are prepared through specialized training. See "Training of Trainers, Peace Generation," July 1, 2014.

17. To "musick" is to take part, in any capacity in a musical performance, whether by performing, listening, rehearsing or practicing, providing material for performance (what is called composing), or dancing.

playing," an audience member said.[18] "I am attracted by the music," says another.[19] Others came to support their friends who were performing. Another group came to support the idea of peace. "I want to promote real peace, not just talk about peace but advocate for real peace."[20] Whatever the reasons, every person played a different role: musician, support crew, organizers, passers-by, or audience. However, once the concert began, everyone melded into one group as participants of the "Rock the Peace" concert. Indeed, the American team leader of NOH was no different from a high school student from Bandung. In this musical space, participants experience a freedom from their daily life routines and their prescribed social identities and enter this space as equals. This phenomenon of leveling and stripping (Turner 1995) sets the stage for transformation to transpire.

Honest Expressions. The youth of Peace Generation use several genres of music to honestly express their inner thoughts, dilemmas, aspirations, and changing identities. From an analysis of nineteen songs used in Peace Generation, the genres of music range from popular music (five songs), pop-rock (three songs), rock (six songs), rap (two songs), and fusion of contemporary-traditional music (three songs).

The use of popular and popular rock music by the youth is not surprising as popular music is a "vital means through which Indonesian youth creatively explore identity and their position in the modern world and the nation" (Wallach 2008, 264). Wallach further points out that popular music is able to "register the ambivalences, allegiances, and emotional attachments different segments of society feel toward the Indonesian nation and the wider world" (264). The texts of the Peace Generation songs articulate some of the dilemmas faced by young Indonesians. First, they are confronted by the choice to either: (1) conform to the majority and choose violence, or (2) to walk the costly path of peace.

> ***Kalau gentlemen, Nggak usah ngegenk* (If you are a gentleman, you don't need to join a gang)**
>
> *Hei Kamu kan bukan hyena* (Hey you are not a hyena)
>
> *Kalau rame-rame jadi Berani* (If in a group you are brave)
>
> *Kalau sendiri jadi banci* (When you are alone, you become wimpy)
>
> *Kalau gentlemen* (if you are a gentleman)
>
> *Nggak usah ngegenk* (you don't need to join a gang)
>
> *Inget, ini hidupmu sendiri* (Remember, this is your own life)

18. Interview with Audience 1. March 24, 2010.
19. Interview with Audience 2. March 24, 2010.
20. Interview with Audience 3, March 24, 2010.

Jangan biarin orang lain pegang kendali (Don't allow others to control you)

Second, "This is your own life" expresses a clarion call for youths to be responsible for their actions and lives. However, the reality is that they are also part and parcel of a community-oriented society where religious and social group pressure can prevent total individual freedom.

Another popular music genre used is rap. *Peace Generation Okk* begins with the sounds of police sirens and gunshots depicting a violent society.

> Peace Generation Okk
>
> *(Sounds of war, sirens in the background)*
>
> *Saling sibuk saling tendang* (Always mutually busy with fighting)
>
> *Guna sibuk dengan perang* (too busy with war)

The song however goes on to assert that the way of violence is outdated and instead brings home the message that peace is "happy and cool."

> *(Sounds of gunshots)*
>
> *Okk anak muda itu masa lalu* (Young people, those are old times)
>
> *Waktu sejarah masih di zaman batu* (Times in the past, during the stone age)
>
> *Sekarang kita lakukan sesuatu* (Now, let us do something different)
>
> *Aiyoh teman teman cubalah ikuti aku* (Friends, come try and follow me)
>
> We are, we are, Peace Generation
>
> At home and at school, Peace Generation
>
> Happy and cool, Peace Generation
>
> When we have problems we will not fight
>
> We choose to forgive and to do what's right

The use of rap as a form of expression is understandable since rap has a history of being the voice of social, economic, and political critique and has a strong appeal to young people in the world. In the United States in the 1990s, rap groups like Public Enemy, through songs such as "Night of the Living Baseheads," directly critique the government, the police, the media, and the black bourgeoisie (Rose 1994, 105). Toni Blackman (2006), a rap lyricist, vocalist, actress, and writer, voices out issues pertaining to violence, racism, and sexism in her community. Following this tradition, Indonesian rap artists like Xaqhala or the Yogyakarta based group, G-Tribe, create rap songs that also critique the social, political, and economic injustice in Indonesia. G-Tribe, for instance, in their song *Hari Berlalu* (The Days Slip By), tells of their alienation and frustration of Indonesia's middle and lower class urban youth and the music becomes distinctly more, "angry and discordant" (Bodden 2005) through the rise of hip-metal music, a fusion between hip-hop and heavy metal in 2001.

Shared Vulnerability, Shared Emotions and Convictions. Listening and performing, two key activities in any music event possess integrative qualities that enhance peace building. During "Rock the Peace," the act of active listening takes place at multiple levels: the audience is listening to the performance, the musicians are listening to other musicians, and the organizers are listening to the overall flow. This listening experience in a social setting is often accompanied by, what Skyllstad describes as, "a physical feeling of total involvement" (2004, 174). With that, the audience is thus moved towards "sympathy, understanding and togetherness" (174). Drawing from Maslow's phenomenon of "peak experience," Skyllstad elaborates that music facilitates these "peak experiences" where "one is able to transcend and integrate splits within the person, within the world." It is this integration that is the glue of any peacebuilding process. Integration also takes place in the interplay between performing musicians, each articulating their own voice through their instrument and also coming together in harmony.

Another integrative element is a shared vulnerability among the participants of the event as students sing and acknowledge their inner struggles. "Many of the (Indonesian) youth only seek for status and for material ways to satisfy their own desires,"[21] says a band member from Te.O.Pe. Conversely in their songs "Peace" and *"Dunia Harta Materi"* (The world and material wealth), they encourage their listeners to search for meaning in love and sacrifice. The song *"Bebas"* (Free) expresses the struggle with two choices in the face of injustice: the way of forgiveness or the way of violence and anger. The Ma'had deals with the illusion that identity and worth is obtained from gang membership. Not only is there a shared vulnerability but there is also a shared conviction such as: "Violence is a language of defeat while peace is the language of victory."[22] This experience of sharing allows students to identify with each other, to "humanize" the other and in so doing, develop feelings of similarity and empathy. As Laurence asserts, this perception of similarity and non-hierarchical relationships enable empathetic relationships to develop (2011, 179).

---

21. Interview with Te.O.Pe band member. March 24. 2010.
22. Interview with choir members, SMP Muhammadiyah 8. March 24, 2010.

Figure 18: The Mahad: Performing at Rock the Peace Concert, 2010

A New Consciousness, The Global-Local. The rich variety of music genres and types of instruments used, the style of dress ranging from Rock the Peace T-shirts and black tight jeans, to the Indonesian sarong and sor-ban (head covering) from the Middle East, to the long shirts and skirts and ḥijāb[23] worn by the girls' choir in Peace Generation music events, all point to the youth in Indonesia belonging to two worlds: the local and global. Their music also demonstrates this dialectic with musicians moving fluidly between four different languages: Indonesian, African-American hip-hop slang (Yo Bro), English, and Javanese youth slang (*nggak usah ngegeng*). Their hybrid rap song, "Peace Generation Okk," also fuses the Indonesian style of poetic verse (pantun) with the new global form of rap. As Bodden aptly surmises that "rap's clever wordplay is similar to older linguistic tradi-tions common across the archipelago: the rhyming jousts such as pantun which allowed youth to exhibit a quick wit and verbal dexterity in courtship and other playful situations" (2005). Notably, this new consciousness fea-tures a local-global identity that is dynamic, flexible, and open.

With that, peace educators and musicians play a role in developing the content of this new consciousnesses and identity. Thus, in terms of content, four positive values are communicated through Peace Generation songs. First, differences exist between people and communities but variety is to be affirmed and appreciated.

23. Ḥijāb is a veil that covers the hair and neck. See http://en.wikipedia.org/wiki/Hijab.

Peace Hymn

Dunia indah karena warna warni (The world is beautiful because it is colorful)

perbedaan ada untuk dihormati (Differences exist to be honored)

bukan alasan saling benci (There is no reason to hate each other)

sambutlah damai yang abadi (welcome this lasting peace)

Second, the reality is that injustice exists in this world. However, one reacts not with violence and anger but with peace, tolerance, and forgiveness. Third, there are religious grounds from which peace values flow and both Muslims and Christians can draw from those spiritual wells. Finally, encounter is encouraged because when different peoples meet and unite in and for peace, walls of false judgment and suspicion are torn down. In an interview with the *Ma'had*, one of the members gave this poignant advice, "If you want to know about Islam (and Indonesia), do not listen to what the media says (about terrorists). Just come and see with your own eyes."[24]

Indeed music and the arts can play a role in the formation of a new consciousness or in John Paul Lederach's term, a "moral imagination" (2005, 29). I would agree that it is this capacity to "imagine and generate constructive responses and initiatives, while rooted in today's challenges of violence, transcend and ultimately break the grip of those destructive patterns and cycles," that should be the ultimate goal.

Music's Relational Capability. Rock the Peace was not merely a musical experience but as Small puts it, "a total social experience" (1998, 44) with multiple levels of encounters taking place between the musicians, audience and support staff. What is pertinent is that levels of relationships are conditional upon (a) the length of relationships prior to the concert, and (b) the intensity of involvement in the event. For example, the most casual of relationships were between strangers as they stood and appreciated the music next to each other. The most intimate relationships were between the organizers and support staff who worked closely to birth and organize this event. For instance, organizing this event was not without its difficulties. The police permit to hold the concert at Ciwalk was granted only twenty-four hours before the event despite several failed appeals. When permission was finally granted, there were huge unified shouts of relief.

Another set of more intimate relationships was evidently built between the musicians from North of Here (NOH), based in Savannah, Georgia, USA, and The *Ma'had* because they had some level of interaction prior to the concert. Earlier, the musicians from NOH had visited the *Ma'had* in

24. Interview with The Ma'had, March 5 2010.

their school in the mountains of Garut, two hours away from Bandung. The band members spent the day at the school, eating and performing together with the Ma'had. Interestingly, the Ma'had had written a song for the concert "We are a Generation." The NOH band members picked up the song, and together began to reshape the song. Ultimately, they recorded the song together. "We learn to be tolerant. We value them (NOH) even though they are from outside and have a different religion. They too value us. During practices when we ask to be excused for prayer, they understand," says a Ma'had band member.[25] This invaluable time spent in an intimate and vulnerable setting, sharing musical ideas, lyrics, improving instrumental skills, and practicing tolerance helped solidify relationships.

What transpired here illustrates a vital peacebuilding dynamic, which Daniel Shapiro describes as "respective of each other's autonomy and building "intertribal affiliation." In his article regarding relational identity theory, Shapiro asserts that "the foundation for integrative problem solving and long term positive relations between conflicting tribes is to have them respect each other's autonomy and build intertribal affiliation." He further states that facing a shared problem rather than seeing the "other" as the problem allows for relationships to be facilitated (2010, 641). Thereby in the process of creating a song together, strangers became partners who shared a similar cause: expressing peace through music. As both groups listened and incorporated mutual ideas, acknowledgement and recognition of expression of group identities were reinforced and autonomy was respected. Through the dynamics of music making, affiliations were then built.

Conclusion

We have discussed the effectiveness of music working with peace education in building and internalizing peace values within individuals and also creating transformative spaces for peacebuilding on a collective level. We have noted how collective listening and performing draws people to total involvement and togetherness. Furthermore, Peace Generation music events are safe places for the youth to explore their identity and to freely express themselves using the genres of music they resonate with. The breadths of these expressions articulate the new consciousness of local roots and global belonging. In all this, a musical peace *communitas* is experienced.

Where do we go from here? We have to remind ourselves that the goal is to create a sustained peace *communitas* among the youth in Indonesia. For this to transpire, what is required is a structure that enables further

25. Interview with Ma'had. March 24, 2010.

opportunities for continued encounters among diverse groups and for increased involvement in music and peace events. What is most heartening is that Peace Generation with their innovative leaders and creative programs is providing this needed structure as they work toward an enduring peace *communitas* in Indonesia.

FOR DISCUSSION

1. This chapter focuses on building a culture of peace among Indonesian youth through effective educational and musical methods. Predict how such methods, again intended for the youth, would or would not be effective in your context.

2. Tan relates in detail how music affects both individual and collective levels to create a peace *communitas*. Examine the collective changes by paraphrasing each one in your own words. Next, create a sample musical event for your context, allowing each of these concepts to be engaged. Present your event to your class or study group for feedback.

3. Compare the communal dynamics present in the Rock the Peace concert to various concerts at the Fes Festival, described in Roberta King's chapter in the previous section. Which dynamics are the same, similar, or different between contexts? Justify your thinking.

4. PROJECT: Go to the Peace Generation website: http://www.peacegeneration.org/. What are the various activities that Peace Generation engages in and how do these activities help foster sustainable peace? Check out other organizations (online) that promote peace education and compare and contrast the work and impact of these organizations with Peace Generation

---

References Cited

Amalee, Irfan. 2008. *Breaking Down the Walls*. DVD. Indonesia: Pelangi Mizan.

———. 2010. Personal Interview. Bandung, Indonesia.

Bertrand, Jacques. 2004. *Nationalism and Ethnic Conflict in Indonesia*. Cambridge: Cambridge University Press.

Bodden, Michael. 2005. "Urban Poetry: Subversive 'underground' voices in Indonesian rap." *Inside Indonesia* 83. http://www.insideindonesia.org/feature-editions/urban-poetry.

Boulding, Ellise. 2000. *Cultures of Peace: The Hidden Side of History.* Syracuse, NY: Syracuse University Press.

Galtung, Johann. 2004. "Violence, War and Their Impact: On Visible and Invisible Effects of Violence." http://them.polylog.org/5/fgj-en.htm.

Harris, Ian M., and Mary L. Morrison. 2003. *Peace Education.* Jefferson, NC: McFarland.

Jordanger, Vegar. 2008. "Healing Cultural Violence: "Collective Vulnerability' through Guided Imagery with Music." In *Music and Conflict Transformation: Harmonies and Dissonances in Geopolitics,* edited by Olivier Urbain, 128–46. London: Tauris.

Laurence, Felicity, Urbain, Olivier. 2011. *Music and Solidarity: Questions of Universaility, Consciousness, and Connection, Peace & Policy.* Vol. 15. New Brunswick, NJ: Transaction.

Lin, Anne. Ucok: March 2, 2008. "Veteran of Indonesian hip-hop." *Jakarta Post.* http://www.thejakartapost.com/news/2008/03/02/ucok-veteran-indonesian-hiphop.html.

Mouw, Richard, and Mark Noll. 2004. *Wonderful Words of Life: Hymns in American Protestant History and Theology.* Grand Rapids: Eerdmans.

Lederach, John P. 2005. *The Moral Imagination: The Art and Soul of Building Peace.* New York: Oxford University Press.

Lincoln, Eric and Irfan Amalee. 2007. *12 Basic Values Of Peace: A Guide Book For Teachers.* Bandung, Indonesia: Pelangi Mizan.

———. 2009. *Beda is Not Bad, Peacesong Mini Album (1).* Peace Generation Indonesia.

Lockard, Craig. 1998. *Dance of Life: Popular Music and Politics in South East Asia.* Honolulu: University of Hawai'i Press.

Pavlicevic, Mercedes, and Gary Ansdell. 2004. *Community Music Therapy.* London: Kingsley.

Peace Generation, Bandung, Indonesia, http://www.peace-generation.org.

Rose, Tricia. 1994. *Black Noise: Rap Music and Black Culture in Contemporary America.* Hanover, NH: Wesleyan University Press.

Skyllstad, Kjell. 2000. "Creating a Culture of Peace: The Performing Arts in Interethnic Negotiation." *Journal of Intercultural Communication* 4. http://www.immi.se/intercultural/nr4/skyllstad.htm.

———. "Managing Conflicts Through Music: Educational Perspectives" in *Music and Conflict Transformation: Harmonies and Dissonances in Geopolitics.* London I.Bl Tauris & Co. Ltd., 2008.

Small, Christopher. 1998. *Musicking: The Meaning of Performing and Listening.* Middletown, CT: Wesleyan University Press.

Shapiro, Daniel L. 2010. "Relational Identity Theory: A Systematic Approach for Transformaing the Emotional Dimension of Conflict." *American Psychologist* 65, no. 7: 634–45.

St. John, Graham. 2008. *Victor Turner and Contemporary Cultural Performance.* Oxford: Berghahn.

"Training of Trainers, Peace Generation." Last modified July 1, 2014. http://www.peace-generation.org/#!teach-peace/c1xne. Accessed July 2, 2014.

Turner, Victor. 1969. *The Ritual Process: Structure and Anti Structure.* Chicago: Adline.

Urbain, Oliver. 2008. *Music and Conflict Transformation: Harmonies and Dissonances in Geopolitics.* London: Tauris.

U.S. Department of State. 01 Aug 2006. "Rap Music Artist discusses Hip Hop, International Diplomacy." USINFO Webchat transcript. http://iipdigital.

usembassy.gov/st/english/texttrans/2006/08/20060801134123xrsma
dao.1899683.html#axzz2k7ztkSl7.

Uncommon Sounds: "The Mahad and North of Here." http://www.songsforpeaceproject.
org/multimedia/test.

Wahid, Kyai Haji Abdurrahman, and C. Holland Taylor. 7 October 2005. "In Indonesia,
Songs Against Terrorism." *Washington Post.* http://www.washingtonpost.com/wp-
dyn/content/article/2005/10/06/AR2005100601559.html.

Wallach, Jeremy. 2005. "Underground Rock Music and Democratization in Indonesia."
http://www.bgsu.edu/downloads/cas/file16892.pdf.

———. 2008. *Modern Noise, Fluid Genres, Popular Music in Indonesia: 1997–2001.*
Madison: University of Wisconsin Press.

PART FOUR

Pathways toward Peace

CHAPTER 13

Musical Pathways toward Peace and Reconciliation

by Roberta R. King and Sooi Ling Tan

As long as your neighbor is in peace, you're in peace.
So wish the best for your neighbor.

—Traditional Lebanese Proverb

Love the Lord your God with all your heart, soul, and mind.
Love your neighbor as yourself.

—Jesus

Living Together as Neighbors through Music

Musical pathways to peace and reconciliation in the early twenty-first century are predicated upon the imperative of living together in neighborly ways, both in close proximity to one another and on a global scale. Today's global world has brought differing peoples and their faiths into new neighborhoods. Indeed, we are experiencing rapid influxes with great migrations of peoples from one corner of the earth to the other. Often they are immigrants escaping war-torn arenas, looking for relief and a place to be safe. They are also those seeking political asylum or opportunities for economic and educational improvements. Peoples who were once called "others" are increasingly becoming our "neighbors." As Volf notes: "Such others live

267

next to us, at the boundaries of our communities and within our nations. Put differently, we live increasingly in culturally and religiously pluralistic social spaces . . . a plurality of cultures is a social reality" (2005, 3). Living together in such close "neighborly" proximity does not have to create barriers, but rather offers opportunities to approach one another in new ways. It is our contention that the convergence of our studies show that music and the arts provide social spaces for approaching, encountering, and living together that shift paradigms and move the conversation from "other" to "neighborly" other (3), to ultimately embracing people, regardless of difference, as "neighbor." The social arenas promulgated through musical events set in specific contexts with the sharing of common and differing cultural musics foster igniting people's imaginations, experiencing healthy relationships, and sustainable peacebuilding.

In seeking to offer nonviolent approaches to sustainable peace in the twenty-first century through music, dance, and the arts, we are affirming Turino's assertion that the "study of expressive cultural practices like music and dance from different societies can help us achieve a balance between understanding cultural difference and recognizing our common humanity" (2008, 3). Further, we assert that such study can also serve to promote mutual understanding, when thoughtfully and discerningly approached, between peoples of differing religions. Indeed, in addressing the topic of songs of peace and reconciliation among Muslims and Christians, we found ourselves turning our focus away from differences between us to discovering the common concerns and practices that we find among us. What allows us to come together as human beings? Three recurring major commonalities drove our investigations and research. We discovered they are located in our mutual desire for peace and acceptance of one another, our religious and spiritual commitment to know and worship God, and our expressive musical traditions that afford opportunities of mutual interaction.

Set within an era of one of the dominant major global-local dialectics, that of international misunderstanding and conflict among and between Muslims and Christians as openly ignited through the events of 9/11, this research project turned to learning from two local contexts outside the United States where conflicts have occurred: Lebanon (and the Middle East) and Indonesia. After experiencing major conflicts, however, each area has seen measured steps of progress in experiencing peace.

Our purpose here is to bring together a convergence of empirical evidence based on our investigations presented in Lebanon and Indonesia that helps us to make sense of how music and related arts contribute to sustainable peacebuilding. While music itself is complex and inextricably linked, we have chosen the metaphor of musical pathways to help us unravel the entangled musical components and interactive processes that facilitate the pursuit of sustainable peace.

Musical Pathways and Peacebuilding

In a seminal ethnographical study of music in daily life, anthropologist Ruth Finnegan (1989) suggests that musical pathways encompass familiar and regular daily activities such as work, worship, and major life events that people encounter in the course of everyday life. She argues that people are dynamically interacting through the formation and changing dynamics of music ensembles, singing groups, and/or bands and further suggests that "hidden musicians" in local societies provide "an invisible structure" through which people process their daily lives (306–7). Looking to musical pathways, we have sought to understand the inner workings of the often neglected, overlooked, and invisible structures promulgated through music available for promoting peacemaking. Related to Finnegan's metaphor of musical pathways is Small's concept of "musicking," which further refines our use of the term musical pathways here.[1] "Musicking" brings together the totality of what occurs whenever music-making is taking place, helping us to address many of the dimensions inherent in the multivalent nature of music, pushing beyond the restriction of musical analysis alone.

Additionally, seen through the lens of communication theory, in this study, we expand the metaphor of musical pathways and "musicking" to encompass multiple dynamics inherent within the processes of musical communication (King 2009). Indeed, music and the performing arts are in essence multivalent in the ways they communicate and process musical significance and meaning. While illusive to comprehensive ways of analyzing how music works, the multivalent nature of music is at the same time one of its greatest strengths.

With such broad considerations of music in society in mind, we propose the forging of five musical pathways: 1) musical events that foster relationships; 2) music-making itself that lays a sonic foundation for processing life; 3) music convergences that heighten and intensify musical experiences; 4) musical peace catalysts who compose, create, and live their expressive art for peaceful purposes; and 5) the spiraling circle of ongoing musical dialogues that are focused on collaboration, spiritual experiences, theological exchange, social action, and everyday life. Within each of these pathways we highlight critical functions of music that move forward relational dynamics between people. Thus, while maintaining that each musical

---

1. See King, "Introduction," in this volume.

pathway is dynamically interlinked and interdependent, musical pathways for this study comprise a broad totality of musical components and dynamic processes that enhance and strengthen transformational impact relative to building peace.

The Musical Event Arena

The musical event arena brings together an interface between musical sound and society, "a set of recognizable behaviors that link music to various broadening social and expressive spheres" and can be viewed as transformative, particularly in the emotional domain (Racy 2003, 11). As Turino argues, "Music, dance, festivals, and other public expressive cultural practices are a primary way that people articulate their collective identities that are fundamental to forming and sustaining social groups, which are, in turn, basic to survival" (2008, 2).

Not only did we benefit from scholars who presented their individual research but we also had the privilege of sponsoring a number of "musicking" events that further confirmed the experiential dynamics, theories, and concepts brought forward in the scholarly presentations. One of these concerts took place in Beirut, Lebanon at the chapel of the Antonine University where Professor Nidaa Abou Mrad led the Classical Arab Music Ensemble in a concert focused on the shared sacred writings between Muslims and Christians, the gospel narrative concerning the "annunciation." From Muslim and Christian religious leaders seated to the one side of the stage, to the performing musicians drawn from both traditions, TV camera men from local stations positioned around the room, students of the university, local community members representing both religious traditions, and two invited guests from the "Songs of Peace and Reconciliation" project from outside of Lebanon, each one was well aware of the identities brought together in the room and who contributed to the totality of the music event, extending out the meaning of "musicking" (Small 1998, 9) in an inclusive way that is productive for understanding the overall dynamics of musical performance. The context of the concert in its larger framework generated a multiplicity of impressions and impacts that facilitated the functioning of music. That is, during musical events, music functions in dynamic ways that foster profound experiences when the actual music-making takes place. Most notably, the musical event arena initiates gathering people together and building interactive relationships, two functions that contribute significantly to the peacebuilding process. Thus, two critical functions of music taking place within musical events are gathering and relating.

Gathering

Musical events provide social spaces for gathering people together. From the Fes Festival on its global, transnational level to two individual musicians, a Libyan and an American whose identities include differing cultures, nationalities, and religions exchanging musical traditions by performing together, musical occasions offer opportunities for encounter, engagement, and personal interaction with "others." Although musical gatherings are most often made up of participants who share music traditions and similar taste affinities for music, people who otherwise might have very little in common or who would not otherwise choose to meet with each other find themselves gathering around a musical event. In such cases, people find themselves released to break out of subscribed boundaries and tear down barriers toward each other psychologically, attitudinally, and in terms of spatial proximity. The mere act of attending a concert in a new location outside of one's normal boundaries, i.e., an American in a North African nation, or Muslims performing in a Christian church setting, moves people into each others' otherwise spatial restrictions as they begin to approach one another. As Volf notes, "We are created not to isolate ourselves from others but to engage them, indeed, to contribute to their flourishing, as we nurture our own identity and attend to our own well-being" (2005, 12–13).

How does the gathering function of music move people toward one another? How does it contribute to overcoming avoidance of one another? Music and the performing arts provide a third arena, one that often lies outside each one's distinct territory and focuses on perceived non-intrusive elements such as the delight and pleasure of music-making. Indeed, questions surrounding music's apparent universal appeal and its ability to move us profoundly, to inspire, elate, and transform listeners and performers alike have occupied a range of "philosophers, religious leaders, politicians, scientists, music critics, and musicians through history" (Racy 2003, xi). Our research observations and data argue that music events, including the actual music-making, engender non-offensive and non-invasive experiences that afford recognition of the "other," give new perspectives toward each other's common humanity, offers dignity and respect, and lays the groundwork for building trust. When seated in the audience and/or when performers find themselves in new configurations together on stage, previously compartmentalized and isolating arenas are denied wherein levels of interactive encounter and engagement provide moments, if only briefly, of peaceful coexistence. A musical third space is created that takes focus off of areas of disagreement, indeed often temporarily ignoring or jumping over differences, and looks toward mutually pleasing experiences of togetherness in ways that avoid initial barriers and walls of avoidance. Strong attractional forces of both music and spirituality tend to propel people toward each other. This was evident during the "Rock the Peace" concert where some shoppers at the mall where the event was held, were drawn by the music to stop and observe. Evidently, a prerequisite to such involvement is that there must be a willingness to place themselves within such events. Music as an attractional agent serves as a motivator that helps to overcome reticence to becoming involved with "others." Based on an energizing motivation derived from music, people bring with them a certain degree of initial openness toward the "other." Thus, musical events open one another to paths that lead to breaking stereotypes and growing together in neighborly ways as they facilitate moving people from positions of enmity and exclusion toward more intimate interaction.

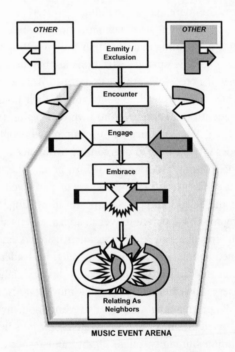

MUSIC EVENT ARENA

Figure 19: Musical Spaces of Relating (King, Tan, 2012)

Furthermore this musical space is an equal one where participants experience a freedom from their daily-life routines, their prescribed social identities, and enter into this musical space consciously or unconsciously as equals. This is well demonstrated at the Fes Festival (see King, chapter

6, above) when a global audience comes together and discovers the lines between Western/non-Western, Muslim/Christian/Jew, and political exigencies are put on momentary hiatus with people coming together with a shared mutual purpose to celebrate life, eat local foods, enjoy the cultural richness of a long 1200-year heritage, and, of course, to listen and participate in sacred musical concerts. While in Indonesia, during the Rock the Peace concert (see Tan, chapter 12, above) an American guitarist was no different from a high school student or a police chief from Bandung. What this engenders is the phenomenon of leveling and stripping that allows barriers to be broken and for bonding to take place.

Musical spaces require a certain degree of volitional willingness to encounter and engage peoples of any kind of difference in meaningful ways. They create space for recognizing the other through performed musics and encourage "inverting perspectives" (Volf 2005, 11) by viewing them as a potential enrichment in one's life rather than an enemy. Where there was once exclusion from and enmity toward one another, musical spaces foster encounters that turn people to see each other in new ways, offer opportunities to engage with each other, and promote a willingness to embrace the other as one's neighbor. Such experiences allow participants to begin to understand the "other" without striving to fully agree with them. Rather, they are enjoying their humanity together, serving as a set of steps toward creating space in oneself and also toward developing a willingness and thus fostering opportunities to "enter the space created by the other . . . (where) the self makes room for the other and sets on a journey toward the other in one and the same act" (Volf 1996, 141–42). Holton in chapter 7 above, for example, describes the experience of reciprocity and growing trust as he performed music for his Libyan friends and they for him. On another level, as they entered into each other's musical spaces by learning music from the other, he notes that trust is deepened and dialogue fostered. Thus, in this way musical events provide social arenas for musical encounter and engagement that move people toward each other, rather than distancing them away from one another. This is a critical dynamic in the peacebuilding process. Indeed, Lederach has observed, "Genuine constructive change requires engagement of the other" (2005, 49) and thus he adamantly argues for a "wide public sphere of genuine human engagement." Musical events are indeed public arenas wherein music and the performing arts naturally and easily occur as they gather people together and engage them in events that facilitate mutual involvement and shared experiences.

Relating

Encounter and engagement through musical events also foster the nurture and growth of dynamic relationships, relating and interacting with one another sometimes for only a brief period and other times on a regular basis. Perhaps the strongest relational links develop among musicians performing together who must agree with one another on the performance and interpretation of the music. When the Arabic Classical Music Ensemble in Beirut performs,[2] Muslim and Christian instrumentalists in conjunction with a Muslim sheik and orthodox priest who melodically and respectively recite common sacred passages from the Qur'an, Hadith, and the Bible have already worked together relationally for long hours of rehearsal as they have sought to come together in performance and to nuance their musical interpretation. They have worked within a musical rehearsal space that has provided opportunity for dialogue about Arabic music, religious texts, and life in general. This in itself is a major step toward embracing one another and contributes on a particular level to peacebuilding, most obviously as the group relates with one another during their public performances that regularly gather two distinct religious communities together in the same room. Here, the ensemble not only performs the musical heritage common to both groups but they also simultaneously function on a metaphorical level that envisions and produces new connections linking both religious groups in new ways. They are making a metaphorical statement that impacts each of their communities in a way that brings interconnection.

Not only does the attending audience engage in deeply listening to the music, but they are also relating with one another as they experience the musical event together. For example, as each religious leader musically recited the Arabic word injīl[3] during the concert, telling the story of the Annunciation, a unanimous response occurred. All the participants, Muslim and Christian alike, stood in respect of the gospel announcement as practiced in their liturgical traditions. Relating with one another through the convergence of common liturgical traditions and sacred texts created a deeply profound moment of unifying solidarity in the midst of a music-cum-worship event.

Thus, music events provide relational spaces where relationships may be initiated and further developed. Significantly, peace scholars consider relationship building to be at the core of successful peacebuilding.

2. See SOPR website, http://www.songsforpeaceproject.org/.

3. The Qur'an talks of the Injīl (لٳنُجِيل) referring to the New Testament of the Bible—usually the Four Gospels. http://wikiislam.net/wiki/Injil, accessed August 30, 2011 9:44 am.

As Lederach reiterates for us, "The centrality of relationship provides the context and potential for breaking violence, for it brings people into the pregnant moments of the moral imagination: the space of recognition that ultimately the quality of our life is dependent on the quality of life of others. It recognizes that the well being of our grandchildren is directly tied to the well being of our enemy's grandchildren" (2005, 35).

Fairuz, for example, is widely recognized for giving public concerts during Lebanon's civil war period (1975–1990) where the song texts raised deeply felt concerns and needs of people. On such occasions, she is known for challenging people to consider what war means for their grandchildren and their future familial welfare.[4] Relational dynamics occur in the midst of music performance that contain seeds for reorganizing relationships. Averted eyes turn to glimmers of the humanity and value of one another in ways that speak of mutual enrichment in each other's lives and ignite the imagination to new possibilities for living together. At work is the building of affiliation as discussed in the Peace Generation project in Indonesia (see Tan, chapter 12, above) where gathering and relating together with a mutual purpose further integrates peoples as they experience music-making within specific time frames that foster respecting the "other" within his or her individual and religious autonomy (see Shapiro 2010).

The Music-making Arena

The gathering and relating of musical events intensifies and produces paradigm shifts that foster change as one enters further into the music-making arena in the midst of performance and the actual musical sounds themselves (see Fig. 20). Indeed, "Musical sounds are a powerful human resource, often at the heart of our most profound social occasions and experiences" (Turino 2008, 1). Repeatedly, we have experienced in our concerts both in Beirut and Yogyakarta, plus in our scholarly investigations (ethnographic case studies), the strength of music to sonically bond people to one another and to initiate or re-establish relationships in a space where recognition of the "other" hangs in the sonic atmosphere. Multiple dynamics are taking place simultaneously, based on inherent functions of music, such as transcending, imagining, and processing. The music-making realm propels participants into transcending the mundane, igniting their imagination, and processing life issues that produce variable types of sonic bonding all as they occur within local musical performance contexts. We argue here that "musicking"

4. Discussion response to a scholarly paper presented at the Southern California chapter of the Society for Ethnomusicology annual meetings, Feb. 2008.

takes place within the experiential arenas and spaces of our lives wherein music-making dynamics are heightened and intensified through a convergence of musical style, song texts, performers, and audience.

Transcending[5]

As musical participants enter into the music-making arena, they come with a plethora of assumptions and expectations for what they will hear and how they will experience music, highly determined by cultural influences and individual associations attached to music. Scholars note that transcendence and trancing is a common experience and a critical element in how music is perceived and conceptualized (Herbert 2011, 201–28; Becker 2004; Rouget 1985). In Arab culture, Racy explains that *tarab*, a genre of music that generically references "the indigenous, essentially secular music of Near-Eastern Arabic cities" (2003, 5), is also commonly used to reference a "musically induced state of ecstasy" (8), an essentially experiential and deeply emotional occurrence that leaves people without words to adequately articulate the phenomenon. He further argues that ecstasy lies at the core of both secular music (*tarab*) and Islamic mystical traditions as are intimately linked through their common Arab culture. Likewise, from the West, the ineffable nature of music also finds psychologists speaking of "entering into an altered state"[6] as one performs and makes music.

> When performing piano I find that often I enter what psychologists would call an "altered state." An altered state is a term used in hypnosis in which your alert awareness of the normal sounds and sights in the moment are suspended. One enters into a trance. In this state there is deeper access to one's internal world . . . including images, sounds, emotions. When I'm performing, I frequently enter this state and am totally focused on the music—marrying my emotions to the elements of the music. I often also feel closer to God . . . deep prayer is also an altered state.[7]

5. Transcendence, trance, and ecstasy are all terms that commonly arise within affiliated discussions (Becker 2011, 54–55). I am using transcendence here in that our main reference is to musics performed within sacred domains, though sometimes desacralized, and is a term often used in association with the study of religious experience (Abernathy 2008, 16).

6. For a literary review into the psychological intersections between altered states of conscious-ness and music, see Herbert 2011.

7. Janice Strength, PhD, Marriage and Family Therapist, e-mail correspondence: September 3, 2011.

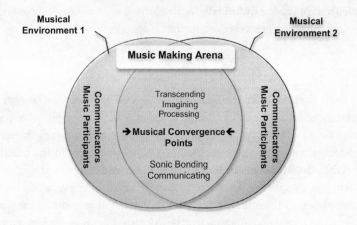

Figure 20. Music Making Arena (King, Tan 2012)

In our investigations, we found that at the forefront of both Muslim and Christian music-making dynamics, religious and spiritual experiences added to the cumulative effect of transcendence,[8] profoundly deepening the musical moments. Ghada Shbeir, the Lebanese singer at the Fes Festival (see King, chapter 6, above) explained singing Syriac early Christian works as a "mystery. There is something hidden that I cannot understand . . . Its a language that is connected with the church, when one sings, one senses direct (immediate) transcendence, in conversation with God himself."

Further, in addressing the Islamic *tawshīh* tradition, Said references transcendence among Sufi spiritual fraternities, pointing to both holy instruments, such as the *nāy* and the human voice, as media through which various Sufi orders achieved "high levels of spirituality" (see Said, chapter 8, above). He also argues that after much study of Qur'anic recitation, the *munshid* (leader) ultimately must reach "a state by themselves through which a spiritual divine gift is imparted only to a person who is pure enough to receive the spirit of the Creator," and additionally notes a continual dynamic interaction and influence of sacred Sufi musical *praxis* upon secular musics, specifying the influence of Mevlevi music on classical Ottoman music itself. Thus, ecstasy and transcendence permeate Arab music-making traditions that build on *samā'*, a practice of religious ecstasy that is musically induced (Racy 2003, 50) and that has also impacted secular Arabic music. When

8. "Aesthetic embeddedness is strikingly evident in sacred music, where music's meanings are so often dependent on its ability to do something, to effect change or to bring about transcendence" (Bohlman 2002, 13).

coupled and practiced within religious, spiritual, and/or liturgical contexts, transcendence is heightened even further.

Imagining

Music and the arts ignite the imagination, especially in relation to ecstasy and transcendence, creating "sensory, emotional and physical effects" (Turino 2008, 13). Often caught off guard or surprised by one's thoughts and feelings, music promotes envisioning possibilities within the realities of specific actualities—political exigencies, time periods, physical locations, and religious differences. The possibility of living together peacefully is and can be sparked in the midst of the actualities of life. It speaks into the well-spring of our moral imagination, which Lederach defines as "the capacity to imagine something rooted in the challenges of the real world yet capable of giving birth to that which does not yet exist" (2005, ix). He further iterates that "transcending violence is forged by the capacity to generate, mobilize, and build the moral imagination" (5).

As participants in musical events function within their own histori-cal backgrounds and cultural contexts, they are freed up to imagine new possibilities that have previously eluded them. As Holton, for example in chapter 7, shared the stage with a Libyan guitarist, he poignantly describes this possibility in his own context:

> For a brief musical moment, there was no conflict between Lib-ya and America. The local guitarist's trust in me was accepted by the audience as a sign that I was trustworthy and our collabora-tion was a visible symbol of burgeoning peace between us, and to some degree our nations and faiths.

Likewise, in Bandung Indonesia, with the programs of Peace Genera-tion, frozen images of unbreakable cycles and habits of violence are shat-tered. Instead young people are offered a new vision, one that is imbued with images of people of differing faiths and ethnicities working together for peace, coexisting and cooperating to form a united leadership for peace. These two examples affirm music-making and musicking as creative acts that, as Lederach posits, are the "source of moral imagination" (2005, ix).

Indeed, participants of musical events enter into a music-making realm of processing their identities, their current life situation and are af-forded the opportunity to reinterpret misperceptions and stereotypes.

Processing

Music and the arts at the same time function as a life processor, by simultaneously connecting previously disjointed thoughts and bringing new clarity and insights in ways that might not have been previously linked. Occurring on multiple levels and in multiple ways, the deeply embedded internal dialogues of individuals in both the cognitive and affective domains are brought into a broader public forum that gives birth to new tentacles of interconnectedness and relational dynamics. Each individual's response contributes to a combined community significance, impacting broader groupings of people whether on the national or global levels. Initiated in the affective domain, the musical events interact with cognitive processing that influences behavioral interaction with others. Thus, assessments of the "other" are given freedom to negotiate for changed perspectives and conclusions that foster overcoming barriers of difference and fear.

The strength of musical processing lies in its integration of both cognitive and affective dimensions in the communication process. The affective dimension of communication exerts more control than normally recognized due to its functioning at a deeper, unconscious level (Smith 1992). Indeed, the integration of the self through music and the performing arts is largely due to the dominance of music's functioning within the affective, emotional realm. Within Arab musical contexts, for example, musicians and their audiences stress that "Arab music must engage the listener emotionally" (Racy 2003, 4), wherein the affective dimension pervasively dominates "certain performance repertoires (thus resulting in) a strong influence upon music related outlooks and behaviors (5).

Yet, the affective dominance of music in the experiential realm is still linked to cognitive processes that often produce a release from inner cognitive-emotional tensions. Dwelling within the realm of emotional understanding engendered by music and the performing arts, new threads of changed behavior and approaches to living are elicited. The relationship of the interaction between the affective, cognitive, and behavioral domains of communication through music contains critical ramifications for the peacebuilding processes, especially in relation to forgiveness and reconciliation where cognitive processes are often inadequate for dealing with the extremities of one's experience. The trauma of war, conflict, and relational brokenness lies buried in the depths of a person, on deeply emotional levels. As Weaver notes,

> Reconciliation gets complicated and compounded when we try
> to address it purely on the intellectual level. Somewhere along

the way we came to think of hurt as lodged in the cognitive
memory. Hurt and brokenness are primarily found in the emotional memory. The reason I like the arts—music, drama, dance,
whatever the form—is precisely because it has the capacity to
build a bridge between the heart and the mind (2003, quoted in
Lederach 2005, 160).

When the children of Peace Generation (see Tan, chapter 12, above),
for example, sing the peace hymn or when Christian and Muslim high
school students met and shared a song during the "Breaking the Walls
concert," it was noted that they were visibly moved. Prejudicial attitudes
and pre-misconceptions of the other that often lie more prominently in the
emotional realm than the cognitive are challenged. A new self-awareness
emerges and new values are implanted and internalized. During Rock the
Peace concert, as songs and music addressed societal injustices, the experience of shared vulnerability, shared emotions, and empathy was felt. The
challenge to respond to injustice with the language of peace and not violence becomes a possibility.

Drawing from this, by addressing the emotional dimension, music
and the performing arts build bridges between the heart and the mind in
ways that process attitudes and engender paradigm shifts in perceptions.
This may include, for example, overcoming barriers of difference, enmity,
and fear. The interpretation filters of both heart and mind are potentially
shifted from closed to open, from exclusive avoidance to embracing acceptance, from demonizing to humanizing, and from negative stereotyping
to new perspectives about people. Such musical processing plays a major,
central role in transactional music communication wherein lie the seeds for
behavioral change/s that can contribute to building sustainable peace.

Musical Convergence Points

During musical events, the dynamics of building affiliation are considerably
heightened due to the convergence of commonalities among performers
and audiences, musical styles and texts. Within this convergence, the dynamics of relating, imagining, processing, sonic bonding, transcending, and
communicating occur in a more intensive manner. Musical convergence
points thus afford the opportunity for people to discover and rediscover
their commonalities within their given contexts, thus providing a strong
grounding for solidarity. And where divergences exist, differences can
be acknowledged, accepted, and better understood. As such, identifying,

developing, and performing common musical styles and texts are vital factors toward sustainable peacebuilding.

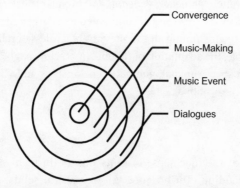

Figure 21: The Centrality of Music Convergences (King, Tan 2012)

The strength of the impact on sustainable peacebuilding lies in the
multiple musical elements and strands woven together through these convergences. Nidaa Abou Mrad asserts that cantillation is the convergence
point of "traditional musical practices related to worship in the Mediterranean region" (see Nidaa Abou Mrad, chapter 5, above). He identifies these
points as the perspective of divine transcendence and prophetic revelation,
theocentric communication channels from the divine to the human, and
subjugating *melos* to *logos*. He poignantly points out that, while there are
verses in the Qur'an and the Bible that diverge on numerous points, what is
similar is the melody of the divine word that plunges deep into the hearts
of the faithful. The strong interconnectedness and shared musical styles and
texts allow for cantillation to be a powerful medium for peacebuilding.

Another example of a strong convergence is Irwansyah Harahap's musical compositions for the band *Suarasama* that reflect resonant texts and
themes among Muslim and Christian communities. In the album *Lebah* he
composes three pieces of music, essentially "praise to the prophets," that
represent the three icons of the Abrahamic tradition in Islam and Christianity. By doing so, he draws from common roots of the traditions and
highlights these icons' intentions to bring peace on earth.

On a broader level, Akiki identifies shared Lebanese musical traditions
including popular traditional Lebanese songs in Mt. Lebanon, wedding
procession songs, and popular neo-traditional songs (see Akiki, chapter 5).
Songs such as *A'tini al-nay* (Give me the flute), a poem by Khalil Gibran
sung by Fairuz to Rahbani-composed melodies, expresses the common
concerns of the Lebanese people. Pertinent imagery such as the *nāy*, Mt.
Lebanon, and the cedars evoke deep emotions of Lebanese identity and

belonging. While in Indonesia, Emha's use of the musical form, *Campur Sari*—a hybrid sound that reflects a beautiful plurality, fusing the elements of *keroncong*, Javanese gamelan, *dangdut*, and popular music, sung in Arabic and Indonesian Javanese and accompanied by a large range of Western and Javanese resonates among all Indonesians regardless of religious affiliations. For example, the adaptation of "Silent Night, Holy Night" in *shallawat* style opened up space for dialogue between Muslims and Christians (see Rithaony, chapter 10, above).

Sonic Bonding

In each scenario, a unique sense of unity occurs through what might be termed sonic bonding (Turino 2008, 2), or musical solidarity (Laurence and Urbain, 2011), as each musical element, plus performers and audience come together in the midst of the convergence providing not only a musical metaphor for imagining possibilities for living together as neighbors, but also momentarily experiencing a Turnerian sense of musical *communitas* that bonds people together. The experience opens peoples to one another in various degrees and triggers for some a willingness to interact with one another on deeper levels in a broadening process that facilitates negotiating understanding of the "other," music's communicating function is taking place.

Communicating

Ultimately, music as an expressive art is about communication, an ephemeral yet memorable, irreversible means of expressing inner thoughts and deeply held emotions of individuals and their communities as they are brought into public domains. The functions of gathering, relating, imagining, and processing life issues through music all take place within a broader dynamic process of what King (2009) has identified as "Transaction Music Communication" where negotiating for mutual understanding occurs; interlinked transactions take place within the emotional, cognitive, and behavioral realms. Drawing from communication theory, communicologists such as Barnlund and Adler in studies over the last few decades no longer view communication as a linear sending of a message. Rather, transactional communication takes place wherein each person participates as a communicator who on a lesser or greater degree simultaneously receives, decodes, and responds to another's communicative behavior. Although musical performers play different roles from the people who make up an audience, there remains a level of being on equal footing. That is, each person brings his or her full identity, both as an individual and as a contributing member of a particular community, to the musical event. Musical sounds, as a special kind of communication and experience, "draw upon and draw out different parts of the self" (Turino 2008, 1–2). In the midst of the musical transaction, participants are always inventing, attributing, and assigning meaning to it. At the same time, there is an interdependency required among the musical participants, whether performers, audience, event staff, for both successful performance and for significant negotiation of meaning that leads to understanding, mutual acceptance, and respect. As Turino argues, "musical participation and experience are valuable for the processes of personal and social integration that make us whole" (1). Whether participating together in performance or listening intently to music, a sense of community occurs where sonic synapses take place and an interconnected sense of "sonic bonding" (see Turino 2008, 2–3) fosters the emergence of interconnected and participatory relationships, what we are calling transformative music communication.

Transformative Music Communication

Transformative Music Communication (see Figure 22) presents a way of understanding music's contribution to working toward peace and offers an initial response to Lederach's question: "How do we transcend the cycles of violence that bewitch our human community while still living in them?" (2005, 5). Taking place within the convergence of synergies promulgated during musical events, transformative music communication is a normative occurrence in the music-making arena; its effects are varied with both positive and negative paradigm shifts in perception. The processing of interactive dynamics at the Fes festival of World Sacred Music, for example, showed an openness and willingness to embrace the "other" that occurred over a period of ten days (see King, chapter 6, above).

Functioning on the experiential level, in each of the four concerts that constituted part of the consultations for the *Songs of Peace and Reconciliation* research project in Lebanon and Indonesia, multiple shifts in attitude and perceptions were observed, from cameraman to performers and audience. Viewed within a context of pursuing peace and reconciliation, transformative musical communication generates changes in perception and attitudes toward the "other" through music, uncovering critical artistic influences in the peace process.

Indeed, music and the performing arts, in particular, are recognized for eliciting unique moments of change, referred to by psychologists and theologians as the "agogic moment" (see Farley 2008, 61–79). Ray Anderson, a scholar in theological anthropology, defines the "agogic moment" as "a human and personal encounter, whether ordinary or extraordinary, that releases a motive power that generates change" (quoted in Farley 2008, 63).

Figure 22: Transformative Music Communication (King, Tan 2012)

Addressing the emotional, affective dimension of communication, Anderson points to the intimate link between emotion, cognition, and motivation and identifies the agogic moment as generating a "recognition," a reworking and rethinking of particular social engagements and perceptions (quoted in Farley 2008, 67). Significantly, "in re-thinking situations, people can change how they understand their experience. This new experience causes new emotional responses, evoking in people relational, cognitive, and motivational changes" (67). Thus, a convergence of all the dimensions within the music-making process fosters an interconnecting synergy between the emotions, the cognitive, and the motivational that catalyze change in attitude and thinking. For example, one such change occurred at the Annunciation concert in Beirut. Hearing that the concert was one based on "classical Arabic music," our young guide and photographer, about twenty-eight years old, did not expect to enjoy the concert. Yet, as the performance took place within familiar traditions that he had heard throughout his life, his attitude changed significantly as he realized what was happening through the performed convergence of Islamic and Christian liturgical traditions. An "agogic moment," probably several, occurred that motivated him to request the concert to be repeated in another part of town. Interestingly, as a Christian, he also emphasized that the *shaykh* who had given a short homily midway in the concert, most definitely needed to be included. In this request, he revealed a desire for additional concerts and opportunities to engage in continued dialogue on multiple levels through music.

Musical Dialogues for Building Peace

Musical events give rise to social spaces for nurturing affiliations on a momentary basis in profound ways. Yet, they are unfortunately limited by time and space. Correspondingly, peacebuilding initiatives, while intensified with the musical event, also appear to end with the event. However, in order to pursue sustainable peacebuilding, the musical event unfolds in a series of dialogues that need to and often do continue beyond the event itself. Bakhtin, the Russian philosopher, underscored the importance of dialogue. He asserted, "My voice can mean but only with others, at times in chorus, but at the best of times in dialogue" (quoted in Clark and Holquist 1984, 12). While music gathers people together in a unifying way, sometimes singing together in chorus, further dialogical elements are inherent in transformative music communication. In the final analysis, continuing dialogue between Muslims and Christians can take place via music and the performing arts as they engender dialogues of musical collaboration, spiritual experience, theological exchange, actions for peace and reconciliation, and life events.[9] These dialogues provide the essential fuel that establishes sustainable peacebuilding, for as Bakhtin (1984, 252) argued, "when the dialogue ends, everything ends."

The Dialogue of Musical Collaboration

Dialogues of musical collaborations arise from shared listening, creating music, rehearsing together, learning music from the other, and performing together. In some instances, musical collaborations enable and foster the development of a relational bonding that endures beyond time-bounded *communitas* as experienced within musical events. For example, Holton recalls how in preparation for a public music festival, he and a Libyan guitarist

9. This typology of music dialogues is derived from interfaith dialogue categories offered by theological scholars including Bevans and Schroeder 2004, 383–84; Kärkkäinen 2010, 3–7; and Thangaraj 1999, 95–96, as appropriate to music.

practiced a simple chord accompaniment with an improvised solo in "gypsy jazz" style.

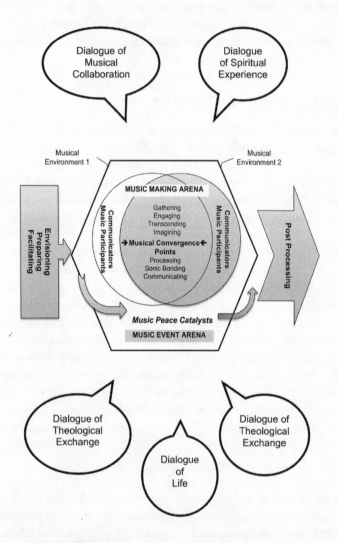

Figure 23: Musical Dialogues for Peace Building (King, Tan 2012)

Working together to fuse music that represented both cultures generated enhanced trust in their relationships as they made mutual decisions about the upcoming performances. In another instance, when the American band members of North of Here and their Indonesian counterparts from the Mahad collaborated to write and record the song, "We are a generation of Peace," we saw the same dynamics at work (see Tan, chapter 12, above). As they listened to each other, helped each other out with guitar licks, and contributed to the writing and styling of the song, mutual respect for each other was established. Finally, the act of performing in general exemplifies musical collaboration. Mustafa Said (see Said, chapter 8, above) argued further how performance of a particular musical genre, such as the *tawshīḥ* that contains interactive dynamics between a leader and responding group, both sonically and metaphorically demonstrates a disposition toward cooperation and acceptance.

Dialogue of Spiritual Experience

An emerging point in this book is the role of spirituality as a moral force for peace. Volf points out that "the will to embrace" (Volf 2005, 11) is the threshold in the movement from exclusion to embrace. The will to embrace is, however, predicated by truth and justice. We cannot have "embrace" if truth is not said and justice is not done. For victims who have experienced destruction and loss, this task of having a will to embrace the enemy proves almost insurmountable, as the issue of truth and justice remain possibly unresolved. However, we have examples such as Father Marcel Akiki who was able to transcend this because of his deep spirituality. Father Marcel Akiki established choirs and musical ensembles incorporating children from diverse social and religious affiliations, often victims of war. He asserts that the ability to desire peace with those who have inflicted harm can only flow out of a vital relationship with the God of peace. For Akiki, peace begins with inculcating peace with God, peace within self, and finally peace with others.[10]

Spirituality also enables the development of healthy attitudes toward "the other." In Indonesia, Marzuki Hasan's personal spirituality and humility toward God is the basis of his philosophy of "others." His conviction is to acknowledge the differences and conflicting ideals while at the same time building bridges to foster "*ikhlāṣ*" or truth and honesty. As such, when teaching *saman* in multicultural and multireligious contexts, Hasan honestly explains about the strong Islamic undergirdings of this performance and in so doing, his sincerity and honesty exudes as he works with other groups. He uses *saman* as a platform to create peace and operates from this conviction that *saman* is meant to draw one closer to God and communicates beauty, love, and brotherhood, thus breaking the stereotypical notions of Islam as a religion of war. Spirituality is also the source of creative musical

10. Akiki, "Music for Peace and Reconciliation from Lebanon," in this volume.

expression. In a similar way, Irwansyah Harahap creates music that flows from his personal interpretations of love and hope toward God.

Within the music-making arena, another set of experiential dialogues of spirituality occurs as peoples from differing religious backgrounds enter into the worlds of musico-religious piety of the "other" in the midst of ' musical performance. This can occur where visualization and embodiment of prayer and worship on the same stage, i.e., Greek Byzantine monks and the *Al-Kindi Sufi Ensemble* from Damascus at the Fes Festival (see King, chapter 6, above), where both Christians and Muslims in the audience alike are exposed to, listen to, and experience each other's musico-religious traditions via concerts and recordings. In this way, the performers themselves are more engaged, both interactively and experientially.

In sum, dialogues of spiritual experience take place in two domains: internally and externally. Internally, experiencing and sharing in musico-religious and secular cultural musics of the "other" promote processing of attitudes toward one another. Externally, and arguably most significant for peacebuilding, musical leaders who practice and live out their deep spirituality by implementing social action through music facilitates and catalyzes the reimagining, reconfiguring, and restoring of relationships. Admittedly, forgiveness, truth, and justice are issues that sometimes have no resolution. Living with the ambiguity of irreconcilable issues requires a deep spirituality. Yet in the midst of such dialogue seeds of hope and further steps toward willing embrace are generated.

Dialogue of Theological Exchange

Dialogues of theological exchange take place at conceptual, scholarly discussions, during pre-concert envisioning and conceptualization for music events, and during concerts, through both musical performance and as part of a concert when religious leaders are given space to discuss the content of the texts and the importance of embodying them through song. The two papers presented by Krabill and Sahiron at the Yogyakarta consultation, for example, are a fruition of theological exchange that took place with other scholars during the Songs of Peace and Reconciliation Conference. This theological exchange revealed a common spiritual and textual basis for peace, and a common quest to seek peace between the two communities. Peace is a valued attribute and upheld highly both in the Bible and in the Qur'an, sacred texts on which Muslims and Christians rest their faiths. Dr. Krabill puts forward the notion that God's nature is that of a reconciler and advocates that peace or the even broader concept *shalom* is God's answer to a broken world. In adjudicating the interpretation of two competing elements of upholding strong Islamic morals for peace and permission for war, Dr. Sahiron (see chapter 4 above) critically concludes that war is only a last resort. Permission for war is only granted when all peacemaking efforts have been exhausted and the goal is to achieve a moral end. Both these tenets provide a strong basis for advocating peace.

Further, the exchange of theology and philosophies of faith traditions, although usually considered solely the domain of experts and officials of specific religions (see Bevans and Schroeder 2004, 383–84), occurs not only in scholarly discussions about music and peacemaking, but also within musical events and music-making arenas. Indeed, at the Fes Festival and during the Beirut Concert, which focused on Divine Love and in which a Muslim *shaykh* gave a short homily as part of the evening's proceedings, direct and immediate dialogues of theological exchange took place. Scholars and religious leaders provided discussion or theological commentary facilitating correctives and clarification in understanding the essence of religious doctrines and perspectives.

Yet, within the musical event and music-making arenas, musical text-based dialogues of theological exchange go further in that they take place quite naturally as performers sing from their Scriptures and holy books. Immediate and direct voicing of Holy Scriptures, devotional materials, and religious poetry are offered within liminal moments of transcendence and the processing of deeply held beliefs. At the "Songs of Divine Love: An Islamic/Christian Spiritual Concert" by the Classical Arabic Music ensemble[11] in Beirut, the theological exchange began with the program notes:

> Christian and Muslim mystical paths have as their goal the sanctifying union of humans with the divine light. These paths serve a quest of human love for God, which responds to the infinite and inconceivable love which God bears for humankind. Mystic poets convey this experience by the use of symbolic lexicons drawn from nuptial mysticism (founded in the Song of Songs) for Christians, and from the chaste and restrained love known as ʿudrī (originating with the desert poets of the Umayyad era) for Muslims
>
> "Songs of Divine Love: an Islamic/Christian Spiritual Concert" endeavors to embody this quest by means of cantillation and the setting to music of religious and mystical texts making

11. This was the first of two public concerts sponsored by the Songs of Peace and Reconciliation Colloquium in 2009 and was conceived and directed by participating scholar, Dr. Nidaa Abou Mrad.

reference to mystical love and illumination, such as St. Paul's "Hymn to Love" (1 Corinthians) and the "Light Sūra" from the Holy Qur'an, along with poems and hymns by St. Roman the Melodist (Beirut, 490 to Constantinople, 551), Abbess Kassiani (Constantinople, 805–807), al-Husayn ibn Mansūr al-Hallāj (Iraq, 857–922), St. Symeon the New Theologian (Constantinople, 949–1024), Muhyīd-Dīn ibn 'Arabī (Andalusia, 1164–Damascus, 1240), and 'Umar ibn al-Fārid (Egypt, 1181–1235).

The program addressed the theological background and indicated the source of the song texts later given voice through musical performance. Thus, song texts and their program notes are of critical significance in that they provide theological exchange that reaches broadly and publicly beyond high-level scholarly discussions. They serve as focal points for the convergence of mutual spiritual and musical traditions by exposing, informing, and correcting false misperceptions as the sacred texts are suspended in the musical environment, raised up for reflection, and contemplated within the parameters of musical performance. All the while, performance and all participants at the musical event are experiencing and relating with one another. Further, song texts reveal longings for peace, raise deep level issues of injustice, facilitate theologizing and interaction with God, integrate interior parts of our differing spiritualities, release the imagination of what is possible in the midst of impossible scenarios, set vision, and offer hope.

Dialogue of Social Action

In the realm of music for social action, dialogues emerge as Muslims and Christians engage in shared projects for peace. Peace Generation's continuing impact in Indonesia is a result of ongoing peace activities. Following "Rock the Peace," other activities such as "Walk the Peace," and now "Kick the Peace," were organized. These events together with the peace education curriculum and the input of invited speakers for peace, all provide a holistic thrust toward peacebuilding. As Tan (see chapter 12 above) argued, such mutual projects foster the building of relational identity and shared affiliations that turn people from perceived adversaries into collaborators in overcoming shared problems. It is important to note that these acts cannot fully erase the harshness of past negative encounters but they afford opportunities to create new narratives of positive encounters that can overcome them.

Dialogue of Life

Dialogues of life need to be pursued in contexts where peoples of faith simply have not mixed with one another or formed neighborly friendships despite living for years within their neighborhoods. Dialogues of life occur regularly within societies where music is a normative feature of the events. Weddings, funerals, baby-naming ceremonies, and religious rituals—indeed all the major and minor life events where musical occasions play significant roles in the daily rituals of life—contribute to nourishing ever-growing webs of interlinked relationships, a critical goal in building sustainable peace. Dialogues of life encompass a lifestyle "where people strive to live in an open and neighborly spirit, sharing their joy and sorrows, their human problems and preoccupations" (Thangaraj 1999, 95–96). More specific to music, musicians and performers gathering together to share music, to listen, to play, to create musical masterpieces, to organize events, and to perform together provide opportunities for relationships to progress further than the performance hall or venue. As barriers are removed, there are moments when musicians share a meal together, invite the other to their house or studios, share the beauty of their land and the magic of their music, talk about difficult issues, share aspirations and dreams, and experience joy and sorrow together. These are dialogues of life, a vision of coexisting and partnership, occurring within the context of musicians and musical enthusiasts interacting with one another. Musicians and performers then contribute further within their community, not only as community members themselves but also more intentionally as musical peace catalysts.

Musical Peace Catalysts

A strident chord in this book is the role of musicians and performers leading as catalysts of peace. Music and its infinite capacity to influence emotions and behavior can either be catalytic toward violence or peace. In this respect, musicians, composers, and performers play a pivotal role in using music either to sow suspicion and incite hatred and violence, or to foster values of respect, tolerance, and peace. Musicians such as Mustafa Said, Marzuki Hasan, Irwansyah Harahap, Rithaony Hutajulu, Nidaa Abou Mrad, and Father Marcel Akiki have not only used music to influence toward peace but are themselves models of peacemakers in their performances, practices, and lifestyle. They are courageously stepping out to play vital leadership roles within their respective artistic traditions and institutions.

Their examples suggest four essential characteristics of musical peace catalysts. First, they are integrous to their art form, their religious, and their musical convictions. In this sense they retain their autonomy as artists. Second, they display an attitude of sincerity and honesty toward keeping true to their art form and a willingness to embrace differences. Third, they have allowed the dynamics of performances and practices to be the ground of intercultural interaction. Working together during intense practices and performances often allows for differences to arise, for conflicts to emerge, and for resolution to take place. A new appreciation for the other is practiced. Fourth, in their creation of music and performances, opportunities arise to write lyrics and music that illuminate the values of peace and harmony or explore common texts and beliefs between Muslim and Christians. This creates a common ground for sharing. Courageously employing their gifting, musical peace catalysts draw from their academic knowledge, religious convictions, and musical expertise to envision the building of relationships in the midst of fearful situations. In essence, they catalyze and design musical means for engaging in dialogues through music and the arts. The role of musical peace catalysts in initiating and nurturing relational interaction and musical dialogues is critically pivotal.

Converging Musical Pathways toward Peace and Reconciliation

In seeking to lift a veil on musical pathways and how they possibly contribute to sustainable peacebuilding, we have identified a number of musical modalities that converge to influence and impact the negotiation of relationships toward peace and reconciliation. These modalities include the ways in which music functions, the social spaces or arenas in which music events take place, the actual music-making itself that brings together multiple components of interaction converging to generate cognitive processing and dialogue within an integrative environment of affect that impacts behavioral transformation, and pivotal musical peace catalysts who conceptualize, envision, and inspire one another and communities at large. They are dynamically interconnected and play off of each other. Thus, the music event and its concurrent music-making enhances, heightens, and deepens dialogues on multiple levels in ways that not only enrich the event but also strengthen affiliation and relational bonding. That is, opportunities for experiencing living together as neighbors within a designated set period of time sets the stage for further integration within communities and moves people toward such relating as a more normative possibility.

Ultimately, each musical pathway feeds into and further nourishes mutual understanding and interreligious encounters as they address people's ways of life. They offer ways of building relationships of trust, respect, and dignity as they approach daily life, its concerns, values, and spirituality authentically and soberly. Always fluid and dynamic as such experiences may be, we recognize that positive movement forward may be thwarted by a number of issues. Yet, we argue here that when intentionally pursued, such musical convergences and dialogues provide pathways toward peace and reconciliation in today's polarized world between Muslims and Christians. The practical implications of this model will be discussed in the following chapter.

FOR DISCUSSION

1. Study the Transformative Music Communication (figure 22) and seek to understand all the parts, as well as the many layers in the "Convergence." In 100 words, paraphrase the meaning and purpose of this figure.

2. Many types of dialogues are mentioned in this chapter. Write them all on a separate sheet of paper and try to add two to three additional types of dialogue that you believe are not specifically included in the types already presented. Give a few examples of each added type of dialogue and share with your class or study group. How would these be effective in the "music making arena"?

3. King and Tan relate three foundational artistic practices that have the potential to overcome conflict, build community, and deepen mutual understanding. Choose one of these practices and write an essay focusing solely on the implementation of this practice in your context, both in community and individually. If King and Tan offer further questions for investigation under the practice you have chosen, then explore ways to respond, either with additional research or personal reflection.

4. PROJECT: Go to the book's website, http://www.songsforpeaceproject.org/, and read the discussions. Add to at least three threads that interest you.

References cited

Bakhtin, Mikhail. 1984. Edited and translated by Caryl Emerson. *Problems of Dostoevsky's Poetics*. Theory and History of Literature 8. Minneapolis: University of Minnesota Press.

Becker, Judith. 2004. *Deep Listeners: Music, Emotion and Trancing*. Bloomington: Indiana University Press.

Bevans, Stephen B., and Roger P. Schroeder. 2004. *Constants in Context: A Theology of Mission for Today*. Maryknoll, NY: Orbis.

Clark, Katerina, and Michael Holquist. 1986. *Mikhail Bakhtin*. Cambridge, MA: Belknap.

Farley, Todd. 2008. "Worship, Dramatic Arts, and the Agogic Moment." In *Worship That Changes Lives*, edited by Alexis D. Abernethy, 61–80. Grand Rapids: Baker Academic.

Finnegan, Ruth. 1989. *The Hidden Musicians: Music-Making in an English Town*. Cambridge: Cambridge University Press.

Herbert, Ruth. 2011. "Reconsidering Music and Trance: Cross-cultural Differences and Cross-disciplinary Perspectives." *Ethnomusicology Forum* 20, no. 2: 201–28.

Kärkkäinen, Veli-Matti. 2010. "Dialogue, Witness and Tolerance: The Many Faces of Interfaith Encounters?" *Theology News and Notes*, 57, no. 2: 29–33.

King, Roberta R. 2009. *Pathways in Christian Music Communication: The Case of the Senufo of Cote D'ivoire*. American Society of Missiology. Eugene, OR: Pickwick.

Lederach, John Paul. 2005. *The Moral Imagination: the Art and Soul of Building Peace*. Oxford: Oxford University Press.

Racy, A. J. 2003. *Making Music in the Arab World: The Culture and Artistry of Tarab*. Cambridge: Cambridge University Press.

Rouget, Gilbert. 1985. *Music and Trance: A Theory of the Relations between Music and Possession*. Chicago: Univeristy of Chicago Press.

Shapiro, Daniel L. 2010. "Relational Identity Theory: A Systematic Approach for Transforming the Emotional Dimension of Conflict." *American Psychologist* 65, no.7: 634–45.

Thangaraj, M. Thomas. 1999. *The Common Task: A Theology of Christian Mission*. Nashville, Abingdon.

Turino, Thomas. 2008. *Music as Social Life: The Politics of Participation*. Chicago: University of Chicago Press.

Volf, Miroslav. 2005. "Living with the 'Other.'" In *Muslim and Christian Reflections on Peace: Divine and Human Dimensions*, edited by J. Dudley Woodberry et al., 3–22. Lanham, MD: University Press of America, 2005.

CHAPTER 14

Employing Musical Pathways
of Peace and Reconciliation

By Roberta R. King and Sooi Ling Tan

In light of the possibilities of implementing musical pathways of peace and reconciliation as discussed in chapter 13, how then do we go about intentionally pursuing sustainable peacebuilding through music and performing arts? Peacebuilding does not simply occur with the signing of a political accord, as significant as such documents and occasions may be. Developing ways of living and relating together as neighbors requires a process where occasions from encountering one another through engaging, embracing, and relating as neighbors are evoked. This is the intersection at which we believe music and the performing arts make a contribution. We believe that musical practices that initiate, nourish, and replenish communities on a daily basis as well as on special occasions provide impetus for changing the entangled realities of contested and conflicted situations.

Artistic Practices for Bridging Differences and Building Communities

We have identified musical events and occasions as proffering public social spaces wherein transformed relationships and new webs of human connectivity occur. We have also attempted to understand how music works in meaningful and profound ways to impact social relationships, as well as the intrapersonal sphere. It is critically important to see and think strategically about the convergence of the musical pathways as they contribute to building sustainable peace. Lederach argues for developing "a capacity to see and think strategically about social spaces. These are the actual places of life where unusual relationships cross and interact" (2005, 86). While approaches to employing music in relation to peacemaking are too numerous to elucidate in this study, we suggest here an initial multiprong approach for strategically including music and the arts in local and global community life. We suggest and focus here on three important practices.

Develop a working philosophy of music as a relational medium

There is a critical need to enhance perceptions about music where musical events, performance, and sound are viewed as significant means for developing webs of relationships. This requires recognizing the critical role of music and arts throughout society and the multiple ways that they contribute to interactive dialogues and holistic approaches to daily life. While music as entertainment in some cultures is at the forefront of popular perceptions about music and is indeed one of its strengths, a considered, more deliberate strategy recognizes the importance of music as a significant participant in the dialogues of everyday life (births, weddings, funerals, etc.) within and between communities, in the dialogues of spiritual experience and religious exchange, and in the dialogues of social action and musical collaboration. As such, music and the arts provide significant platforms for interfaith encounter and engagement that contribute to overcoming fear of the "other," dispelling demonization, and breaking stereotypes. Further, the integrating relational dynamics inherent within music foster recognizing one another's common humanity, acknowledging differences and coming to live within such parameters. Most importantly, music-as-relationship-building promotes a respect for each person and each community, and promotes the ascription of dignity and autonomy on each other.

An Intentional Approach

While the ubiquitous nature of musical occasions proliferate in our daily lives and regularly contribute to healthy relational dynamics quite spontaneously, we suggest an intentional, considered approach in light of music and the arts. Intentional approaches are required on three levels in the peacemaking process: pre-conflict (everyday life and society), during conflict, and post-conflict. In the pre-conflict domain, when society is functioning well, promotion and performance of music and the arts foster the prevention of conflict and misunderstanding as they provide arenas for healthy dialogue, particularly in relation to working through differences. During conflict, cultural dialogues through music and related arts provide "agogic" moments that trigger motivation toward overcoming the conflict (see Adeney-Risakotta 2005) and initiate the settling of conflict and healing relationships. In post-conflict settings, the re-establishing and restoring of relationships are nurtured as musical occasions are designed and planned within specific contexts.

The corroboration of our findings points to two critical, often missing elements that need to be pursued as part of the overall process: listening and post-processing. Relational engagement requires two-way expression where each party or group listens deeply to the other. Listening is critical to forming healthy, dynamic relationships (Smith 1992). Facilitating and encouraging "deep listening" of the other should be given top priority in the overall process. Closely linked to deep listening, what we perceive as the other sorely lacking strategy in musical event arenas, is that of post-processing. When musical events take place, people are impacted. However, one must ask: What are people doing with this event after they have entered into the music-making realm and experienced the dynamics of transcending, relating, imagining, and processing the "agogic" moments of transformation? How long does the impact last and what perceptions, attitudes, and behaviors have changed? Here lies an area for further research and investigation that will help us to go further in our quest.

Strategically, however, the practice of post-processing should include listening and responding to feedback on the part of participants. Post-processing should also include thinking beyond a one-time, stand-alone musical event, to initiating further musical and relational dialogues on a normative basis. These include initiating a series of concerts and/or forming community ensembles that bring people together in dynamic ways and that are designed to promote the restoration of broken relationships and the further nourishment of reconciled relationships that have already occurred.

Identifying and Promoting Musical Peace Catalysts

Perhaps the most surprising finding was uncovering the significant roles and impact of musical peace catalysts, many who are quietly, unpretentiously contributing to bridging differences and shaping healthy communities both in local and global contexts. Depending on cultural perceptions of their roles, i.e., musicians in some societies are attributed low status while other societies think predominantly of musical sound, musicians (including liturgical musicians), some composers, musicologists, and ethnomusicologists are actively taking the initiative. They are giving leadership to forming musical occasions and interactions that impact individuals and communities in healthy ways. They serve as agents and visionaries in composing, select-ing, and performing the songs texts that pique our imaginations and trigger transcendence. They initiate and envision dynamic music events and make recordings that continue the dialogues of our spiritual and daily lives far beyond the bounded timeframes of musical occasions. In their song texts, musical peace catalysts as composers and performers reveal longings for peace, raise deep wounds of injustice for dialogical interaction, and facilitate theologizing and transcendence in the spiritual realms. They provide spaces for not only relating with the "other" but also for interacting with God on deep levels through liturgical, spiritual, and religiously-informed musics. Forming integral parts of our spiritual experiences, musical peace catalysts release the imagination in the midst of impossible scenarios and thus offer renewed vision and hope. Many model living neighborly with the "other" by courageously moving into settings of conflict, composing and design-ing music events, and discovering and creating regular moments of *com-munitas*. As they work collaboratively, they themselves practice and model neighborliness. In this respect, there is a need to pursue intentional ways of identifying and developing musical catalysts who are knowledgeable in the fields of ethnomusicology, peace studies, and performance practice who can integrate and engage in holistic peacebuilding.

From (un)Common Sounds to Common Sounds

In conclusion, the converging commonalities achieved through the forg-ing of musical pathways offer means for building community and living together as neighbors. "(un)Common Sounds" of the "other" can turn into "Common Sounds" of encounter, embrace, and appreciation of one another. Indeed, we are not in any way suggesting that one musical concert alone will necessarily dissolve political tensions within and between societies. Steps forward and backward in the development of harmonious and healthy rela-tionships among individuals, communities, nations, and in global interac-tions are inherent in any process. Yet, when combined and intentionally pursued music and the performing arts make significant contributions to building peace. Musical pathways engender moving us further into local and global neighborhoods where we live our everyday lives. They foster initiating and restoring webs of relationships in ways that no longer allow us to freely stereotype, dehumanize, demonize, or criticize. We come to see one another as human beings to be acknowledged and respected for who we each are.

Figure 24: Songs of Peace Participants Who Sang in *Kita Berbagi* (We Share)

We close with two song texts addressing peace and reconciliation that reveal a synthesis of ancient and modern expressions of people seeking God in the midst of dealing with life issues. In the first one, performed for the first time at the Yogyakarta "(un)Common Sounds" concert in April 2010, Irwansyah Harahap envisioned and summarized a convergence of our scholarly considerations and personal convictions, *Kita Berbagi.*

Kita berbagi (We Share)[1]

(A Song of Peace and Reconciliation)

We share the same world (earth)
We share the same sun
We share the same air
Everything has its origins in The One
We see because of The One
We hear because of The One
We bear witness to all things
The One has Power, over everything
If we lie, The One will Know (that we lie)
If we are arrogant, The One is the Highest
If we pray, The One listens
(And Grants Our Prayers)

1. © Lyrics and Music by Irwansyah Harahap, Maret, 2010. See appendix 1 for the original words in Bahasa Indonesia.

We all originate from The One
We are created from The One's Nature
We should not cause pain in this existence
We all shall return to The One
We should be as one, to share this life
We should be without suffering, without anger
We should be of one voice, and quarrel no longer
Sending forth to all, love for one another

Irwansyah's song of peace and reconciliation is a contemporary expression reminiscent of another song formulated centuries earlier, one that also reveals longings and desires for peoples to live together in peace.

The second is drawn from the Psalms, a sacred book common to both Muslim and Christian traditions. In it, the psalmist poignantly expresses our longings and prayers as we have pursued songs of peace and reconciliation among and between two religious groups and have begun to glimpse a horizon where one can see the possibility of

how wonderful and pleasant it is
when God's people,
live together in harmony!
Ps 133:1

FOR DISCUSSION

1. Plan your own intentional series of musical events that foster peace-building and interfaith dialogue.

2. Form a group of composers, musicians, peacebuilding and interfaith dialogue specialists, along with local community participants. Discuss and develop ways that musicians can contribute to the local community toward peacebuilding through music.

3. Do an analysis of your community and identify two or more groups that often are at odds with one another. Then survey and analyze musical genres that can be employed and adapted for peacebuilding and interfaith dialogue.

References Cited

Adeney-Risakotta, Farsijana R. 2005. "Politics, Ritual and Identity in Indonesia: A Moluccan History of Religion and Social Conflict." PhD diss., Radmoud University, Nijmegen.

Lederach, John Paul. 2005. *The Moral Imagination: the Art and Soul of Building Peace.* Oxford: Oxford University Press.

Smith, Donald K. 1992. *Creating Understanding: A Handbook for Christian Communication across Cultural Landscapes.* Grand Rapids: Zondervan.

Kita Berbagi

(We Share)

Kita yang berbagi bumi yang sama
Kita yang berbagi surya yang sama
Kita yang berbagi udara yang sama
Semua itu berasal dariNya

Kita yang melihat sesuatu dariNya
Kita yang mendengar sesuatu dariNya
Kita yang menyaksikan segala sesuatunya
Dia yang Kuasa, atas segalanya

Seandainya kita berdusta,
Ia yang Maha Mengetahui
Seandainya kita sombong,
Ia yang Maha Tinggi
Seandainya kita sama berdo'a,
Ia yang Maha Mendengarkan (Mengabulkan)

Kita yang semua berasal dariNya
Kita yang tercipta dengan fitrahNya
Kita 'tak semestinya menyakiti di antara
Kita semua 'kan kembali padaNya

Seharusnya kita bersama, 'tuk berbagi kehidupan

Seharusnya tanpa derita, tanpa rasa amarah

Seharusnya kita sama berkata, tiada lagi yang bersengketa

Sampaikanlah kepada semua, berbagi cinta untuk sesama

Glossary
(Arabic)

adhān	the Call to Prayer in Islam
ahl al-dimmah	"the people of the protection covenant": non-Muslims living in a Muslim country, granted protection in exchange for paying a tax
Aḥmadīyah	reformist movement in Islam
'amal	work, labor, activity
'arūḍ	rhythmic rules for poetry, also applied in vocal improvisation using poetry
asbāb al-nuzūl	"the reasons or occasions of the descent from heaven" (of passages in the Qur'ān): historical context identifiable in passages in the Qur'ān
aṣīl	authentic, genuine, proper (of melodic modes)
al-awzān al-ḫalīliyah	the Khalilian poetic meters. see also *wazn*
bāb	door, gateway; area in an old city around a gate or the former location of a gate (pl. *abwāb)*
biṭānah	group of singers taking part in *tawšīḥ* performance
al-buḥūr al-ḫalīliyah	see *al-awzān al-ḫalīliyah*
al-ḍamīr al-mustatir	in Arabic grammar, the unstated but implied pronoun
darajah	degree or tone of a musical scale (pl. *darajāt)*
ḍarb	rhythmic unit or period
dārij	"current, prevalent, common": possibly a former synonym for *tawshīḥ*
dawr	type of vocal performance genre using a colloquial text, with pre-composed sections, but featuring extensive improvisation by a vocal soloist (pl. *adwār)*
dhikr	remembrance (of God); mention (of God's name); collective ritual in some *Ṣūfī* orders consisting in constant repetition of certain words or phrases, especially the name of God, often accompanied by movement.
dhimmī	non-Muslim living under a covenant of protection in a Muslim country
dīwān	the interval of the octave, which is normally divided into seven main scale degrees
du'ā'	prayer of supplication (pl. *ad'iyah)*
ḥadīth	"report": narrative recounting a deed or saying of the Prophet Muḥammad or his companions, documented and established as a guiding text; Hadith (pl. *aḥādīth)*
al-ḥarakat al-qabḍīyah	the appropriation procedure by which derived modes are generated
ḥarām	prohibited

305

ḥijāb	woman's veil
Hijrah	the migration of the Prophet Muḥammad from Mecca to Medina in AD 622, the beginning of the Muslim era; Hegira, Hijra.
ḥurrīyat al-ikhtiyār	freedom of choice
iʻādah	"reiteration, resuming": pre-composed phrase sung by the *biṭānah* as response to each improvised phrase by the soloist in *tawshīḥ*
ʻibādah	service; worship
Ibāḍī	of or relating to the Ibāḍīyah, a denomination of Islam
ibdāʻ	creative ability; achievement of distinctive results
ijāzah	license or authorization, such as that accorded to a *munshid* by a guild
ikhlāṣ	sincerity, purity, fidelity
ʻilm al-ʻarūḍ	the science of poetic meter; prosody, metrics
ʻilm al-nagham	the science of melodic lines
ʻilm al-samāʻ	the science of listening
imām	prayer leader, spiritual leader; imam (pl. *aʼimmah*)
injīl	gospel (pl. *anājīl*)
inshād	hymnody
īqāʻ	rhythmic mode, rhythmic cycle (pl. *īqāʻāt*)
ʻIrfān	mystical cognition; Islamic Gnosis
iṣlāḥ	reconciliation
iṣlāḥ baynahum	"reconciliation between/among them": peacemaking
Islām	"submission [to God]": the religion originating with the Prophet Muḥammad; Islam
Ismāʻīlī	of or relating to the branch of Shīʻī Islam named for Ishmael, son of Abraham
jihād	struggle, fight; war of religious motivation
al-jihād bi-al-qawl	*jihād* by oral statement
jihādī	of or relating to *jihād*; someone engaged in *jihād*
jizyah	tax paid by a *dhimmī* to a Muslim authority
Khārijī	adherent of the Khārijīyah, an early sect of Islam
madḥ	"praise": public, folkloric type of *inshād*

madīnah	city
al-Madīnat al-Munawwarah	"the Lighted City": Medina
maghzá	significance
ma'lūf	"familiar, customary": prestigious repertoire of traditional music of North Africa
maqām	melodic mode (pl. *maqāmāt*)
maqāṣid	intentions, meanings, import (of passages in the Qur'an) (sing. *maqṣid*)
mashāyikh	plural form of *shaykh*, used to refer to respected elders or masters as a
Mashriq	"place of sunrise": the eastern Mediterranean region of the Arab world
Mawlawī	a member of the order of Jalāl al-Dīn Rūmī; Mevlevi
Mawlid al-Nabī	the Prophet's birthday
miftāḥ	key (to a door, etc.)
miḥnah	inquisition, trial
muḥkam	accurate, precise, reinforced, clear (of passages in the Qur'an) (pl. *muḥkamāt*)
mukhallafūn	"those left behind": shirkers, those not going to war (sing. *mukhallaf*)
munshid	vocal soloist with an improvisatory role; cantor (pl. *munshidūn*)
muqri'	reciter of the Qur'an
murīd	novice, aspirant, student, disciple (pl. *murīdūn*)
murshid	instructor, leader, spiritual guide (pl. *murshidūn*)
mutashābih	obscure, not clearly intelligible (of passages in the Qur'an) (pl. *mutashābihāt*)
muwallad	generated, derived (of melodic modes)
muwashshaḥ	a type of vocal composition in measured rhythm; the form of poetry used in such compositions (pl. *muwashshaḥāt*)
nagham	the concept of melody in Arabic music
Nahḍah	"awakening, rebirth": the Arab cultural renaissance period occurring between approximately 1798 and 1939
naḥw	grammar, syntax
nāy	end-blown flute, usually of bamboo, produced in various sizes for different pitch levels (pl. *nāyāt*)
qā'idūn	"those remaining seated": shirkers, those not going to war (sing. *qā'id*)
qānūn	box zither of trapezoidal shape, with strings in triple courses

	plucked by two plectra attached to the player's fingers (pl. *qawanīn*)
qawā'id	foundations, bases; rules, theories (sing. *qā'idah*)
qawā'id al-tilāwah	the rules for public reading or recitation (of the Qur'an)
qawālī	popular devotional music in the form of love songs based in the concept of human-divine love; the environment or performers of such music
qirā'ah bi-al-alḥān	melodic reading
qirā'ah maqāṣidīyah	reading oriented to intentions or import of the text
al-qitāl bi-al-silāḥ	armed contention, war
qiwālah	saying or speaking (through music)
Qur'ān	the sacred book of Islam; Qur'an, Koran
raḥmah	mercy
Ramaḍān	the ninth month in the Muslim calendar, a time of important religious observances
rīshah	feather, quill, plectrum (pl. *rīshāt*)
al-sab'ah al-sulṭānī	"the sovereign seven": the seven main notes of the musical scale
Ṣā'iqah	Palestinian Ba'athist political/military organization
Salafī	adhering to the Salafīyah Islamic reform movement; Salafist
ṣalāh	Islamic ritual prayer carried out five times each day (pl. *ṣalawāt*)
salām	peace, well-being
samā'	listening, hearing; *Ṣūfī* ceremony involving music
samā'ī	of or relating to listening
ṣarf	inflection, as it applies to proper declamation
sha'bī	popular, of the people, folk
Sharī'ah	the canonical law of Islam; the Sharia
shaykh	a person possessing special knowledge of religious concepts and practices, a person respected for special religious knowledge in Islam, an elder or head of an administrative district, a master of a *Ṣūfī* order (pl. *mashāyikh*)
Shī'ī	of or relating to the Shī'ah or branch of Islam recognizing the Prophet Muḥammad's son-in-law 'Alī as his true successor; a Muslim adhering to the Shī'ah; Shi'i, Shiite
shirk	polytheism
silm	peace

Ṣūfī	of or relating to any of various mystical or ascetic practices in Islam; a member of an order devoted to such practices; Sufi
ṣulḥ	reconciliation, peacemaking
Sunnah	the deeds and words of the Prophet Muḥammad, compiled as authoritative precedent and particularly important in Sunnī Islam
Sunnī	of or relating to the branch of Islam accepting the caliph successors to the Prophet Muḥammad; a Muslim adhering to *Sunnah*; Sunni, Sunnite
sūq	market (pl. *aswāq*)
Sūrah	a chapter of the Qur'an (usually printed as *Surat* when the name of the *Sūrah* follows immediately) (pl. *Suwar*)
taf'īlah	metrics of poetry
tafrīd	improvisatory solo passage interpolated by the *munshid*
taḥlīl ittijāhī	orientational analysis (of a text)
tajwīd	the art of Qur'an recitation according to rules of intonation and diction in an elaborate, melismatic presentation
taqsīm	"partition": instrumental improvisation (pl. *taqāsīm*)
ṭarab	ecstasy or elevated state resulting from a deep experience of musical performance; category of music performance genres associated with this state
tartīl	Qur'an recitation in steady, deliberate, largely syllabic style
Taṣawwuf	mystical or ascetic practice in Islam, Sufism
tawshīḥ	a type of vocal performance genre within *inshād* making responsorial use of a soloist (*munshid*) and a group of singers (*biṭānah*) (pl. *tawāshīḥ*)
'ūd	short-necked lute without frets
'ulamā'	Muslim scholars with recognized knowledge of Islam
'umrah	pilgrimage to Mecca other than during the Ḥajj
Wafd	"arrival": former secular nationalist party in Egypt
waḥdah	"unit": beat or pulse in music
waṣlah	suite or sequence of individual compositions and improvisations presented as a performance unit (pl. *waṣlāt*)
waṣlat inshādīyah	performance suite in the context of *inshād*
wazn	measure, rhythm; pattern, form (pl. *awzān*)
wiṣāl	"reunion, communion": the notion of human-divine union

wuṣūl	attainment, achievement, accomplishment
Yathrib	the original name of the city of Medina
zajal	type of popular traditional strophic poetry; music sung to such poetry (pl. *azjāl*)
zajjāl	performer of *zajal*
zukrah	type of music and dance of Libya frequently performed during wedding festivities; reed instrument prominently featured in this music
ẓulm	oppression, unfairness

Glossary
(Indonesian)

abangan	Literally means "red" or earth colored. This term is generally used to designate peasants and farmers; and also Muslims who are not very strict and combine Islamic rituals with local animistic practices.
Bahtera	sails
bebas	free
bersamaan	togetherness
Bintang Wetimu	East Star
Campur sari	An Indonesian musical style that combines the gamelan ensemble, regional Indonesian forms of music and instrumentation, and Western diatonic instruments such as guitars and keyboards.
communitas	community
dakwah	religious moral teaching
dangdut	a popular musical style based on Hindustani, Arabic, and Malaysian popular music
dhikr	remembrance of God; Allah's name or short formulas repeated often
dunia harta materi	the world and material wealth
Fajar di atas awan	Dawn above the clouds
gambus	Arabic style lute or 'ūd
gamelan	a traditional Indonesian musical ensemble
Jalali wa Ikram	God is most Bountiful
jejurun	a type of grass
jihād	war, hard work, order to preach Islam to unbelievers

311

kendhang (kendang)	a cylindrical, double-headed drum
kekompakan	friendship
kemufakatan	social consciousness
Kenduri Cinta	ritual gathering that involves a common meal
keroncong	an Indonesian musical style that combines musical influences from Java and Portugal.
kesatuan kemasyarakat	unity within society
Kita Berbagi	We Share
lagu gerriyet	virtuoso gestures
lagu selalu	basic gestures
Lebah	Bee
Lembaga Indonesia Perancis	Indonesian-French cultural center
macapat	Javanese six-line verse form
Maiyayah	meeting
Malam Kudus	Silent Night (christmas carol)
membina kerukunan	building social balance and solidarity
meunasah	mosque
mistik	mystical
nyanyian	singing
Pancasila	five basic principles of the Indonesian republic
Partai Komunis Indonesia	Communist Party of Indonesia
pengangkat	raiser
pengapit	locker
penupang	holders
penyepit	the ones who act in between
perbedaan	differences
pesantren	Islamic school
rateb meusekat	a female song (with religious texts) and dance (body percussion) genre from Aceh, Indonesia.
rebana	Malay-Indonesian frame drum

Reformasi	Reformation
rindu damai	longing for peace
sama	equal, together, ear of the heart
saman	a traditional dance performance originating from the Gayo people in Aceh, Indonesia.
Santri	Term used to designate pious Muslims who are more strict in following Islamic laws and rituals.
saron	Musical instrument used in gamelan consisting of six or seven keys placed on top of a wooden resonating frame.
sebuah tafsir tentang misteri perjalanan sebuah peradabanan	An interpretation of the mystery of the long journey/history of civilization.
seni baca al-Qur'an	the art of reciting the Qur'an
sepuh	elder
seudati	standing vocal dancing
shalawat	religious songs, often in praise of the prophet Muhammad
sruti box	a small wooden drone instrument
suara	voice, sound, opinion
suling	Inodnesian bamboo flute
sumbang	wrong, off-track
syafaat	religious meditation
syair	textual poetry expressed in a call-response style
Tanah Air Ku	My Homeland
tarian	dancing
tarian duduk	sitting dance
ulama	Islamic religious leaders
Untuk mu berperang	For those who go to war

Index of Names, Terms, and Subjects

315

Scripture Index

Song Title Index